MW01691233

# ALICE NEEL

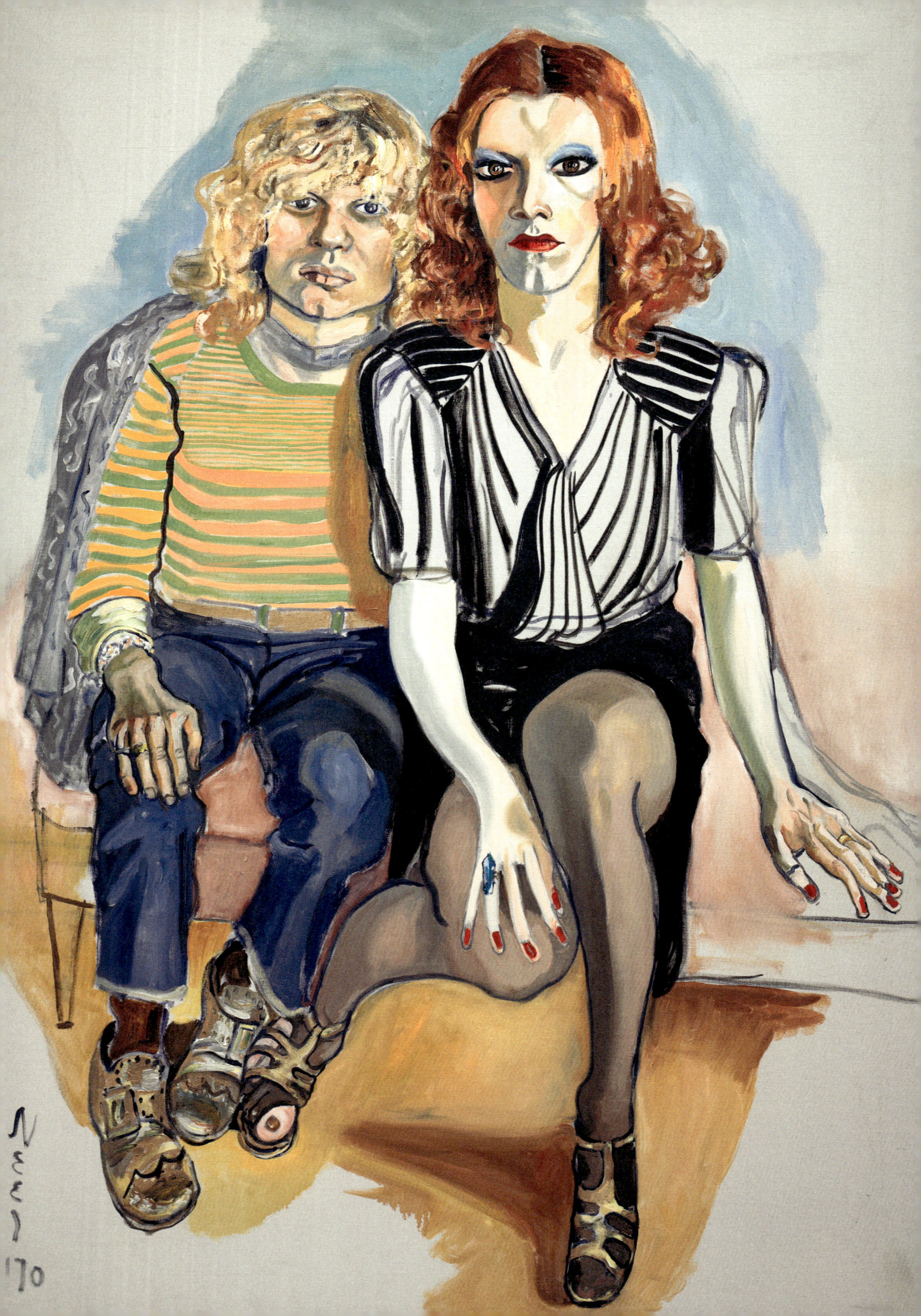
NEEL
'70

# ALICE NEEL

## PEOPLE COME FIRST

**KELLY BAUM** and **RANDALL GRIFFEY**

with contributions by

**MEREDITH A. BROWN, JULIA BRYAN-WILSON,**

and **SUSANNA V. TEMKIN**

THE MET

**THE METROPOLITAN MUSEUM OF ART, NEW YORK**

DISTRIBUTED BY YALE UNIVERSITY PRESS

NEW HAVEN AND LONDON

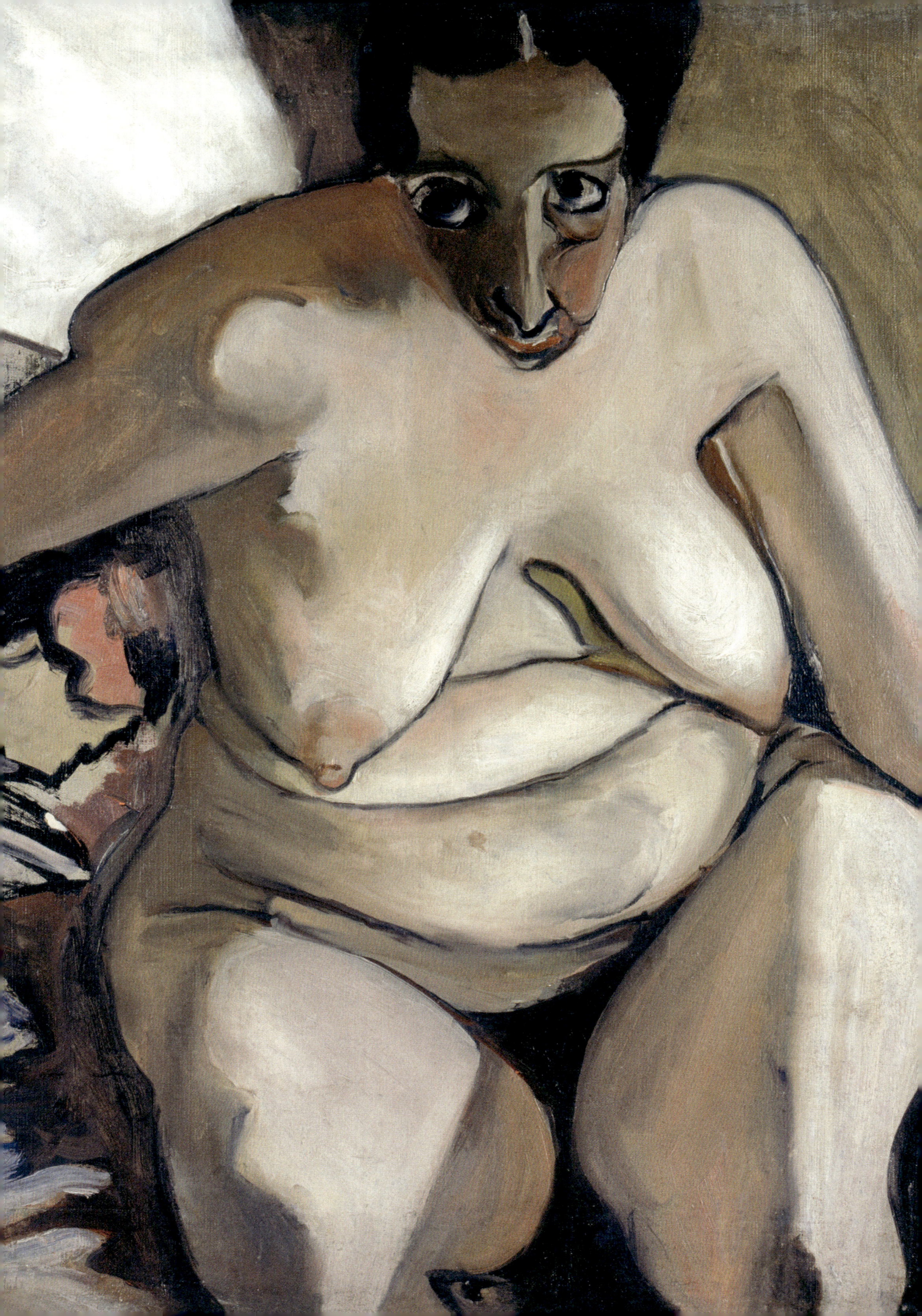

# CONTENTS

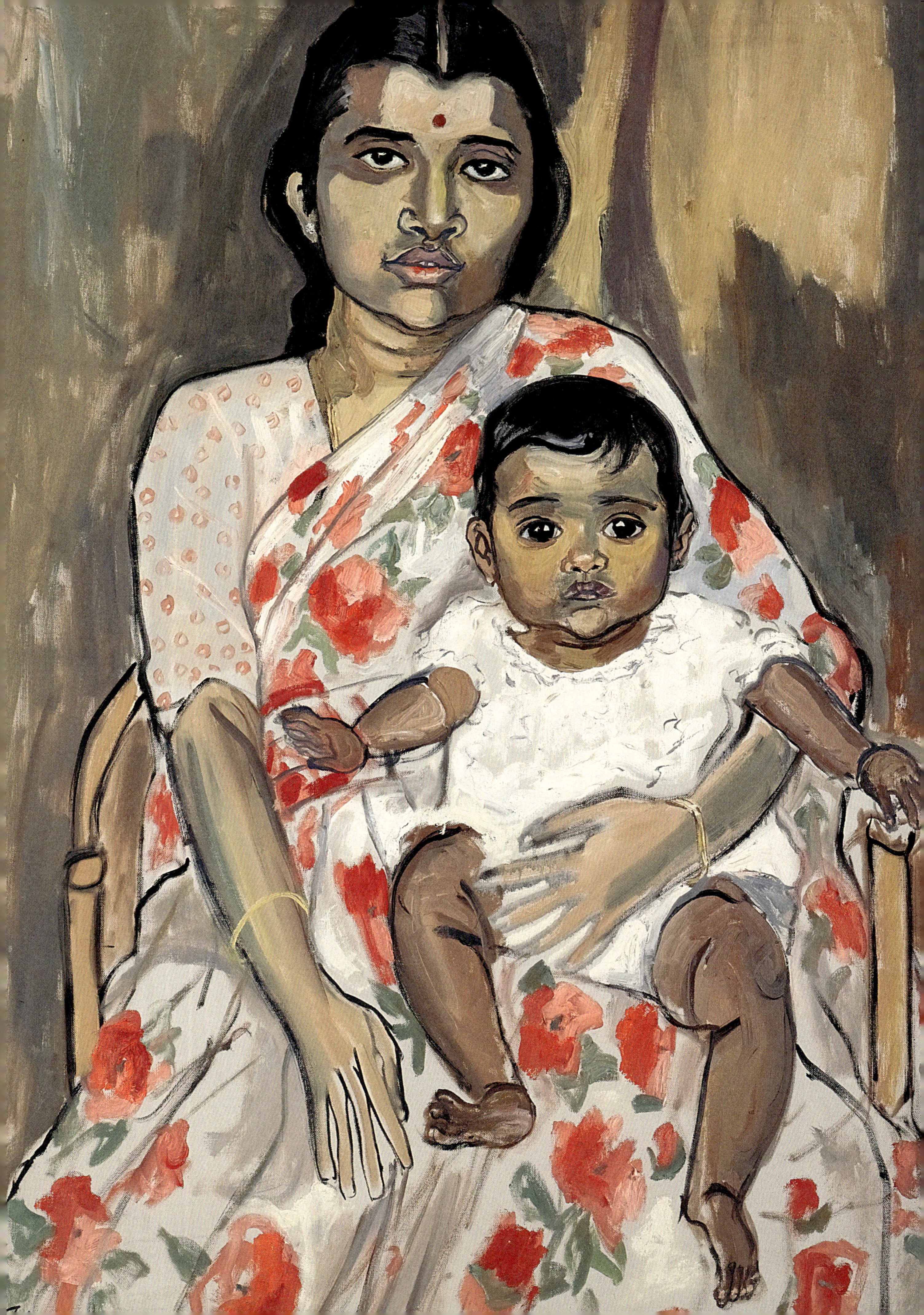

# DIRECTOR'S FOREWORD

The rich story of Alice Neel's prodigiously creative life is one of tremendous perseverance, of an outstanding painter with a defining body of work remaining true to her own vision despite many obstacles over her nearly seven-decade career. The first retrospective of this extraordinary artist's work to appear in a New York museum in over twenty years, *Alice Neel: People Come First* places Neel's life and her art within the larger cultural history of the twentieth century, considering them both in relationship to the major events and upheavals of the time. It also positions her as a radical artist whose commitment to civil rights and social justice defined her personal and public identities, her decision to paint in a representational manner, and especially her choice of subject matter.

We are grateful to Sheena Wagstaff, Leonard A. Lauder Chairman of Modern and Contemporary Art, who initially conceived of a retrospective of Neel's work at The Met. Kelly Baum, Cynthia Hazen Polsky and Leon Polsky Curator of Contemporary Art, and Randall Griffey, Curator of Modern and Contemporary Art, developed the curatorial vision and content of the exhibition, conducting extensive research in the Neel archive and uncovering many new revelations, in conjunction with Meredith A. Brown, former Senior Research Associate, who provided essential support. This project was only possible because of the countless contributions from many other colleagues, both within the Museum's walls and beyond.

I especially want to extend my deep gratitude to the artist's family, in particular Hartley and Ginny Neel, and to all of our institutional and private lenders, without whom this project would have been inconceivable. Thanks are also due to the important donors to the exhibition, including the Barrie A. and Deedee Wigmore Foundation, the Adrienne Arsht Fund for Resilience through Art, Agnes Gund, and the Jane and Robert Carroll Fund. This publication is made possible by the Samuel I. Newhouse Foundation, Inc., Sueyun Locks, the Locks Foundation, and the Antoinette Kraushaar Fund. The opening celebrations are sponsored by Phillips. I also want to acknowledge our exhibition touring partners, the Guggenheim Museum Bilbao and the de Young Museum, Fine Arts Museums of San Francisco, who will bring Neel's art to even wider audiences.

Neel believed that her portraits captured the zeitgeist of her era. Infused with the artist's humanism and commitment to social equity, her imagery now also resonates with our own challenging cultural and political circumstances. The vast majority of this catalogue was written during The Met's shutdown due to the COVID-19 pandemic from March to August 2020 and amid renewed, urgent calls for social justice and antiracism in the United States. In this context, Neel's fierce personal belief in humanity's inherent dignity combined with her steadfast social conscience seem all the more relevant.

Max Hollein
*Director*
*The Metropolitan Museum of Art, New York*

# ACKNOWLEDGMENTS

This exhibition and catalogue position Alice Neel as one of the twentieth century's most radical artists, a champion of equality whose enduring commitment to humanist principles inspired her art as well as her life. Although work on the project began in 2018, much of the writing for the catalogue commenced in March 2020, continuing through the end of August, a period of extreme duress in the world at large, which suffered the outbreak of a global pandemic, and in the United States in particular, as a torrent of police violence against people of color and ensuing protests ignited across the nation. Completing our book during this time proved challenging, but it also gave us a great sense of purpose, since Neel herself surely would have found a way to register today's predicaments in her art, just as she did the turmoil of her own era. We also found inspiration in the artist's indomitable spirit, her sheer perseverance, and her well-honed sense of justice, all attributes that feel more relevant than ever.

*Alice Neel: People Come First* benefited from the wisdom and encouragement of numerous individuals. Foremost, enormous thanks are due to the Estate of Alice Neel. Hartley and Ginny Neel were our constant companions on this journey, and their tireless enthusiasm, continuous support, and willingness to answer every question and open every archive helped us immeasurably. Sheena Wagstaff, Leonard A. Lauder Chairman of Modern and Contemporary Art, was this exhibition's earliest advocate—indeed, it was Sheena who realized the world was due for a major retrospective on Neel. We owe a debt of gratitude to Daniel H. Weiss, President and Chief Executive Officer, and Max Hollein, Director, for their endorsement of this project. Quincy Houghton and Katy Uravitch provided important counsel and worked to secure our two additional venues, while Katy brought her usual brilliance as project manager. Former Senior Research Associate Meredith A. Brown was a key partner. Brinda Kumar, Assistant Curator, graciously assumed planning and organizational duties at a critical stage of the project.

The colleagues who helped bring this exhibition to fruition are among the best in the world, and we are grateful to each and every one of them. Aislinn Hyde ensured the safe movement of art around the globe and within the galleries. Fabiana Weinberg brought extraordinary creativity to the exhibition's design, as did graphic designers Betsy Tsai, Tiffany Kim, and Anna Rieger. Neel's art was expertly cared for by conservators Diana Diaz Canas, Shawn Digney-Peer, and Rachel Mustalish. In Communications, Kenneth Weine, Alexandra Kozlakowski, and Micol Spinazzi played a vital role in refining the exhibition's message and in generating excitement about it. Amy Desmond Lamberti and Nicole Sussmane from the Counsel's Office offered help, as did Marci L. King from Exhibitions and Brian Healy from Merchandising and Retail. For the crucial role they played in fundraising, we thank Clyde B. Jones III, Jennifer M. Brown, Julie Hamon, Jason Herrick, Denali Kemper, Kimberly McCarthy, Kate Thompson, and John L. Wielk.

Much gratitude is owed our colleagues in Publications and Editorial, led by Mark Polizzotti, Peter Antony, and Michael Sittenfeld, without whom this catalogue and the exhibition's interpretative material would not exist. Anne Blood Mann helped shape the book's content, providing invaluable editorial support in the process; Lauren Knighton oversaw the book's production and printing; Josephine Rodriguez-Massop sourced well over a hundred images for the book; and Elizabeth Benjamin coordinated the show's interpretative material. Michelle Lee Nix, of McCall Associates, is the creative mind behind the book's design. The catalogue is enriched by the contributions of our two outside authors, Susanna V. Temkin and Julia Bryan-Wilson.

In the Department of Modern and Contemporary Art, Cynthia Iavarone, Catherine Burns, Lionel Carre, Jeff Elliott, Brooks Shaver, Elizabeth Doorly, Kolleen Ku, and Jasmine Kuylenstierna Wrede provided sustained assistance of many kinds. For supporting loans from within The Met, we thank Jeff L. Rosenheim, Joyce Frank Menschel Curator in Charge, Meredith Reiss, and Karan Rinaldo in Photographs; Sylvia Yount, Lawrence A. Fleischman Curator in Charge, and Catherine Mackay in the American Wing; and Dita Amory, Curator in Charge of the Robert Lehman Collection. In the Thomas J. Watson Library, Melissa Raymond facilitated the acquisition of books and ephemera for the exhibition, while Sophia Alexandrov and Shayla Nastasi helped prepare items for installation.

Special thanks are due to David Zwirner, Bellatrix Hubert, Rebecca Holmberg, Priya Parthasarathy, and Britta Nelson at David Zwirner Gallery, who gave aid and advice at critical junctures. We are also indebted to the staff at Aurel Scheibler, LA Louver, Victoria Miro, and Xavier Hufkens.

For sharing their insights on Neel, we are grateful to Penny Arcade, Brigid Berlin, Donna De Salvo, Charles C. Eldredge, Mary Garrard, Pedro Juan Hernández, Phoebe Hoban, Miguel Luciano, Patricia Mainardi, Virginia Miller, Cindy Nemser, Jasmine Ramirez, and Edward J. Sullivan.

We owe an enormous debt to the institutions, galleries, and private collectors, all of them listed at the beginning of this book, that lent works to this exhibition, and to the associated directors, curators, registrars, conservators, collection managers, technicians, and shippers. We extend great appreciation to our touring partners, Daniel Vega, Carolina Erdocia, Lucía Agirre, and Xabier Urberuaga at the Guggenheim Museum Bilbao and Thomas P. Campbell and Krista Brugnara at the de Young Museum in San Francisco, for hosting this exhibition at their institutions.

Finally, we offer our heartfelt thanks to the Barrie A. and Deedee Wigmore Foundation, the Adrienne Arsht Fund for Resilience through Art, Agnes Gund, and the Jane and Robert Carroll Fund for their gifts in support of the exhibition. We are indebted to the Samuel I. Newhouse Foundation, Inc., Gene and Sueyun Locks, of the Locks Foundation, and the Antoinette Kraushaar Fund, whose generosity made this publication possible. We are grateful to Phillips for its sponsorship of the opening celebrations. We cannot imagine better philanthropists—smart, judicious, discerning—to help bring *Alice Neel: People Come First* into being.

Kelly Baum
*Cynthia Hazen Polsky and Leon Polsky*
*Curator of Contemporary Art*
*The Metropolitan Museum of Art, New York*

Randall Griffey
*Curator of Modern and Contemporary Art*
*The Metropolitan Museum of Art, New York*

## CONTRIBUTORS TO THE CATALOGUE

Kelly Baum
Cynthia Hazen Polsky and Leon Polsky
Curator of Contemporary Art,
The Metropolitan Museum of Art, New York

Meredith A. Brown
Director of Museum Affairs and Chief Curator,
Planting Fields Foundation, Oyster Bay, New York

Julia Bryan-Wilson
Doris and Clarence Malo Professor of
Modern and Contemporary Art,
University of California at Berkeley

Randall Griffey
Curator of Modern and Contemporary Art,
The Metropolitan Museum of Art, New York

Susanna V. Temkin
Curator, El Museo del Barrio, New York

# LENDERS TO THE EXHIBITION

Barbara and Theodore Alfond

Art Berliner

Baltimore Museum of Art

Blanton Museum of Art, The University of Texas at Austin

The Brand Family Collection

John Cheim

Cheim and Read, New York

The Cleveland Museum of Art

COMMA Foundation, Belgium

Defares Collection

Lonti Ebers

Equitable Holdings, Inc., New York

Estate of Alice Neel

Diane and David Goldsmith

Francie Bishop Good and David Horvitz

Catherine Gund

Institute of Contemporary Art, Boston

The Antonia Johnson Family Collection

James Kenyon

The Locks Foundation, Philadelphia

Louis-Dreyfus Family Collection

Nancy Magoon

Lillian and Billy Mauer

Anne McNamara

The Metropolitan Museum of Art, New York

Minneapolis Institute of Art

Museum of Contemporary Art, Los Angeles

Museum of Fine Arts, Boston

The Museum of Modern Art, New York

Museum of the City of New York

National Gallery of Art, Washington, D.C.

National Museum of Women in the Arts, Washington, D.C.

National Portrait Gallery, Smithsonian Institution, Washington, D.C.

Oklahoma City Museum of Art

Pennsylvania Academy of the Fine Arts, Philadelphia

Philadelphia Museum of Art

Private collections

Marcia Rafelman

Rennie Collection, Vancouver

Daryl and Steven Roth

San Francisco Museum of Modern Art

Smithsonian American Art Museum, Washington, D.C.

Tate, United Kingdom

Tia Collection, Santa Fe, NM

Tufts University Art Galleries, Medford, Mass.

Whitney Museum of American Art, New York

Doug Woodham and Dalya Inhaber

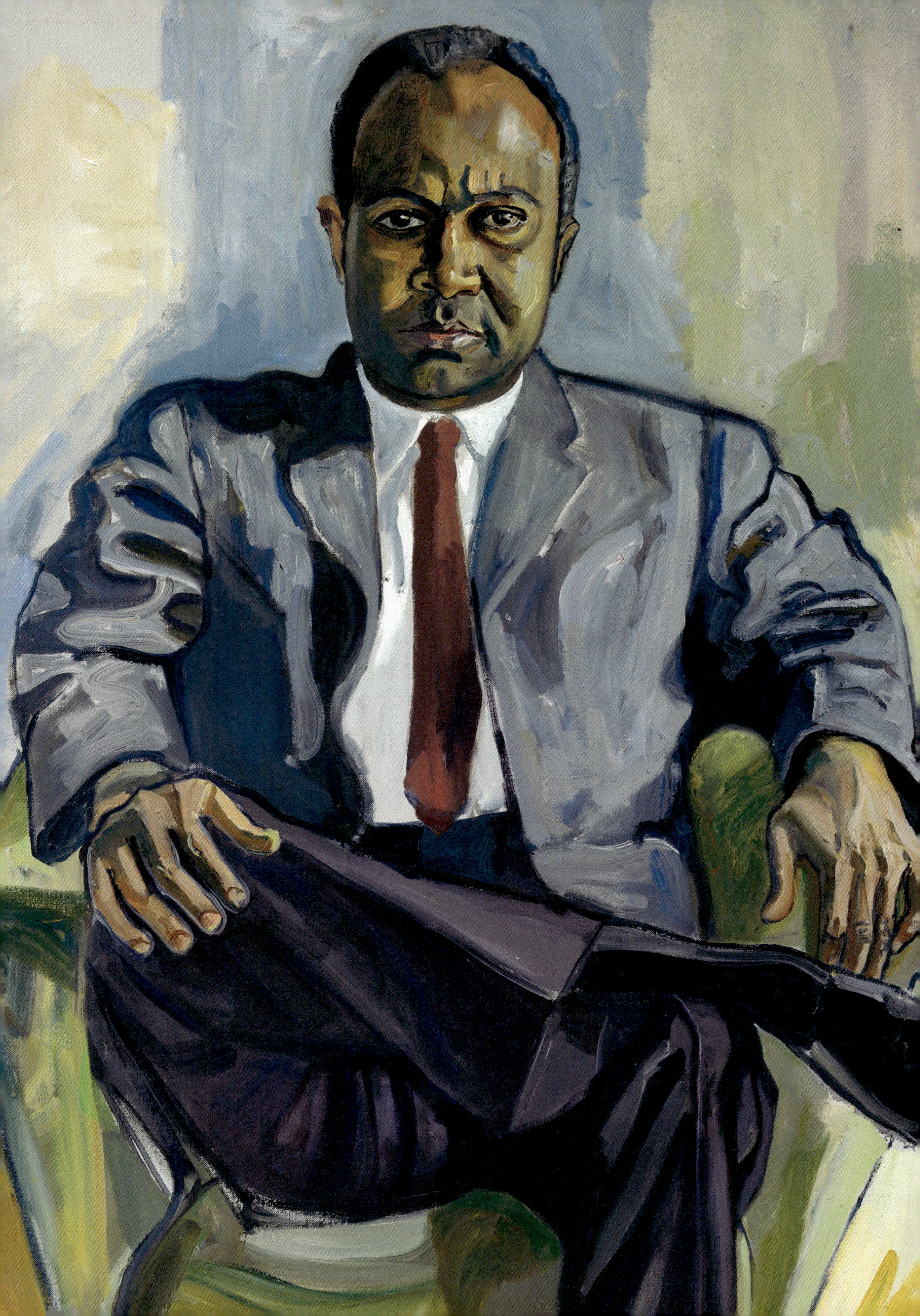

# ANARCHIC HUMANIST

**KELLY BAUM** and **RANDALL GRIFFEY**

Born in Merion Square, Pennsylvania, and raised nearby in Colwyn, American painter Alice Neel (1900–1984) possessed, among other distinctive attributes, a stalwart sense of purpose in her dedication to an ethic of radical humanism.[1] "For me, people come first," she declared in 1950 to journalist and activist Mike Gold in the Communist periodical the *Daily Worker*. "I have tried to assert the dignity and eternal importance of the human being."[2] Neel reprised this mission statement many times, and within her overarching, politically inflected humanism lies the key to understanding both her life and her work. For Neel, humanism was as much an outlook—or even a philosophy—as a practice and a responsibility, one that was distinct from both the academic discipline of the humanities and the study of classical antiquity in the Renaissance period. Active during a century obsessed with political and stylistic "isms"—that is, of categorically defined belief and aesthetic systems—Neel proudly upheld her raison d'être, proclaiming late in her career, "You know what I am really? I'm an anarchic humanist."[3] This identity was well earned, the culmination of a life filled with struggle, loss, betrayal, and neglect, but also adventure, discovery, perseverance, and, eventually, recognition for her abundant talent.

Offering a holistic, integrated view of her practice, *Alice Neel: People Come First* spans the breadth of Neel's career, from her enrollment in the Philadelphia School of Design for Women (now Moore College of Art and Design; 1921–25; fig. 1) to her formative sojourn in Havana, Cuba (1926–27), to her long residency in New York (1927–30 and 1931–84). It features more than 100 paintings, drawings, and watercolors from all of the seven decades in which she worked in a range of genres, including portraits, still lifes, landscapes, and cityscapes. Besides foregrounding her often under-recognized artistic accomplishments, this publication positions her as an artist who engaged with progressive politics throughout her lifetime and attends to her place in the larger cultural history of the twentieth century.

Neel demonstrated her humanism most explicitly in her focus on the human figure. Throughout her career, Neel rendered women and men, children and adults, paupers and princes with the same unflinching intensity. She also depicted people of many different races and ethnicities, especially after moving to Spanish Harlem (East Harlem/El Barrio) in 1938. "There isn't much good portrait painting being done today," Neel said, "and I think it is because with all this war, commercialism and fascism, human beings have been steadily marked down in value, despised, rejected and degraded."[4] The dehumanization of people, in other words, resulted in their effacement from art, which served only to prolong and deepen humanity's crisis. Neel sought to counter such a state of affairs by creating pictures of human beings, which she understood very

Detail of *James Farmer*, 1964 (p. 172)

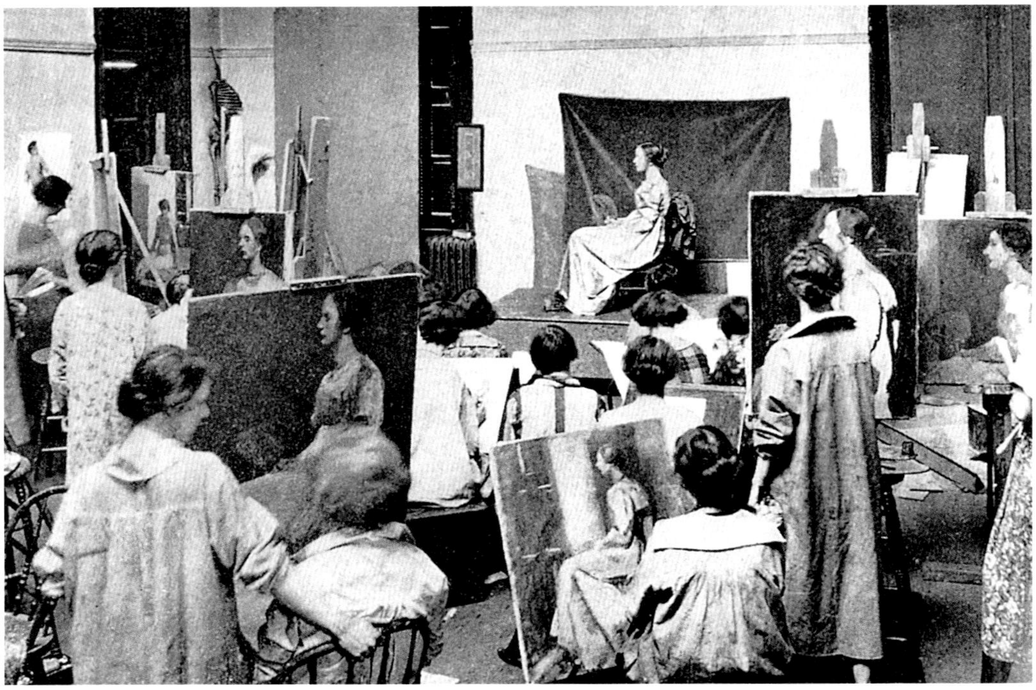

FIG. 1 An art class at the Philadelphia School of Design for Women, published in the school's yearbook, 1925–26

much as a reflection of, as well as a weapon in, her fight for humanism. As Gold proclaimed in an essay for the artist's 1951 exhibition at the New Playwrights Theatre in New York, "Alice Neel has never allowed them to dehumanize her. This is heroic in American painting, where for the past fifteen years Humanity has been rejected, its place given to the mechanical perversions, patent-leather nightmares and other sick symbols of a dying social order."[5] For Neel, adopting a humanistic approach to art was an ethical responsibility.

Revealingly, Neel resisted the label "portrait painter," primarily due to lingering perceptions of portraiture as a staid, conservative genre that served to flatter those individuals portrayed. Although she certainly painted portraits, she tended to describe her work as "pictures of people" that constituted, in both part and sum total, a kind of history painting.[6] As she said to art historian Patricia Hills, "People's images reflect the era in a way that nothing else could. When portraits are good art they reflect the culture, the time and many other things. . . . Art is a form of history. . . . Now, a painting is [a portrait of a person], plus the fact that it is also the Zeitgeist, the spirit of the age."[7] Whom Neel chose to paint and when and how she painted them all served her larger purpose of bearing witness not just to the unfolding of history over time but to instances of cruelty and oppression in the present as well. This led her to depict both the victims of injustice and the individuals who dedicated their lives to overcoming it.

Neel's humanism was initially forged in the crucible of 1920s Cuba (fig. 2). There, her husband, Carlos Enríquez, introduced her to philosopher José Ortega y Gasset's "La deshumanización del arte" ("The Dehumanization of Art"; 1925), a critique of the antihuman impulse behind modern abstract art. In his polemic, Ortega defined modernism as antagonistic to human presence, complaining, "The young set has declared taboo any infiltration of human contents into art." He added, "In foregoing to emulate reality the [modernist] painting becomes . . . an image, an unreality. Expressionism, cubism etc., are . . . attempts at executing this decision. From painting things, the painter has turned to painting ideas."[8] Given her dedication to painting the human figure, Neel appears like a veritable apostle of Ortega's text, with the notion that humanist art necessarily cuts against the dominant grain of modernism–especially abstraction–a critical takeaway. Later Neel herself described Ortega as "prophetic" and credited his book as having predicted "a whole era of art."[9]

Encounters with socialist and Communist activists in the United States in the late 1920s and 1930s further shaped Neel's humanism. She joined the Communist Party in 1935 and was intermittently affiliated with the group for the rest of her life.[10] Marxist literature, including contemporary newspapers and journals such as the *Daily Worker* (1924–58), *New Masses* (1926–48), *Art Front* (1934–37), *Masses & Mainstream* (1948–56), *Mainstream* (1956–63), and the *Daily World* (1958–86), copies of which appear in the artist's archive, serve as an indispensable index of her political worldview with regard to class, race, and gender equality. Neel was a friend to many union organizers, left-leaning writers, and Communists. She painted some of these individuals, like Mike Gold (p. 166) and Pat Whalen (p. 124), and provided illustrations for their books and journals. Moreover, a powerful synergy exists between these texts and Neel's art. For example, her moody street scene of longshoremen returning from work (p. 125) evokes the longshoremen's strike of 1936–37, an uprising reported widely by Communist newspapers,

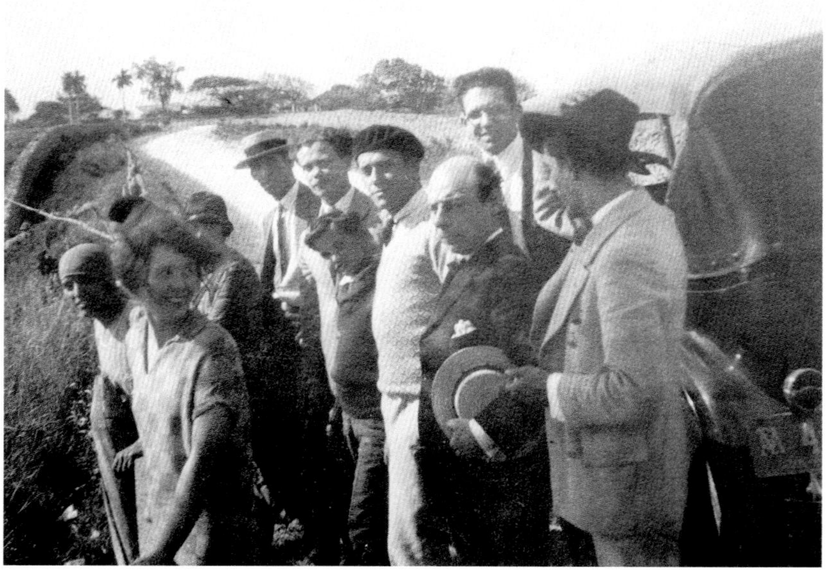

FIG. 2 Alice Neel (near left), Marcelo Pogolotti (center in distance), and Carlos Enríquez (far right in profile), with family and friends in Cuba, ca. 1926. Alice Neel Archive, Stowe, Vt.

including the *Daily Worker*. The quasi-journalistic but sympathetic images of economically disadvantaged children appearing in *Masses & Mainstream*—including, for one, the photograph of a Puerto Rican boy on the cover of its December 1949 issue (fig. 3)—seem to be iconographic siblings of Neel's images of kids in Spanish Harlem, such as *Puerto Rican Girl on a Chair* (p. 130) or, even more, *A Spanish Boy* (p. 155). The same issue of *Masses & Mainstream* also features Neel's *The Martyr* (fig. 4), a "courtroom sketch" of Judge Harold Medina, who presided over the controversial Foley Square Trial, at which eleven members of the Communist Party were convicted of sedition. Eventually, Neel's politics evolved to encompass the civil rights and feminist movements, which had homes of their own within Communism of the 1930s and beyond, a complex subject that Kelly Baum explores in her essay in this volume.

Neel identified as a humanist out of a disgust with all that served to dehumanize people, especially ethnic minorities and members of the lower and working classes. This also explains her investment in progressive ideologies that strove to ameliorate inequality and oppression. Indeed, Neel pitched her humanism as the antidote to the anti-humanism of the modern world, what she described as the "rat race" we endure.[11] Neel meant not only to affirm the fundamental dignity and legitimacy of people in the face of an unjust world but also to recognize their agency and autonomy in the face of numerous threats, from the forces of self-interest and consumerism to those of technology, racism, sexism, and, above all, capitalism. Doing so, however, involved neither idealizing nor romanticizing her subjects. To the contrary, Neel sought to capture all the complexity of human experience. As she said in 1976, "I paint to try to reveal the struggle, tragedy and joy of life."[12]

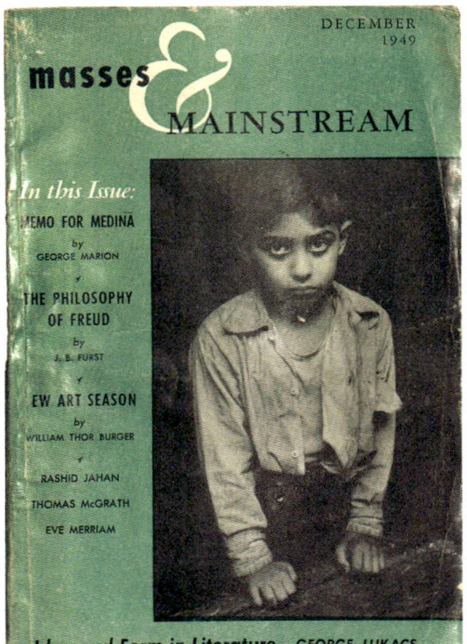


FIG. 3 Cover of *Masses & Mainstream*, December 1949

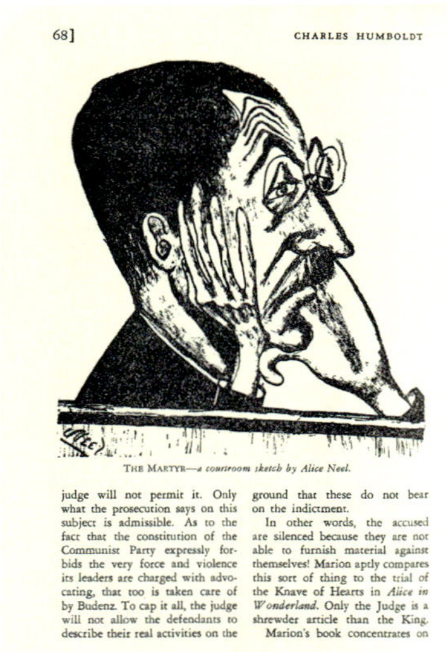
68] CHARLES HUMBOLDT

THE MARTYR—*a courtroom sketch by Alice Neel.*

judge will not permit it. Only what the prosecution says on this subject is admissible. As to the fact that the constitution of the Communist Party expressly forbids the very force and violence its leaders are charged with advocating, that too is taken care of by Budenz. To cap it all, the judge will not allow the defendants to describe their real activities on the ground that these do not bear on the indictment.

In other words, the accused are silenced because they are not able to furnish material against themselves! Marion aptly compares this sort of thing to the trial of the Knave of Hearts in *Alice in Wonderland*. Only the Judge is a shrewder article than the King.

Marion's book concentrates on

FIG. 4 Alice Neel's illustration *The Martyr* as reproduced in *Masses & Mainstream*, December 1949, p. 68

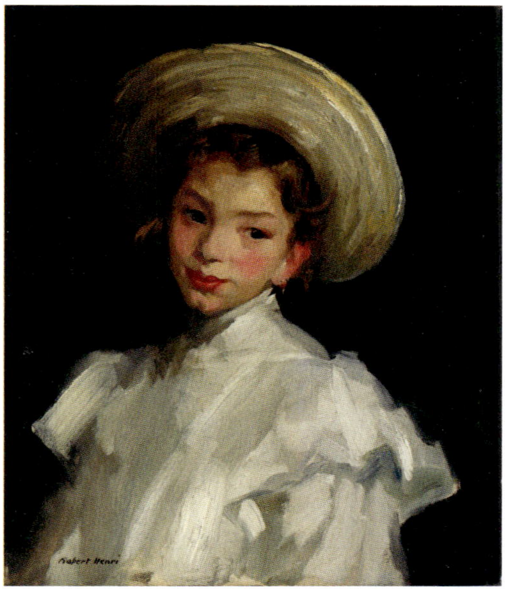

FIG. 5 Robert Henri (American, 1865–1929). *Dutch Girl in White*, 1907. Oil on canvas, 24 × 20 in. (61 × 50.8 cm). The Metropolitan Museum of Art, New York, Arthur Hoppock Hearn Fund, 1950 (50.47)

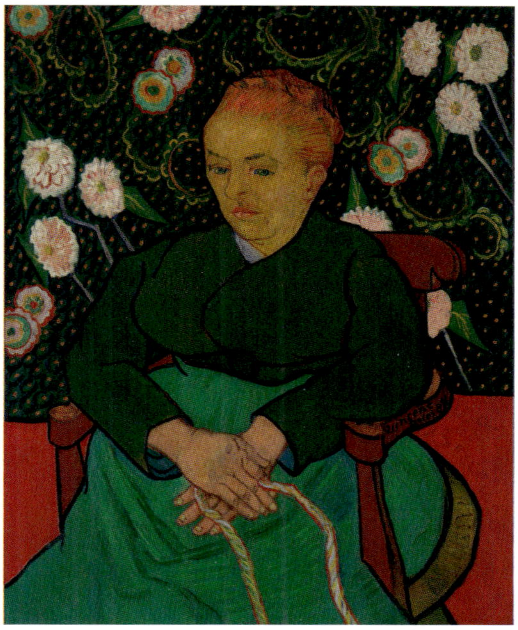

FIG. 6 Vincent van Gogh (Dutch, 1853–1890). *La Berceuse (Woman Rocking a Cradle; Augustine-Alix Pellicot Roulin)*, 1889. Oil on canvas, 36 1/2 × 29 in. (92.7 × 73.7 cm). The Metropolitan Museum of Art, New York, The Walter H. and Leonore Annenberg Collection, Gift of Walter H. and Leonore Annenberg, 1996, Bequest of Walter H. Annenberg, 2002 (1996.435)

Neel's humanism permeates not only what she painted but also how. From 1921 to 1925, she studied at the Philadelphia School of Design for Women, where she developed a style of painterly realism loosely in the manner of Robert Henri, whose tenure as a teacher at the school, from 1892 to 1895, left a strong legacy (fig. 5).[13] Moreover, Henri's *The Art Spirit* (1923) deeply impacted the aspiring artist, particularly the manifesto's assertion of the primacy of human experience and feeling in the creation of art. "Life and art cannot be disassociated, nor can any artist, however he may desire it, produce a line of 'sheer beauty,' *i.e.*, a line disassociated from human feeling," Henri proclaimed in *The Art Spirit*. "We cannot, and we should not, desire to get away from our feelings."[14]

Elaborating on Henri's philosophy, Neel fused careful observation from nature with painterly flourishes to evoke personality and character, both the sitter's and her own. This delicate but potent combination of analysis and intuition is evident even in her earliest extant works, such as *French Girl* (p. 221), likely the product of a student exercise with a model in the classroom studio. While Henri's imprint endured over the course of her career, Neel's paint handling and palette became bolder, more expressionistic in subsequent years, especially during and just after her time in Cuba, as seen in *Mother and Child, Havana* (p. 208), a subject to which the artist would famously return again and again, or in the claustrophobic interior *Bathing in a Furnished Room* (p. 142). Another early high-water mark in Neel's formal experimentation, but quite different in approach, is *Futility of Effort* (p. 185), a hauntingly spare, quasi-abstract representation of the death of a child.[15]

Over the course of the 1930s, Neel gradually broke from the aesthetic principles she had inherited from Henri, especially his emphasis on painterly flair. Embracing many of the objectives of Social Realism, which, broadly defined, focused on modern American life, she increasingly eschewed conventional bravura in painting and embraced imperfection as part of her technique. In the context of her work, such an approach signifies the intrinsic humanity of her subjects as well as her own subjectivity. Neel went on to evolve a distinctive mode of direct painting-as-drawing, reminiscent of Vincent van Gogh's technique, from the 1960s onward (fig. 6). Consequently, the viewer is almost always aware of Neel's (left) hand at work, a characteristic that distinguished her output from not only the slick, streamlined Machine Age aesthetics (such as Precisionism) that defined so much of American art and design before and during World War II (fig. 7) but also geometric abstraction of the 1960s and representational painting of the kind included in the Whitney's 1970 exhibition *22 Realists* (fig. 8).[16] While her loose, sometimes seemingly careless manner of painting occasionally ran afoul of conservative critics, it more often earned the artist plaudits (if not often sales) for its boldness and originality.[17]

Neel typically represented people within her immediate circle, individuals who were near at hand, at heart, and in mind. Her images from the late 1920s and early to mid-1930s, made in Cuba, Philadelphia, and New York, focus almost exclusively on her closest intimates: her husband and their two daughters; her female friends; her mother, father, and brother; and her male lovers, Kenneth Doolittle, John Rothschild, and José Santiago Negrón. Many of these works are poignant in the extreme. These decades also witnessed Neel's first experiments painting the nude figure—adult and juvenile, male and female—and the creation of a number of small self-portraits. Here, Neel

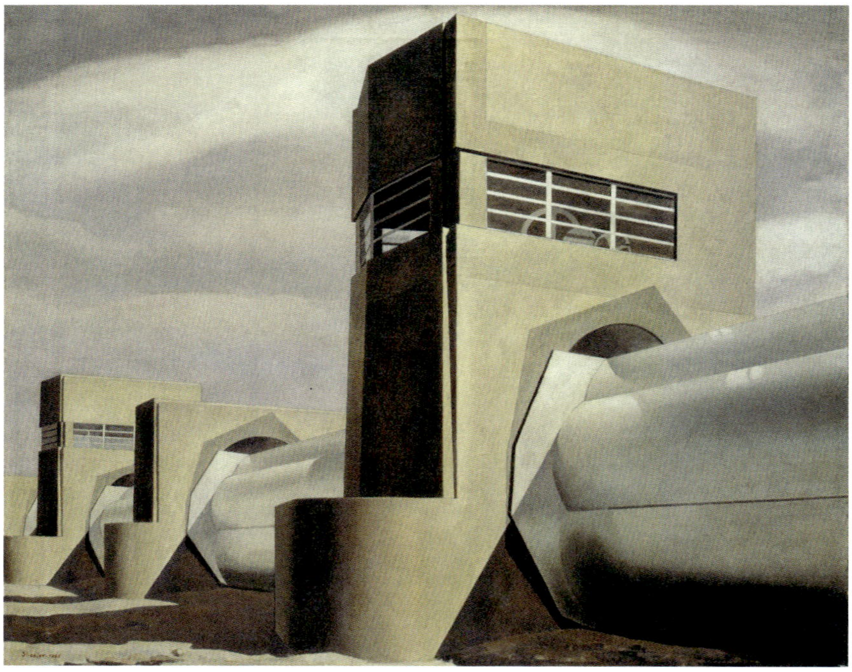

FIG. 7 Charles Sheeler (American, 1883–1965). *Water*, 1945. Oil on canvas, 24 × 29 in. (61 × 74.3 cm). The Metropolitan Museum of Art, New York, Arthur Hoppock Hearn Fund, 1949 (49.128)

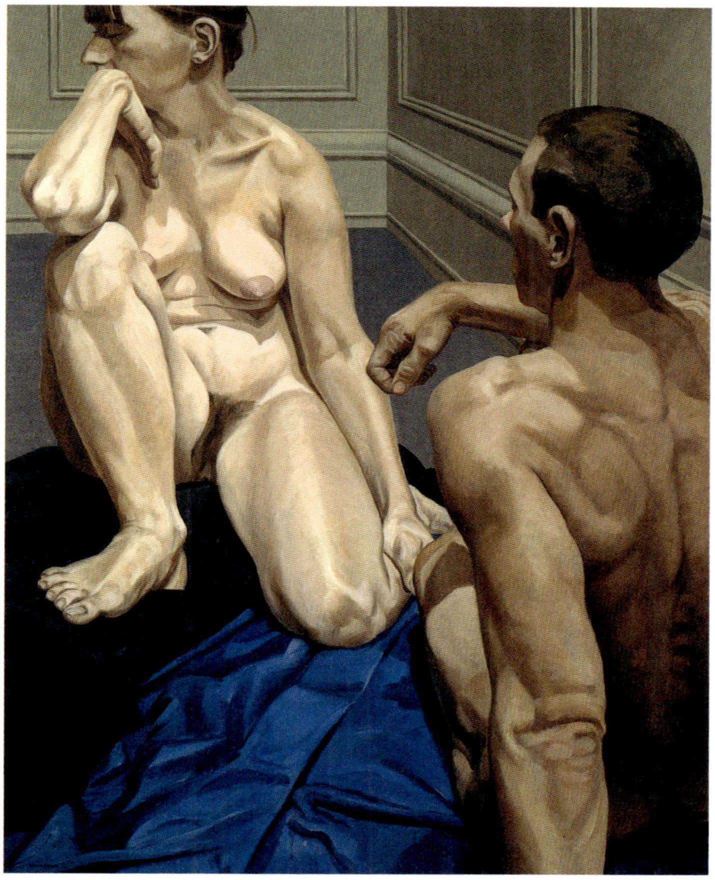

FIG. 8 Philip Pearlstein (American, born 1924). ***Male and Female Models Sitting on the Floor***, 1964. Oil on canvas, 60 × 48 in. (152.4 × 121.9 cm). The Metropolitan Museum of Art, New York, Purchase, The Mrs. Claus von Bülow Fund Gift, 1987 (1987.4)

referenced experiences of a profoundly private nature, such as mental distress, childbirth, motherhood, loss, and solitude, and often signaled her disenchantment with bourgeois ideology and conventional gender roles, correlating the personal with the political.

As Neel established herself in Greenwich Village (fig. 9), where she moved in late 1931–early 1932, not far from the headquarters of both the NAACP and the Communist Party USA (CPUSA), she devoted more time to painting and sometimes collaborated with what we might think of as her extended family—that is, a group of like-minded, left-leaning white people, almost all of them activists and intellectuals, such as Max White (p. 163) and Dick Bagley (p. 123). Interspersed with these portraits are still lifes, interiors, street scenes (p. 121), urban landscapes (p. 120), and images of strikes and political rallies. Neel created many of these under the auspices of the Public Works of Art Program (PWAP) and then the Works Progress Administration's (WPA) Federal Art Project, part of President Franklin Delano Roosevelt's New Deal, which she joined in 1934, along with artists such as Jacob Lawrence (fig. 10), and with which she remained until its dissolution in 1943. Once Neel established herself in New York permanently, the city became her most faithful, most constant subject. Indeed, her work serves in aggregate as a portrait of the last century as it played out on the compact, vibrant island of Manhattan, the perfect setting for what

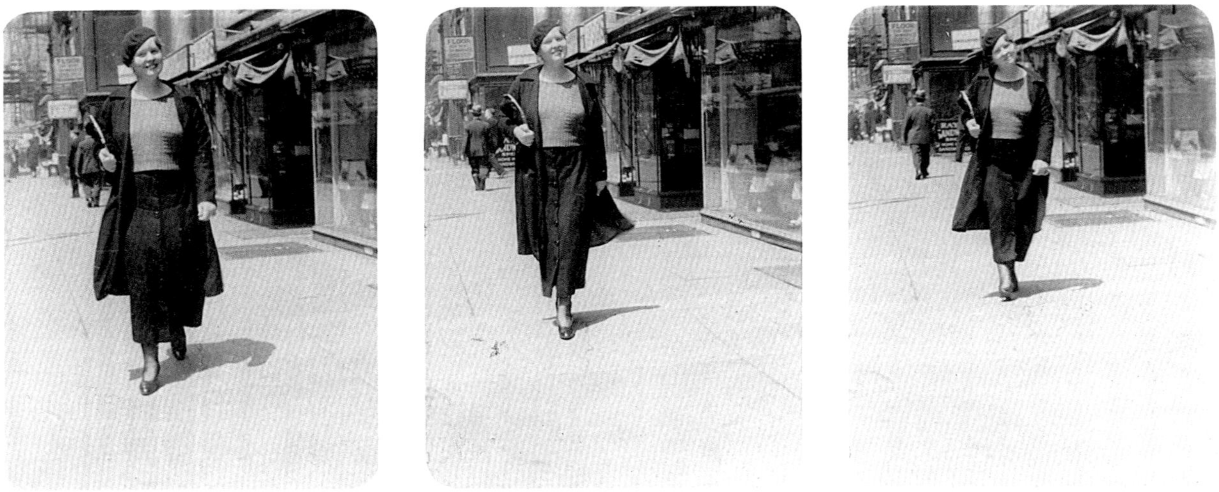

FIG. 9 Alice Neel in Greenwich Village, 1932. Alice Neel Archive, Stowe, Vt. Photographs by Kenneth Doolittle

she described, in a nod to Honoré de Balzac, as her "human comedy."[18] As the critic for *Time* magazine wrote in 1969, "each picture [by Neel is] a devastating microcosm of all that is both magnificent and maddening about the megalopolis of Manhattan."[19] After becoming familiar with Neel's art, it is impossible not to experience the city and its inhabitants through her vision.

In 1938 Neel left Greenwich Village and moved with her partner José Santiago Negrón to Spanish Harlem, a community in the midst of a dramatic demographic shift, as increasing numbers of people from Puerto Rico, Cuba, and the Dominican Republic moved into the neighborhood. In addition to painting scenes of and participating in El Barrio's lively street culture, as Susanna V. Temkin discusses in her essay, Neel, for the first time since residing in Cuba, painted African American, Afro-Caribbean, and Latino subjects.[20] Many belonged to the same group of progressive, usually Communist intellectuals she had been depicting since the early 1930s and almost all were involved in the civil rights struggle, but a large number were, simply, her neighbors. "I have never felt strange in East Harlem," Neel reminisced, "because of the fine and hospitable humanity I find all around me. . . . East Harlem is like a battlefield of humanism, and I am on the side of the people there."[21] Many of the individuals Neel painted in Spanish Harlem would probably not be known today, at least outside their families, if not for her images, given the climate of white supremacy, male hegemony, and class privilege that was prevalent then as now. After she moved uptown, moreover, her home, which had always served as her studio, began to make its presence felt *and* seen, both as a setting that occasioned particularly intimate encounters with sitters and as a protagonist in the mise-en-scène itself.

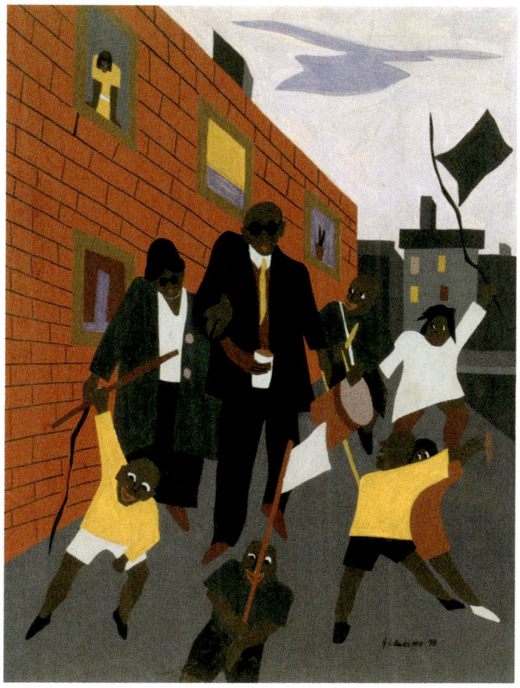

FIG. 10 Jacob Lawrence (American, 1917–2000). *Blind Beggars*, 1938. Tempera on illustration board, 20⅛ × 15 in. (51.1 × 38.1 cm). The Metropolitan Museum of Art, New York, Gift of New York City W.P.A., 1943 (43.47.28)

Neel's time in Spanish Harlem, where she resided until 1962, coincided with the rise of Abstract Expressionism, which gradually but decisively supplanted the work of WPA-era Social Realist artists like Neel. During this period, Neel framed her artistic practice as a critique of and remedy for the presumed anti-humanism of contemporary abstraction. In 1950, when Jackson Pollock's "drip" paintings were defining a new avant-garde in American art (fig. 11), Neel declared in the pages of the *Daily Worker*, "I am against abstract and non-objective art because such art shows a hatred of human beings. It is an attempt to eliminate people from art, and as such it is bound to fail."[22] While Neel's relationship to the abstract painting of her day was more nuanced than this statement would indicate, as Julia Bryan-Wilson explores in her essay, the artist's pointed refusal to acquiesce to the compulsory critical bias in favor of nonobjective and expressive abstraction contributed mightily to the neglect she endured throughout the 1950s, a decade during which she also found herself under surveillance by the FBI for her political activities.[23] That Neel's most pointed rejection of abstraction appeared at the height of the Cold War, inside a Communist periodical, is of great relevance. Indeed, it seems likely that Neel was participating in a political and artistic polemic specific to that time, which pitted Communism against capitalism, the USSR against the USA, and Social Realism against abstraction. As the Cold War waned, interestingly so too did Neel's rejection of abstraction, so much so that by the last decade and a half of her life she was signaling regularly and publicly her embrace of a stylistic mode she once denounced.[24]

In 1962 Neel moved from East to West Harlem, renting an apartment at 107th Street and Broadway (fig. 12). Formal and stylistic changes followed: besides working on a larger scale than before, Neel began to experiment with bolder, brighter colors and an ever-greater economy of means. Her subject matter evolved and expanded too. Then as now, the Upper West Side was a diverse neighborhood, home to large Black and Latino communities as well as immigrants and Columbia University students. Situated amid a global diaspora, Neel painted her first images of people of South Asian, Middle Eastern, Japanese, and South Korean descent, some of whom had settled in the United States by virtue of the 1965 Immigration and Nationality Act. In West Harlem Neel also launched one of her most groundbreaking bodies of work: pregnant nudes. This subject is rare in the history of Western art, but Neel's blunt, forthright manner of representing the distended bellies of expectant mothers is simply without precedent. Equally radical are Neel's paintings of mothers. In these works, the artist gave expression to the emotional complexity and psychological strain of caring for children, an experience with which she herself grappled as the mother of four children, two of whom she raised into adulthood on her own, all the while struggling to realize her ambitions as an artist, as Meredith A. Brown explores in her essay.[25]

Occupying a much broader stage than she had previously enjoyed, Neel added into her picture gallery of the 1960s and 1970s images of celebrated artists, performers, critics, curators, and filmmakers of the day, most of them a generation or two younger than her. No less eccentric and dissident than the intellectuals and activists she painted in the 1930s,

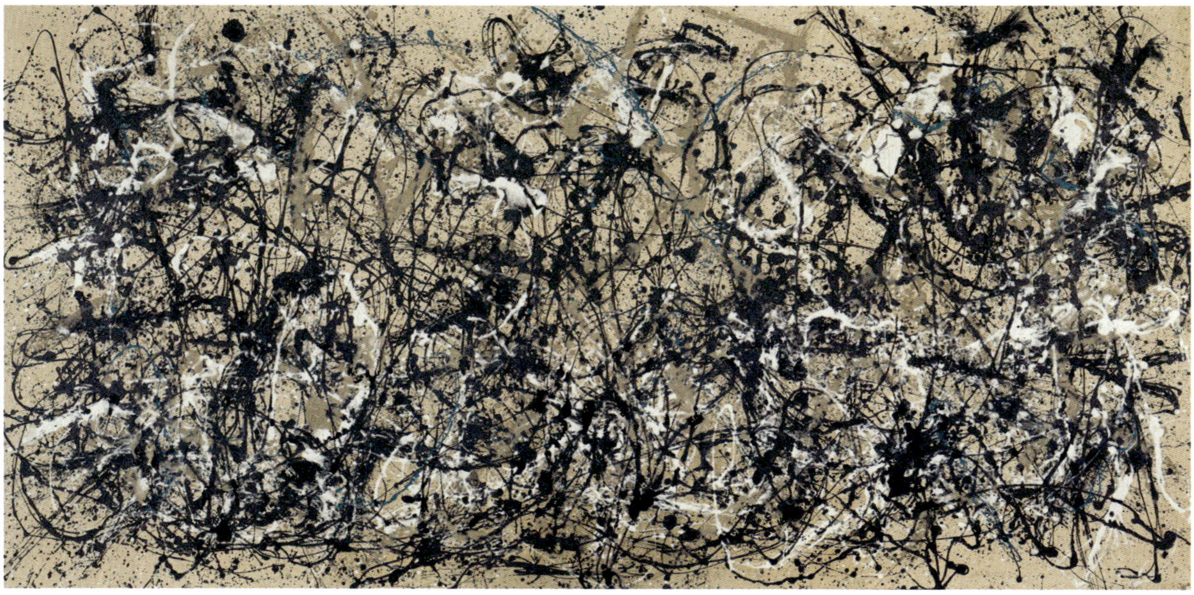

FIG. 11 Jackson Pollock (American, 1912–1956). *Autumn Rhythm (Number 30)*, 1950. Enamel on canvas, 105 × 207 in. (266.7 × 525.8 cm). The Metropolitan Museum of Art, New York, George A. Hearn Fund, 1957 (57.92)

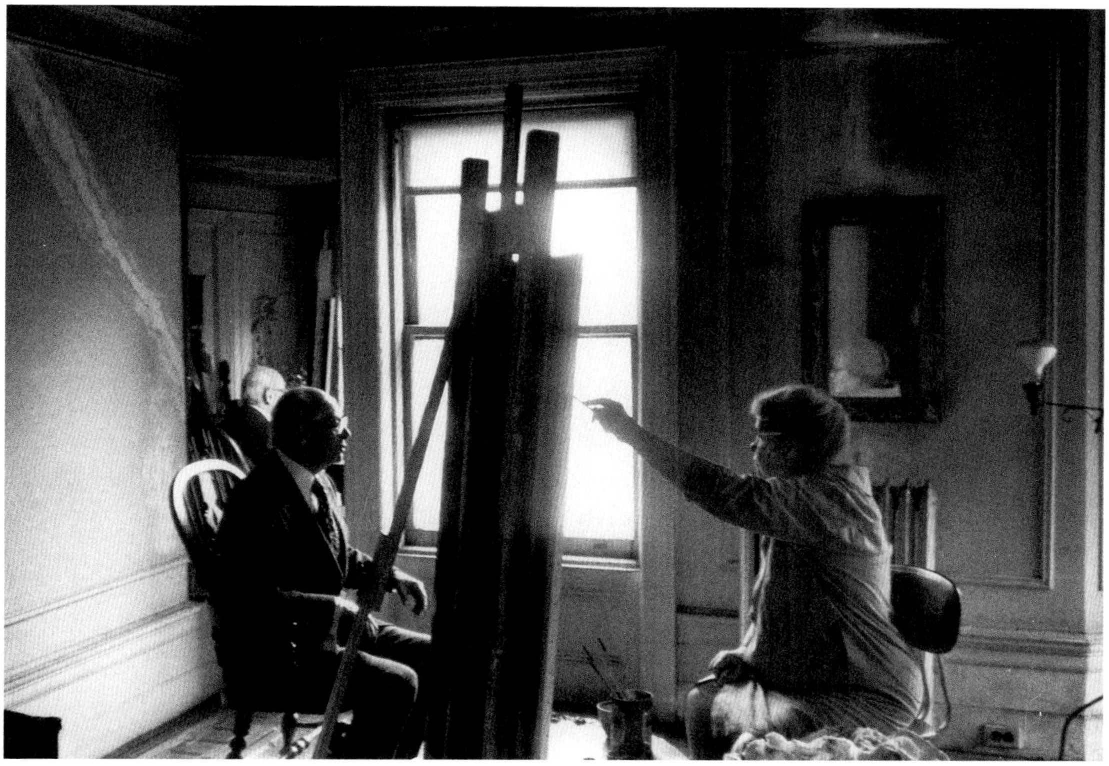

FIG. 12 **Alice Neel painting Edward Weiss in her apartment at 300 West 107th Street, ca. 1976. Alice Neel Archive, Stowe, Vt.**

1940s, and 1950s, these new subjects were considerably more unconventional in appearance and demeanor than their predecessors. Among them were numerous known LGBTQ individuals (mostly gay men), whom Neel painted throughout the early years of the gay rights movement, a coincidence that has led many scholars to adopt and exalt her as an avowed straight ally, as Randall Griffey explores in his essay. In the 1970s, Neel also created portraits of feminist critics and curators, who rallied around the artist's life and work and contributed to her late-career ascendancy.

During this period, Neel was often on the road, giving slide lectures around the country, although she also spent increasing amounts of time with her two sons—Richard and Hartley—daughters-in-law, and grandchildren, whom she painted in New York, at her home in Spring Lake, New Jersey, and on Hartley and Ginny Neel's property in Vermont. These works chronicle in loving, uncompromising detail the growth of the Neel family. They also capture broad social changes, from the explosion of counterculture in the 1960s to the conservative retrenchment of the 1970s. In these and other images from the last decade and a half of her career, moreover, Neel realized the full potential of an unfinished aesthetic.[26] Because she generally eschewed the use of preparatory drawings, choosing instead to draw directly on the canvas with paint, her work had always lacked a high degree of finish.[27] Later, however,

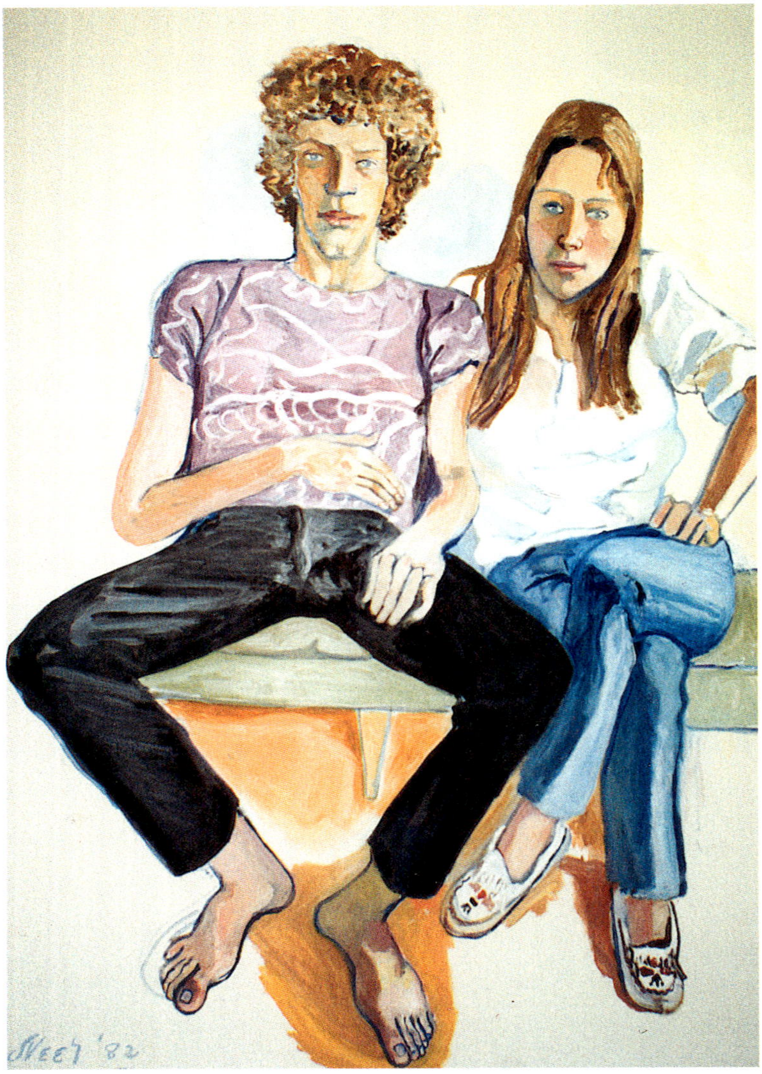


FIG. 13 *David and Catherine Saalfield*, 1982. Oil on canvas, 55 × 40 in. (139.7 × 101.6 cm). Collection of Agnes Gund

Neel deliberately began to allow even more traces of her process to remain visible and left ever larger portions of her canvases empty, with the bodies of her sitters roughly sketched in and the backgrounds barely articulated (fig. 13). She associated this approach with a modern sensibility. "In old-fashioned art," Neel once said, "they drew things in, but they hid their tracks; they finished everything. Of course, that finish is to me insipid. But the characteristic of modern art is to let the drawing show through. Look at Matisse. . . . And Cézanne's late work—a lot of it was very unfinished."[28] The more unfinished Neel's paintings, the more abstract they invariably are.

In 1956—during the nadir of her career—cultural anthropologist Stephen Porter Dunn published an adoring paean to Neel, exalting her artistic commitment to and presumed identification with all of her sitters, no matter how different they were from her. Portraying Neel as a kind of

Mother Teresa in a painter's smock, Dunn deified the artist, a seeming martyr to unpopular and unfashionable causes:

> You belong / Among the people you paint, the sad people / Who'd be better off dead, or in some other world / Than this, since nobody likes them or calls them / human, / No one who counts, that is, but you and me / You say only / These outcasts are your friends: the Communist, / the radical poet who has lost his faith, / The Village character, the lesbians, / And even the lone Park Avenue matron, rich as sin. / Though they inhabit a country unknown to others, / You carry a passport to it; / the people trust you. / You can cross the border without being suspected. / You look like one of them, / To us like one of us.[29]

Neel's aura as an irreproachable champion of all those she painted, likewise her limitless powers of empathy, has only increased since her death in 1984. Her uncompromising artistic vision, her unconventional life, and her disarming, slightly quirky personality have earned her new admirers, among them a host of contemporary artists, including Jordan Casteel (see fig. 42), Moyra Davey, Barkley L. Hendricks, Simone Leigh, Sharon Lockhart, and Shirin Neshat. Indeed, in an era of record income inequality, resurgent white nationalism, and xenophobia, Neel's painterly advocacy of humanity in its multiracial and multicultural manifestations, her inclusive, democratic spirit, and her commitment to social justice all serve to enhance her posthumous reputation, making her art seem all the more relevant, even urgent.

Yet Neel wasn't a martyr or a saint, and we should not expect her to be. Like the individuals who appear in her "pictures of people," she was a compelling, complicated person possessing admirable virtues but also blind spots, many of which were symptomatic of the time in which she lived. Neel embraced imperfection as intrinsic to the human condition, and we are wrong to assume perfection from her. Just as Neel understood and pursued her mission to visualize the "human comedy," *Alice Neel: People Come First* seeks to provide a complex, honest, and unflinching portrayal of her art.[30]

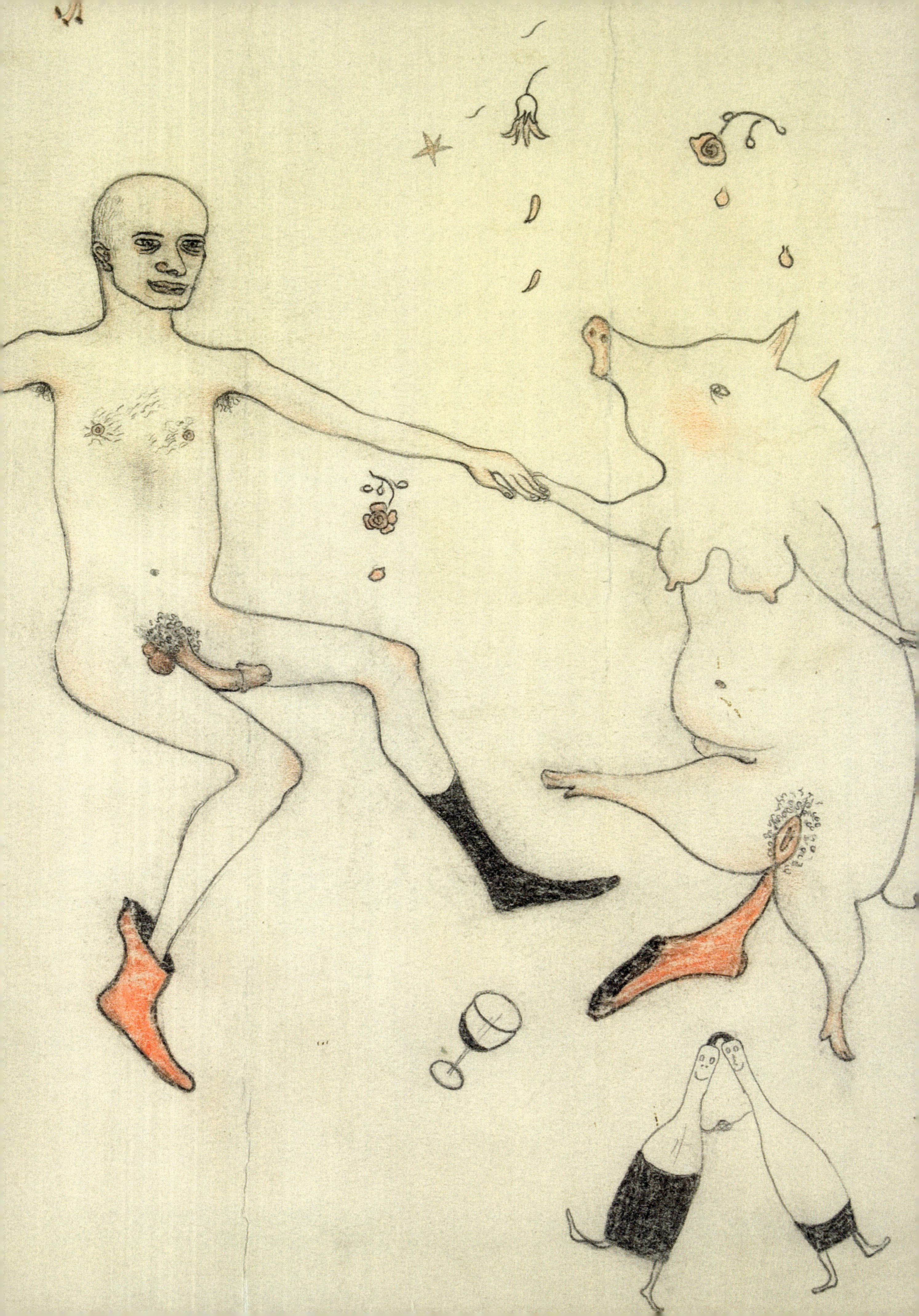

# POLITICAL CREATURES

**KELLY BAUM**

Alice Neel was a political creature through and through—a radical humanist, this book proposes. But when was she at her most radical? We might presume it was in her paintings of Communist luminaries and Popular Front demonstrations. Here she parades her commitment to social and economic justice. Yet these images are only the most obvious and, in some ways, the most conservative manifestations of Neel's politics. The artist was at her most radical when she was at her least didactic and least declarative—that is, when she did not seem to be making political statements at all.[1] Indeed, if we truly want to find the "radical" in Neel's "humanism," we must look in unexpected places, in her depictions of interspecies bacchanals, for instance, and her renderings of suicide wards and pregnant bellies. By considering "elsewheres" such as these, we will also retrieve the artist's feminism, which similarly has taproots in sources both familiar and unfamiliar.

## PAINT YOUR PLACE

When she settled in New York in the early 1930s, Neel chose to reside at the epicenter of progressive politics in the city: Greenwich Village, a community dominated by left-leaning activists and intellectuals. Neel was first introduced to the neighborhood between 1927 and 1930, when she lived uptown with her husband, Carlos Enríquez, but commuted downtown to work in Fanya Foss's store. After returning to New York with her lover Kenneth Doolittle, in 1931–32, Neel rented a home on Cornelia Street. A few years later, in 1934, she moved to West 17th Street. Both apartments were a short walk from the headquarters of the Communist Party USA (CPUSA), at 35 West 12th Street. A wide range of party-affiliated organizations rented space in the same building, including the newspaper the *Daily Worker*, the New York Workers School, the Workers Bookshop, the Young Communist League, and the National Negro Congress. Also based in the area were the offices of *Art Front*, the mouthpiece of the Artists' Union and the Artists' Committee of Action; *New Masses* and, later, *Masses & Mainstream*, both Communist publications; and the NAACP, from whose window a banner reading "A MAN WAS LYNCHED YESTERDAY" hung regularly in the later 1930s (fig. 14).[2] Neel's residence in Greenwich Village, where encounters with socialists and civil rights advocates were routine, simultaneously reflected and cemented her commitment to radical politics. It is little wonder that she joined the CPUSA in 1935 (as did many other women at this time) and supported Black liberation her entire life.[3]

Neel's arrival on Cornelia Street also marks the beginning of what she called her "revolutionary paintings."[4] These canvases often depict real-life revolutionaries, most of whom were

Detail of *Joie de Vivre* (fig. 19)

members of the CPUSA, which advocated for not only economic justice and workers' rights but also Black and Puerto Rican liberation. (From almost the moment of its founding in 1919, the CPUSA recognized African Americans as an oppressed class, openly embracing a broad civil rights agenda.)[5] A few of Neel's sitters from the 1930s through the 1950s were strictly political actors, including labor organizers Pat Whalen (p. 124), Ella Reeve "Mother" Bloor (pp. 168, 169), and "Brother" Bill McKie (1953). The vast majority, though, were artists and intellectuals who excelled at class warfare and civil rights as much as creativity. Such was true of journalist Art Shields (1951), translator Sam Putnam (1933), scholar Harold Cruse (fig. 15), playwright and actress Alice Childress (p. 165),[6] poet and novelist Kenneth Fearing (p. 122), educator and historian Mercedes Arroyo (p. 131),[7] writers Hubert Satterfield (1952 and p. 171) and Alvin Simon (1959), and editors and authors Phillip Bonosky (p. 164) and Mike Gold (p. 166).

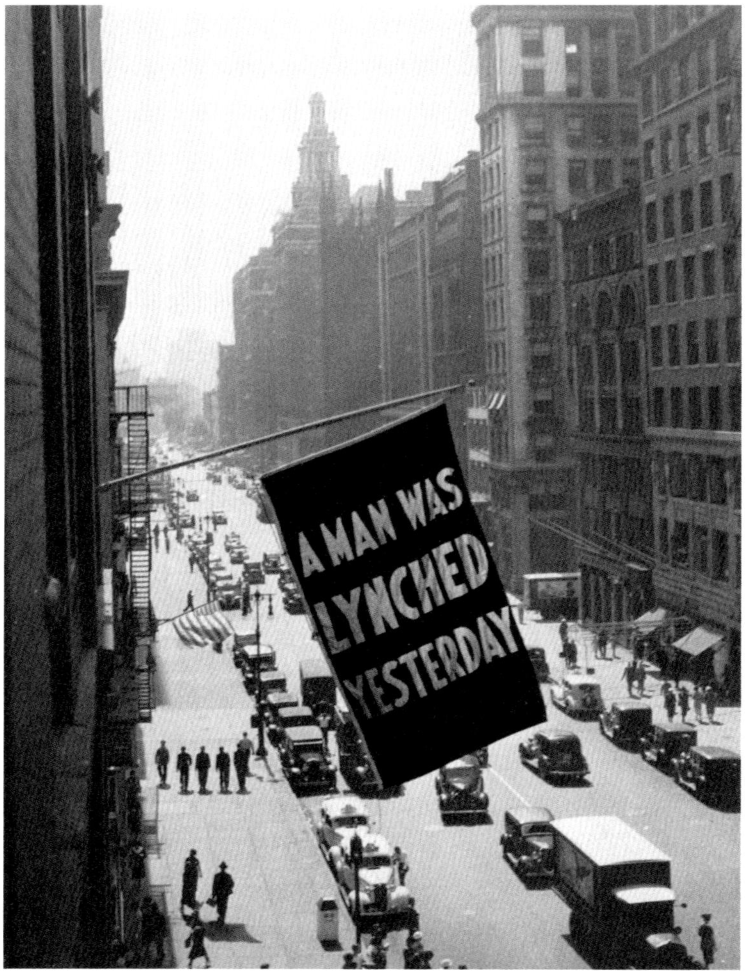


FIG. 14 A banner flown from a window of the NAACP headquarters on 69 Fifth Avenue, New York, announcing, "A man was lynched yesterday," 1936. Library of Congress

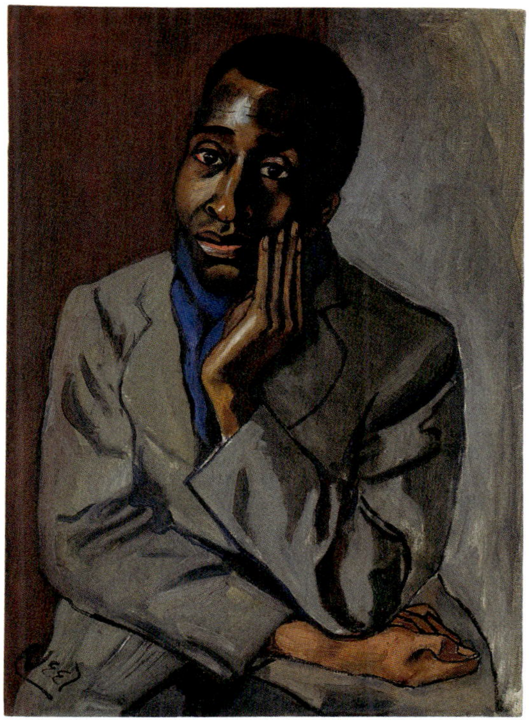

FIG. 15 *Harold Cruse*, ca. 1950. Oil on canvas, 31 × 22 in. (78.7 × 55.9 cm). Private collection

Neel knew some of her sitters in name only, such as Mother Bloor, whose deathbed portrait she might have based on a photograph from *Life* magazine, but others she collaborated with on ventures both militant and artistic, whether in Greenwich Village or in Spanish Harlem, where she relocated in 1938. Indeed, Neel traveled in many of the same circles as the dissidents she depicted. Proving an especially rich source of subject matter were the political and intellectual communities that coalesced around a handful of left-leaning organizations.[8] Gold and Childress served on the board of the New Playwrights Theatre, for example, which hosted an exhibition of Neel's work in 1951, for which Gold wrote an accompanying essay. Childress and Arroyo taught at the Jefferson School of Social Science, where Neel took classes in the 1940s and 1950s and delivered one of her earliest slide lectures, in 1953.[9] Putnam, Shields, and Gold reported for the *Daily Worker*, for which Bonosky served as an editor and for which Gold once wrote an essay on Neel. Bonosky, Childress, and Gold each contributed to *New Masses* and *Masses & Mainstream*, two publications that Bonosky and Gold also edited. Such periodicals make appearances in Neel's portraits: Mike Gold rests his hands next to an issue of *New Masses*,[10] while Pat Whalen holds his clenched fists above a copy of the *Daily Worker* and a figure in the far-left background of *Kenneth Fearing* carries a copy of the same newspaper under his arm. Neel herself provided the occasional illustration to *Masses & Mainstream*, likewise its successor, *Mainstream*.[11]

Neel continued to paint revolutionaries after she moved to the Upper West Side in 1962, favoring leaders in the civil rights and feminist movements, both of which had established organizations independent of the CPUSA by the 1960s. Hugh Hurd (1964) falls into this group, as do Kate Millett (fig. 29), Benny Andrews (p. 183), Irene Peslikis (p. 175), Linda Nochlin (p. 219), and Faith Ringgold (fig. 30). Neel's drawing of Marxist insurgent Che Guevara (p. 170), made shortly after he was executed in Bolivia and based on one of the photographs released to the press as evidence, dates from this period as well. With the exception of Guevara, Neel's sitters all lock eyes with the viewer, addressing and implicating all at once. Consider James Farmer (p. 172), for instance, whom Neel captured the same year he and other members of CORE (Congress for Racial Equality) were arrested while protesting at the World's Fair in Flushing Meadows, Queens.[12] A study in focus, determination, and intensity, Farmer's brow is furrowed, his body clenched tight like a fist. Neel felt a strong sense of political kinship with Farmer, as she did with the other radicals she depicted. Indeed, it was their shared commitment to equality that led her to represent them in the first place.

The rank and file of the "Old Left" figure in Neel's pictures as well, but almost always in the context of group demonstrations. This holds true for *Uneeda Biscuit Strike* of 1936 (fig. 16), in which mounted police officers beat striking workers, and *Nazis Murder Jews* (p. 126), painted the same year, which documents a protest against fascism and genocide that Neel herself attended.[13] *Save Willie McGee* of about 1950 (p. 127) depicts a rally on behalf of a Black man from

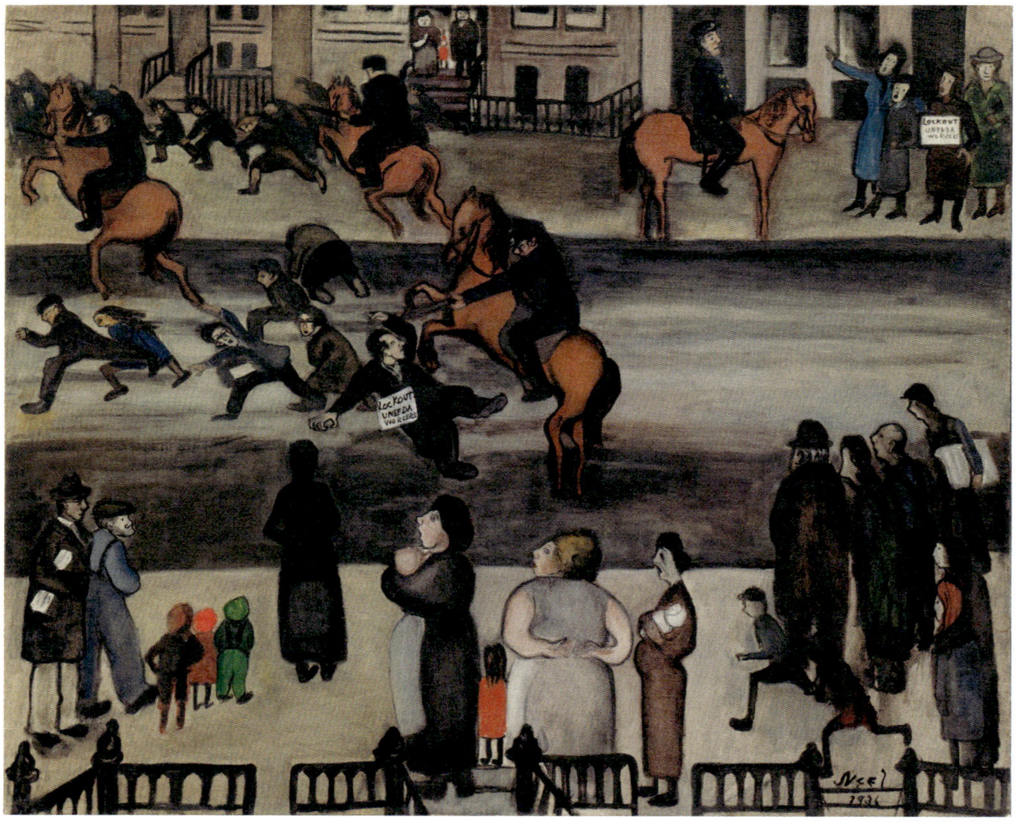

FIG. 16 *Uneeda Biscuit Strike*, 1936. Oil on canvas, 36 × 43 in. (91.4 × 109.2 cm). Estate of Alice Neel

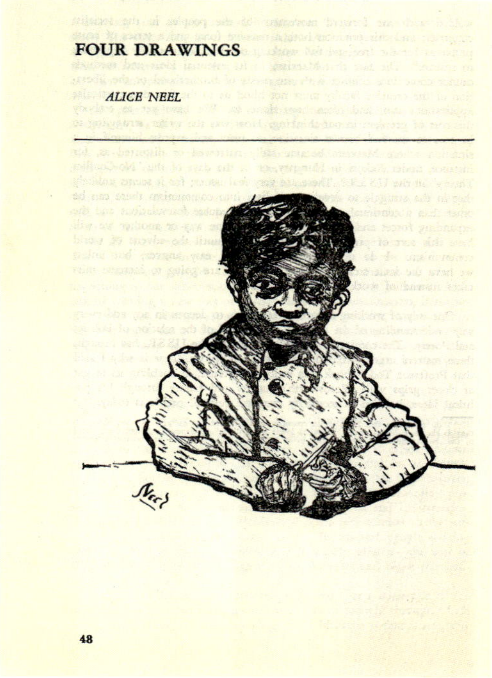


FIG. 17 Neel's drawing of Georgie Arce as reproduced in *Mainstream*, June 1958, p. 48

Mississippi who had been convicted, unjustly, many believed, on charges of rape, attracting the attention of both Communists and civil rights advocates. McGee was memorialized as a political prisoner in the July 1950 issue of *Masses & Mainstream*, and his trial was covered extensively in both that journal and the *Daily Worker* between 1950 and 1951, the year he was executed.

In addition to painting the agents of political change, Neel devoted a great number of pictures to what art historian Hal Foster has called the "precariat," a class of people particularly vulnerable to violence and discrimination.[14] Neel tended to paint the most precarious of the precariat: poor people of color, especially women and children, most of them immigrants, whose simultaneous exposure to poverty, sexism, and ethnophobia compounded their suffering. These are the same individuals for whom the dissidents Neel memorialized were fighting, and she gravitated to them out of a sense of solidarity and responsibility. The artist first began to represent ethnic minorities of the lower and working classes while living in Havana with her husband between 1926 and 1927 (see p. 208). She returned to the theme after moving to New York during the peak of the Great Depression. Neel's paintings from this period reference concrete, identifiable subjects, as in *Investigation of Poverty at the Russell Sage Foundation* of 1933 (p. 119), in which a homeless mother of seven and two indigent men plead their cases to the foundation's members. Such works tend to be didactic and moralizing, demonstrating Neel's more conservative side.

Far more affective are Neel's portraits from Spanish Harlem, which depict her Black and Puerto Rican neighbors, some of them members of her extended family, alone or in small groups. Shorn of contextual detail and absent the rules of conventional storytelling, such images communicate in an especially direct manner. Many were originally disseminated through extra-artistic spaces affiliated with the CPUSA: while the New Playwrights Theatre featured *Mercedes Arroyo* (p. 131),

*The Spanish Family* (p. 210), and *T.B. Harlem* (p. 187) in Neel's 1951 exhibition, *Mainstream* included a drawing of Georgie Arce in its June 1958 issue (fig. 17).[15] Neel was well aware of the difficulties that plagued Spanish Harlem before and after World War II—hunger, infirmity, illiteracy, and underemployment among them. She references this cluster of hardships explicitly in *T.B. Harlem*, a haunting portrait of Carlos Santiago Negrón, her lover José's brother, pictured after receiving treatment for tuberculosis, an illness that disproportionately impacted (and still does) poor communities of color.[16] Neel represents Carlos as a contemporary martyr, his bandaged chest a sign of both injury and persecution. In the residents of Spanish Harlem, however, Neel saw more than just victims. Fittingly, her portraits strike a delicate balance, acknowledging the physical and psychological toll of poverty while affirming her sitters' innate dignity and agency. In so doing, they grant visibility to subjects who remained largely absent from the precinct of fine art, breaking the monopoly that white, upper-class men had long enjoyed on the category of human being as well.

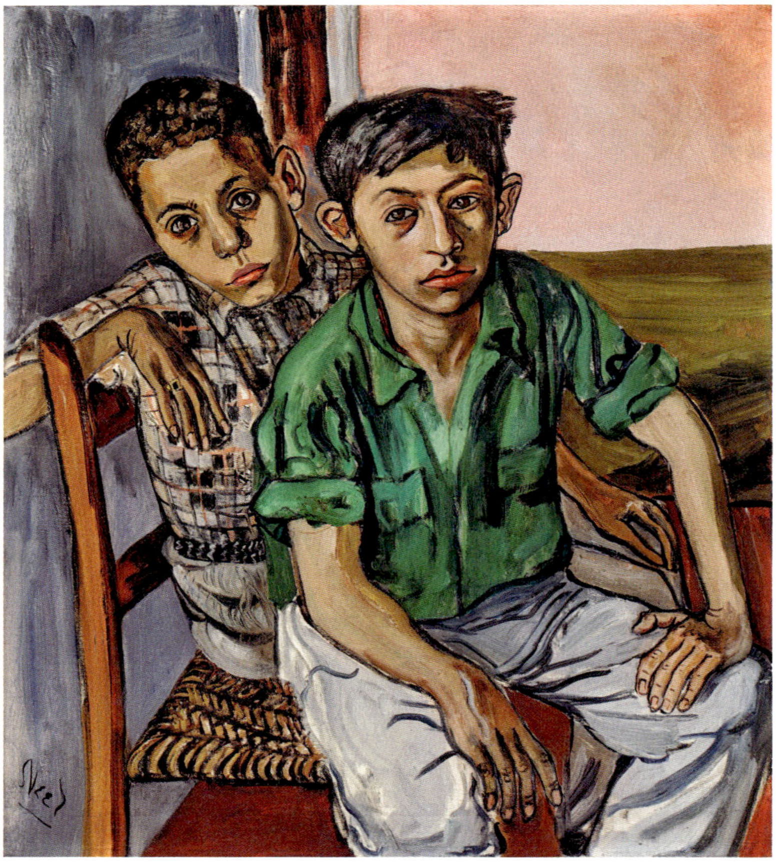

FIG. 18 *Two Puerto Rican Boys*, 1956. Oil on canvas, 32 × 28 in. (81.3 × 71.1 cm). Jeff and Mei Sze Greene Collection

Paintings such as *T.B. Harlem* also signal an important change in Neel's practice. The artist had almost always worked from home, but until 1938, with very few exceptions, those homes were in predominantly white neighborhoods and hosted exclusively white sitters, most of them intimates with whom she enjoyed professional ties. The resulting portraits document unions on common ground between "like" and "like." Different conditions were at play in Spanish Harlem, however, where familiarity between artist and sitter was harder fought. For her part, Neel tended to romanticize her relationship to El Barrio. The story she told was one of belonging, appreciation, and hospitality: that is, of cross-racial, cross-ethnic harmony. She was no mere "tourist" or voyeur in a neighborhood of Black and Latino people, as she put it.[17] To a certain extent, this was true. José, the father of Neel's first son, Richard, was Puerto Rican, and his extended family lived near Neel's building. Neel, who spoke Spanish quite well, participated actively in the cultural and political life of El Barrio, where she resided for twenty-four years, leaving only after her landlord offered her a larger apartment for the same price. That said, as a white woman from a middle-class suburb, the artist would necessarily have always remained a little out of place in El Barrio, neither a stranger, exactly, nor an insider. The same held true for her sitters, in fact. As recent immigrants and first-generation citizens, they too would have experienced an incomplete sense of belonging, both a part of and apart from the island of Manhattan. Indeed, for artist and sitter to have met where they did—in Neel's home, in the middle of El Barrio—each had to have "traveled abroad," so to speak, to have crossed a threshold into unfamiliar territory, whether a home, a neighborhood, a city, or a country.

This, in turn, set the stage for the charged drama that plays out repeatedly in the paintings themselves. Again and again, we witness artist and sitter confronting each other across either side of a canvas. The distance between them is small, but the social and cultural gulf is considerable. It was always Neel's intention to forge a connection with her subjects, but misrecognition turns out to have been just as likely an outcome as identification. In the most intimate of her portraits, sitters lean into the picture plane and fill the edges of the canvas, creating the impression of physical and, by extension, emotional proximity. Consider *A Spanish Boy* of 1955 (p. 155), which depicts Georgie Arce, a young child Neel painted many times over the course of several years and with whom she was quite close. Arce's face is open, searching, while his posture is suggestive of trust and familiarity. *The Spanish Family* of 1943 (p. 210) pitches in a different direction, with its sitters—José's sister-in-law and three of her children—receding deep into the background. Despite the family connection, no current of affection travels between Neel and the Négrons. The young boy is weary, the mother detached, and the girl distracted. More ambivalent is *Two Girls, Spanish Harlem* of 1959 (p. 135). Here Antonia and Carmen Encarnación, both of them curious but uncertain, squirm under Neel's gaze, especially Carmen, who closes her body like a clamshell. Other portraits seem more like standoffs, with the sitters conveying suspicion, defiance, even hostility. Such is true of *Two Puerto Rican Boys* of 1956 (fig. 18), *Georgie* of 1950, and *Georgie Arce No. 2* of 1955 (p. 133). In the latter, an older Arce reciprocates Neel's scrutiny from under a furrowed brow, brandishing a knife in her direction, the same one Neel recalled he used when pretending to cut her throat, perhaps.[18] That the knife was rubber and Arce was playacting in no way diminishes the animosity he projects, not least because its target is the uninitiated viewer as much as it is Neel.

Such portraits serve as important object lessons, suggesting as they do the myriad ways in which "radical" operates in Neel's work, some less obvious than others. Indeed, as evidenced by the pictures above, the artist's honesty was just as provocative as her politics, especially when it came to the intricacies of human relationships and the intensities of cross-cultural exchange. Sometimes, Neel's pictures tell us, we are just as likely to prove incomprehensible to one another as intelligible. Sometimes intersubjective communication results in refusal as much as acceptance, in conflict as much as unity. Philosophers Judith Butler, Simon Critchley, and Thomas Keenan have all identified this very predicament—the "intolerable complexity" of our encounters with others—as central to the work of ethical activity.[19] "Perhaps most importantly," Butler writes, "we must recognize that ethics requires us to risk ourselves precisely at moments of unknowingness. . . . To be undone by another is a primary necessity, an anguish, to be sure, but also a chance—to be addressed, claimed . . . to be moved, to be prompted to act. . . . If we . . . try to give an account from this place, we will not be irresponsible, or if we are, we will surely be forgiven."[20] Neel took these very risks throughout her career, but nowhere more overtly than in her portraits from El Barrio.

## PAINT YOUR DESIRE

Throughout her career, Neel consistently depicted subjects that few artists—especially women—had dared represent before, and she did so with a candor and irreverence equally rare in the history of art. Many such themes are intensely private, ranging from the joyful to the fantastical to the harrowing. In making them the focus of her art, Neel gave visual expression to categories of female experience that had long been ignored, belittled, or even censored by patriarchal culture. These are not necessarily her best-known works, but they are some of her most radical, precisely because they address topics long considered taboo. Among the most extraordinary are the erotic images she created in the 1930s, all of which dramatize her sexual agency.[21] So singular is their content that Linda Nochlin recognized in Neel that rarest of species: a female artist who claimed territory previously monopolized by men—the erotic—for herself.[22]

Neel's erotica is of two general types: images of her lovers, seen alone, often asleep, and images of the artist in the company of a partner. Consider, for instance, a watercolor of Neel and José Negrón nude, painted about 1935 (p. 150). Neel places her hand behind her head in the manner of an odalisque, while Negrón stands upright, his left hand positioned suggestively near his penis. Facing the viewer head-on, the couple parade their extramarital affair without guilt or apology. In the poignant *Alice and José* of 1938 (p. 149), the two lie cuddled in bed, their eyes closed, with Negrón's head resting on Neel's shoulder and Neel's luxurious hair spread across the pillow. In other examples, the artist herself is absent, but her presence as both author and protagonist is nonetheless implied. Indeed, the perspective in Neel's erotica is invariably her own. Such is true of

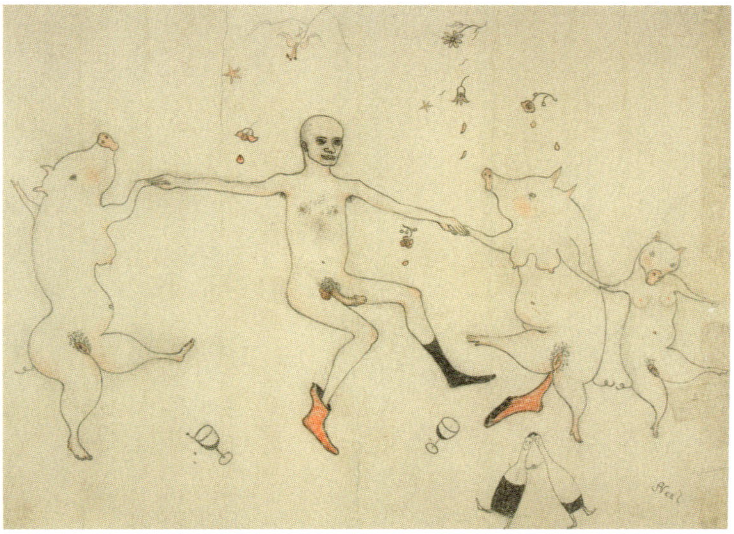

FIG. 19 *Joie de Vivre*, 1935. Graphite and wax crayon, 11 15/16 × 15 15/16 in. (30.4 × 40.5 cm). Yale University Art Gallery, New Haven, Purchased with the aid of funds from the National Endowment for the Arts and the Susan Morse Hilles Matching Fund (1978.120)

*Kenneth Doolittle* of 1932 (p. 196), whose subject is drawn from above looking down. This particular mise-en-scène, in which Doolittle lies sleeping under a carved crucifixion, his legs splayed and his genitalia exposed, is as kinky as it is blasphemous. Far more tender but just as covetous are the artist's images of Negrón, especially the 1938 pastel *José Asleep* (p. 151). Thanks to the perspective Neel assumed, we imagine ourselves seated on the bed just next to Negrón. Taking advantage of his vulnerability, our gaze, like Neel's, lingers over his body and indulges in his beauty.

Created in between the drawing of Doolittle and the pastels and watercolors of Negrón is a remarkable series of watercolors depicting Neel with another lover, John Rothschild. These are more stories than snapshots, and together they tell a far more complicated tale. *Joie de Vivre* of 1935 (fig. 19) is a raucous interspecies bacchanal, a scene of polymorphic pleasure between a man, John, and three pigs endowed with female anatomy.[23] John's erect penis points in the direction of one of the pigs, an avatar for Neel. His left boot, which has detached from his foot and sailed across the paper, tickles her clitoris. Around the lovers a cacophony of flowers and glasses swirl, while two bottles of wine dance a tango. Part pornographic postcard, part Disney animation (the parallels with *Flowers and Trees*, of 1932, one of the *Silly Symphonies*, is especially suggestive), *Joie de Vivre* might be cloaked in allegory, but it remains one of the most uninhibited representations of female pleasure in twentieth-century art. Indeed, that Neel felt emboldened to create such a work in 1935 is truly remarkable.

The two related watercolors are equally extraordinary, albeit more for their candor and irreverence than their libidinal charge. *Untitled (Alice Neel and John Rothschild in the Bathroom)* (p. 145) represents either the routine preamble to or the banal aftermath of a sexual encounter. Rothschild pees into a sink, while Neel urinates into a toilet. He inspects his nails, while she adjusts her coiffure. Their reciprocal disinterest borders on the severe. Even more sobering is *Alienation* (p. 144), which Neel painted in Spring Lake, New Jersey, where she and Rothschild rented a house over the summer.[24] A scene of postcoital malaise, *Alienation* shows Neel lying unclothed on a bed. As with Negrón, she assumes the pose of an odalisque, but here, it seems strained, affected. Rothschild stands naked beside her. Projecting utter defeat, he crosses his legs at the ankle and wraps his arms protectively around his torso. Just as Neel looks away from him, he turns away from her, their estrangement complete. Considered in conjunction with *Joie de Vivre*, *Kenneth Doolittle*, and *José Asleep*, these last two watercolors epitomize Neel's tendency to demystify–to deromanticize–sex. Whether representing the heat of a passionate encounter or the flaws of an erotic relationship, Neel always steered clear of sentimentality, adopting an ethic of radical honesty that links her work across subject matter.

As it happens, the Hays Code went into effect the same decade Neel created her erotic images. Signed into law in 1930 but not enforced until 1934, the code regulated morality in motion pictures, signaling a new era of conservatism. Along with scenes of childbirth, it prohibited "complete nudity," "adultery and illicit sex," "sex perversion" (or same-sex desire), and "dances suggesting or representing sexual actions or indecent passion."[25] Neel's erotica falls foul of both the spirit and the letter of the code. As such, it evokes a much earlier moment in the history of Greenwich Village, when sexual liberalization was widespread. Indeed, the conditions of possibility for a work like *Joie de Vivre* lie very much in the 1910s, within a community that coalesced around sisters Ethel Byrne and Margaret Sanger and writers Floyd Dell and Max Eastman, who edited the left-leaning monthly *The Masses*, to which Neel's friend Mike Gold contributed some of his earliest essays. These progressive, Village-based feminists espoused not only socialism but also "sexual modernism,"[26] whose tenets included free love and erotic equality for women.[27] Consciously or not, Neel was channeling just this generation of dissidents when she started making her own sexual revolution two decades later.[28] So radical was the art she produced in the process, none of it would see the light of day until the 1970s, when the interdiction against the expression of female sexuality began to loosen.[29]

## PAINT YOUR OPPRESSION

Neel was equally expert at visualizing "female maladies."[30] Guided by her own experience, she gave form to some of the most private and painful aspects of women's lives, no more so than in the late 1920s and early 1930s, when she was a young wife, mother, and artist whose relationship with both the nuclear family and conventional gender roles was under severe strain. Such pictures exemplify what scholar Jacqueline Rose has called "scandalous feminism." Relying on the strategies of revelation and disclosure, scandalous feminists like Neel surface the "scars of oppression," acknowledging what women "in their dreams and nightmares" have endured at the hands of patriarchal society.[31] Despite their origins in autobiography, Neel's works have profound political currency, foregrounding as they do the injustices propagated by extra-personal ideologies and institutions.

Consider, for example, the operatic *Well Baby Clinic* of 1928–29 (p. 184). Set in the hospital where Neel gave birth on November 24, 1928, while living in dire financial straits in the Bronx, the painting addresses the ignominy of childbirth, specifically among poor women. Neel herself appears at the far middle right. Projecting both composure and serenity, she peers down at

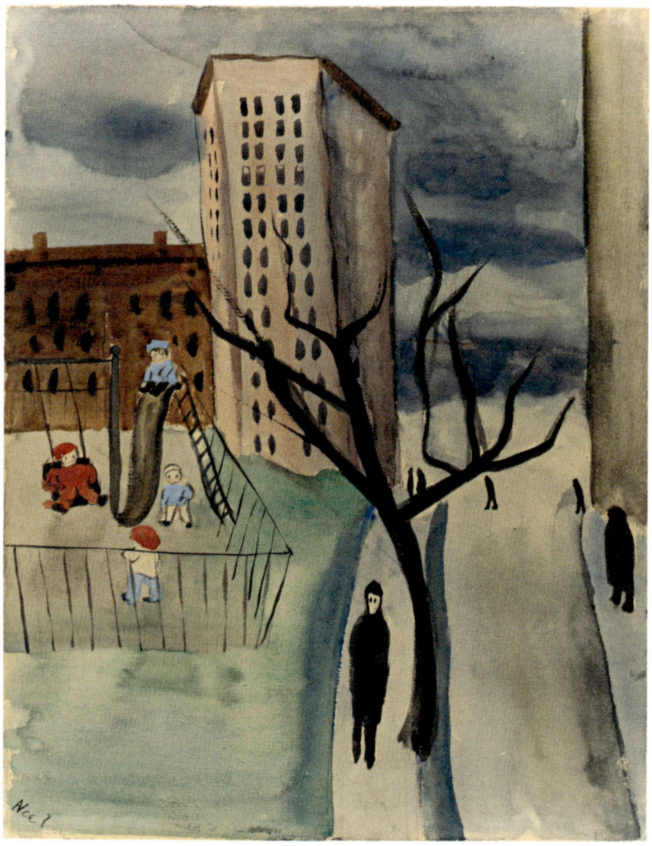

FIG. 20 *After the Death of the Child*, 1927–28. Watercolor, gouache, and graphite on paper, 11 3/4 × 8 3/4 in. (29.8 × 22.2 cm). The Frances Lehman Loeb Center, Vassar College, Poughkeepsie, N.Y., Gift of Mrs. John Benson Brooks (Frances K. B. Jones, class of 1940) (1990.19.6)

her second daughter, Isabetta, who returns her gaze beatifically. This is the work's only nod to romantic sentiment, however. Surrounding artist and child is a nightmare of decrepitude: ugly, misshapen babies squirm, while their mothers, deformed by fear and privation, sit in varying degrees of dismay. The wild grin and ravaged body of the woman at center left signals emotional instability. Her green dress falls from her shoulder, ripped by the insatiable infant in her lap, who pulls impatiently at one of her nipples. In a society based on economic inequality, Neel's painting implies, privacy and dignity are privileges reserved for upper-class women alone.

That said, *Well Baby Clinic* is thick with ambivalence, betraying as much antipathy for poor mothers as it does sympathy. Neel might buck a long-standing tradition and de-idealize the institution of motherhood, to her credit, but she does so at the expense of the families therein.[32] The artist's account of a visit to the maternity ward ("a very dismal place"), written shortly before she began work on *Well Baby Clinic*, expresses similar sentiments.[33] Besides lamenting the physical discomfort of pregnancy ("my own back aching") and the challenges of indigence ("you who do not know bitter poverty can little realize the powerful feeling I have, when like today, I am capable of paying the milk bill"), Neel struggles to recognize herself in the expectant mothers around her. "I have not yet attained that splendor of mind that revels in its oneness with all humanity," she confesses. "I feel sorry for them all—can realize their hard burdens—but I hate their stupid faces and I hate like hell to be their thin white robed companion." Neel ends by imagining the fate that awaits her cohort (a lifetime of "labor" and "grief"), expressing dismay that sex ("that so enjoyable privilege") leads only to suffering, at least for the poor, who too often lack ("for want of an oil stove . . . or a doctor in time") the ability to care for their young.[34]

A slightly later work also limns the relationship between motherhood, struggle, and grief. According to Neel, *Futility of Effort* of 1930 (p. 185) was inspired by two tragedies.[35] In December 1927, the artist lost her first daughter, Santillana, to diphtheria, an event that occasioned *After the Death of the Child* (fig. 20) and *Requiem*, of 1928, as well. Shortly after Santillana's passing, Neel learned of an infant who had choked on the bars of its crib while its mother was ironing in the kitchen. From this event she derived the picture's iconography. Here a small child faces straight ahead, its body suspended between the crib's rungs. A thin black line crosses the child's midsection, severing its upper torso from its lower half. The two parts are displaced left to right, a slippage in both space and logic that serves to intensify the work's haunting atmosphere. Rendered with an extreme economy of means, in which all visual activity is confined to a single plane, *Futility of Effort* distills the experience of loss, both personal and vicarious, into a dreamscape of grays, blacks, and whites. Much as she employed wildly expressionistic brushwork in *Well Baby Clinic* to accentuate the drama of childbirth and motherhood, so too does Neel rely strategically on style, in this case abstraction, to convey meaning and affect in *Futility of Effort*.

The three years between December 1927 and December 1930 were filled with tragedy and hardship for Neel. Besides losing Santillana and suffering intractable poverty, she was abandoned by her husband, Carlos Enríquez, who took their second daughter, Isabetta, back to Cuba in May 1930. In August Neel suffered a nervous breakdown, which resulted in her hospitalization over the course of the next year in four different clinics.[36] Created shortly after her return home in September 1931, *Suicidal Ward, Philadelphia General Hospital* (p. 186) recreates in lurid, harrowing detail the "frightful" conditions of Neel's confinement.[37] Though the artist herself is absent from the scene, Neel telegraphs her experience through a series of avatars—her fellow patients, "poor scraps of humanity," she called them.[38] At the front left is a woman who had sequestered herself in her room for ten years, at the back right an individual whom doctors force-fed with a tube every day. The older women at the front right "were not mentally ill, but they had nowhere else to put them."[39] The suicide ward, as Neel remembered it, was essentially a landfill with walls, a junkyard where society discarded the ill, the elderly, and the broken.

As much as *Suicidal Ward* documents a particular episode in the artist's life, likewise the cruelty of mental illness,[40] it also dramatizes a venerable prejudice that pits feminine irrationality against masculine reason. According to this logic, women possess particularly fragile psyches. Their predisposition to madness threatens the social order and nuclear family alike, demanding constant vigilance, a task historically entrusted to male doctors. With the aid of female nurses, these guardians of sanity simultaneously treat and control, cure and police. As such, they occupy positions of great authority vis-à-vis women. The man at the center of *Suicidal Ward*, Neel's psychiatrist, Dr. Breitenbach, lords this very power over his female patients. Master of his domain, he administers advice and treatment, all with the aim of containing, much like the barred windows

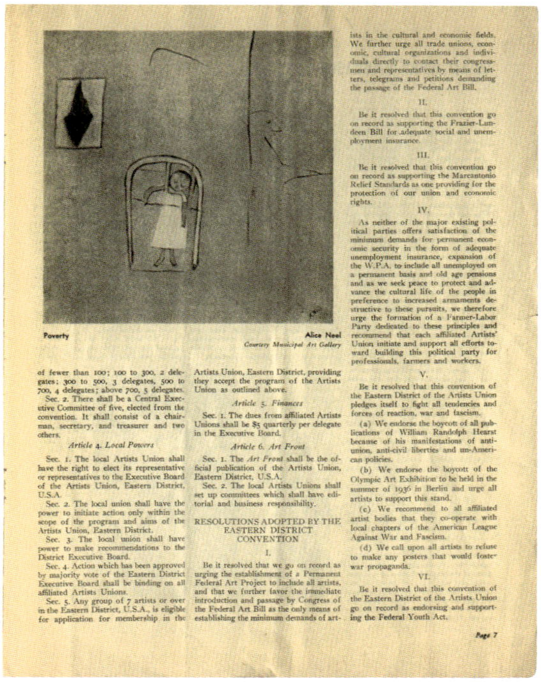

Poverty

Alice Neel
*Courtesy Municipal Art Gallery*

of fewer than 100; 100 to 300, 2 delegates; 300 to 500, 3 delegates, 500 to 700, 4 delegates; above 700, 5 delegates.

Sec. 2. There shall be a Central Executive Committee of five, elected from the convention. It shall consist of a chairman, secretary, and treasurer and two others.

*Article 4. Local Powers*

Sec. 1. The local Artists Union shall have the right to elect its representative or representatives to the Executive Board of the Artists Union, Eastern District, U.S.A.

Sec. 2. The local union shall have the power to initiate action only within the scope of the program and aims of the Artists Union, Eastern District.

Sec. 3. The local union shall have power to make recommendations to the District Executive Board.

Sec. 4. Action which has been approved by majority vote of the Eastern District Executive Board shall be binding on all affiliated Artists Unions.

Sec. 5. Any group of 7 artists or over in the Eastern District, U.S.A., is eligible for application for membership in the Artists Union, Eastern District, providing they accept the program of the Artists Union as outlined above.

*Article 5. Finances*

Sec. 1. The dues from affiliated Artists Unions shall be $5 quarterly per delegate in the Executive Board.

*Article 6. Art Front*

Sec. 1. The *Art Front* shall be the official publication of the Artists Union, Eastern District, U.S.A.

Sec. 2. The local Artists Unions shall set up committees which shall have editorial and business responsibility.

RESOLUTIONS ADOPTED BY THE EASTERN DISTRICT CONVENTION

I.

Be it resolved that we go on record as urging the establishment of a Permanent Federal Art Project to include all artists, and that we further favor the immediate introduction and passage by Congress of the Federal Art Bill as the only means of establishing the minimum demands of artists in the cultural and economic fields. We further urge all trade unions, economic, cultural organizations and individuals directly to contact their congressmen and representatives by means of letters, telegrams and petitions demanding the passage of the Federal Art Bill.

II.

Be it resolved that this convention go on record as supporting the Frazier-Lundeen Bill for adequate social and unemployment insurance.

III.

Be it resolved that this convention go on record as supporting the Marcantonio Relief Standards as one providing for the protection of our union and economic rights.

IV.

As neither of the major existing political parties offers satisfaction of the minimum demands for permanent economic security in the form of adequate unemployment insurance, expansion of the W.P.A. to include all unemployed on a permanent basis and old age pensions and as we seek peace to protect and advance the cultural life of the people in preference to increased armaments destructive to these pursuits, we therefore urge the formation of a Farmer-Labor Party dedicated to these principles and recommend that each affiliated Artists' Union initiate and support all efforts toward building this political party for professionals, farmers and workers.

V.

Be it resolved that this convention of the Eastern District of the Artists Union pledges itself to fight all tendencies and forces of reaction, war and fascism.

(a) We endorse the boycott of all publications of William Randolph Hearst because of his manifestations of anti-union, anti-civil liberties and un-American policies.

(b) We endorse the boycott of the Olympic Art Exhibition to be held in the summer of 1936 in Berlin and urge all artists to support this stand.

(c) We recommend to all affiliated artist bodies that they co-operate with local chapters of the American League Against War and Fascism.

(d) We call upon all artists to refuse to make any posters that would foster war propaganda.

VI.

Be it resolved that this convention of the Eastern District of the Artists Union go on record as endorsing and supporting the Federal Youth Act.

Page 7

FIG. 21 Neel's *Futility of Effort* reproduced under the title *Poverty* in *Art Front*, June 1936, p. 7

above his head, the riot of distress around him. Breitenbach seems avuncular enough, but Neel remembered him as "the enemy," blaming him for the indignities to which she and the other patients were subjected under the guise of therapy.[41] Neel found one of his so-called remedies especially offensive: the ban on art. It was not until this particular embargo was lifted that Neel began to recover, an experience with striking parallels to that of the protagonist in Charlotte Perkins Gilman's 1892 short story "The Yellow Wallpaper."[42] Ultimately, Neel's drawing positions the suicide ward as a quintessentially patriarchal institution.

That Neel's depictions of private suffering, and the private suffering of other women, whether in a suicide ward or a maternity hospital, were of political consequence is confirmed by her decision to display such works when and where she did. Indeed, Neel strategically guided these pictures into the public sphere, prioritizing progressive venues that served to frame the personal as an extension of the political. *Futility of Effort*, for example, was exhibited in a 1938 exhibition at ACA Galleries alongside scenes of eviction, images of railroad workers, and portraits of political activists, all of them by male artists.[43] *Childbirth* of 1939 (p. 209), one of the first paintings in the history of Western art to represent a woman giving birth (at a moment, no less, when society had little tolerance for the subject), appeared in a 1940 exhibition organized by the left-leaning group United American Artists.[44] Mission-driven print culture also proved an appealing method of distribution to Neel.[45] In 1936 she published *Futility of Effort* under the title *Poverty* in the June issue of *Art Front* (fig. 21). There it appeared on a page devoted to the Eastern District Convention of the Artists' Union, an organization devoted to defending the economic security of artists and battling the "forces of reaction, war, and fascism."[46] By reproducing *Poverty* in this periodical, Neel effectively transformed a private lament into a weapon of class warfare.

The timing of this makeover was deliberate. One year earlier, in 1935, Neel had joined the CPUSA. Long focused on unionizing male-dominated factories, the party was beginning to allocate more resources to supporting women and children and to ameliorating poverty, hunger, and illness.[47] By virtue of her newfound intimacy with Communism, Neel would have been exposed to ideas and books that framed indigence as the logical outcome of an unjust economic system. From the very beginning, the artist blamed penury for Santillana's illness ("you see if I'd had the money . . . the baby maybe wouldn't have caught it like she did—and then if I could have paid a doctor I wouldn't have been so slow to call one"[48]), but it wasn't until the mid-1930s that she came to understand poverty as a political, not just a personal, condition, an evolution in thinking that prompted *Futility of Effort*'s appearance in *Art Front* and its temporary change in title.

Interestingly, Neel always preferred the first title over the second,[49] and when she declared *Futility of Effort* one of her most "revolutionary" paintings, she failed to mention its fleeting romance with the Old Left. "I don't think that anyone was doing anything like that," Neel claimed in 1975. "It was an experience felt and painted."[50] Such is the political imagination of a scandalous feminist, "for [whom] making visible the invisible histories of women has always been a key task."[51] Ultimately, one of Neel's greatest contributions as an artist lies here, in her determination to publicize and, by extension, to politicize the private afflictions of women.

## PAINT YOUR POWER

Neel continued to probe the deepest recesses of female subjectivity in the 1960s and 1970s, when she focused on one drama in particular: motherhood. Although she had previously painted the occasional mother—notably in *Couple on a Train* of 1930, *Blanche Angel Pregnant* of 1937 (fig. 22), and *The Spanish Family* of 1943—she only began to concentrate on the subject in earnest in the mid-1960s.[52] The resulting body of work is more dispassionate than *Well Baby Clinic*, but it is no less incisive. Here Neel's goal was sincerity without sentimentality, and in this she succeeded, rebuffing stereotypes that had long plagued representations of mothers, from the beatific caregiver (fig. 23) to the saintly Madonna.[53] Unlike the fanciful, cloying facsimiles that appear in art and popular culture, all of them sanitized, domesticated, and disembodied, Neel's mothers are both frank and concrete.

Among her gallery, which frequently features her daughters-in-law Nancy and Ginny as well as several of her grandchildren, are pictures of nursing mothers, their breasts exposed to the mouths of hungry infants, as in the drawing *Mother and Child* of 1956 (p. 211) and the painting *Nancy and the Twins* of 1971 (p. 218). Joining them are images of mothers, most but not all white, cradling heavy infants in their arms, from *Mother and Child* of about 1962 (p. 214) to *Nancy and Olivia* of 1967 (p. 215) and *Ginny and Andrew* of 1978 (fig. 24). Feeding and holding are the only two activities in which Neel's mothers engage. Insofar as they require the flexibility of a contortionist and the expenditure of vast reserves of energy, both are apt metonyms for the hard, ongoing labor of motherhood. (Neel, who preferred to communicate economically, probably

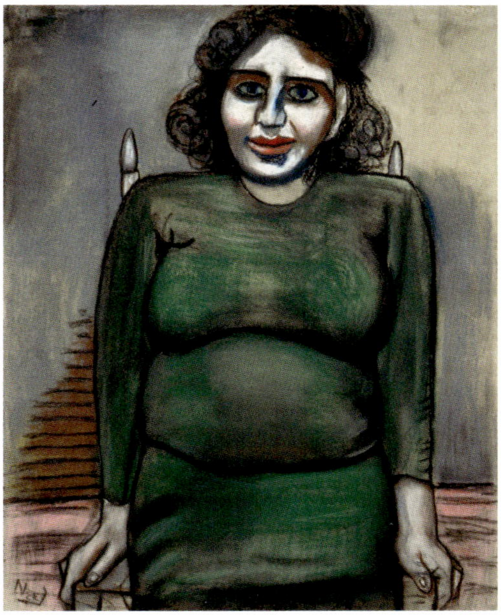

FIG. 22 *Blanche Angel Pregnant*, 1937. Pastel on paper, 26 × 20½ in. (66 × 52.1 cm). Whitney Museum of American Art, New York, Purchase, with funds from the Drawing Committee (87.53)

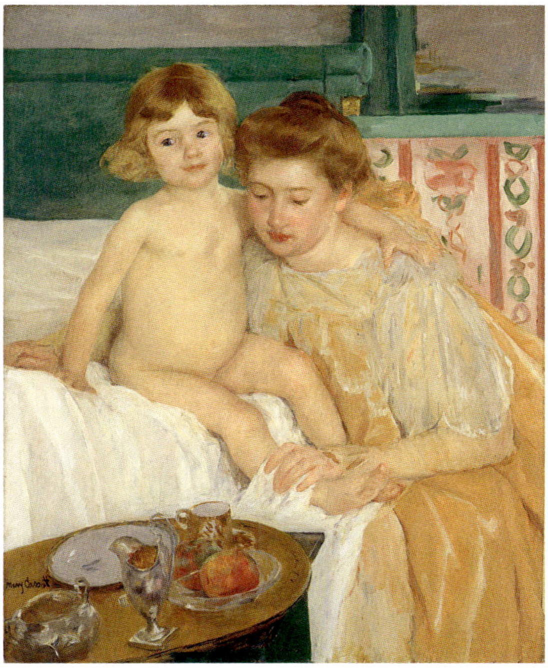

FIG. 23 Mary Cassatt (American, 1844–1926). *Mother and Child (Baby Getting Up from His Nap)*, ca. 1899. Oil on canvas, 36½ × 29 in. (92.7 × 73.7 cm). The Metropolitan Museum of Art, New York, George A. Hearn Fund, 1909 (09.27)

chose them for just this reason.) Fittingly, the mothers' faces register a range of emotions, from resolve and tenacity to stoicism and solemnity. More than a few seem resigned, even beleaguered, straining under pressures both physical and psychological. Not a single one smiles.

Especially powerful is *Carmen and Judy* of 1972 (p. 217), in which a mother, Carmen Gordon, is seen cradling her limp, emaciated daughter, Judy. In the baby, life barely stirs, just enough for her to wrap her tiny hand around her mother's fingers but not enough for her to latch onto the proffered breast, a symptom of the disease that would contribute to her passing a few months later.[54] As a portrait that doubles as a deathbed scene, *Carmen and Judy* differs considerably from Neel's other pictures of mothers and children, and as one of the very few people of color she ever represented in a state of undress, along with Carlos in *T.B. Harlem* (p. 187) and possibly Maria in *Pregnant Maria* (p. 201), Carmen and Judy are unique among her gallery of sitters.[55] Carmen's relationship with Neel, for whom she kept house and whose granddaughters she babysat, was equally complex. A professional caregiver, Carmen played the role of surrogate "mother" to Neel and her brood, tending (like so many other Black, working-class women in the United States) a white family. What makes *Carmen and Judy* so extraordinary, therefore, is precisely what makes it so fraught, implicated as it is in a power dynamic that advantaged Neel but disadvantaged Carmen. Sitter and artist might have been intimates of a sort, witness to each other's frailties, and they might even have enjoyed a bond forged in common tragedy, but the fact remains that Carmen, as Neel's Black employee, was very much at the artist's mercy, far more so than such white personalities as Cindy Nemser (p. 203) and Andy Warhol (p. 194), whose clothes Neel also removed and

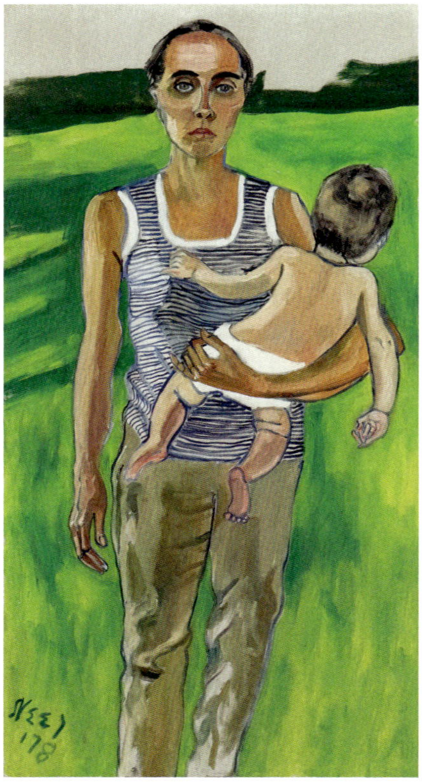

FIG. 24 *Ginny and Andrew*, 1978. Oil on canvas, 48 1/4 × 25 1/8 in. (122.6 × 63.8 cm). Estate of Alice Neel

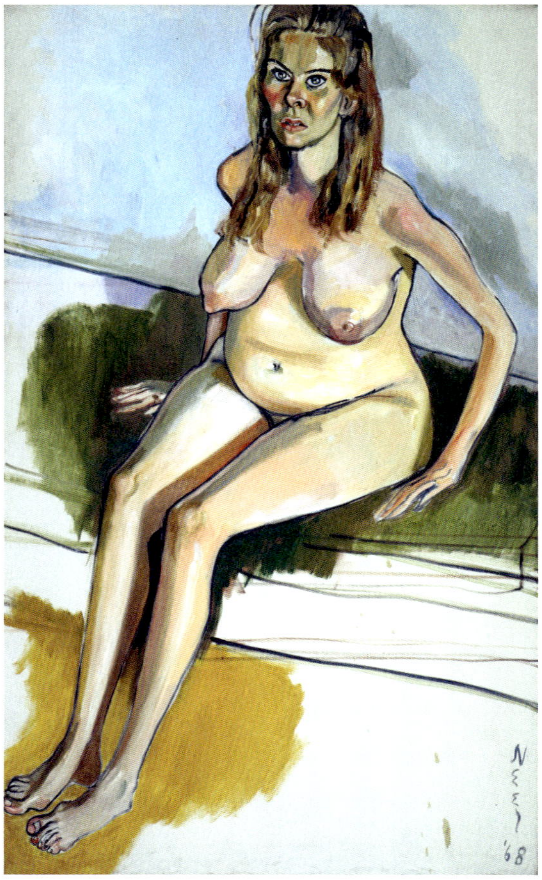

FIG. 25 *Pregnant Betty Homitzky*, 1968. Oil on canvas, 60 × 36 in. (152.4 × 91.4 cm). Collection of Sandra and Gerald Fineberg

whose afflictions she similarly dramatized, at least in Warhol's case.[56] Carmen and Judy, on the other hand, had little privilege to spare, with only the artist's sympathy to insulate them from her probing brush. Ultimately, their vulnerability proved irresistible to Neel: in the process of committing their suffering to canvas, she also exposed them, laying them bare, literally, for all to see.

Neel was neither particularly kind nor particularly cruel to the mothers she painted, as seen in her extraordinary series of pregnant nudes from the 1960s and 1970s.[57] The first, *Pregnant Maria* (p. 201), in which the sitter is posed provocatively like a model in a *Playboy* centerfold, dates to 1964, and the last, *Margaret Evans Pregnant* (p. 205), in which another model is perched on a yellow chair, to 1978. Four of the paintings show the women alone, as in *Pregnant Betty Homitzky* of 1968 (fig. 25), while the remaining two—*Pregnant Julie and Algis* of 1967 (pp. 212–13) and *Pregnant Woman* of 1971 (p. 200)—include their partners. Generally speaking, Neel depicted expectant mothers near the ends of their pregnancies, when their bodies were at their most unruly and their curves at their most dramatic. She relished the formal challenge such individuals presented, confessing, "plastically [pregnancy] is very exciting."[58]

Each work from the series is remarkably, if subtly, individualized, with no one woman projecting precisely the same emotion. The subjects in *The Pregnant Maria* and *Claudia Bach Pregnant* (fig. 26) seem confident and self-possessed, while in *The Pregnant Woman* (1967), *Pregnant Woman* (1971), *Pregnant Betty Homitzky*, and *Margaret Evans Pregnant*, they appear alternately indifferent, apprehensive, alarmed, and dazed.[59] Most importantly, the balance of power between mother and pregnancy varies from painting to painting. Only Maria and Claudia truly own the bodies with which they have been endowed. The other sitters are nearly overwhelmed by their conspicuous abdomens, which seem poised to detach themselves from their hosts. As Nochlin astutely recognized in 1974, Neel's pregnant nudes defy "the comforting mystique of childbearing" and dwell on the "very unnaturalness" of "incipient motherhood."[60] Nemser concurred, writing one year earlier for *Ms.* magazine, "These paintings record the confusion, discomfort, and resentment usually sidestepped by artists who have been brainwashed into believing that pregnancy and motherhood are purely beatific experiences."[61] Yet even when they signal discomfort, Neel's expectant mothers remain dignified and unabashed, never appearing in the least bit ashamed.

For Neel, pregnancy was a lived, embodied experience above all. Indeed, she would always insist on pregnancy's stubborn facticity, consistently depicting real mothers, not myths, allegories, stereotypes, or political slogans, refusing, moreover, to either moralize or pontificate. As Neel once said, "[Pregnancy] isn't what appeals to me, it's just a fact of life. It's a very important part

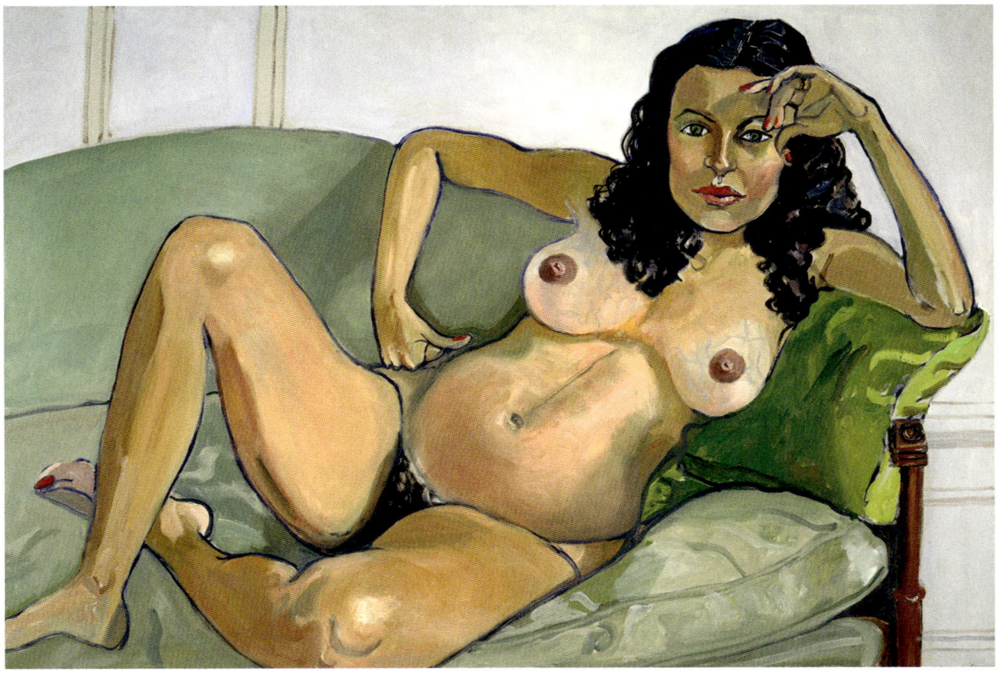

FIG. 26 *Claudia Bach Pregnant*, 1975. Oil on canvas, 32 × 45 7/8 in. (81.28 × 116.5 cm). Pennsylvania Academy of the Fine Arts, Philadelphia, Art by Women Collection, Gift of Linda Lee Alter (2011.1.23)

of life and it was neglected. I feel as a subject it's perfectly legitimate, and people out of false modesty, or being sissies, never showed it."[62] Paint was Neel's ally in this endeavor. A sensuous material, it allowed her to give substance to each of her sitters and to concretize the physical reality of pregnancy. For Neel, every detail warranted attention, especially those considered too unsightly for public consumption, from the *linea nigra* and enlarged nipples to the thickened veins and engorged, mottled flesh of the lower extremities. The artist lavished particular attention on her sitters' swollen stomachs, no more so than in the case of Margaret Evans, whose abdomen is composed of layer upon layer of yellow, pink, purple, and green paint. (Because it emblematizes both the metamorphic potential of pregnancy and women's reproductive capacity in general, Neel might also have recognized in the distended belly a metaphor for her own work as an artist—that is, for her ability to create something out of nothing.) Aside, perhaps, from Imogen Cunningham's and Emmet Gowin's photographs of pregnant nudes of the 1950s, 1960s, and 1970s (fig. 27), no more honest, declarative representations of the prepartum body exist in Western art, either before or during the postwar period, than Neel's.

The majority of Neel's mothers were painted during the height of the feminist revolution, but posters for women's liberation they were not, despite receiving the occasional nod from feminist critics and curators.[63] For many feminists, motherhood was the very source of women's oppression. As Shulamith Firestone postulated in *The Dialectic of Sex: The Case for Feminist Revolution* (1970), the "natural reproductive difference between the sexes led directly to the first division of labor based on sex, which is at the origins of all further division into economic and cultural classes and is possibly even at the root of all caste." The "heart of woman's oppression," she concluded, "is her childbearing and childrearing roles."[64] Freeing women from their reproductive systems, likewise their responsibilities as mothers, was thus considered a crucial first step on their path to political, economic, and erotic freedom. This explains the importance feminists attached to universal day care, the legalization of abortion and chemical contraceptives, and, in Firestone's case, the development of new technologies of procreation and the elimination of the nuclear family. For these same reasons, though, motherhood writ large was never held in especially high regard by feminists, who mostly considered it a problem to solve, with a few, like Firestone, looking upon it with outright disgust.[65]

This skepticism accounts for the relative absence of mothers from feminism's visual and discursive culture, which devoted much greater attention to sexuality, self-determination, marriage, housework, gender roles, wage discrimination, and violence against women.[66] A few exceptions exist, among them Barbara Carrasco's *Pregnant Woman in a Ball of Yarn* of 1978 (fig. 28), Judy Chicago's *Birth Project* of 1980–85, Susan Hiller's *Ten Months* of 1977–79, Mary Kelly's *Post-Partum Document* of 1973–79, Léa Lublin's *Mon fils* of 1968, and the interventions staged by the collective Mother Art, formed in 1973.[67] In contradistinction to Neel, these artists were mostly affiliated with conceptual and performance art, and they tended to abstract, anonymize, and politicize motherhood, folding it into a clear-cut narrative of female oppression to which Neel never subscribed. Among feminist writers, Adrienne Rich, whose book *Of Woman*

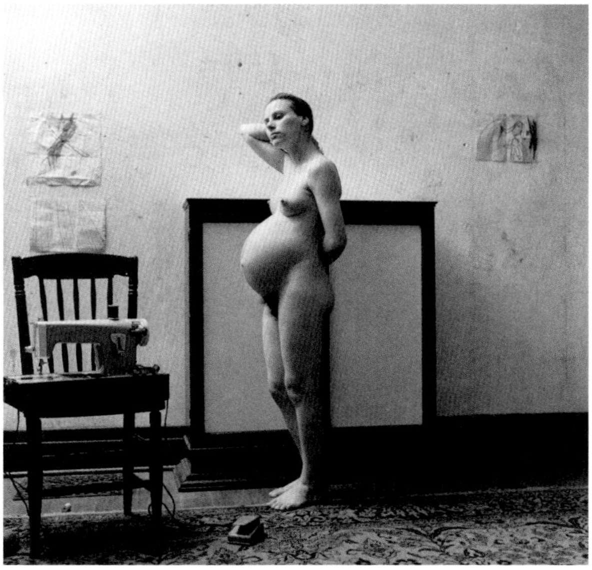

FIG. 27 Emmet Gowin (American, born 1941). *Edith, Dayton, Ohio*, 1967. Gelatin silver print, 9 1/8 × 5 3/16 in. (23.2 × 13.2 cm). Princeton University Art Museum, Gift of Mrs. Saul Reinfeld (x1982-396)

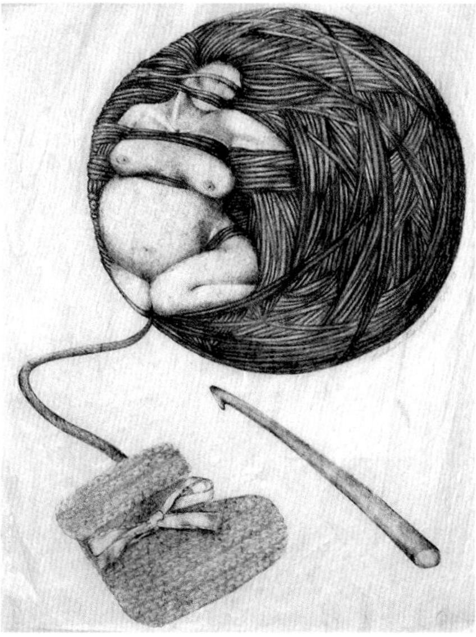

FIG. 28 Barbara Carrasco (American, born 1955). *Pregnant Woman in a Ball of Yarn*, 1978. Lithograph, 12 5/8 × 9 1/4 in. (32.1 × 23.5 cm). Collection of the artist

*Born: Motherhood as Experience and Institution* appeared three years after Neel drew her portrait (p. 174), is particularly noteworthy. Rich takes pains to distinguish between motherhood as an institution, which reflects and perpetuates the "imbalance" of power between women and men, and female reproductive ability, which serves as a source of great personal and political potential.[68] For the most part, however, Neel was alone in giving motherhood the amount of airtime she did, asserting the visibility, even validity, of maternal labor at the exact moment feminism had imposed a virtual embargo on the subject. Cutting against the grain of so much feminist discourse, Neel's pictures of mothers read more like spirited rebukes to than gestures of solidarity with the larger movement.[69] Put another way, the artist painted mothers in spite of feminism, not because of it.[70]

## PAINT YOUR POLITICS

Nevertheless, Neel was very much a cause célèbre among feminists, who recognized in her a symbol of perseverance and excellence: a living example of a great artist denied recognition because of her gender. Feminists not only lobbied on her behalf, they also recruited her into the movement. Neel's own relationship to feminism was neither incidental nor superficial. Indeed, the artist identified just as strongly with women's liberation as she did with socialism.[71] As she said to Ted Castle in 1983, "Well, it's an obvious fact that women were second-class citizens, but you didn't have to be that. I fought that, but in a subterranean way. I never fought right out on the barricades although I've always been a women's libber. I was just born like that, I was that way back in the 30's before there was any women's lib."[72] Neel aligned more

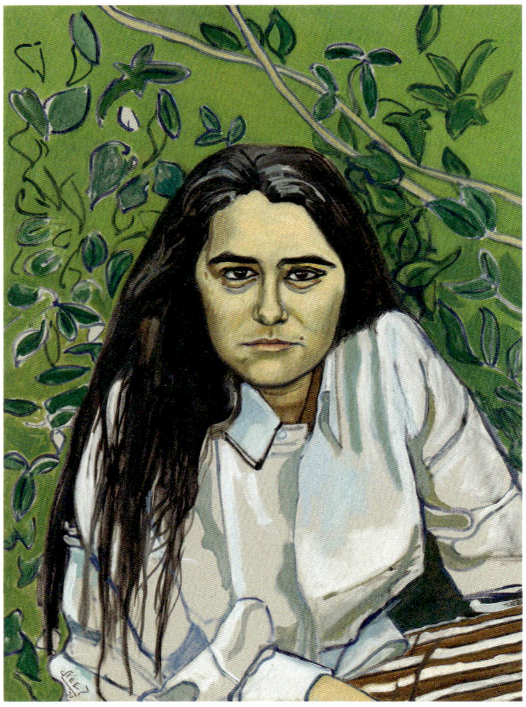

FIG. 29 ***Kate Millett***, 1970. Acrylic on canvas, 39 3/4 × 28 1/2 in. (101 × 72.4 cm). National Portrait Gallery, Smithsonian Institution, Washington, D.C., Gift of *Time* magazine (NPG.78.TC588)

than one of her paintings with feminist politics, including two nudes, *Ethel Ashton* of 1930 (p. 198) ("Look at her, she's women's lib already") and *Joe Gould* of 1933 (p. 197) ("that's women's lib").[73] She also participated actively as a luminary, fellow traveler, and exhibiting artist in a broad network of feminist endeavors throughout the 1970s and 1980s.

Neel's first rendezvous with modern feminism occurred in 1970. That year, she was commissioned to paint a portrait of activist, artist, and author Kate Millett (fig. 29)—whose book *Sexual Politics* had recently been published to great fanfare—for the cover of *Time* magazine's August 31, 1970, issue, "The Politics of Sex."[74] One year later, a discussion with Neel appeared in the inaugural issue of *Women and Art*, alongside a transcript of her 1971 doctoral address at Moore College of Art and Design and a petition, spearheaded by Women in the Arts, demanding her representation in the forthcoming Whitney annual. In 1972 Mary Beth Edelson featured Neel in her pantheon of female artists, *Some Living American Women Artists*, a photomontage based on Leonardo's *The Last Supper*. Between 1973 and 1976, Neel exhibited in six group shows held at or curated by the Women's Interart Center, an organization founded in 1970 by members of WAR (Women Artists in Revolution) and Feminists in the Arts, with the goal of ending gender discrimination in the arts.[75] (One of the six exhibitions, *Women Choose Women* (1973), included her *Pregnant Woman* of 1971.) In addition to taking part in the center's programs, Neel was a donor to its 1973 benefit exhibition *ArtLift 549*. Her collaborations with feminists continued to mount as the decade wore on. In 1975 Neel was featured in *The Year of the Woman*, co-organized by Nemser for the Bronx Museum of the Arts, and one year later in *Women Artists: 1550–1950*, co-curated by Ann Sutherland Harris and

Linda Nochlin. To the *Sister Chapel* (1978), a collaborative project conceived by Ilise Greenstein, she contributed a painting of progressive lawyer and politician Bella Abzug, which hung alongside twelve other pictures of female heroes.[76] In 1980 Neel participated in a program honoring "women of courage" that was sponsored jointly by the Women's Caucus for Art and the Coalition of Women's Arts Organizations on the occasion of the passage of the Equal Rights Amendment. Then, in 1982, she sent an early nude, *Nadya Olyanova* (1933), to *Sexuality in Art: Two Decades from a Feminist Perspective*, one of sixteen exhibitions coordinated by the Women's Caucus for Art.[77] Around the same time, Neel's name appeared among a list of advisers to the New York Feminist Art Institute, a school devoted to the teaching of "art in a feminist environment."[78] Importantly, Neel drew many of her sitters from the feminist organizations with which she partnered, including Mary Garrard (p. 174), Linda Nochlin (p. 219), Irene Peslikis (p. 175), and Faith Ringgold (fig. 30).[79]

That said, Neel practiced feminism differently than did many of the individuals she painted, and not only because she was one generation older.[80] As with Communism, her feminism was idiosyncratic, not programmatic. She also disagreed with certain feminist orthodoxies, especially the tendency to prioritize gender inequality over other forms of injustice and to frame women's oppression as a battle of the sexes.[81] "Injustice has no sex," Neel declared in 1971.[82] Later, when Nemser asked about the possibility of "anti-male" sentiment in *Joe Gould* (p. 197), Neel replied, "I never was like that. . . . In fact that's one thing that's wrong with some women liberationists." She continued, "I don't think we should fight each other because we are all creatures in a way, aren't we? Both men and women are wretched and often it's a matter of how much money you have rather than what your sex is."[83] Neel penned a similar statement in 1973, writing, "The enemy perhaps is not men but the very system itself which also encourages men to oppress each other."[84] By system, Neel undoubtedly meant capitalism.

Tellingly, Neel's only written statement on feminism, from 1971, appeared in the Communist newspaper the *Daily World*, and it was illustrated not with a portrait of a feminist, but with a picture of labor organizer Pat Whalen. Her short, mostly autobiographical essay begins, "It's a great thing to see women demanding the right to be human beings and to have their product taken just as seriously as that of men." Note Neel's use of "product," a term associated with Marxism. In a capitalist society, Marxists maintain, the working class is alienated from the fruits—or products—of its labor. Unacknowledged and undercompensated, workers make without owning and produce without possessing. Women, Neel suggests, occupy an analogous position vis-à-vis patriarchy. Later on, she again uses Marxist phrasing to explain women's predicament:

> It is true that women's real liberation cannot occur without some change in the social organization which, of course, would include a change in thinking. Property relations, which reduce everything to the status of "things" and "objects," have also reduced women to the status of "sexual objects," and have bound them and crushed them in many ways. This has been and still is largely a male world. In an office, a man is boss—a woman is secretary. In the museums it is the same thing.[85]

According to Neel, then, as long as patriarchy and capitalism share the same ends—the monopoly of money, power, and status by men—and the same result—the disenfranchisement of women—advocates for social justice will need to employ the tools of both feminist and socialist critique.

As her statements here and elsewhere imply, Neel's feminism was shaped in fundamental ways by the left-wing milieu in which she operated during the first three decades of her career. Indeed, her feminism owes a considerable debt to the Old Left—that is, to early twentieth-century Communism, which gave birth to what historian Kate Weigand has called "red feminism."[86] The latter was forged in the crucible of the Bolshevik Revolution of 1917–23, the founding of the CPUSA in 1919, and the achievement of women's suffrage in the United States in 1920.[87] Together these incidents instilled a thirst for justice and a robust political consciousness among a budding generation of left-leaning women. Red feminists operated from within the CPUSA, and, unlike most of their male comrades, they confronted the specificity of women's experience under capitalism. In so doing, they triangulated the inequities of class, gender, and race,[88] expounding a theory of compound or "intersectional" discrimination very much ahead of its time.[89]

Many of the party-affiliated organizations in which Neel participated during the first three decades of her career took up "the woman question," as it was then known, with relative enthusiasm. *New Masses* published multiple essays on the subject, including Meridel Le Sueur's "Women on the Breadlines" in 1932, Rebecca Pitts's "Women and Communism" in 1935, and Betty Millard's "Woman against Myth" in 1947 and 1948.[90] In spring 1949, the Jefferson School began holding regular conferences on subjects about women, including women of color, and sponsoring additional classes through 1956, most of them taught by red feminists.[91] International Publishers, whose books Neel read, issued Grace Hutchins's *Women Who Work* in 1934 and *The Woman Question: Selections from the Writings of Karl Marx, Frederick Engels, V. I. Lenin, Joseph Stalin* in 1951.[92] Ultimately, Neel's feminism (or its origins, at least) lies here, at the intersection of *New Masses*, the Jefferson School, and International Publishers, where capitalism met patriarchy and class met gender. If the artist's relationship to the women's liberation movement of the 1970s was vexed, it was because Neel was more "red feminist" than "second-generation feminist."

In the 1940s and 1950s, Neel painted two women who qualify, on the basis of their work and advocacy, as red feminists: Mother Bloor and Alice Childress.[93] These portraits were followed many years later by a picture of Irene Peslikis, curiously titled *Marxist Girl* (p. 175)—curious because Peslikis, a well-regarded activist, artist, educator, and editor, was known at the time not as a Marxist but as a feminist. Indeed, Peslikis belonged to three of the country's earliest feminist organizations—New York Radical Women, established in 1967, Redstockings of the Women's Liberation Movement, formed in February 1969, and Redstocking Artists, which she co-founded with Patricia Mainardi in 1971, the same year she helped launch the periodical *Women and Art*.[94] To christen Peslikis "Marxist Girl" in 1972, therefore, would seem to disidentify her with the very movement she was helping lead.

In truth of fact, Neel's title merely turns back the clock on Peslikis's biography and, by extension, on feminism itself. After all, many second-generation feminists, Peslikis among them,

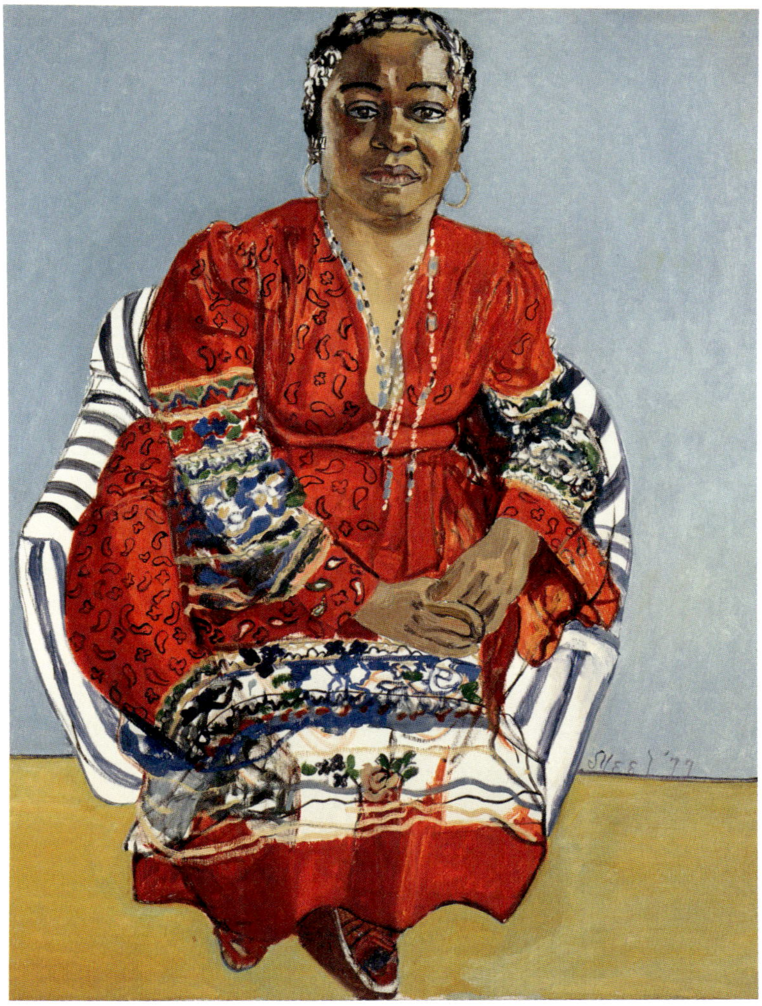

FIG. 30 *Faith Ringgold*, 1977. Oil on canvas, 48 × 36 in. (121.9 × 91.4 cm). Private collection

entered politics by way of the New Left, a broad coalition of activists organized against racism, militarism, and capitalism in the mid- to late 1960s.[95] Even when they started forming feminist alliances and proclaimed patriarchy the world's most pervasive system of oppression, Peslikis and others continued to use socialist terminology in their writing, as in the 1969 manifesto of the Redstockings of the Women's Liberation Movement, which proclaims women "an oppressed class."[96] *Marxist Girl* might have been an anachronistic title for Neel's portrait of Peslikis, but it was not inaccurate.

*Marxist Girl* is also unique among Neel's paintings of women, the clothed ones, at least. No matter how outspoken their politics or forceful their personalities, the artist's female sitters very often signal propriety and respectability—in a word, femininity. Many sit upright or bend slightly forward, their knees pressed together or their legs or ankles crossed, as in Neel's portraits of Linda Nochlin, Ellen Johnson (1976), Faith Ringgold (fig. 30), and Marisol (1981). Even Mercedes

Arroyo and Alice Childress are depicted as paragons of female presentability. Not Peslikis, however. In *Marxist Girl*, she leans back into her chair. One arm reaches above her head, exposing her unshaved armpit, while her right leg hangs over an armrest, forcing her legs apart.[97] With very few exceptions, only Neel's male sitters project this much bravado and insouciance. Indeed, the closest comparison to *Marxist Girl*—so close, in fact, it might be a pendant—is *Benny and Mary Ellen Andrews*, painted in 1972 (p. 183). Like Peslikis, Benny Andrews too commands the stage of the picture, and like Peslikis, he too traveled in the same left-leaning circles as Neel, who not only joined him and others from the Black Emergency Cultural Coalition (BECC) at protests in front of The Met in 1969 and MoMA and the Whitney in 1971 (fig. 31) but also contributed a drawing to *The Attica Book*, issued by the BECC in conjunction with Artists and Writers Protest against the War in Vietnam in 1972.[98] Almost exact mirror images of each other, Peslikis and Andrews present in an especially formidable, commanding manner. Each is a paragon of political authority, as comfortable in their own skin as they are with their respective belief systems.

The only sitters whose confidence rivals Andrews's and Peslikis's are a few of the women whom Neel depicted unclothed, such as those in *Ruth Nude* of 1964 (fig. 32) and *Annie Sprinkle* of 1982, both of whom flaunt their pudendum, turning their most private parts into instruments of moral and ideological warfare. Neel elides disinhibition with defiance in two other paintings as well, one of her daughter Isabetta, nude, of 1934–35 (p. 199) and another of her granddaughter Olivia, in a bikini, of 1974 (*Olivia in a Red Hat*). With their arms akimbo, legs splayed, and feet planted firmly on the ground, each of these prepubescent girls positions herself like a warrior,

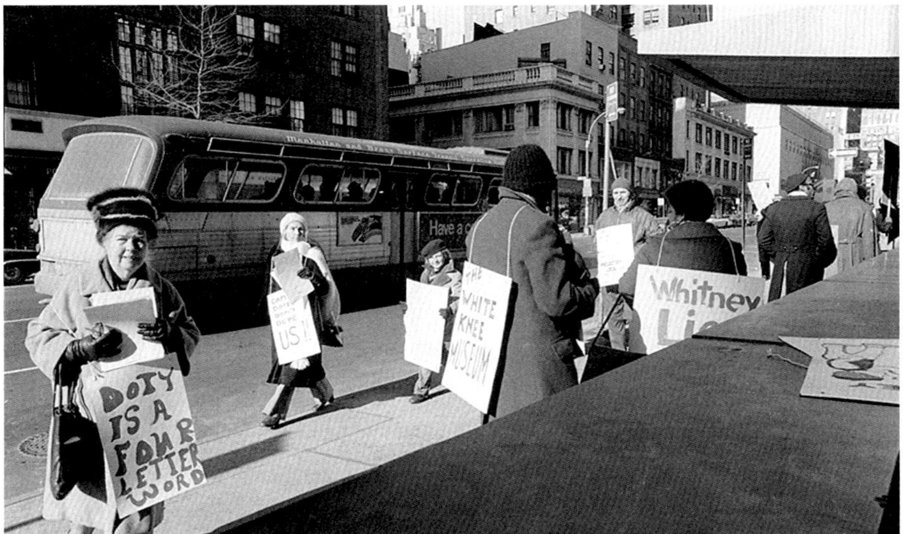


FIG. 31 Alice Neel protesting at the Whitney Museum of American Art, January 1971

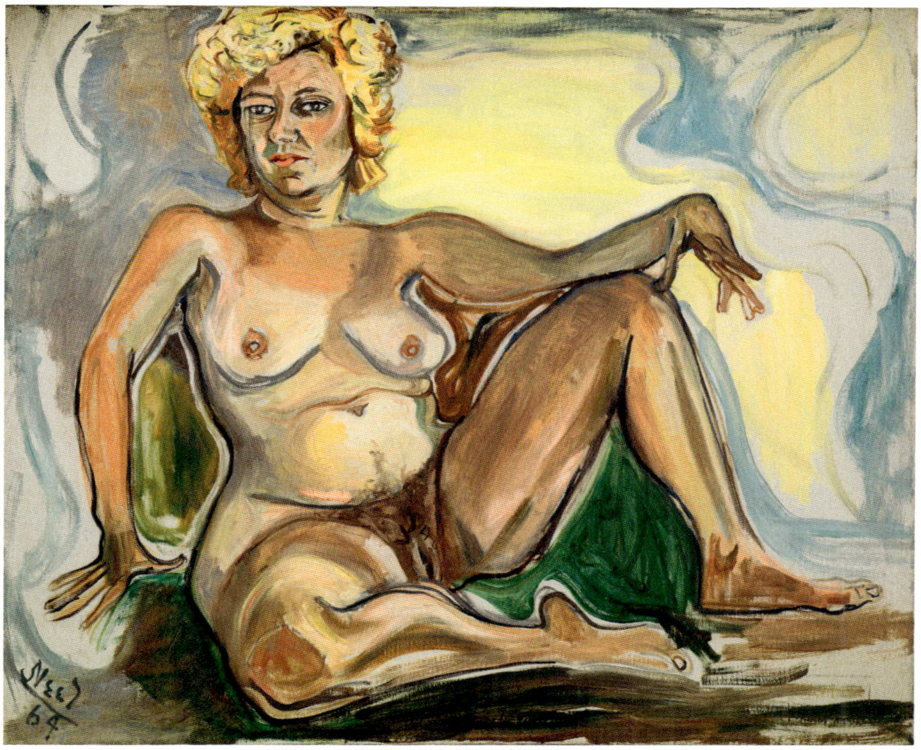

FIG. 32 *Ruth Nude*, 1964. Oil on canvas, 40 1/8 × 48 in. (101.9 × 121.9 cm). Estate of Alice Neel

steeling herself for confrontation. According to the artist, *Olivia in a Red Hat* doubled as both a portrait and a political icon. Olivia "is a child born in the middle of the great struggle of Women's Liberation," she wrote, "and shows the fearlessness and aggression of the new woman."[99] Neel, who turned twenty the year women gained the right to vote in the United States and who consistently defied prescribed gender roles, most certainly identified with Olivia, seeing in her (and perhaps Isabetta also) a genetic and symbolic avatar as well as a new generation of revolutionaries.[100] In these and other works, moreover, Neel expresses her politics indirectly, through the disposition of limbs and chins and the choreography of composition and brushwork. Here, bodies—painted bodies, more specifically—do the work of communicating politically. By drawing as she does on a common inventory of gestures, Neel forges, whether consciously or not, an intersectional, multigenerational alliance uniting socialism, feminism, and Black liberation.

Like her sitters, Neel was a political creature par excellence. Sometimes she practiced her radical humanism openly, through actions; sometimes she expressed it covertly, through painting. "Should thoughts be said plain or wasn't it more fun to play hide and seek—to hide them artfully in little corners?," Neel once queried.[101] The answer lies in the subtle qualities—the myriad "elsewheres"—of *Marxist Girl*, *Benny and Mary Ellen Andrews*, *Ruth Nude*, and *Olivia in a Red Hat*, which together constitute a painted manifesto declaring Neel's idiosyncratic brand of scandalous red feminism.

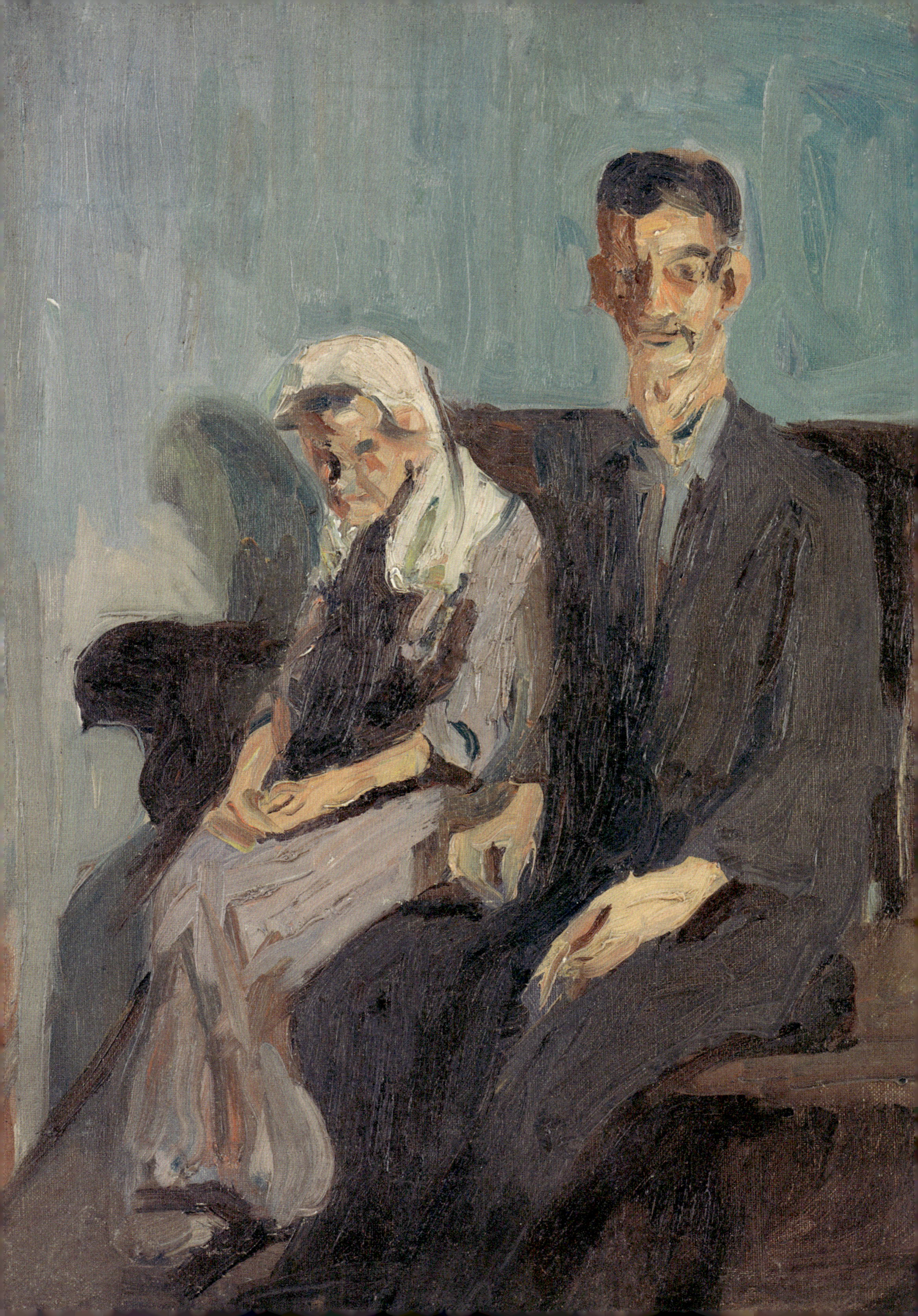

# SIEMPRE EN LA CALLE

**SUSANNA V. TEMKIN**

In a 1975 interview, Alice Neel invoked the Spanish phrase "*siempre en la calle*" (always in the street) while reflecting on her brief but formative time in Havana, where she was launched into bourgeois Cuban society through her marriage to artist Carlos Enríquez.[1] Ever the rebel, Neel surely relished this intended insult directed toward independent women like herself, who struggled to balance domestic responsibilities with artistic aspirations. Indeed, although Neel's practice has long been associated with the intimate environment of her home studio, the phrase brings to light the impact of the street as a site and source for her art. Such imagery appears throughout her oeuvre, including in the work she created in Spanish Harlem (East Harlem/El Barrio).[2] Despite the fact that she lived in this neighborhood for more than twenty years, much of the literature on this period emphasizes Neel's separation from the downtown art scene in New York, describing her location uptown as one of exile and isolation or even as a retreat into an "alien world."[3] Beyond exposing the racism undergirding these analyses, such language also implies that Neel was somehow disconnected from her surrounding environment. While more concerted attention has been dedicated to this body of work since the 1990s, culminating in Hilton Als's revelatory 2017 exhibition,[4] only three paintings from Spanish Harlem were featured in the artist's major 2010 retrospective at the Museum of Fine Arts, Houston, evidence of the lingering oversight of this aspect of her career.[5] Positioning Neel both physically and conceptually "*siempre en la calle*," this essay offers a novel approach to Neel's practice by foregrounding her proximity to, active participation with, and observation of the street and urban culture.

## CUBAN PRELUDE

Critics have frequently interpreted Neel's sojourn in Havana as a primer for her future experience in Spanish Harlem; yet, while Cuba and Puerto Rico have been called "two wings of the same bird,"[6] such assertions overlook the striking differences between Neel's life in Havana as a pregnant newlywed to a man from a wealthy, well-connected family and her life as a single mother in a working-class Manhattan neighborhood. These biases also occlude the profound impact her time in Cuba had on her approach to and observation of daily life and culture. In fact, Neel's arrival in Havana in 1926 coincided with an important moment in the young republic's artistic development.[7] Her husband, Enríquez, was not simply an anonymous amateur but rather one of the nation's foremost modernist artists, and shortly after coming to Havana, the young couple was catapulted to the center of the island's artistic and intellectual avant-garde.[8]

FIG. 33 *Beggars, Havana*, 1926. Oil on canvas, 20 × 18 in. (50.8 × 45.7 cm). Estate of Alice Neel

Together, they associated with such internationally renowned figures as novelist Alejo Carpentier, to whom Neel is believed to have gifted Robert Henri's *The Art Spirit* (1923).[9] They also explored Havana's neighborhoods with Enríquez's childhood friend, the painter Marcelo Pogolotti, sketching the people, places, and urban landscape of the capital city.[10] Neel sometimes invited those whom she encountered in the streets to sit as models, as in the expressionistically rendered *Beggars, Havana* (fig. 33); she would continue this practice upon her return to the United States while living in Philadelphia, and later in Spanish Harlem.

While Neel's excursions were interrupted by the birth of her first child, Santillana, in late 1926, her involvement in the Cuban art world did not wane. She presented her paintings publicly for the first time at the *XII Salón de Bellas Artes* in March 1927. Though the show was mostly panned for its academic bent, Neel's and Enríquez's contributions were singled out in the press as "the best of the Salon," and evidence of "an extraordinary marriage."[11] Later that year, she submitted some eight paintings to the *Exposición de Arte Nuevo*, an event regarded as the starting point for modern art on the island.[12] It is remarkable that Neel, a non-Cuban (and woman) artist, contributed to this groundbreaking exhibition, establishing her role as part of the legacy of Cuban art history.[13] However, her connection to Cuba remains underexamined, in part because Neel left the island soon after the opening of the *Exposición de Arte Nuevo*, a situation made permanent following the dissolution of her marriage; nevertheless, Havana stayed with her, for as she later declared, "my life in Cuba had much more to do with my later psychology. It conditioned me a lot."[14]

## COMMUNITY, FAMILY, AND FRIENDSHIPS IN SPANISH HARLEM

Neel's return to the United States in 1927 ushered in a period of profound personal trauma. After briefly reuniting with Enríquez in New York, the artist traveled home to Pennsylvania where she suffered a mental breakdown; following her recovery, she moved to New York's Greenwich Village. Here, Neel painted the streets and elevated subway lines peopled by the working class. Such scenes as *Longshoremen Returning from Work* (p. 125) allude to Neel's political sympathies and growing associations with radical artists and intellectuals during the 1930s, which were perhaps fueled by her experiences in Cuba. Alongside peers from the Works Progress Administration (WPA), Neel participated in meetings at the Artists' Union and John Reed Club; it is also during this time that she first began to take part in public protests. Depicting a torch-lit Communist parade that Neel attended, the canvas *Nazis Murder Jews* (p. 126) reveals how such street-based politics informed her compositions during this period.[15] In 1938 Neel left Greenwich Village for Spanish Harlem, a timeline that seems to coincide with Susan Rosenberg's assertion that "in the 1940s Neel abandoned the painting of city streets, retaining her social commitment to the representation of urban life by painting people."[16] The street did continue to inform her work, however, and may be found subtly embedded within the very portraits that Rosenberg cites.

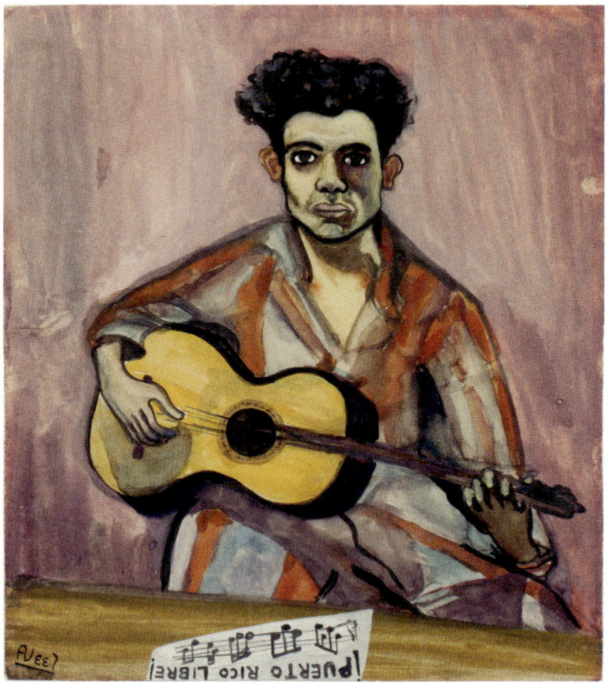

FIG. 34 *Puerto Rico Libre!*, 1939. Watercolor on paper, 16 × 13 in. (40.6 × 33 cm). Estate of Alice Neel

Although Neel would later romantically attribute her arrival in Spanish Harlem to a search for "more truth," her relocation was largely connected to her then partner, José Santiago Negrón.[17] Neel's infatuation with the Puerto Rican musician, whom she met in 1934 at a nightclub where he was performing, is palpable in the striking portrait *Puerto Rico Libre!* (fig. 34), in which Negrón tenderly clasps his instrument while looking outward with a dark, penetrating stare. Set against a vibrant pink background, the painting belongs to an extended series of artworks that seems to chart the lovers' relationship and offers a glimpse into the culture of Neel's new life. Bedecked in the colors of his national flag–*la bandera bonita*[18]–Negrón sings from sheet music with lyrics that point to the colonial status of Puerto Rico as a US territory, first "acquired" by the United States from Spain in the wake of the Spanish-American War. In 1917 all Puerto Ricans were officially granted statutory US citizenship, facilitating migration to neighborhoods like East Harlem, where many moved to pursue greater economic opportunities.[19] This demographic influx accelerated in the 1940s and 1950s, prompting the area to become known as Spanish Harlem and coinciding with Neel's own life in El Barrio. Neel chronicled her move uptown in the nocturnal *Flight into Egypt* (fig. 35), her pregnant stomach indicating what ultimately impelled the young couple to relocate to be closer to Negrón's family. Gloomy and even somewhat sinister, the canvas perhaps reflects Neel's anxieties about motherhood after having lost her first child as an infant, being separated from her second daughter, Isabetta, and suffering a miscarriage of a child with Negrón. The painting's biblical title, however, offers a reprieve from this dismal tone through its promise of refuge.

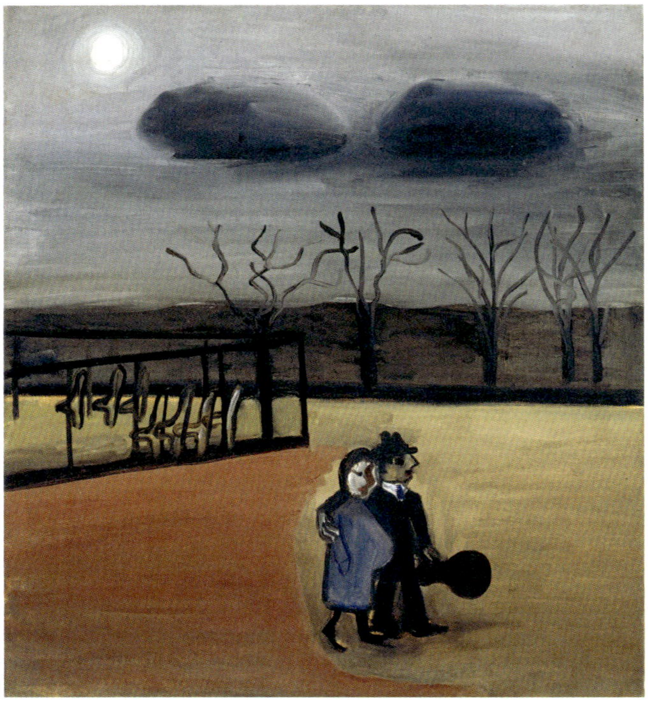

FIG. 35 *Flight into Egypt*, 1939. Oil on canvas, 31 × 27 in. (78.7 × 68.6 cm). Estate of Alice Neel

The Negrón family helped root and connect Neel into the community of Spanish Harlem. Even though Negrón left Neel for another woman shortly after the birth of their son, Richard, in 1939, the artist retained contact with her ex's kin. His brother, Carlos, and sister-in-law, Margarita, appear in a number of Neel's paintings, although this familial relationship has been obfuscated by the generic titles by which the canvases have become known. Thus, the simple description *The Spanish Family* (p. 210) hides the fact that the work portrays *her* "Spanish" family: Margarita with her eldest son, Carlos, daughter, Margarita, and newborn, Tommy. Similarly, Neel's direct and intimate relationship with her sitters is elided in *Two Girls, Spanish Harlem* (p. 135), which depicts Antonia and Carmen Encarnación, the children of her neighbors.[20]

Notably, in many of Neel's canvases from this period, like *The Spanish Family*, women and children are the main protagonists.[21] Pamela Allara has pointed out that this is in keeping with the traditional gender roles and matrifocal emphasis of Latino families;[22] moreover, these are the people who Neel most likely encountered in her daily life. Neel was a single mother with two young boys (her second son, Hartley, was born in 1941), and these women and children were her peers and neighbors, with whom she shared relationships as members of the same community. Although Neel's sitters were frequently invited into her home to sit for a painting, the initial encounter between artist and subject often took place in the streets. Such was the case for Georgie Arce, a young boy whom Neel recalled meeting while walking her dog, and who became her friend and the subject of numerous canvases and drawings.[23]

## ARCHITECTURE AND PUBLIC SPACES

There may be no better proof of Neel's participation in the daily life of Spanish Harlem than her 1947 painting *Fish Market* (p. 129).[24] This bustling scene is divided into dynamic diagonals that are anchored at center by the market stall's tray. Filled with heaping piles of silvery-blue fish, the tray neatly separates the many figures populating the canvas along gender lines: at right, five men (and maybe one woman in green) work the counter; at left, a more animated group of women and children go about with their groceries. These characters are truly anonymous, and despite some individualized features and differentiated clothing, they are somewhat cursorily executed. Although perhaps lacking the psychological connection conveyed in her more intimate images of family and neighbors, this canvas reflects a different sense of familiarity, offering a raw, yet realistic, collective portrait of quotidian life in the neighborhood.

Portrayed from above, *Fish Market* positions the viewer (and thus Neel) on the precipice of a staircase, on the verge of descending into the crowd. This perspective highlights the market's architecture, bringing attention to the tiled wall at back, the long lamps hanging from the ceiling, and most especially the large bank of multipaned windows that overlook the space. As corroborated by vintage photographs, such features identify the seemingly generic market scene as taking place in Spanish Harlem's beloved La Marqueta (fig. 36). Located under the railroad tracks on Park Avenue between 111th and 116th Streets, the Park Avenue Retail Market was built in 1936; it was part of a New Deal project conceived by Mayor Fiorello La Guardia to improve

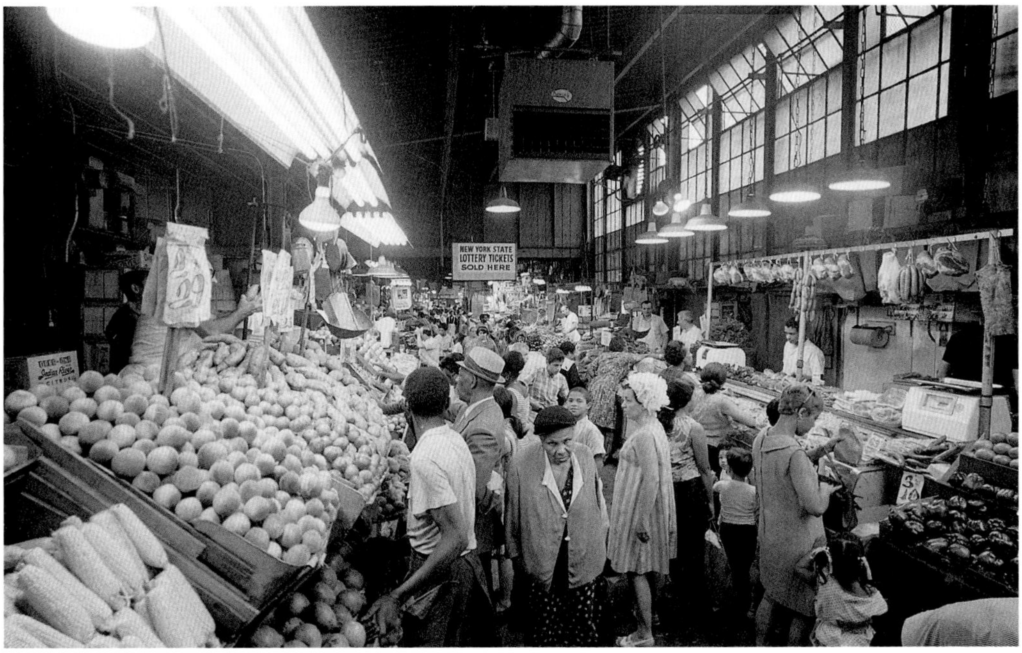


FIG. 36 La Marqueta in Spanish Harlem, 1968

public hygiene through the consolidation of street vendors and pushcarts into a network of public markets across the five boroughs.[25] In the years after World War II, it earned its nickname, La Marqueta, and by the 1950s had become the prime shopping destination for New York's Latino population, who traveled there from throughout the city to purchase familiar goods from home. Still in operation today, albeit at a reduced scale, it has been called East Harlem's "most recognizable symbol" by the *New York Times*.[26] Neel's portrayal of this local landmark is in keeping with her other New York cityscapes, which favor domestic architecture over modernist skyscrapers or the more grandiose building projects of the era, such as the Chrysler and Empire State Buildings.[27] Turning instead to public spaces, Neel captured the streets of the local communities that she and her fellow citizens inhabited.

Coincidentally, the type of street vendor that La Marqueta was meant to replace appears in an earlier Neel streetscape that dates to around the time of her arrival to the neighborhood. Simply titled *Spanish Harlem* (p. 147), the painting presents a glancing view from Neel's apartment on 107th Street, where she first moved with Negrón. As the peddler trundles his cart down the snowy street, the building across the way seems to press upon the picture plane, emphasizing its proximity. Such physical closeness is reiterated in the presence of Neel's neighbors, whose private lives are on public display: a woman sits at a sewing machine in one of the windows and a young couple with a newborn enters Neel's building. While these various personalities suggest a certain allegorical reading (particularly bearing in mind that the artist was pregnant when this painting was executed), they remain strangely peripheral. Instead, emphasis is placed on the modest entryways, corbeled windows, fire escapes, and repeated facades of the apartments. Neel's attention to such seemingly innocuous details from the built environment is evident in other works, such as *East 249 Street Entrance* of about 1938, and even more compellingly in *The Spanish Family*, in which the heart-shaped iron grillwork surrounding Margarita and her children not only situates the scene as taking place outdoors but also signifies familial love.

In the wintry *Spanish Harlem*, the prominent entry column and iron gate restrict the view, conveying a sense of claustrophobia. This sense of loneliness and even existential angst has been discussed in relationship to Neel's depictions of the cityscape by such art historians as Allara, Barry Walker, and Rosenberg.[28] These scholars, however, have tended to focus on the perspective from which Neel painted—namely, from inside her apartment looking out, thereby reinforcing her separation from local life. Yet, the artist also created artworks that attest to the neighborhood's lively sense of community. For example, *Building in Harlem* (fig. 37) portrays a city block under an exuberant blue sky with a group of figures talking on the corner. Considered alongside such compositions, the earlier *Spanish Harlem* may be regarded as a more muted image of street life in keeping with the winter season.

Two years after her separation from Negrón in late 1939, Neel changed apartments and eventually settled one block north, where she lived until 1962. This slight variation in scenery provided the backdrop for her canvas *Dominican Boys on 108th Street* (p. 132), which centers on the two young protagonists whose cultural identification attests to the presence of other

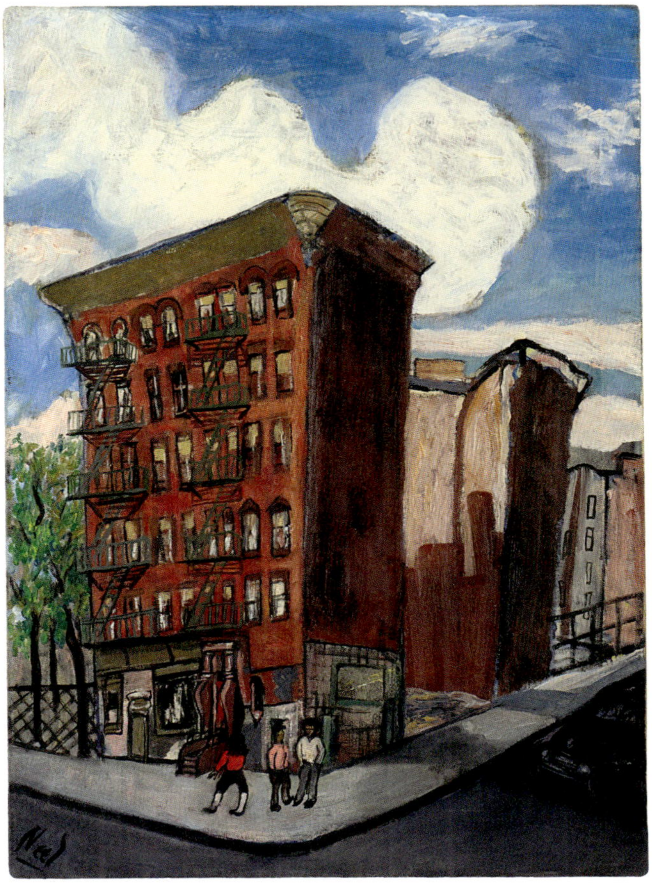

FIG. 37 *Building in Harlem*, ca. 1945. Oil on canvas. 34 × 24 in. (86.4 × 61 cm). Estate of Alice Neel

nationalities within the largely Puerto Rican neighborhood. The work's outdoor setting plays an essential role in communicating aspects about the boys' personalities, their wide-legged, hands-in-pocket poses suggesting a studied, streetwise swagger. Although their pudgy faces retain a sense of childish innocence, their bold presence within the urban environs signals a maturity beyond their years—or, at least a pretense of confidence.

Standing at the front of the picture plane as if on a proscenium stage, the boys are literally on the street, with a cropped view of the sidewalk and apartment buildings behind them. Again, Neel's attention to vernacular details is apparent in the decorative grillwork of the iron gates; the advertisements presented in the windows of the corner bodega; the bit of graffiti reading "Felipe" over the boy's head at right; and perhaps most significantly, the group of people gathered on a stoop, from where the two boys may have originally wandered. In her sketchbooks, Neel captured these and other characteristic features of uptown culture and community, particularly through drawings of children and adults in conversation and at play on stairs, columns, and balustrades. Since Neel typically did not paint outdoors, such sketches and her own intimate knowledge of the neighborhood helped inform her canvases once back in her apartment, with works like *Dominican Boys on 108th Street* reflecting the influence of her location in Spanish Harlem on her art.

## ARTISTIC PEERS AND LEGACY

Although Neel's paintings have earned her acclaim as "the first clear and beautiful voice of Spanish Harlem," she is not the only artist to have looked to the neighborhood's streets for inspiration.[29] Yet, perhaps her closest colleagues in terms of subject matter turned to the camera rather than the brush. While curator Helen Molesworth has rightfully written about the media specificity of painting versus photography in relation to Neel, comparisons of her work with that of photographers from both within and outside of the community reiterate how Neel's lived experience inflected her practice.[30]

In the 1940s, Neel's one-time peer on the WPA Helen Levitt used the camera lens to document Spanish Harlem, and with Janice Loeb and James Agee produced the appropriately titled 1948 short film *In the Street*. Akin to Neel, Levitt depicted the racially diverse children of the area, whom she often captured at play, as in *New York (Two Children Dancing)* (fig. 38). The majority of Levitt's images are candid, and she retained a certain distance from her subjects,

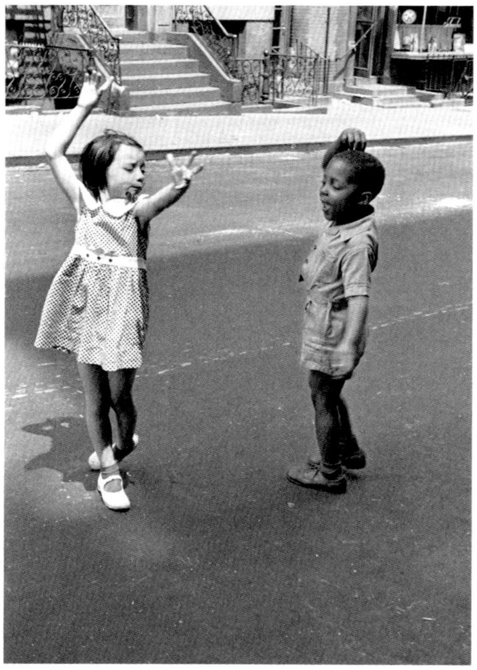

FIG. 38 Helen Levitt (American, 1913–2009). *New York (Two Children Dancing)*, ca. 1940. Gelatin silver print, 12 1/2 × 8 5/8 in. (31.8 × 21.9 cm). Courtesy Thomas Zander Gallery, Cologne

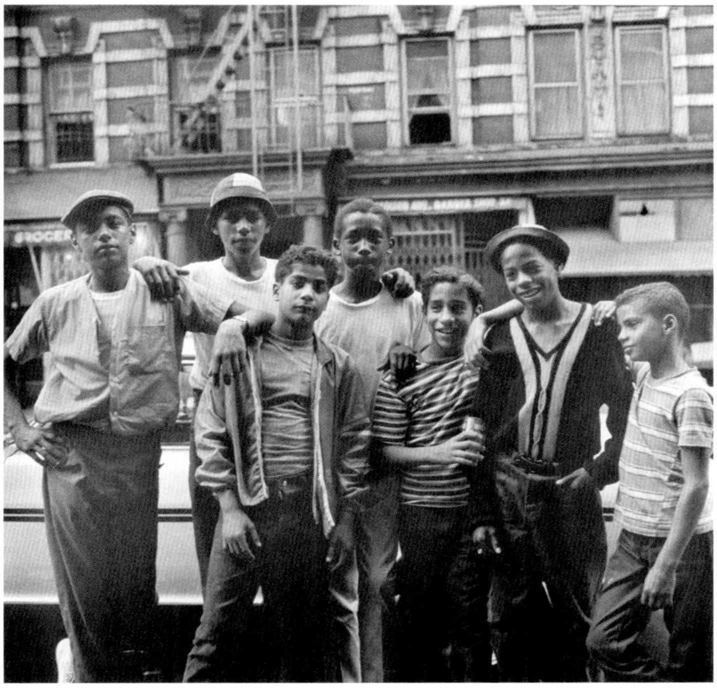

FIG. 39 Hiram Maristany (American, born 1945). *Group of Young Men on 111th Street*, 1966, printed 2016. Gelatin silver print, 14 7/8 × 15 in. (37.8 × 38.1 cm). Smithsonian American Art Museum, Washington, D.C., Museum purchase through the Smithsonian Latino Initiatives Pool, administered by the Smithsonian Latino Center (2016.30.8)

who seem either unaware of or indifferent to her presence.[31] While this reflects Levitt's methodology, which included employing a right-angle viewfinder in an effort to conceal her camera from her subjects, her studied detachment differs from Neel's more personally engaged relationship with the people she painted; it perhaps also reflects Levitt's outsider status within the neighborhood, apart from the rhythms of its daily life.[32]

Nearly thirty years later Bruce Davidson took images of the area as part of his *East 100th Street* suite, a two-year-long project focused on the residents of this single address. A selection from the series was exhibited at the Museum of Modern Art (MoMA) in 1970, where the images' stark emphasis on the neighborhood's poverty sparked controversy over the artist's perceived voyeuristic perspective, or, because, as critic A. D. Coleman bluntly put it, "Davidson is inarguably not only an outsider but an alien. He is neither black nor Puerto Rican, but white; he may, like the block's residents, 'love and hate' this ghetto—but, unlike them, he has the option of leaving."[33] Coleman's critique was published in the *New York Times* alongside a review by Puerto Rican photographer Felipe "Phil" Dante, who shifted the argument away from the artist's background and instead accused Davidson of exploitation, asking simply "where is our soul?"[34]

Significantly, while Dante directed readers to Levitt's photographs as evidence of an artist who succeeded where Davidson had failed, he could have also pointed to the work of his peers

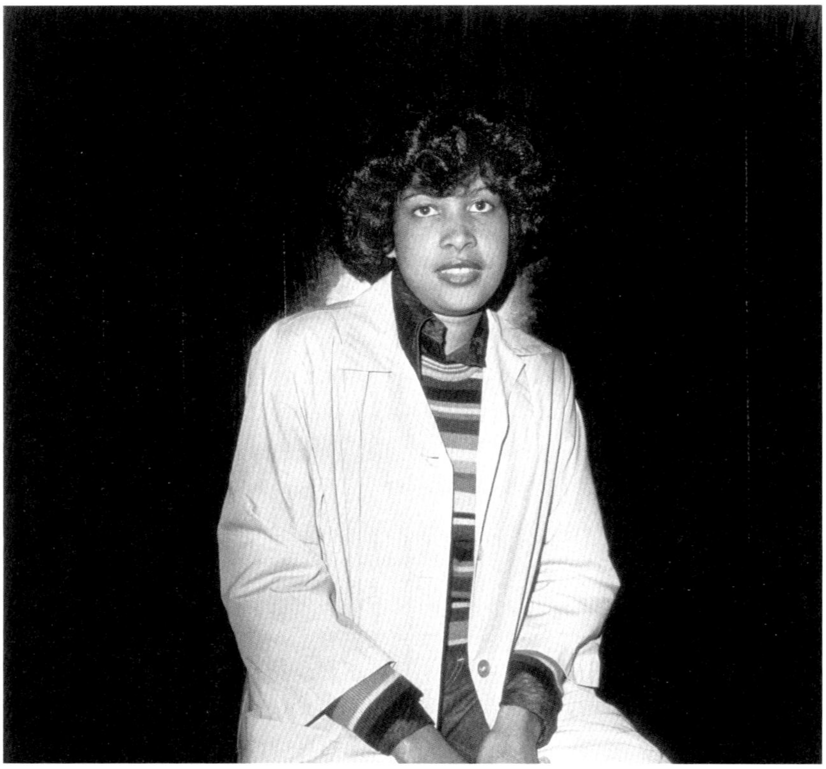

FIG. 40 Sophie Rivera (American, born 1938). *Untitled*, 1978, printed 2006. Gelatin silver print, 48 × 48 in. (121.9 × 121.9 cm). Smithsonian American Art Museum, Washington, D.C., Museum purchase through the Luisita L. and Franz H. Denghausen Endowment (2011.24.1)

Hiram Maristany and Sophie Rivera. A lifelong resident of Spanish Harlem who grew up just streets away from Neel, Maristany captured the children and young adults of his neighborhood in incisive photographs that bear significant aesthetic resonances with Neel's paintings. Indeed, in pose and location, the adolescents portrayed in his *Group of Young Men on 111th Street* (fig. 39) appear as the next generation of Neel's subjects in *Dominican Boys on 108th Street*. Basing her practice in her Bronx neighborhood, Rivera, like Neel, similarly encountered her sitters on the streets, and her *Nuyorican Portraits* series (fig. 40) shares a conceptual link to Neel's work as a visual record of the local community. For this project, Rivera asked the people who passed her home if they were Puerto Rican, and if they answered in the affirmative, she would invite them into her studio for a photoshoot. Though Neel's background as a white woman would have excluded her from Rivera's project, the artist nonetheless shares an important correspondence with Rivera and Maristany in that all three created images of the neighborhoods in which they lived.

Unlike Levitt and Davidson, whose photographs of Spanish Harlem were presented at MoMA during their lifetimes,[35] neither Maristany nor Rivera nor Neel received the same degree of critical attention.[36] In fact, between 1968 and 1971, Maristany and Neel both participated in protests at the Whitney and The Met over the lack of representation of Black and Latino artists at these venerable institutions (fig. 41).[37] In a continuation of her earlier participation in public protests during the 1930s, Neel's concern for civil rights and the equal treatment of minority artists prompted her to again take to the streets in the 1960s and 1970s. Though it is perhaps unsurprising that the two Puerto Rican photographers are still awaiting their due, Neel's belated fame, as well as the recent reevaluation of her Spanish Harlem works, has come to influence subsequent generations. Painter Jordan Casteel openly affirms Neel as an inspiration to her practice, which also centers on portraits of the people she encounters in her own Harlem neighborhood and in the streets of New York (fig. 42).[38] Neel's images of queer men and women find a contemporary parallel in the paintings of David Antonio Cruz, whose intersectional approach to portraiture renders often-forgotten and/or marginalized bodies visible. Cruz's recent series of slain, trans-identifying individuals resonates with the same quiet, powerful dignity intuited in Neel's work (fig. 43). The recent resurgence in figuration continues to propel Neel toward greater recognition, particularly among emerging artists from diverse backgrounds who see in her work a model for portraying both themselves and their surrounding communities.

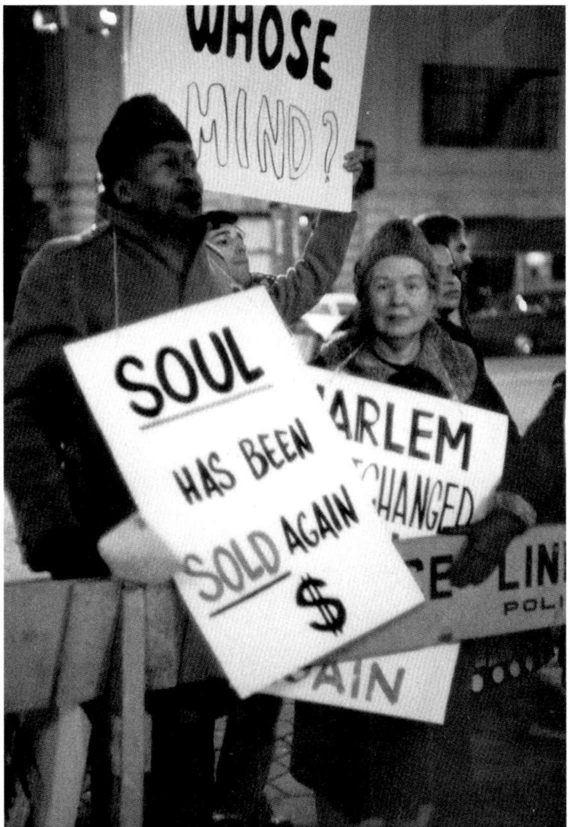


FIG. 41 Alice Neel at a demonstration to protest the exhibition *Harlem on my Mind* at The Metropolitan Museum of Art, January 16, 1969. Photograph by Fred W. McDarrah

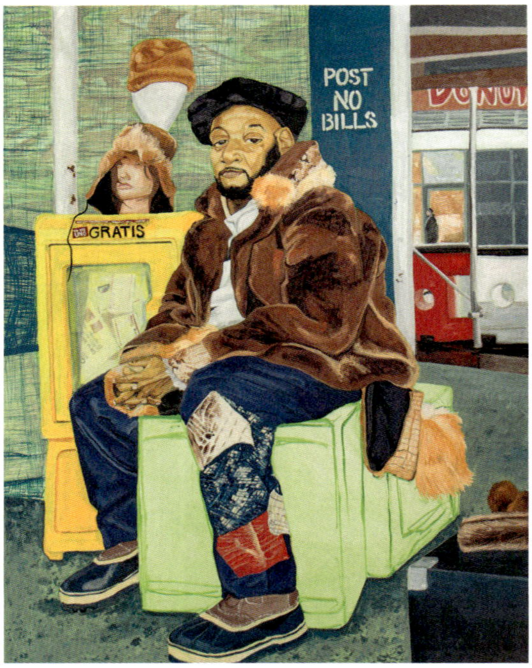


FIG. 42 Jordan Casteel (American, born 1989). *Charles*, 2016. Oil on canvas, 78 × 60 in. (198.1 × 152.4 cm). Courtesy Casey Kaplan Gallery, New York

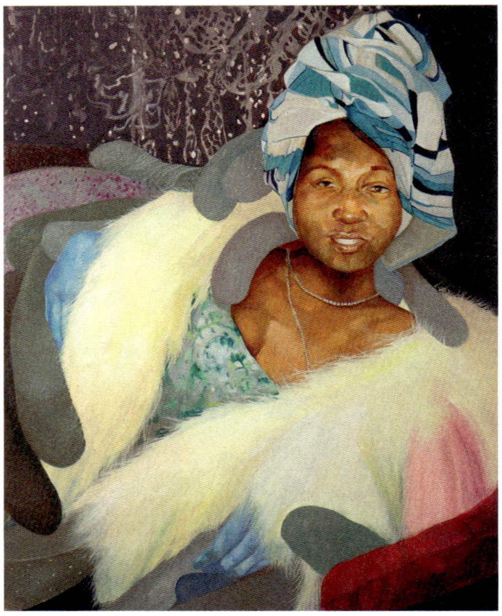

FIG. 43 David Antonio Cruz (American, born 1974). *iguessyoudidntlearnyourlessonandyouhavereturned, Portrait of Derricka*, 2018. Oil and enamel on wood, 20 × 16 in. (50.8 × 40.6 cm). Courtesy Monique Meloche Gallery, Chicago

## LEAVING SPANISH HARLEM

Interspersed amid his poetic vignettes of personal reminiscences and imagined narratives, writer Hilton Als addresses the essence of Neel's relationship to Spanish Harlem in the exhibition catalogue *Alice Neel, Uptown*:

> Harlem was her home. There was struggle, but goodness in the struggle, and there was poverty and love, too. As a single mother of two trying to make ends meet, she recognized the struggle on her neighbors' faces, because children clung to her skirts, wrapped their arms around her neck as well. She was needed and was needy. She would not wait to see if it was "appropriate" to diversify or not–to be part of a community that was not supposed to be her own, as a white woman, an educated girl from Pennsylvania who had all sorts of chances, but so few chances, too. No matter what, she was a woman–she would just do it. Because East Harlem was what she felt like, or identified with, no matter what she looked like.[39]

Getting to the heart of her insider-outsider status, Als attests to the important place of Neel's community in her life. *Harlem was her home.* Alongside her friends, family, and neighbors, she suffered the ails that plagued the neighborhood, and also relished in its joys. Ironically, Neel's shared fate with her community came to a head in 1962, when she was forced to move by her landlord. According to the artist, "I was just put out. I never would have left. They divided the whole house in half and rented each half for much more."[40] Casting herself as the victim of gentrification–the effects of which continue to plague El Barrio–Neel was certainly not alone in her displacement; beginning in the late 1950s and extending into the 1960s, East Harlem experienced large-scale so-called slum clearing. Low-rise tenements were bulldozed block-by-block and replaced by the massively scaled public housing that today characterizes much of the neighborhood's physical landscape.[41]

With the help of her landlord, Neel moved almost laterally across Manhattan to an apartment located on 107th Street and Broadway, just south of Columbia University. Although it should be noted that this area was itself experiencing a demographic change, including a growing Latino population, Neel seems to have not connected with the culture on the streets as before. Indeed, while Neel produced some of her most celebrated portraits during this time, her encounters with her (mostly white) sitters were markedly different than they had been in Spanish Harlem. Whether due to the new neighborhood, her age, or her surging fame and the accompanying travel that it brought, it seems that Neel was no longer *siempre en la calle* upon her move to the Upper West Side.

Would this have been different had Neel remained in East Harlem? Although she was absent during the height of urban neglect suffered in the area, she also missed the concomitant radical actions of the militant Young Lords Party, with whose politics she would almost certainly have been aligned.[42] Neel also did not witness the neighborhood's florescence in the visual arts through the establishment of El Museo del Barrio, the artist collective Taller Boricua, and other Puerto Rican–led community organizations that emerged in the late 1960s and early 1970s. While Neel's role in this history must be left to conjecture, her affinity for the neighborhood is evident in such works as *Sunset in Spanish Harlem* (p. 223), which, painted four years prior to her departure, retrospectively reads as a poetic goodbye. Depicting humble tenement buildings against a swirling late afternoon sky, the canvas is a paean to Neel's East Harlem; portrayed slightly askew, the buildings seem to dance as if to the sound of Negrón singing "Puerto Rico Libre!"–a song linked with Neel's arrival to Spanish Harlem nearly twenty years earlier.

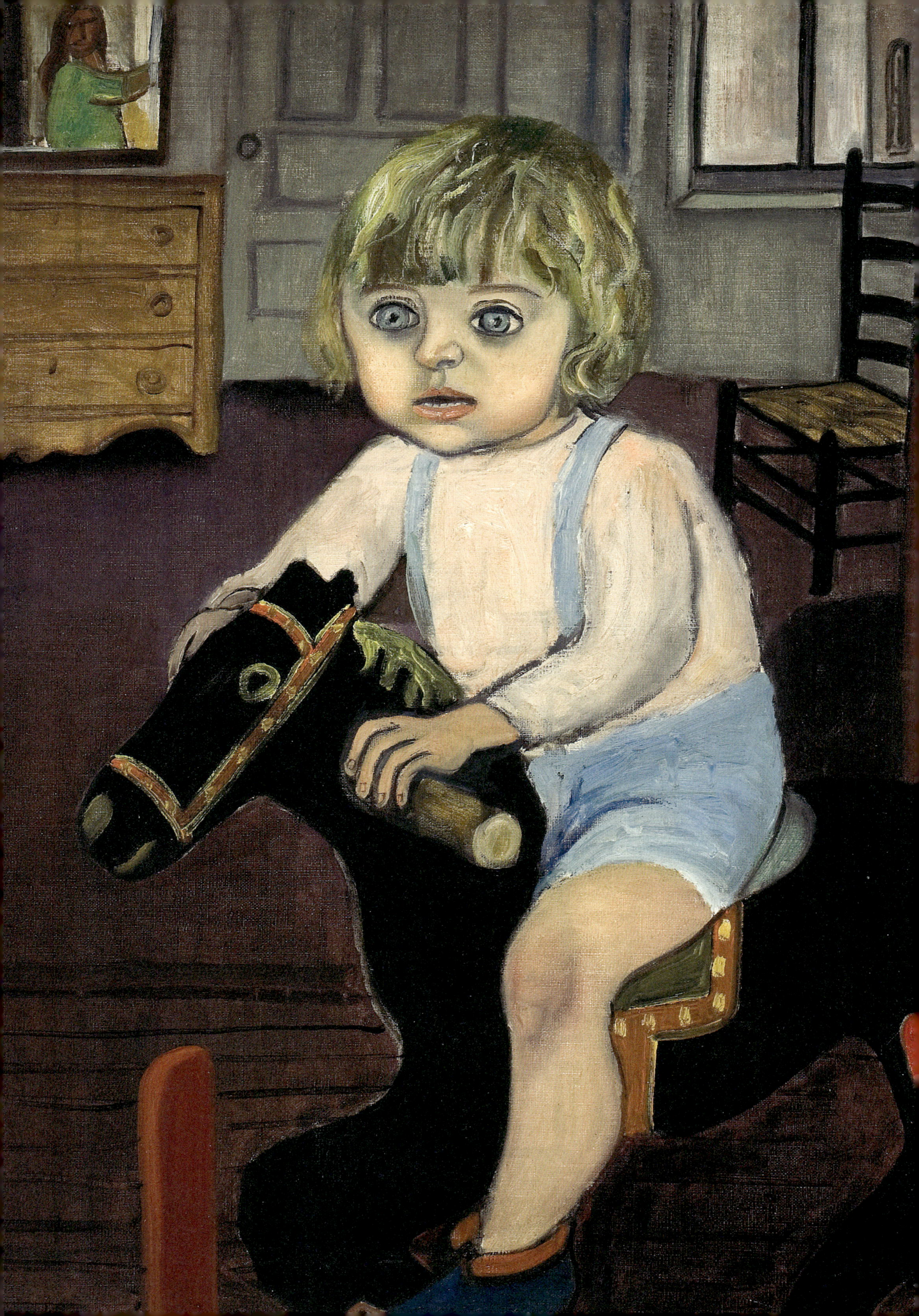

# "I'LL SHOW EVERYBODY": AN ARTIST-MOTHER AT HOME

**MEREDITH A. BROWN**

Stacks of newspapers, magazines, and books, a plush couch and some chairs, hearty houseplants, family photos, and framed artworks commingle with a row of cans and pots filled with brushes and rags on the mantel, while an easel, tubes of paint, and a large palette sit in the center of the floor (fig. 44). From this crowded living room, Alice Neel directs Nancy Neel, who was both her assistant and her daughter-in-law, to bring paintings out from the racks built in the hallways to show to her guests who have come to discuss art, drink wine, and eat a take-out pizza lunch. So begins *Portrait of Alice Neel, 1976–1982*, a film collage by Neel's friend, New York–based French filmmaker Michel Auder.[1] Auder not only recorded Neel painting and talking about her work but also focused in on household objects, peeling paint on the walls, the view of the city out the window. Each domestic vignette is treated as an artistic one. As the film and its title suggest, a study of the artist, of her remarkable images, would be incomplete without a discussion of the rooms in which she read, entertained, mothered, and painted.

Like many artists who were women, Neel never had an independent studio. The strictures placed on women beginning in the nineteenth century served to deny them access to many of the professional opportunities, affiliations, and spaces afforded to their male peers. Domestic and familial responsibilities further confined women to the home, leaving little time or social support to pursue professional artistic ambitions in a space apart from the home.[2] Moreover, for Neel, economic hardship and the responsibilities of being a single mother necessitated she set up her easel in her apartment. Throughout her long career, she painted at home in a physical environment where her identity and duties simultaneously included those of daughter, mother, and grandmother. In Neel's pictures of her own interior spaces—which always functioned both as domestic rooms and as professional areas in which she welcomed neighbors, acquaintances, and members of the public to sit for her—she crystallized an important ambivalence between her gendered, embodied familial work, especially motherhood, and her artistic ambitions.

"I was a pathfinder in those days," Neel told Taylor Mead, a writer and performer who was part of Andy Warhol's Factory, as they were being recorded by Auder in 1976.[3] She was talking to Mead in her apartment about free-spirited choices she had made in her personal life in the 1930s and 1940s. Seated at a messy desk, an image of a bear head taped to the wall behind her, her own distinctive canvases leaning against the walls nearby, discussing her sex life with a queer underground movie star twenty-five years her junior for an art film that would see public release, Neel surely understood her use of the past tense—*in those days*—would land with great irony. Neel's entire life was marked by unconventional choices, including her decision to have a creative career at all. Women like Neel from white middle-class suburban families were discouraged

Detail of *Hartley on the Rocking Horse*, 1943 (p. 153)

from harboring ambitions beyond finding a husband and raising children. Indeed, the influential American journalist Dorothy Thompson warned women against pursuing careers outside the home in her monthly column in *Ladies' Home Journal*, which ran from 1937 to 1961. In a 1939 piece addressing an imagined daughter with aspirations to be a writer, Thompson advised the young woman to focus on raising "a fine man" rather than writing "a second-rate novel," implying not only that marriage should be a woman's priority but also that creative geniuses can only ever be male. The ability of women to succeed in both a demanding profession and a happy family life was, Thompson declared, "an illusion."[4] Although Neel was more likely to be reading the daily newspaper or left-wing journals like *New Masses* than a women's magazine like *Ladies' Home Journal*, she had received–and rejected–such sexist messages throughout her childhood: "My mother used to say to me, 'I don't know what you expect to do; you're only a girl.' But this, instead of destroying me, made me more ambitious because I'd think, you know, I'll show them, I'll show her, I'll show everybody."[5]

One of Neel's earliest depictions of her home, a small watercolor entitled *The Family* (p. 141), painted during the summer of 1927 when she had returned to visit her parents, dramatizes the psychological structure of her childhood household through architecture. Divided unevenly into three horizontal panels, the watercolor shows a cross section of her parents' house, each level teetering on the one below. In the lowest compartment, the basement, a wash of shades of gray, the large black boiler on the left extends its oversized pipes toward Neel's pathetic-looking

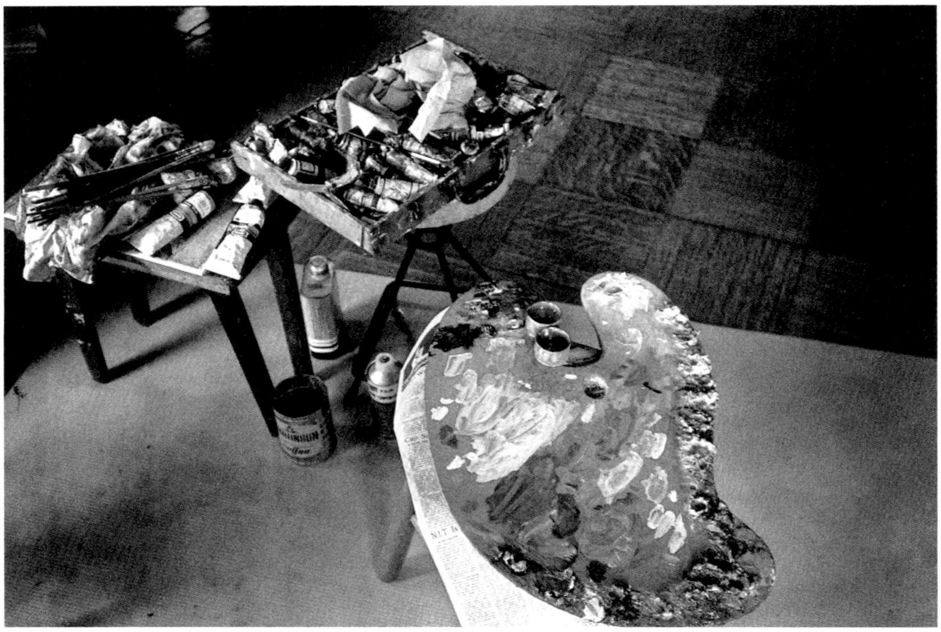

FIG. 44 Alice Neel's palette and tubes of paint in her Upper West Side apartment. Alice Neel Archive, Stowe, Vt.

father, George Washington Neel. A thin man with thinner hair, he trudges up the stairs with a bucket full of coal, his face downturned, his body precariously balanced on the step's edge. "My little, gray father," Neel called him, worn down by drudgery.[6] Above him, in a room filled with warm-colored patterns, are the women. Neel painted herself preternaturally large, seated in a pink housedress, resting with closed eyes, cradling her chubby-cheeked infant daughter in her lap. Crouched under the oval table, its surface tipped up toward the viewer, a bespectacled, simian-looking woman—the elder Alice Neel—frantically scrubs the floor. She stretches the toe of her left shoe over the uneven black line to impinge on the level below as if ready to kick her husband back down the stairs should he ever reach the top. In the uppermost room, Neel's younger brother, known as Peter, leans back in a rocking chair; his feet and head extend out of the frame. He studies his book while producing a thick ribbon of dark smoke from the cigarette dangling from his mouth, aloof and unaware, or unconcerned, with the activities of the floors below. Compartmentalized by gender, the generations are also divided by work, with the parents exhausted by the menial physical tasks of maintaining a house and the children engaged in intellectual or nurturing pursuits. Neel depicted herself absorbed in an activity (the bodily labor of cuddling her young daughter); her work in *The Family* is not the work of an artist, it is the work of a mother. Meanwhile, her own mother's physical labor has turned her into a wild-eyed hysteric, a frightening prediction for the newly married, postpartum Neel. These isolated rooms inhabited by three generations of the Neel family, rendered as simplified spaces with flattened forms and multiple perspectives, create a picture of discomforting domesticity.

Neel gave a name to this psychological discomfort years later when recounting the fraught position in which she found herself following the death of her first daughter in December 1927 and subsequent birth of her second child, Isabetta, in November 1928. She described it as an "awful dichotomy": "I loved Isabetta, of course I did. But I wanted to paint."[7] Neel was not alone in her maternal ambivalence. "Any mother of young children . . . who wants to do serious creative work," wrote literary critic Susan Rubin Suleiman in 1979, "with all that such work implies of the will to self-assertion, self-absorption, solitary grappling—must be prepared for the worst kind of struggle, which is the struggle against herself."[8] The constant battle between writing and motherhood, Suleiman argues, is both a struggle against the ideologies and institutions that hold the two as mutually exclusive and an internal fight between the artist-mother's creative needs and her guilt-ridden desires to abandon her children.[9] By the time Suleiman was writing about it in the late 1970s, this issue of combining the work of a mother with the work of an artist was being tackled by many feminist artists.[10] In the mid-1930s, however, vocalizing that conflict and representing that experience in art must have seemed nearly impossible. Neel literalizes this splitting in her 1929 satirical watercolor *The Intellectual* (p. 143), in which two women chat while a third figure stands behind them as Neel, on the far left, uses all three of her arms in a frantic attempt to keep up with her active young daughter and the "intellectual" conversation.[11]

Neel's internal conflict between her art and her maternal duties was temporarily relieved, in a way, when her husband, Carlos Enríquez, abandoned her and took their infant daughter

Isabetta with him to Cuba. Following an intensely difficult year in which Neel suffered and recovered from a nervous breakdown, she moved to an apartment on Cornelia Street in Greenwich Village and entered the employment of the Works Progress Administration's (WPA) easel division. Accordingly, most of Neel's works that remain from this period are primarily socially concerned pictures of the street, public life, or public figures. One significant exception is a portrait of her daughter begun in 1934 when Isabetta came to spend the summer with her mother and grandparents at the beach in Belmar, New Jersey. There, Neel painted her nearly six-year-old daughter standing naked on a pink-and-red striped throw rug in front of a wood-paneled wall (p. 199). Isabetta's self-possessed pose and pronounced nudity caused controversy at the time the work was created. Throughout her career, Neel was committed to depicting the body as she saw it, without concern for societal norms. Gallerists in the 1930s, on the other hand, found the stark nudity of the young child disquieting. "The galleries would not show it," Neel recalled, "as they said it was indecent."[12] The girl's hands are placed firmly on her hips and her exaggeratedly large feet point out, not unlike those of Edgar Degas's well-known and controversial sculpture *Little Dancer Aged Fourteen* (1878–81, National Gallery of Art).[13] The pose is also reminiscent, as art historian Jeremy Lewison has asserted, of Paul Cézanne's *The Bather* (ca. 1885, Museum of Modern Art), a painting Neel likely would have known.[14] Whereas Cézanne placed his figure within a vast landscape, Neel articulated the setting of *Isabetta* in a way that is distinctive from her other extant works from the mid-1930s, as if to firmly situate the scene within her own familial sphere. Neel's parents had rented a home on the New Jersey shore for summer vacations since Neel was young, and she continued the tradition with her own family,

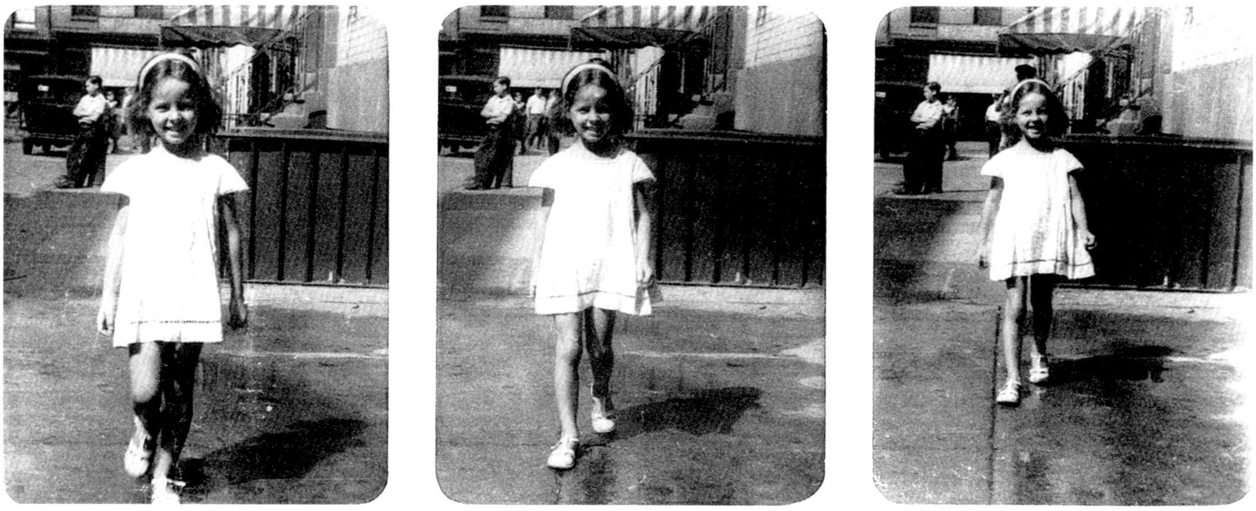

FIG. 45 Isabetta Enríquez during a summer visit to her mother, Alice Neel, in New Jersey, 1934. Alice Neel Archive, Stowe, Vt.

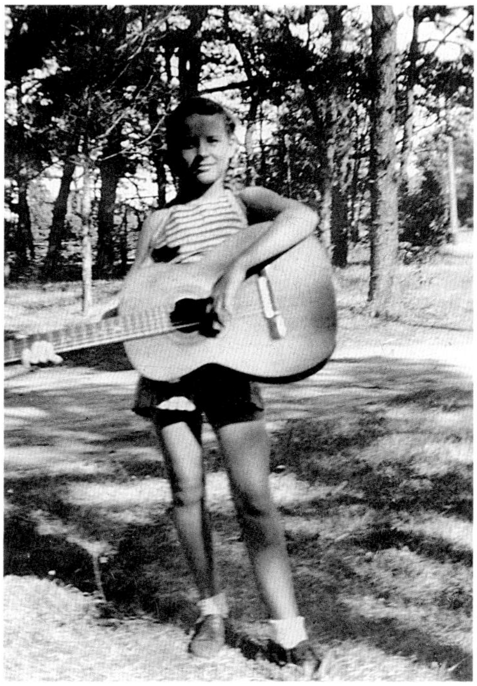

FIG. 46 Isabetta with José's guitar, 1939. Alice Neel Archive, Stowe, Vt.

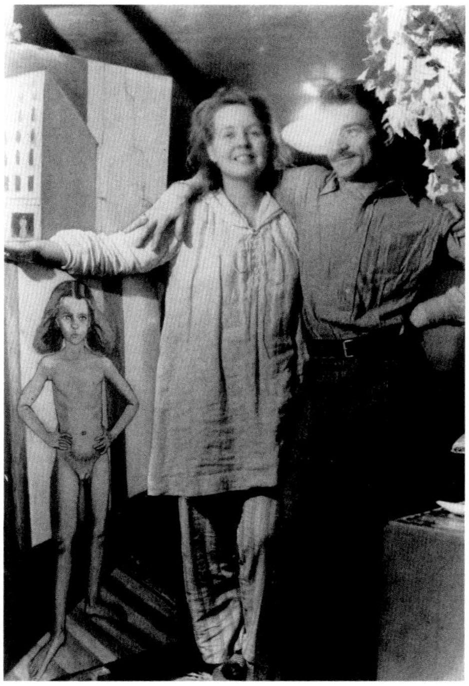

FIG. 47 Alice Neel and Kenneth Doolittle with *Isabetta*, 1934. Alice Neel Archive, Stowe, Vt.

first in various rental homes, like the one depicted here, then, from 1935 until her death, in a cottage she purchased in Spring Lake, New Jersey. The sharp angles and diagonal lines that activate the shallow interior space of *Isabetta*, combined with the little girl's unwavering gaze, create a sense of closeness that is both loving and unnerving.

Although family photos from Isabetta's two summer visits show a beautiful girl in possession of a confidence uncharacteristic for her young age (figs. 45, 46), a sense of self-assurance that Neel captured in paint, *Isabetta* also reveals the power imbalance inherent when an artist (clothed) depicts a nude figure. This dynamic is further compounded when that artist is the parent and the nude model their child.[15] The intimacy engendered by Isabetta's nakedness within a domestic space is countered by her unabashed exposure; Neel's confident and unapologetic rendering of her young daughter's body may be read as both an act of maternal pride and an erotic provocation. These opposing forces gain a particular and perhaps troubling intensity in the case of *Isabetta*, for there remains an additional unsettling element to this maternal-child relationship and, therefore, to the work: for most of their lives, including when this painting was made, Neel and Isabetta were estranged. Their complicated, and in many ways heartbreaking and mysterious, mother-daughter relationship remains difficult to divorce from the canvas itself.[16]

As a record of Neel's labor as an artist and as documentation of an infrequent meeting between mother and daughter, *Isabetta* held special significance for Neel, becoming almost a surrogate for her absent child. Not only did she have the work photographed for posterity shortly after it was completed, she also posed with it in a photograph taken in the apartment she shared with her lover Kenneth Doolittle in 1934 (fig. 47). In this image, Neel proudly drapes her arm over the canvas as if she were embracing her once-again faraway daughter. Her other arm

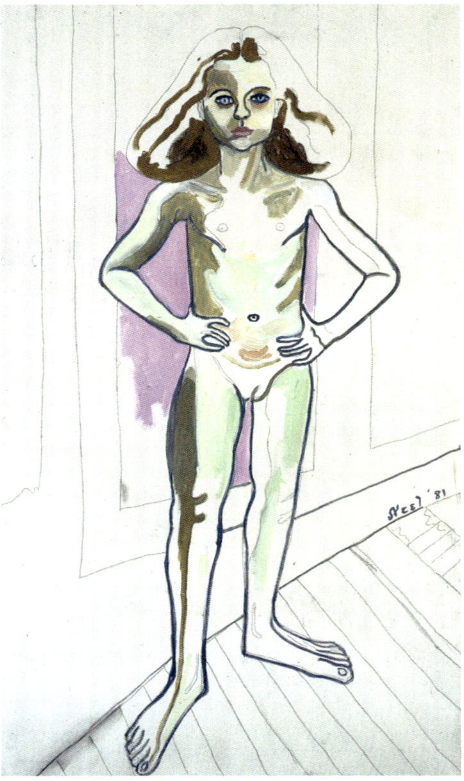

FIG. 48 *Memories*, 1981. Oil on canvas, 43 × 25 in. (109.2 × 63.5 cm). Private collection, Belgium

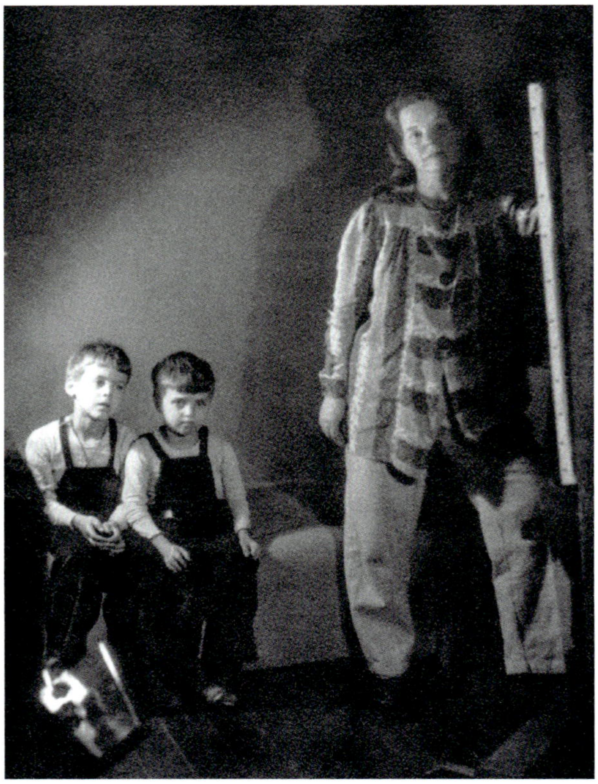

FIG. 49 Richard, Hartley, and Alice Neel, 1946. Alice Neel Archive, Stowe, Vt. Photograph by Sam Brody

wraps around Doolittle. In 1935 Doolittle destroyed some 350 of Neel's paintings, drawings, and personal photographs in a rage, including *Isabetta* and another painting of the girl made at the same time. Following *Isabetta*'s destruction in this traumatic domestic episode, Neel created an almost exact replica of the striking nude portrait, based on the photograph and her recollections of her daughter. The confidence of Isabetta's pose in both the original and its replacement is matched by the bold line of Neel's brush, physical proof of a mother at work depicting her daughter in a shared domestic space. Although several of Neel's slashed canvases were able to be semi-repaired (including a painting of Isabetta as a baby that Neel made from memory in 1930 shortly after Carlos had taken their daughter to Cuba), most of her work was completely destroyed. Already missing her actual daughter from her daily life, Neel now found her painted daughter obliterated in a violent attack in and on her home. The act of repainting *Isabetta* was one of recuperation, as Neel symbolically worked to heal the doubled loss of her daughter and her art. Having held on to the picture for some thirty-five years, Neel sold *Isabetta* to Jonathan Brand, the son of her friend, novelist and poet Millen Brand, in 1971 or 1972, telling him, "I love the *Isabetta*. Do you know why? Her elegance."[17] In 1981—now a grandmother of six—Neel painted "the *Isabetta*" once again, this time in a remarkably unfinished sketch of her young, naked daughter standing inside their summer rental cottage at the Jersey Shore nearly fifty years before (fig. 48). The painting is evocatively titled *Memories*.

Beginning in 1938 (after she had left Doolittle and begun a relationship with the musician José Santiago Negrón), and for the next twenty-four years, Neel lived and worked in the ethnically mixed, impoverished neighborhood of Spanish Harlem.[18] From within the confines of a railroad apartment on the third floor of a tenement building at 21 East 108th Street, where she settled as the mother of two young sons in 1942, Neel struggled to balance caretaking responsibilities with professional ambitions, stealing moments to paint while her toddlers napped during the day or slumbered at night.[19] Now a single mother with limited funds, time, and space, she set up her canvas and paints in the living room, the kitchen, the bedroom, reflecting her domestic duties in her art, blurring the boundaries between home and work, or, as Second Wave feminists would make plain thirty years later, the personal and the political.

A photograph from 1946 taken by Sam Brody, the father of Neel's younger son and a professional photographer and documentary filmmaker, captures the muddling of their domestic life, of Neel's simultaneous mothering and painting. In it, Neel stands at her easel in a smock, her left hand touching the canvas while her sons, Richard and Hartley, ages six and four and dressed in their matching school uniforms, huddle together on the couch behind their mother (fig. 49). In contrast, a 1944 photograph by Brody of Neel seated cross-legged on the floor, surrounded by a

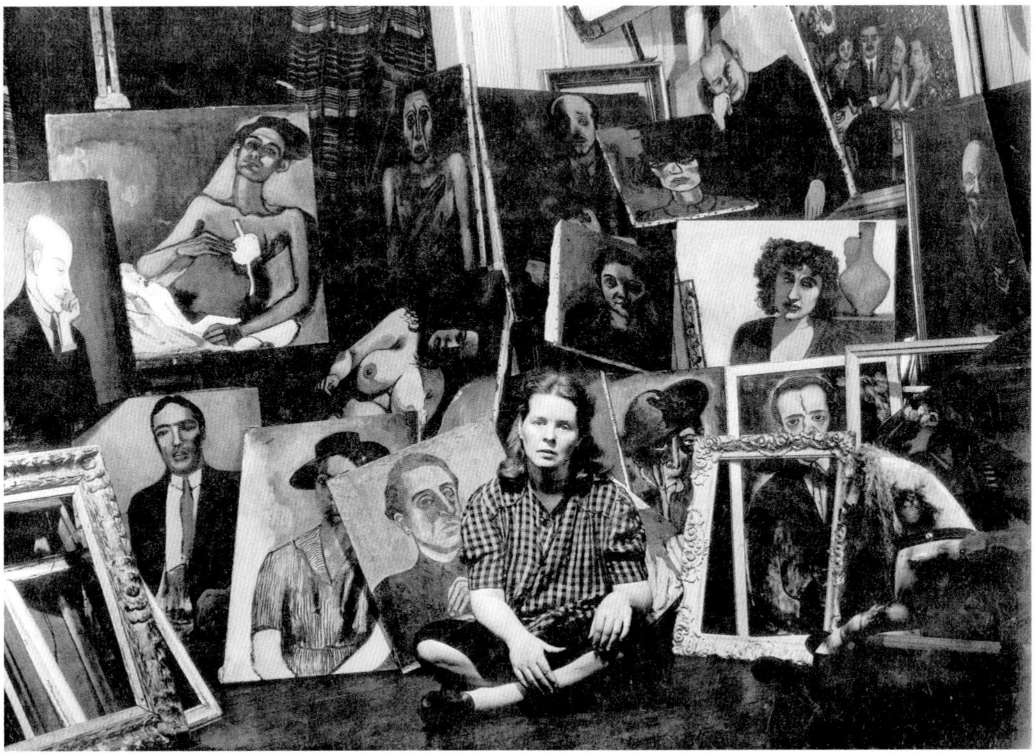

FIG. 50 Alice Neel, 1944. Alice Neel Archive, Stowe, Vt. Photograph by Sam Brody

swell of her paintings and empty frames piled in front of striped curtains, presents a portrait of a prolific woman artist, alone with her work (fig. 50). In both pictures, Neel looks unsmilingly into the camera with the seriousness of an artist and the weariness of a mother. The photographs capture an interior space that is obviously domestic (the presence of children, the couch, the decorative curtains) *and* incontrovertibly artistic (the easel, the canvases, the frames). In the 1940s and 1950s, women who conceived of themselves as ambitious artists, as Neel did, were encouraged by teachers and male peers to separate their female-lived experience from their art practice in order to have any hope of professional success.[20] Neel must have understood this implicitly; while both photographs show her with her art at home, she used the 1944 portrait—the one without her children—for the invitation to her first solo exhibition in six years, held at Rose Fried's Pinacotheca Gallery on West 58th Street from March 6 to 22, 1944. She employed it again in 1960 as part of her contribution to Alfred Leslie's anthology of Beat literature, *The Hasty Papers*, where the image was captioned "Alice Neel, in her studio."[21] By identifying the space in the photograph as her studio, the caption presents an artist where we expect to find them. But it omits a crucial aspect of the setting: for Neel, the studio and the home were one and the same. As feminists would argue beginning in the 1970s, the inseparability of the domestic from the artistic for modern women artists generated a painful, split identity.[22]

Particularly for women, the home is a psychologically charged space, the site of internal and inter-relational comfort and conflict. Louise Bourgeois, who also worked to make art at home while raising young children in New York, explored this theme in her *femme maison* paintings and drawings from 1946–47, which depict female bodies with houses for heads (fig. 51). These surrealistic figures represent the predicament of the artist-mother, as art historian Mignon Nixon has argued, a housewife-housewoman who is "struggling to free herself from the burdens of displacement and domesticity, motherhood and masculine desire."[23] In the United States in the 1940s and 1950s, the struggle between a woman's artistic desires and her maternal duties was dismissed, if not pathologized. The prominent American psychologist Helene Deutsch even theorized in *The Psychology of Women* (1944–45) that in "normal" female psychological development, a woman's "urge to intellectual and artistic creation" is replaced "in favor of the reproductive function."[24] In other words, a normal "woman" is naturally creative, but those impulses, which may find outlets in literature or art in her youth, are supplanted by her procreative efforts until her child-rearing is complete. In her transformative book on motherhood, feminist writer and poet Adrienne Rich, whose portrait Neel drew (p. 174), refuted this prescriptive definition of female creativity as being the result of patriarchal culture, not biology, arguing that the "envy, awe, and dread of the male for the female capacity to create life has repeatedly taken the form of hatred for every other female aspect of creativity. Not only have women been told to stick to motherhood, but we have been told that our intellectual or aesthetic creations were inappropriate, inconsequential, or scandalous."[25]

Like Bourgeois and Rich, Neel rejected this formation of woman as *either* artist *or* mother and used her art practice to push against such limitations. By depicting her domestic life, she

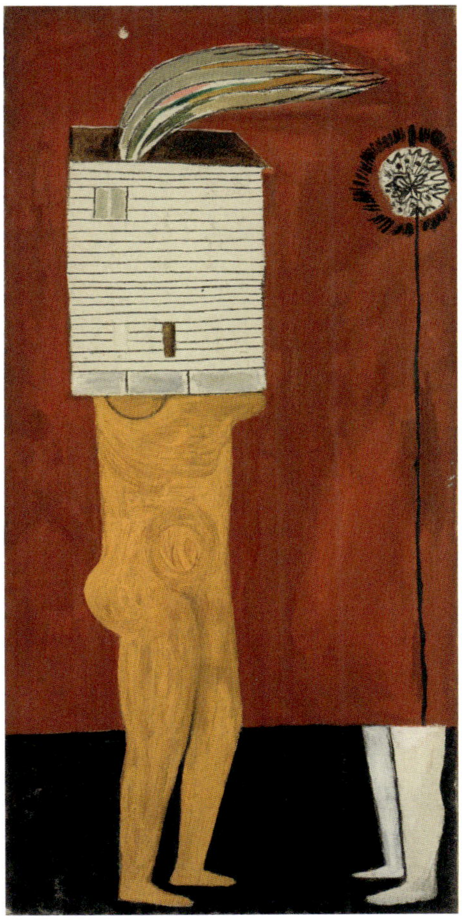

FIG. 51 Louise Bourgeois (American, born France, 1911–2010). *Femme maison*, 1946–47. Oil and ink on linen, 36 × 14 in. (91.4 × 35.6 cm). Collection of Agnes Gund

refused to sacrifice creativity for procreativity, professional work for maternal labor.[26] For example, in a 1950 painting of Richard and Hartley (fig. 52), Neel created her own version of the 1946 photograph by Brody (see fig. 49). In her version, she is the agent, not the static object of another artist's image. Neel has made her own picture rather than stand inside someone else's. This is her own familial scene: her two somber, wide-eyed sons seated on the same couch in front of the same wall as in Brody's photograph. Hartley rests his hand on Richard's shoulder in a fraternal gesture while Richard knits his fingers together into a Gordian knot, a physical manifestation of the "awful dichotomy" under which they all lived. This is not a scene of domestic bliss but rather of familial ambivalence. The dark colors and flattened space compress the figures, emphasizing a closeness between the brothers, while their carefully rendered faces expose the scrutiny of the maternal gaze.

Perhaps surprisingly, Neel only once portrayed herself in the midst of laboring as an artist and as a mother in the contested space occupied by those bifurcated roles, in *Hartley on the Rocking Horse* of 1943 (p. 153). Unusual in Neel's oeuvre for its depth of field, the canvas shows her younger son, then two years old, astride a small rocking horse in the living room. Neel had found the horse on the street near their apartment and, according to Hartley, brought it inside,

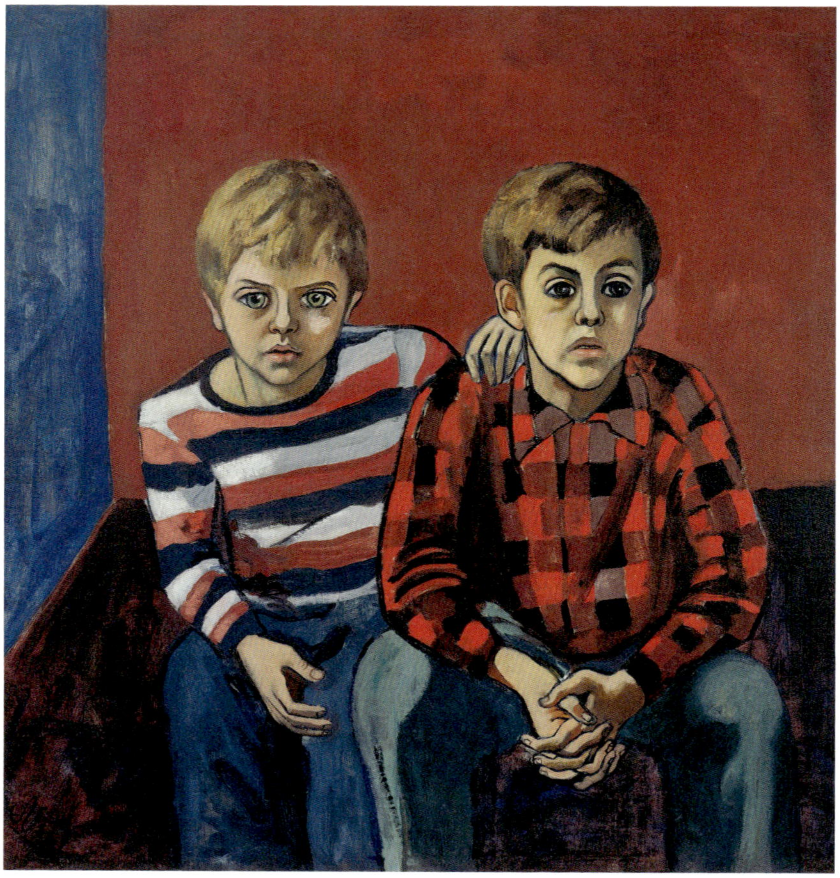

FIG. 52 *Richard and Hartley*, 1950. Oil on canvas, 38 × 36 in. (96.5 × 91.4 cm). Private collection

cleaned it up, and repainted it so that her sons would have a toy; the artist-mother at work.[27] Large in the foreground, with his wide, light eyes prominently outlined in black and a row of tiny baby teeth visible in his open mouth, the toddler tensely grabs onto the handles. Behind the rocking horse on the right is a horizontally striped curtain (the same one evident in the 1944 photograph of Neel), which divided the living room from Neel's bedroom.[28] Stranded in the background is a ladder-back chair with a rush seat. This chair (or another in the set) appears in several of Neel's portraits from this period, including *Still Life with Fruit* of 1940 (p. 152), *Mercedes Arroyo* of 1952 (p. 131), *Cut Glass with Fruit* of 1952 (p. 154), and *Georgie Arce No. 2* of 1955 (p. 133); it is a visual reminder that *all* of Neel's portraits, not just those of her family, were painted in her home. Neel's friend, journalist and activist Mike Gold, celebrated her home studio in his essay for her 1951 exhibition at New Playwrights Theatre: "Alice has for years lived with her children in a Harlem tenement. Her studio is the kitchen and her models the neighbors and the streets. She comes from an old Philadelphia family dating back to the Revolution. But her paintings reveal that here is her true family."[29] Gold, a committed Communist, valorized the economic status of Neel and her sitters; he also emphasized her constant dual role as an artist-mother, identifying the artist as a parent and her studio as her home.

Neel, too, inscribed these lived identities into *Hartley on the Rocking Horse*. In the upper-left corner, reflected in the mirror hanging over the chest of drawers, she depicted herself, long hair down her back, arm raised to the canvas: a woman creating a picture of her son in their domestic environment. Well-versed in art history, Neel would have been familiar with the device of incorporating a reflected figure in the mirror, used most famously by Diego Velázquez in *Las Meninas* (1656, Museo Nacional del Prado, Madrid) and by Henri Matisse in such works as *Carmelina* (1903, Museum of Fine Arts, Boston), where the artist's visage is part of the reflected image.[30] The presence of the artist-mother's reflection, a self-portrait set within a larger portrait of Neel's son playing at home, adds to the complexity of the composition.[31] In *Hartley on the Rocking Horse*, Neel makes visible the work of the artist *as* the work of the mother. The psychological spaces of the studio and the home, the identities of the artist and the mother, have collapsed.

In the fall of 1962 Neel moved into an eight-room apartment at 300 West 107th Street at Broadway.[32] She once again set up her easel in the living room, into which lots of light streamed through its north-facing bay window. With more space and more time in which to work, Neel changed her practice as well: she increased the size of her canvases, incorporated more of the figure, and distilled her new environment down to a few lines suggestive of a baseboard or doorframe. Moreover, with her children now grown, Neel herself was no longer caught so acutely in the "awful dichotomy" of being a mother and an artist. Instead, she captured its drama in others who came to sit for her. In the 1960s and 1970s in particular, Neel painted many portraits of women who were both mothers and professionals. Often, she depicted the mother in the act of caring for her child.[33] For example, in *Nancy and Olivia* of 1967 (p. 215), her daughter-in-law Nancy nervously clutches her first child to her chest. In *Nancy and the Twins* of 1971 (p. 218), Neel shows the weary mother, partially reclining on a maroon daybed. Nancy's white shirt is unbuttoned to reveal her left breast, proffered for the nourishment of her chubby, naked twin babies. That Neel chose to portray this young woman nursing her children within the space where she helped out as Neel's assistant and that she did so in the heyday of the women's liberation movement does not point to a reification of traditional motherhood. Rather, in these frank, unromanticized portrayals of the physical work of mothering, of the toll taken on both the mind and the body, Neel used her own artistic labor to reveal and counter the conflict of the working mother: her desire for "a self-realization that has nothing to do with her being a mother" and her selfless love for and commitment to her child, who needs her as she needs work beyond mothering.[34]

Art historian Linda Nochlin, who in the late 1960s and early 1970s was a professor at Vassar College, a doctoral student at the Institute of Fine Arts in New York, a wife, and a mother to two young daughters, described this conflict in herself: "If I had to correct papers, I felt guilty about not doing research for a seminar report in graduate school; if I worked on the seminar report, I felt haunted by neglected shopping; if I shopped, I felt I wasn't paying enough attention to my child."[35] After being introduced to the radical writing of *Redstockings*, *Everywoman*, and other journals of the burgeoning women's liberation movement, Nochlin would come to join a growing group of women (and some men) who challenged the status quo in the art world, advocating for greater representation and recognition of contemporary and historic female artists, publishing her groundbreaking essay, "Why Have There Been No Great Women Artists?" in *ArtNews* in January 1971.[36] Nochlin and others saw in Neel's paintings a depiction of the gendered struggles they were attempting to overcome and in Neel herself a fierce, unconventional role model.[37] Neel, in turn, saw in Nochlin and other professional women a manifestation of the very dichotomy she had experienced since her first daughter was born.

In her 1973 portrait of Nochlin and her four-year-old daughter, Daisy (p. 219), the two figures, in their colorful clothing, sit close together on Neel's green silk Empire sofa. Neel rendered in great detail the sofa's delicate floral brocade upholstery, the brass buttons, the clawed feet, and the curved, carved mahogany frame. As curator Ann Temkin has asserted, "Neel's house and her art went together,"[38] and in portraits like this one, the artist's treatment of furniture takes on a symbolic quality, revealing something of the psychological dynamics of the composition. She situated Nochlin and Daisy on a specific couch that held meaning for her.[39] Perhaps she sat them on the Empire sofa in a nod to Nochlin's professional expertise in nineteenth-century French art. Regardless of the reason, Neel's commitment to the intersubjectivity of portraiture was aided by the fact that she was painting portraits not in the homes of the sitters but in her own home, an environment over which she exerted control.

In *Linda Nochlin and Daisy*, the mother and daughter stare intently out at the viewer, Daisy with rapt attention and Nochlin with the studied, scrutinizing eye of an art historian watching an artist at work. Neel's presence as the artist is visible, too, not only in the gazes of the sitters, who look back at her, but also in her brushwork and in her particularly detailed rendering of her own sofa, which Nochlin grasps emphatically with her left hand. Daisy's hand echoes her mother's, a visual representation of generational time.[40] As Nochlin recalled, Neel was surprised by the anxiety she saw in her face, exclaiming, "'You know, you don't *seem* so anxious, but that's how you come out.'"[41] Although Neel entertained Daisy with stories to counter the boredom of sitting for hours, Nochlin struggled to contain her daughter's restless body by pressing her right hand firmly into the little girl's thigh. Art historian Tamar Garb has argued that in this image Nochlin becomes Neel's surrogate: "Nochlin's furrowed brow and tense, upright posture may register the strain of motherhood, but it is the mother/artist in front of her who mirrors her anxiety with her own."[42] The tension Neel captured in Nochlin's face, then, is that of the "awful dichotomy" of the mother struggling to balance her maternal and professional duties simultaneously. Though it was no longer an acute issue for Neel the grandmother, the artist nevertheless recognized in her sitter a troubled condition she remembered well.

Having absented her own body as the artist-mother from the canvas for nearly forty years, Neel completed her self-portrait in 1980 (p. 207), a remarkable portrayal of an artist-(grand) mother at work. Many photographs of Neel in the late 1970s and early 1980s show her sitting in her living room studio, reading the newspaper or painting, surrounded by her canvases and sometimes one or more of her grandchildren (fig. 53). In these images—and in much of the writing that accompanied them in newspapers and magazines—Neel is portrayed as a quirky

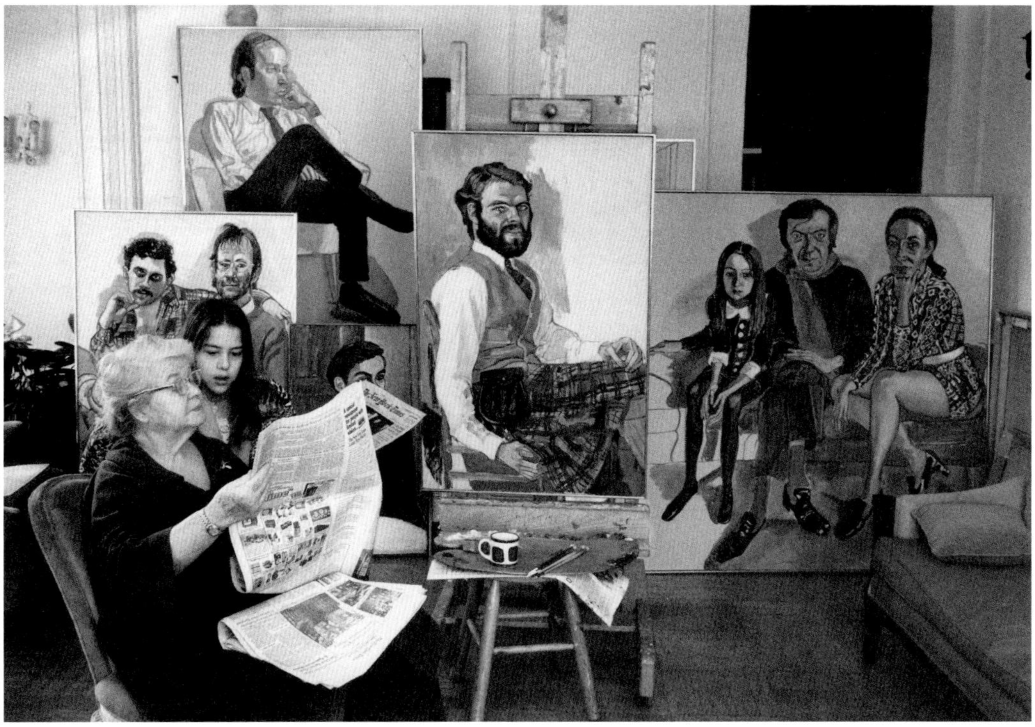

FIG. 53 **Alice Neel with granddaughter Olivia in her home/studio at 300 West 107th Street, January 5, 1979**

grandmother with white hair, a gentle face, sparkling green eyes, and an unexpectedly brash mouth.[43] While this version of Neel perpetuated in both the art press and the mainstream media was no doubt an aspect of the artist's personality (and one that she used to her advantage to garner the critical and popular attention she deserved), in her *Self-Portrait*, Neel depicts herself unflinchingly. Seated naked at the edge of her blue-and-white striped chair—the chair in which she most often asked other artists to sit and which must have been a particular favorite—Neel holds the tools of her trade: a brush in one hand and a rag in the other. Neel countered the overwhelmingly male tradition of the virile artist wielding his brushes like phallic tools with her unabashed portrayal of an elderly female form. Her eighty-year-old body, with sagging breasts and protruding belly, is the body of a woman who birthed four children, raised two sons, and worked at an easel for over six decades. The concentration of her stare, emphasized by the glasses that her aging eyes needed in order to see her reflection, is the serious and steady gaze of a great artist. Unlike in *Hartley on the Rocking Horse*, where the little boy at play is the focus of the painting and the reflected image of the artist-mother is small in the background, here Neel is the central—and sole—subject. By presenting her aged maternal body engaged in creative labor, in her home-cum-studio, Neel, in *Self-Portrait*, marked the culmination of a sixty-five-year career in which she learned to harness her domestic space to dramatize the experience of navigating the "awful dichotomy," that seemingly impossible dynamic between maternal and artistic work.

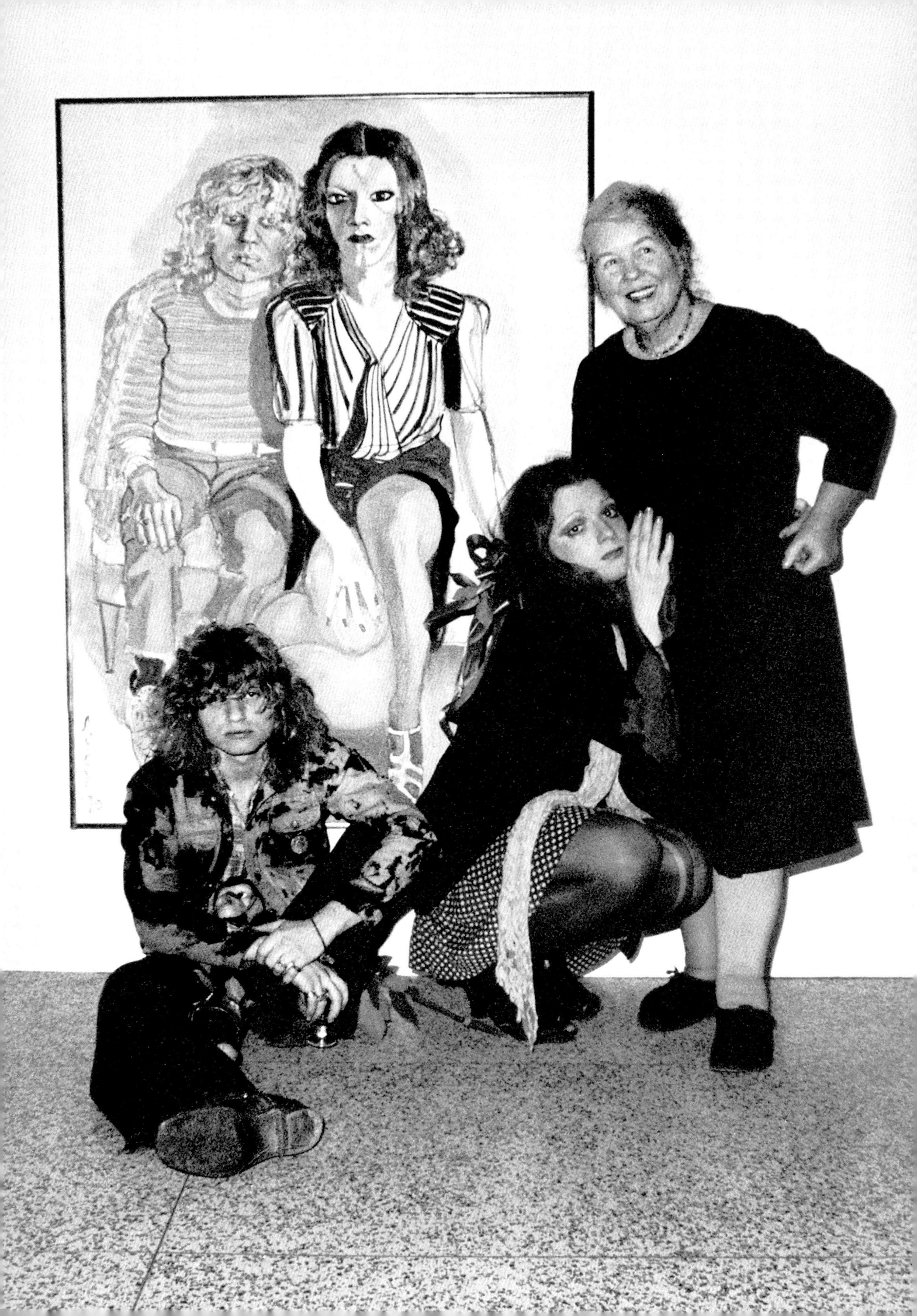

# PAINTING FRUIT(S)

## RANDALL GRIFFEY

*Should thoughts be said plain or wasn't it more fun*
*to play hide and seek–to hide them artfully in little corners?*[1]
–Alice Neel

In a 2012 interview, Fluxus artist Geoffrey Hendricks recalled sitting for Alice Neel with his partner, fellow artist Brian Buczak, at her Upper West Side apartment.[2] Like other firsthand accounts by Neel's former sitters, such as Mary Garrard and John Perreault, Hendricks's recollection provides interesting insight into Neel's process. The three met in the fall of 1977 at Rutgers University (where Hendricks taught), when the couple offered Neel a ride back into the city after she had delivered a slide lecture on campus. She returned the favor with an invitation up to her apartment for coffee. "She was a great story teller," Hendricks reminisced. "Just as in her portraits, she really gets in and extracts the essence of a person's personality." As it turned out, Neel was not yet finished with her guests when they said goodbye that evening. The next morning, they received a call from the artist's daughter-in-law Nancy indicating that Alice would like to paint them later that afternoon. And she wanted them to wear the same clothes as the day before.

The resulting double portrait (p. 177) is a disarmingly casual representation of same-sex affection–it is almost sweet, an adjective not often applied to Neel's portraits, especially of adults. The painting shows the couple seated at her kitchen table, a corner of which likewise appears in *Black Bottles* of 1977 (p. 159). Wearing a light-green pullover, the bespectacled Hendricks meets the viewer's gaze with a smile framed by late-day scruff. With his dreamy eyes and red-plaid shirt opened up to reveal abundant chest hair, Buczak imparts a sensual charge to the composition. Buczak wraps his arm around Hendricks's shoulders in a loving embrace that compresses their bodies, which are further bound and energized by a yellow-green halo, a signature trait of Neel's late style. A veritable orgy of phallic bananas overfills a bowl in the foreground, with one curving around an avocado in a manner that echoes Buczak's embrace of Hendricks. Neel moved this still life element into place midstream, Hendricks recalled, "with a little twinkle in her eye," discreet admission that it functions as a playful, slightly dirty visual pun that encodes her sitters' sexual identities as gay men and lovers.

"While she was painting," Hendricks explained, "her focus was totally on the painting. It was not a conversational situation at all–that came before and after." Communication between Neel,

FIG. 54 **Ritta Redd, Jackie Curtis, and Alice Neel at her exhibition opening at the Moore College of Art and Design, Philadelphia, January 1971. Alice Neel Archive, Stowe, Vt.**

Hendricks, and Buczak continued, in fact, well beyond their sitting in 1977.[3] Indeed, mementos of their friendship are found among Neel's personal effects in the Archives of American Art, including a heart-shaped valentine Buczak designed for Neel and both men signed. "Would you mind if Geoff and I come up and visit you sometime?" he queried Neel in an undated note, adding, as an affectionate enticement, "We'll bring some cookies with us."[4] Neel painted Buczak again (without Hendricks) in 1983 (fig. 55).

As two of several younger artists whom Neel charmed and who became part of her personal network, even if they had little in common with her aesthetically or generationally, Hendricks and Buczak belong to a notable roster of gay individuals whom Neel depicted over her career, with even more who remained—and remain—unidentified as such.[5] LGBTQ sitters populate some of Neel's most celebrated works, from *Andy Warhol* (p. 194) to *Kate Millett* (fig. 29) and *Jackie Curtis and Ritta Redd* (p. 178).[6] Generally speaking, Neel's queer subjects were predominantly white and male, characteristics symptomatic of the racial and gendered demographics of her sitters' respective professions within the literary, art, music, and fashion industries, arenas that provided them relatively greater visibility as queer people. Many of her sitters in the 1970s were also part of overlapping personal and professional circles in New York, some of whom were connected to Warhol.

While Neel painted prominent Communist and African American leaders in prior decades, very few of her LGBTQ sitters were associated publicly with the gay rights movement, which was active when she executed the vast majority of these pictures. That said, at least two of her subjects, Congresswoman and civil rights advocate Bella Abzug (1975) and New York City Mayor Ed Koch (1982), were responsible for key gay rights legislation, while others, such as Perreault, Garrard, and David Bourdon, were activists in the context of their professional work as curators and art historians, advocating for gay people, women, and people of color. Some of her queer sitters, such as Hendricks and Buczak, were romantic couples, but other pairs Neel painted were involved in nontraditional relationships that diverged from heteronormative, monogamous models, despite many assumptions to the contrary. In addition to sharing in common the experience of sitting for Neel, a number of these young men would become joined in history by succumbing tragically to the AIDS epidemic not long after Neel's own death in 1984. One of these was Buczak, who died on July 4, 1987.

Neel's portrayals of LGBTQ subjects flowed from her broad and steadfast humanism, her commitment to capture life's complex diversity. These sitters were not only marginal as sexual minorities, but, for the vast majority of her lifetime, they were criminalized, subject to discrimination in society in addition to state and federal punishment. As a broad category of humanity for whom hiding and deflection were often necessary, LGBTQ people offered the painter poignant opportunities to occasionally play "hide and seek" with ideas. To this end, Neel, a bit of a sexual nonconformist herself, frequently embedded signs of desire and identity through visual codes and puns in her depictions of queer sitters. In other instances, she explored more obvious and somewhat typical tropes of gender and androgyny.

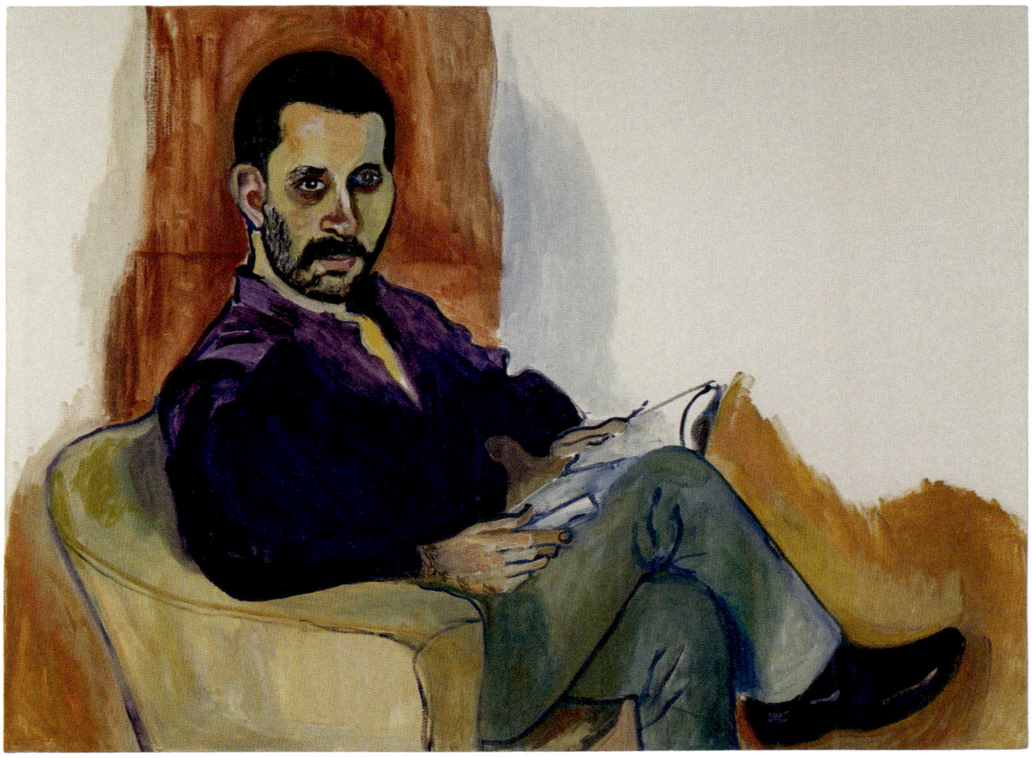

FIG. 55 *Brian Buczak*, 1983. Oil on canvas, 36 × 47 3/4 in. (91.4 × 121.3 cm). Estate of Alice Neel

"I'm very aware of the political scene," Neel admitted in 1974, "but . . . I hate obvious political paintings because they're stereotyped and they're boring."[7] The ambiguity of Neel's work is a source of its rich complexity and appeal, but it has also encouraged some misunderstanding and misinterpretation among viewers, and this pattern pertains especially to her depictions of LGBTQ people. Neel's paintings certainly acknowledge their lives and identities, but they should not be assumed to be necessarily affirmative from a sociopolitical perspective. Neel's accommodation of LGBTQ subjects in her life and art contained limits and inconsistencies, and while she spoke and even marched in support of African American and feminist causes, her engagement with LGBTQ culture and politics throughout the 1970s seems to have transpired more at arm's length. Like her position vis-à-vis feminism, the artist's personal attitudes regarding sexual and gender identity and expression were in many instances more complex than they are usually presumed to have been.[8]

As a witness to multiple social, political, and cultural revolutions that defined much of the twentieth century, Neel likewise beheld throughout her lifetime a dramatic evolution in the public construction of LGBTQ identity and vacillations in queer visibility. Her earliest exposure to out gay individuals likely transpired in Greenwich Village, which, throughout the 1920s and 1930s, served as a locus of the city's self-styled bohemians and sexual minorities, with some overlap between them.[9] The neighborhood was home to—as it still is today—several gay-friendly establishments, which included, as one well-known example, Stewart's Cafeteria (later Life Cafeteria) at 116 Seventh Avenue South. Having earned a reputation for scandal that attracted locals and tourists alike, Stewart's is likely the inspiration for a rare representation of queer culture in early cinema. A scene in the 1932 film *Call Her Savage* follows Clara Bow's character, Nasa Springer, on an eventful date "slumming" in the Village, where she and her beau enter a smoke-filled cafeteria at which the waitstaff has just completed a flamboyant show in partial drag (before other mayhem ensues). Stewart's is more obviously the setting of *Greenwich Village Cafeteria* of 1934 (fig. 56), a bawdy scene by Paul Cadmus, who painted it while employed (as Neel had been) by the Public Works of Art Project (PWAP).[10]

Whether Neel ever patronized Stewart's is unknown, but the likelihood seems high, as the cafeteria was a popular gathering spot for artists, and it stood only three and a half blocks north of her apartment on Cornelia Street. An even more likely customer would have been Christopher Lazare, whom one can easily imagine passing through its doors and taking a seat. Neel's 1932 watercolor of Lazare, an author and editor she met through her lover Kenneth Doolittle, is one of her earliest depictions of a known gay subject (p. 162). Perhaps to rankle any uptight listeners, the artist later divulged unjudgementally the fact that he liked "rough trade," an allusion to his apparent desire for men he would pay for sex, the availability of which increased in the 1930s due to growth in prostitution amid record economic hardship.[11]

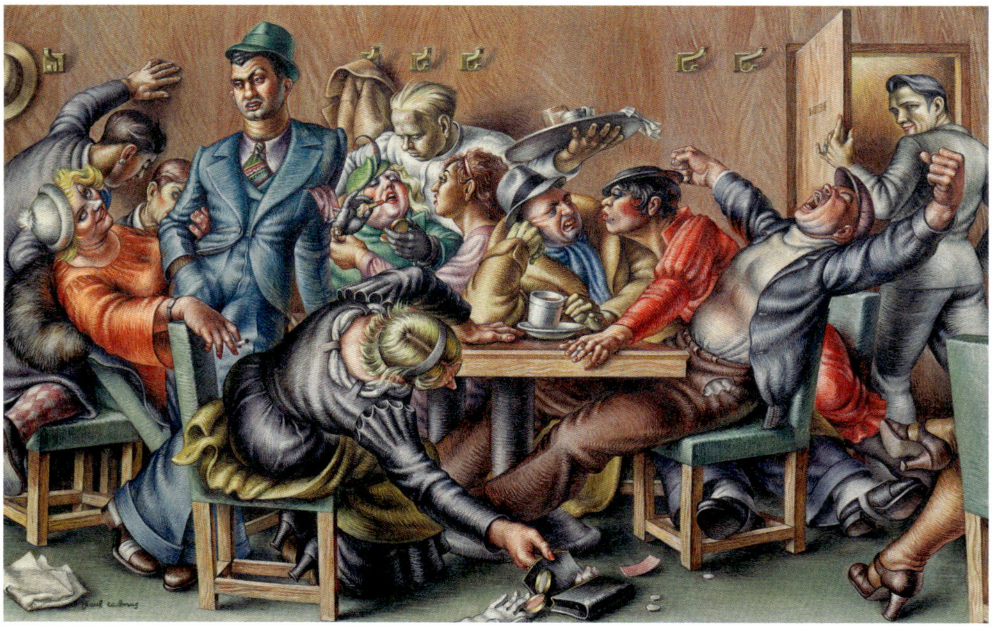

FIG. 56 Paul Cadmus (American, 1904–1999). *Greenwich Village Cafeteria*, 1934. Oil on canvas, 28 × 40 in. (71.1 × 101.6 cm). Museum of Modern Art, New York, Extended loan from the United States WPA Art Program. Fine Arts Collection, Public Buildings Service, General Services Administration

Like so many of Neel's "pictures of people," this portrayal of Lazare defies conventional notions of portraiture as presenting a singular, coherent, and flattering image of the sitter. Instead, she depicted Lazare, bespectacled and unsmiling, three times across the page, with a fourth portrait pasted on top as a collaged element in the lower right corner. Along the composition's left-hand side, Lazare stands facing the viewer, striking an elegant, self-possessed, hand-on-hip pose. He appears here as a modern dandy, an updated Oscar Wilde type as he might be seen in public, sporting a fashionable driving or flat cap, whose herringbone pattern Neel evoked with staccato black marks, and a Breton-striped shirt, a garment that the painter rendered with direct blue lines, which would become a signature motif later in her career. Elsewhere he seems to be in more private, vulnerable states. At the far right, the author wears a loose-fitting robe (or scarf) that reveals his rash-covered chest, an unknown ailment and early manifestation of Neel's empathetic interest in states of bodily distress, which would recur with Carlos Santiago Negrón's gruesome wound in *T.B. Harlem* of 1940 (p. 187) and Andy Warhol's scarred torso in his portrait of 1970. In the center, Lazare, turned at profile, folds in on himself while a phallus sprouts surreally out of his head, an unambiguous pun that invokes his gay identity and desire: he literally has sex on his mind.

Neel portrayed another queer literary bohemian in 1932, albeit more conventionally than she did Lazare. *Martin Jay* (fig. 57) shows the young, enigmatic publisher and Communist sitting against a deep red ground, hands folded, wearing a dark turtleneck, and staring plainly at the viewer with bright blue eyes. Jay, who was given the name Ronald Lane Latimer at birth and mysteriously employed multiple aliases and pseudonyms, championed the work of contemporary American poets, especially Wallace Stevens, whose canonical *Ideas of Order* he released in 1935.[12] Neel rendered Jay with flattened, somewhat abstracted forms enhanced by thick contours, signifiers of artistic naivete associated with early American "folk" art, which was very much in vogue among galleries and museums in the 1930s (fig. 58). While Neel omitted symbolic accoutrements from this portrait, she notably included the blemish on Jay's left cheek, an indicator that she understood imperfection to be intrinsic to the human condition.

With few exceptions, known queer subjects largely disappeared from Neel's work after the 1930s, resurfacing only after she moved to the Upper West Side in 1962.[13] The precise reasons for this gap are unclear, however. "I loved Greenwich Village. It was wonderful," Neel reminisced in 1975. "Although I finally left it because so many lesbians walked up and down the block. And I don't know, maybe I should have been more tolerant."[14] Characteristically provocative, this statement also suggests the degree to which her relocation to Spanish Harlem in 1938 reduced her proximity to and engagement with queer culture, but it also highlights the artist's regret about her former feelings toward her lesbian neighbors. A range of personal and cultural variables—from her increased domestic responsibilities to the suppression of personal visibility due to widespread public vilification and criminalization of gay men and women as perverts and predators throughout the Cold War—surely contributed to queer people fading effectively from her oeuvre for nearly three decades.[15] Instead, Neel devoted much of her portraiture during that time to Communist Party leaders and activists in the civil rights movement, most of whom presented as cis and straight.

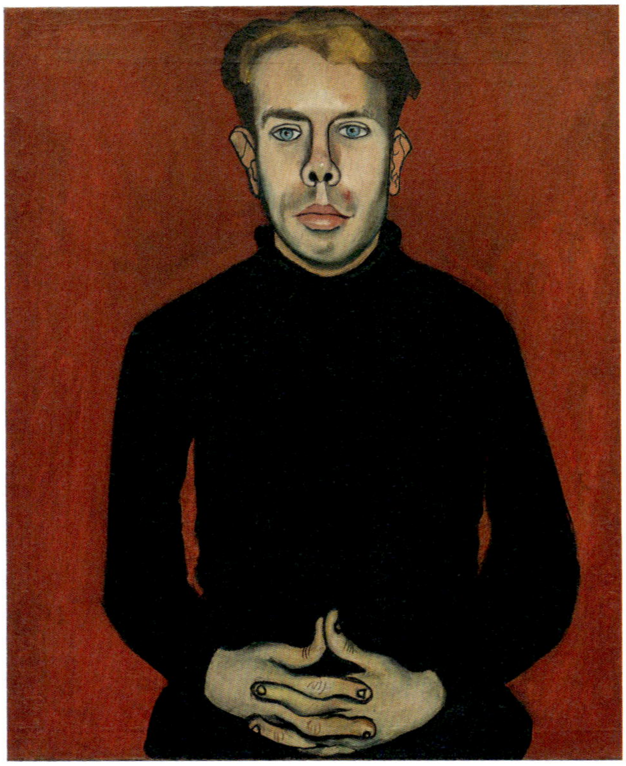

FIG. 57 *Martin Jay*, 1932. Oil on canvas, 25¼ × 20¼ in. (64.1 × 51.4 cm). Estate of Alice Neel

Neel's enduring concerns for gender equality and racial justice intersected with her alliance with Communism, but her acceptance of gay men like Lazare and Jay, whom she depicted unflinchingly and unapologetically, has roots within her own unique humanism. As Robert Shaffer has emphasized, "communists in the 1930s viewed homosexuality as a sexual aberration or vice brought on by the tension of life under capitalism."[16] Indeed, Communist activist and journalist Mike Gold, Neel's friend and champion, would launch homophobic critiques of the work of authors he rejected, such as multiple Pulitzer Prize–winner Thornton Wilder.[17] Allergic to bureaucracy and dogma, Neel was, by her own admission, "never a good Communist,"[18] and, by refusing to perceive LGBTQ people to be dangerous threats to society, she was, whether she realized it or not, disregarding party dogma, including the homophobia espoused by Gold and other Communist leaders.

Moreover, Neel belonged to a generation of American artists for whom the production and reception of modern art were often circumscribed by intersecting discourses about national identity, gender, and sexuality.[19] Gold was not alone in issuing feminizing and homophobic attacks on cultural productions he deemed undesirable, unnatural, or foreign. Prominent artists, like Thomas Hart Benton, wore their macho homophobia as a badge of honor as well. Art critics—especially those antagonistic to the more avant-garde aspects of European modernism washing up on

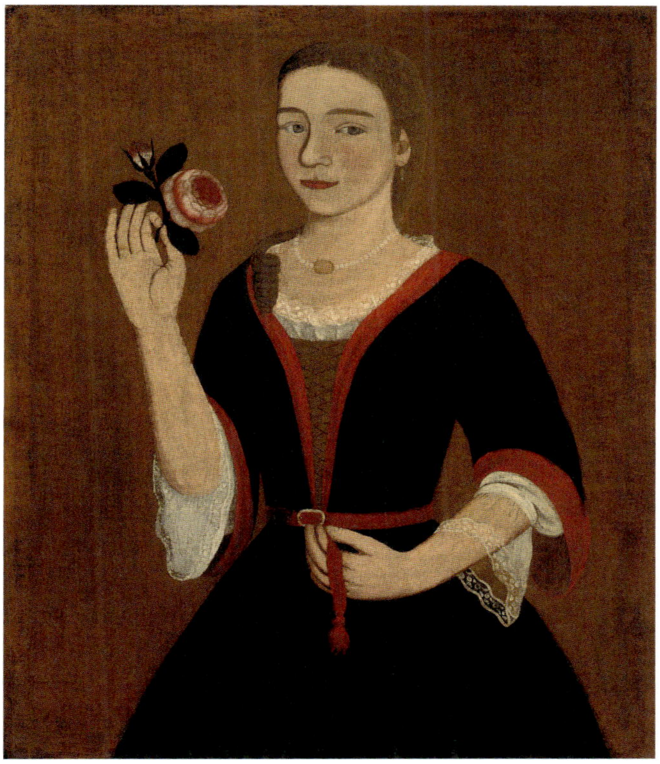

FIG. 58 The Gansevoort Limner (possibly Pieter Vanderlyn). *Miss Van Alen*, ca. 1735. Oil on canvas, 31 3/16 × 26 1/8 in. (79.2 × 66.4 cm). National Gallery of Art, Washington, D.C. Gift of Edgar William and Bernice Chrysler Garbisch (1956.13.14)

American shores—laced their writing with xenophobic and gendered criticism against male artists. Author Malcolm Cowley recalled the fear of being the victim of such assaults in his memoir *Exile's Return* (1934):

> I had nightmares in which I suffered from the malice directed against contemporary art. Was there a general conspiracy of slander? . . . I came to believe that a general offensive was about to be made against modern art, an offensive based on the theory that all modern writers, painters, and musicians were homosexual.[20]

In this regard, Lazare and Jay could seem to represent an archetype that haunted Cowley and many other male artists, a stereotyped conflation of bohemianism, intellectualism, and sexual deviancy that threatened to contaminate American culture, including art, and to undermine American society. However, Neel's relatively progressive views regarding sexuality stood in stark contrast to such prevalent and homophobic cultural elisions throughout this period.

The reemergence of visible LGBTQ subjects in Neel's work in the 1960s and 1970s was symptomatic of—and, to a degree contributed to—increased queer visibility resulting from the homophile and gay liberation movements. Advocacy and organizing to mitigate oppression, discrimination, and violence against gay people spiked first in San Francisco in the wake of widely publicized uprisings against authorities with the famed Compton's Cafeteria Riot in 1966, and, closer to home for Neel and other New Yorkers, with the transformational Stonewall Riots in 1969. Key milestones (and setbacks) punctuated the following decade, including the American Psychological Association's removal of homosexuality from its official list of disorders in 1973, and Harvey Milk's political ascendancy as the first openly gay elected official in US history in 1977 (and his assassination the next year). Miami-Dade County's passage of a nondiscrimination ordinance in January 1977 became a particular flashpoint over the battles for gay rights, especially after Anita Bryant's successful nationwide "Save Our Children" campaign that led to its revocation that June. In New York, Mayor Koch advocated for legislation barring discrimination of gay men and lesbians among city agencies, which passed in January 1978 and about which Neel, a voracious consumer of news, was keenly aware.[21]

In this context, Neel not only portrayed LGBTQ people, but she also promoted her images of them. She regaled audiences with anecdotes about Lazare, Warhol, Curtis, and others, thereby cleverly ensuring the cultural currency of and public interest in her art–"old-fashioned" easel paintings–to a new generation. She could speak for hours about her paintings (and often did), demonstrating an innate ability to connect to younger audiences with her work.

One of the mainstays of Neel's slide lectures was her tender portrait of Andy Warhol (p. 194).[22] Warhol, seminude, sits with his eyes closed and hands clasped in a seemingly meditative or prayer-like state. He submits to the viewer's inspection of his pale, unathletic body; the open space he occupies facilitates, even encourages this scrutiny. Neel's painting technique accentuates her subject's vulnerability; indeed, the slender lines register metaphorically as precarious lifelines threatening to trail off completely. An irregular block of light blue buttresses him on his left side, while an elongated passage of a desaturated variant of the same hue more lovingly caresses his right contour. Showing Warhol in a serene void, Neel's portrait, which commenced on the afternoon of August 12, 1970,[23] casts her subject in an existential guise, unmoored from his celebrity and the quotidian, consumerist character of his art.

The scars crisscrossing Warhol's torso like rivulets of stitched and healed flesh, compressed by the corset he wears for abdominal support, occupy much of the center of the composition. Famously, his disfigurement resulted from Valerie Solanas's assassination attempt on June 3, 1968, and the multiple surgeries necessary to save his life.[24] As Neel rendered them, his scars are both literal and metaphoric marks of his enduring trauma. "I'm so scarred I look like a Dior dress," Warhol confided to journalist John Leonard: "I'm afraid to take a shower. It's scary. I close my eyes. But it doesn't look so bad. The scars are really very beautiful; they look pretty in a funny way. It's just that they are a reminder that I'm still sick, and I don't know if I will ever be well again."[25] Warhol's comments are confessional, but they are also discreetly (and characteristically) self-promotional; his description of his scars stokes the reader's curiosity.

Warhol simultaneously cultivated and satiated such public interest in his scarred body not only in the press but also through photography. Factory member Brigid Berlin began taking Polaroids of Warhol's torso soon after his recovery and sold them (for five dollars each) to

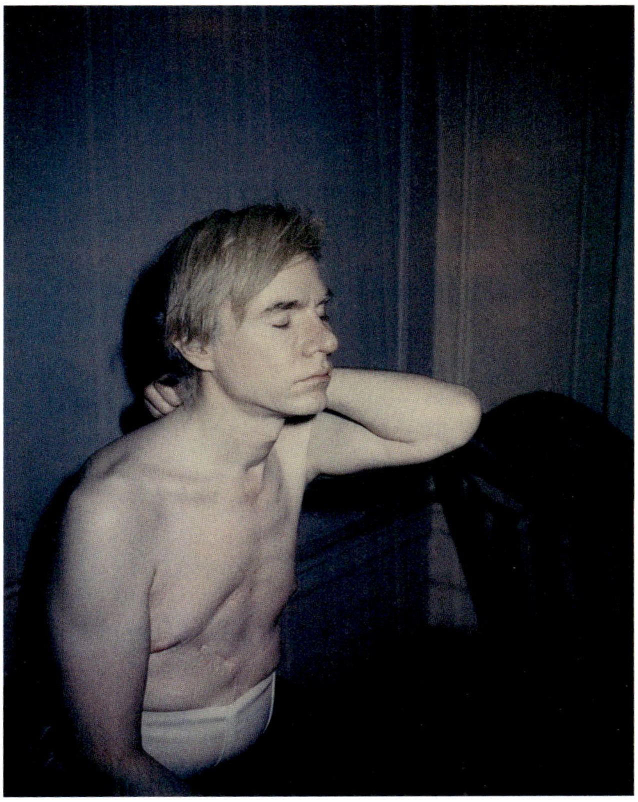

FIG. 59 Brigid Berlin (American, 1939–2020). *Andy Warhol*, 1970. Polaroid

random passersby on the street. In 1969 Richard Avedon produced studio portraits of Warhol that explore the artist's relationship with his transformed body. One of these shows Warhol facing the camera, his shirt rolled up to unveil his scars and his hands extended in a borderline-clichéd Christ-like pose. Such conspicuous tropes of martyrdom prompted critic David Bourdon later to characterize Warhol's wounds as "the stigmata of his celebrity."[26] In *Andy Warhol, Artist, New York City*, Avedon more jarringly focuses on his subject's torso, cropping his head in the process; Warhol's right hand provocatively slides down his lower abdomen and his left thumb peels back the hem of his corset to reveal just a bit more flesh. His scarred white skin registers here as a sewn hide, not unlike his black leather jacket that frames this more fetishistic portrayal of his body. Such imagery constructed his post-attack personal reality and public identity: As Daniel Morris has asserted regarding the Avedon portraits, "Warhol wanted to exist as an 'after' image in the realm of appearances alongside such celebrated survivors of cultural violence as Jackie O."[27]

Warhol's self-exposure in Berlin's and Avedon's photographs precipitated his sitting with Neel, which Berlin documented (fig. 59). His closed eyes in Neel's portrait and Berlin's Polaroids evoke not only a meditative state, but also his admitted reluctance to gaze upon his own altered body. Moreover, Warhol's sitting with Neel manifests his growing comfort with—even desire for—*others* to gaze upon it.

In stark contrast to Avedon, Neel desexualized her subject, presenting him as passive, victimized, and feminized. The painting manifests Neel's belief that Warhol's queerness lay in his apparent androgyny, a trait she frequently mentioned when discussing the portrait.[28] Rendered with extended highlights and shadows, his chest appears to consist of sagging breasts, flesh succumbing to gravity in a way that presages Neel's representation of her own aging physiognomy in *Self-Portrait* (p. 207) ten years later. Her treatment of her subject struck at least one critic as a bit cruel when the work made its debut at the Graham Gallery in 1970. As Gerrit Henry of *Art International* complained, the portrait "makes Andy Warhol out to be more of an androgyne than he really deserves."[29] Perhaps this is one reason, too, Warhol described the picture evocatively in his diary as "a closet painting," suggesting, among other inferences, his preference that it not be seen at all.[30]

Gender bending returns more explicitly in Neel's psychologically nuanced and often misunderstood double portrait of performer, playwright, and poet Jackie Curtis with friend and occasional collaborator Ritta Redd, painted in 1970 (p. 178). Curtis and Redd snuggle head-to-toe in Neel's portrait, the upright confines of which ensure their closeness. The pair stares somewhat unnervingly at the viewer; Curtis's eyes, highlighted with dark eyeliner and blue eye shadow, are particularly penetrating. While their faces radiate with intense specificity encroaching on realistic likenesses, the environment they occupy (including the bench on which they rest) fades into a schematic haze. A dirtier, desaturated variant of Curtis's blue eye shadow surrounds the two in an irregular halo, further binding them together. Neel's direct, attenuated linear application of paint accentuates Curtis's reptilian features and elongated limbs; indeed, Curtis's garish elegance is disturbed only by the tear in the sheer black pantyhose, through which a toe has humorously broken through. "See that toe?" Neel later queried an interviewer. "That's a male toe."[31] Sporting a mop of blonde hair and wearing a long-sleeve shirt and blue jeans, Redd appears as a boyish "masculine" foil to Curtis's parodic, performative (if ultimately unconvincing) femininity. Almost conjoined, Curtis and Redd register as an inseparable duo of hip nonconformity.

Given the name John Holder, Jr. at birth, Curtis was a prominent figure in Manhattan's Lower East Side counterculture and had catapulted to underground notoriety in the late 1960s and early 1970s, entering the orbit of Warhol, who introduced the performer to Neel. By the time of Curtis and Redd's sitting with Neel, the performer was an acknowledged Warhol "superstar," having starred with Joe Dallesandro and Candy Darling in the now-iconic *Flesh* (1968). Curtis would also later perform, with Penny Arcade, in *Women in Revolt* (1971), an irreverent send-up of "Women's Lib" and a film that Neel, who harbored some mixed feelings about contemporary feminism, would recommend heartily to audiences.[32] In 1969, a lengthy profile in the *New York Times* described the performer as "probably the East Village's first indigenous playwright."[33] "[I'm] not a boy, not a girl, not a faggot, not a drag queen, not a transsexual–just me, Jackie," Curtis declared, disavowing all limiting categories of gender and sexuality and, with them, the mainstreaming of gay identity Curtis associated with the gay liberation movement.[34] In contrast to Curtis, Redd–whose given, non-stage name was Richard Zollo[35]–is known today almost solely by virtue of his appearance in Neel's painting. As a performer, he was often cast in supporting roles, participating, for example, in Curtis's Off-Off Broadway musical *Vain Victory, the Vicissitudes of the Damned* (1971). Redd even penned a gossipy profile of Curtis in the 1970s, in which he

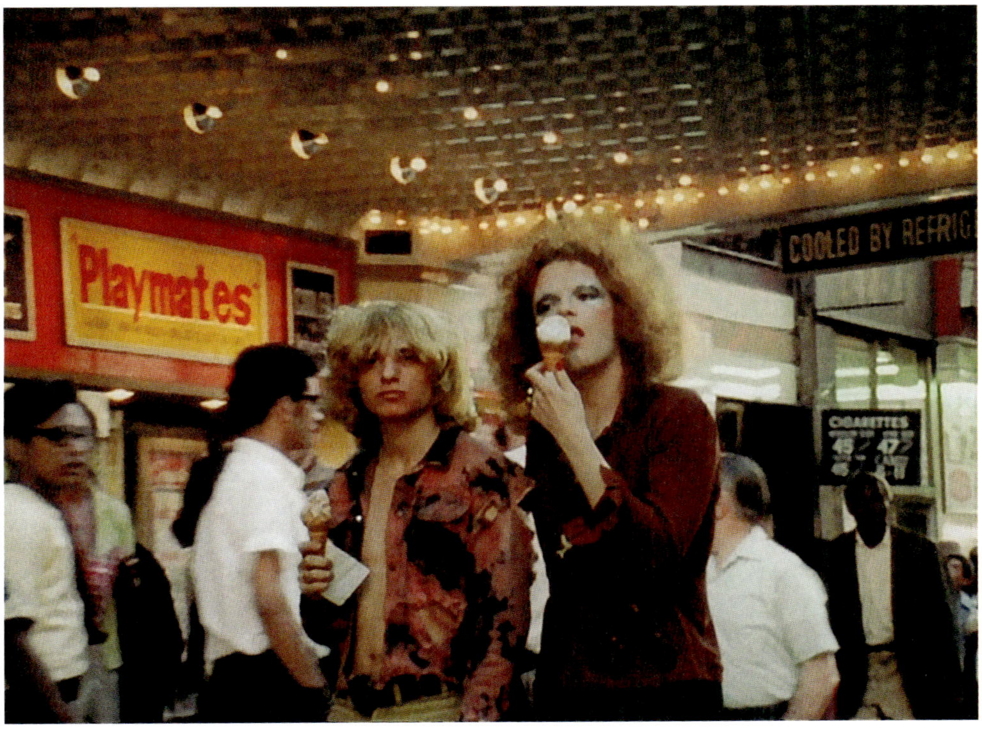


FIG. 60 Dušan Makavejev (Serbian, 1932–2019).
*WR: Mysteries of the Organism*, 1970. Film still, approx. 27:15

reminisced about a party they attended at which Redd divulged "fooling around" with playwright Edward Albee, author of *Who's Afraid of Virginia Woolf?*[36]

Neel's double portrait commemorates Curtis and Redd's friendship, particularly their close connection around 1970, but it also reinscribes Redd's role as a handmaid to Curtis and testifies to Curtis's irrepressible personality, increasing fame, and lust for the spotlight. Curtis leans toward the viewer, moving around and in front of Redd, who consequently falls quite literally in Curtis's shadow. Curtis's right foot pushes Redd's left leg off to the side, as if attempting to shove him out of the composition altogether, even as Redd visually supports Curtis like a buttress.[37]

Nevertheless, their physical intimacy here has fueled misunderstanding regarding their off-stage (and off-canvas) relationship, which, according to Penny Arcade, never resembled anything like a committed romance.[38] For their sitting with Neel, Curtis and Redd ostensibly reprised their roles in *WR: Mysteries of the Organism*, a documentary and fictional recreation of the writings of sexologist Wilhelm Reich by avant-garde Serbian director and screenwriter Dušan Makavejev.[39] Curtis and Redd, who shot their scenes for Makavejev's project in July (approximately two months before sitting for Neel in September),[40] play a couple composed of a transsexual (Curtis, who appears in multiple scenes) and an anonymous boyfriend (a nonspeaking Redd, who appears in only two). In a parody of heteronormative, monogamous coupledom, they stroll through Times Square enjoying ice cream (fig. 60), while a male voice-over advertising artificial eyelashes and

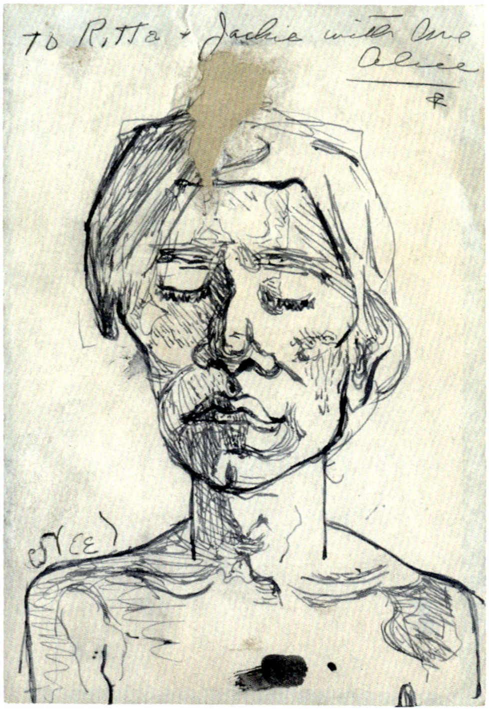


FIG. 61 *Andy Warhol*, ca. 1970. Pen on paper, 6 × 4 in. (15.2 × 10.2 cm). Collection of Craig Highberger

suntan lotion asserts American commercial standards of feminine beauty, which the conspicuously made-up Curtis ironically seems to exemplify.[41] Curtis later returns alone and shares the character's first experience of erotic love, a confession that continues as voice-over to footage showing Curtis and Redd kissing in the back of a station wagon. As Curtis reflects on the eventual demise of this relationship, complicated by the character's reported sex change, this scene with Redd, as the unnamed, mute ex-boyfriend, registers as a wistful flashback.

While Neel, like many others, frequently misidentified Curtis as a transvestite, she clearly admired Curtis's obstinate nonconformity. The story of her meeting Curtis and Redd at the then gender-segregated Harvard Club became one of her favorites to share with audiences.[42] Additionally, in an interview with Patricia Hills, Neel recalled the scene Curtis made at her exhibition opening at Moore College of Art and Design in 1971: "Wasn't he frightful!" the painter exclaimed with delight. "He tried to make dates with all the teachers. And then went in the Women's Room with me. . . . I mean it was really quite a performance."[43]

A photograph from the Moore College opening demonstrates Neel and Curtis's mutual admiration and inadvertently reproduces Curtis and Redd's asymmetrical relationship (fig. 54). Posed in front of the double portrait, Redd and Curtis playfully recreate the composition, though Curtis turns away from Redd and toward Neel. With Curtis cowering worshipfully at her feet, Neel assumes the role of a maternal figure, offering a gentle embrace as she smiles for the camera. Perhaps surreptitiously but nonetheless remarkably, their arrangement roughly mimics

Redd's and Curtis's own comportment in the painting, with Curtis momentarily playing the supporting role of Redd to the star Neel. Meanwhile, Redd's glum expression may convey some awareness of his nominal consequence.

As a likely gesture of gratitude for their attendance at her exhibition opening, Neel gave Redd and Curtis an intriguing drawing related to her portrait of Warhol (fig. 61).[44] As a memento, this sketch not only commemorates their friendship, it also materializes the means by which they met one another and would be bound together for posterity through art. Focused on Warhol's face, the composition notably omits the sitter's scarred torso, though the worn and tattered paper surreptitiously evokes his fragility. Despite the painter's warm inscription to both of them across the top of the sketch ("To Ritta + Jackie with love / Alice"), the work descended down as part of Curtis's personal effects, a sign of seniority. Another meaningful triangulation between them occurred in 1984, when Curtis phoned Warhol to convey the news of Neel's death.[45]

In 1970 Neel also painted David Bourdon and Gregory Battcock (p. 176), two friends, art world colleagues, and likely occasional sexual partners. Unlike other couples and pairs Neel depicted, Bourdon and Battcock do not even touch; they are connected only by horizontal lines Neel added in the background to suggest wainscoting. In effect, the work is a study of stark and quite humorous contrasts. Sporting a suit and tie, Bourdon, who would later publish a key study of Warhol, sits upright and alert with hair neatly coiffed, as if ready for an office meeting relating to his duties at *Life* magazine, where he worked as an assistant editor.[46] Wearing only underwear and socks and staring blankly into space, an unshaven Battcock, his hair tousled, looks like he

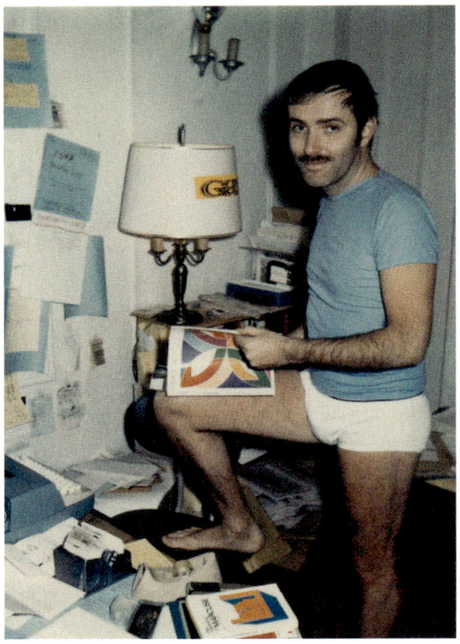

FIG. 62 Gregory Battcock, 1970. David Bourdon papers, Museum of Modern Art Archives, New York

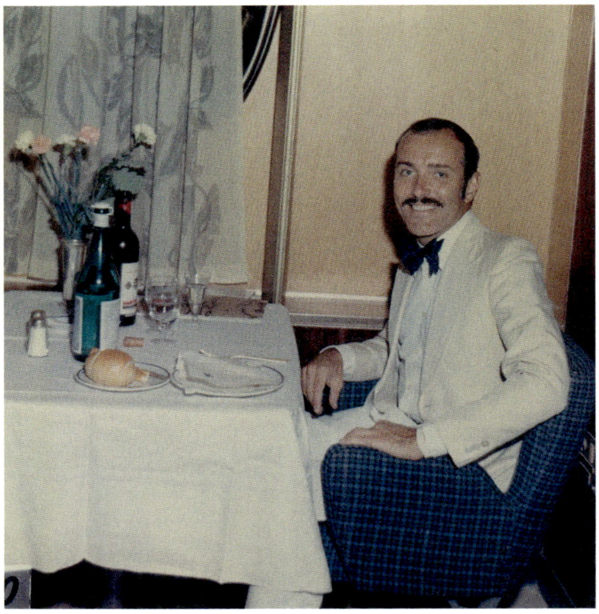

FIG. 63 Gregory Battcock aboard the cruise ship *The Michelangelo*, 1970s. Gregory Battcock papers, 1952–circa 1980. Archives of American Art, Smithsonian Institution, Washington, D.C.

has just woken up or is preparing to turn in after a long night out. In a conversation with film-maker Michel Auder, Neel recalled that Bourdon recommended that she paint Battcock in this outfit,[47] a suggestion perhaps inspired by Battcock's preference for lounging and working at home in his French underwear (fig. 62).[48] Viewers of the painting who knew Battcock as a debonair, intellectual bon vivant (fig. 63) would have been particularly amused by his depiction here.

While Neel's double portrait ostensibly gives both men equal billing, the wonderfully indecorous Battcock, a sex-positive proponent of non-monogamy, steals the show.[49] Battcock had eclectic intellectual interests, both mainstream and underground; he wrote on contemporary art and cinema and contributed to the underground newspaper *Gay* and the *New York Review of Sex*.[50] In fact, his liminal state of partial undress can be interpreted as signifying the in-betweenness of his practice, his blurring of boundaries between personal and professional, "high" and "low," and, especially, the cerebral and carnal. This reading hinges in part on David Joselit's exploration of another, slightly earlier image of Battcock, seminude and spread-legged, that appears on a cover designed by Warhol for *Arts Magazine* (fig. 64). Warhol's design was, in addition to three related photo-collages the magazine also reproduced, the culmination of *Time Piece*, a commissioned collaborative project with Battcock and Bourdon, who traveled to Paris at Warhol's expense and documented their trip (Bourdon took the original Polaroid of Battcock). According to the magazine, *Time Piece* "reflects the banality of the 'family album,' while commenting ironically on space as a factor in art."[51] For Joselit, however, Battcock's eroticized countenance discreetly manifests the critic's expansive, quite subversive approach to his life and work:

> [Battcock's] anthologies were intended to make difficult art practices accessible and intelligible to a general public, and his columns in the underground press not only addressed audiences beyond the art world but also developed a writerly voice that dispensed with standard forms of morality, just as the "new art" moved beyond normative models of objecthood. His *Arts* cover blithely collapsed the boundary between these related but distinct practices, making *Arts* into *Gay* just as Battcock's columns sought to make *Gay* into *Arts*.[52]

Reprising his unpolished appearance on the cover of *Arts*, Neel's painting similarly evokes the cross-fertilization of his unconventional practice, which stands (or, in this instance, sits) in distinct contrast to Bourdon's more traditional example, one that could also more easily "pass" as straight.

"Passing" also seems to play a role in Neel's *Jackie Curtis as a Boy* (p. 179), her second portrait of the star. Far from the cross-dressing trash-glam queen Neel painted two years earlier, Curtis here averts the viewer's gaze and wears no makeup, just jeans, a blue-and-red undershirt, and a loose white sports jersey. Unassuming, if a bit remote, and clothed in patriotic colors, Curtis appears conspicuously "All-American," a decidedly ironic projection given Curtis's unapologetically subversive predisposition and lifestyle. As a foil to *Jackie Curtis and Ritta Redd*, the boyish portrait of 1972 reveals the other side of the performer's expansive play with gender, as, depending on mood and the day, Curtis would don men's drag rather than women's, assuming male personae that were similarly rooted in desire.[53] The addition of "as a boy" to the title

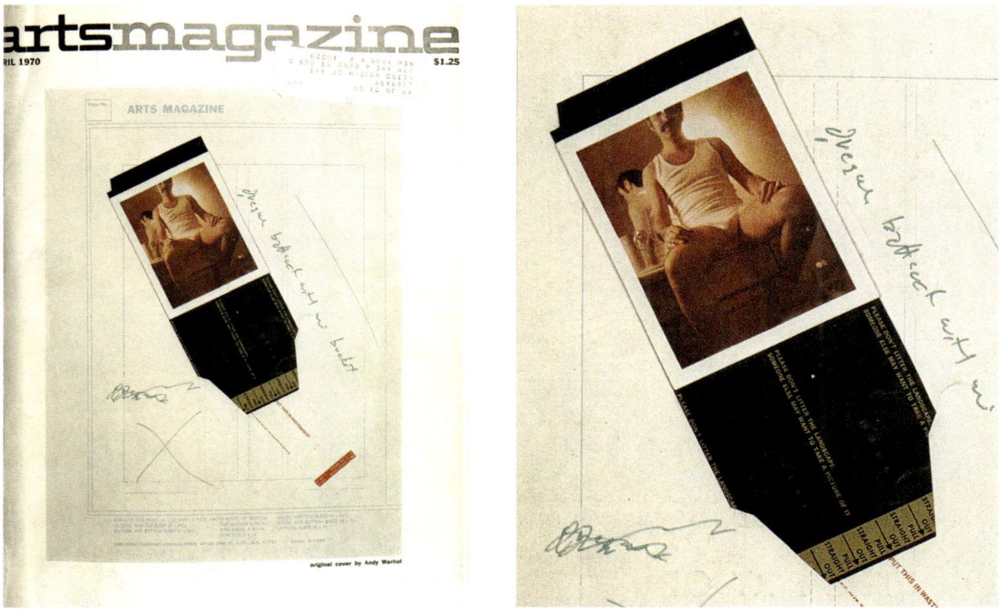


FIG. 64 Cover design by Andy Warhol for *Arts Magazine*, April 1970 (left); detail of cover (right)

underscores this ongoing performance of gender. Moreover, the relative wholesomeness of *Jackie Curtis as a Boy* is deceptive. According to gallerist John Cheim, Neel described the space outlined by the band of piping surrounding the neck of the jersey and running down the torso as an elongated phallus.[54] Likewise, she interpreted the manner in which Curtis's left hand grasps the post of the armrest in sexual terms. More discreet than the phallus emerging from Lazare's head, these details nonetheless speak to Neel's occasional tendency to embed in her composition sexual innuendo to allude to her subject's queer desire and identity.

For her 1972 nude portrait of John Perreault (p. 202), Neel dispensed with all manner of embedded code or innuendo. Perreault had initially approached Neel to lend her notorious 1933 painting of Joe Gould (p. 197) to his forthcoming exhibition on the male nude, but Neel was loath to be represented only by an early canvas in a show that included recent works by such artists as Sylvia Sleigh and Philip Pearlstein. Neel proposed that she also execute a new painting featuring the fledgling curator himself, an offer he could not refuse. "When she painted me, she was Alice Neel, the icon," he recalled in 2000. "She was 72 and looked like a Norman Rockwell grandmother, but with a wicked twinkle in her eye and a fiery tongue. How could I have denied a request by my grandmother? Pose nude? Sure."[55]

As a counterpoint to the idealized male nude prevalent in the history of Western art, *John Perreault* is humorously unceremonious but also disconcertedly frank. Perreault's gangly, hairy limbs splay across Neel's final composition and his thin frame runs diagonally from corner to corner. Like Warhol, Perreault is vulnerable; he submits his body to the viewer's gaze. But Perreault also stares back; his piercing blue eyes underscore his complicity in this episode of invasive anatomical spectatorship. Shown in a strikingly relaxed pose, one that the curator claimed to have originated, Perreault lets his knees fall widely apart, an egregious demonstration of manspreading that culminates in the full display of his genitals near the center of the canvas. Neel painted this area like a delicate still life, albeit one consisting of a lumbering penis, plump testicles, and a nest of pubic hair, all framed by a summer tan line. The cool environment he occupies, consisting simply of a white wall and sheet with light-blue shadows, enhances the warmth and sensuous potential of his body, even as Neel's active brushwork imparts a taut, somewhat nervous energy throughout the composition.[56]

By the time Neel painted Perreault, the subject of the male odalisque had become, like the male nude more generally, a familiar trope of contemporary feminist painting, pursued by, among others, Sylvia Sleigh, Martha Edelheit, and Marion Pinto.[57] While Sleigh later argued that Neel was following her lead,[58] the feminist engagement with the male body in the 1970s likely struck Neel as somewhat unexceptional because she herself had created male nudes and several intimate drawings of her male companions as early as the 1930s. In the context of Perreault's show, the presence of *Joe Gould* along with the curator's recent portrait would have made Neel's long-standing claim on the subject clear to visitors and participants alike, as she surely desired.

While Neel's objectives in depicting Perreault in this way were not necessarily erotic in intent, their sessions together, culminating with the painting's public debut in February 1973, unfolded amid a gradual proliferation of images of male flesh that extended well beyond venues for high art. Indeed, the emphatically horizontal dimensions of Neel's portrait, combined with her hairy subject's bodily arrangement, call to mind the period's most famous male odalisque: actor Burt Reynolds's centerfold for *Cosmopolitan* magazine's April 1972 issue (fig. 65). Widely hailed as a triumphant feminist appropriation and reversal of the commercial (female) centerfold, the

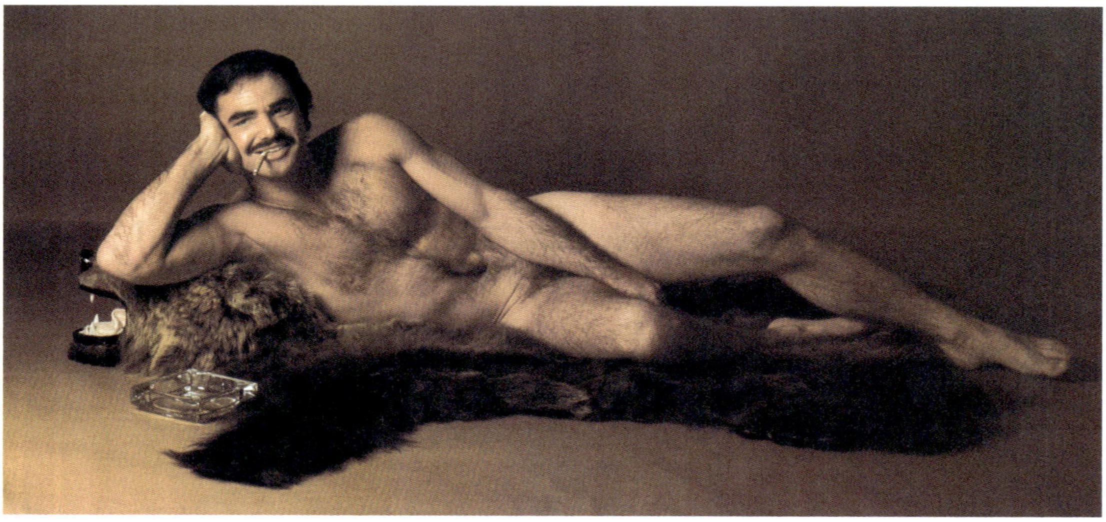

FIG. 65 Burt Reynolds in *Cosmopolitan*, April 1972

photograph shows Reynolds smoking a cigarillo while lying on a bear rug. This spread, the brainchild of editor Helen Gurley Brown, catapulted the actor to a new level of fame and revealed a robust, hitherto neglected market for images of male nudity for heterosexual women.[59] In the months that followed, it spawned numerous imitations and precipitated the publication the following January of an early iteration of *Playgirl*, which soon thereafter made history by selling upward of two million copies.

Given the renown of Reynolds's centerfold and the widespread discussions about it, particularly in the context of contemporary feminism, Neel likely knew of its existence (despite the fact that she did not regularly read popular magazines), as the record shows that Perreault himself did.[60] Moreover, many visitors to *The Male Nude* would have viewed *John Perreault* through the lens of contemporary soft-core pornographic images underpinned by feminist-driven consumerism. Of course, Neel was not constrained by the same degree of public decorum that compelled the publishers of *Cosmo* and *Playgirl* to conceal their male models' sexual anatomy early on. This, too, would change quickly, however, as demand for uncensored male nudity proved strong enough to shift industry standards to become more graphic. In this respect, the prominent still life of genitalia in Neel's portrait of Perreault, a kind of indiscreet centerfold in paint, was a sign of more things to come.

For feminist critic Cindy Nemser, *John Perreault* embodied Neel's political support of LGBTQ people and their civil rights. "Artists such as Alice Neel, Lowell Nesbitt, and John Button," Nemser asserted in 1975, "have struck a blow for gay and women's liberation by presenting us with a straightforward depiction of the male nude."[61] Naming Neel in the context of Nesbitt and Button, gay artists whose work also featured in *The Male Nude*, Nemser assumed similar artistic intent between them, thus framing *John Perreault* as a statement of Neel's political beliefs.[62] However, Perreault himself admitted later that he was unsure whether or not Neel even knew he was gay.[63] The subject of his sexuality never came up during their sessions, he said, adding, "We talked about her lovers, not mine." Like other paintings she produced, this nude portrait functions less as a reliable index of Neel's affirmative feelings for LGBTQ people than it serves as a screen onto which Nemser and others have projected their own assumptions and desires.

Throughout her career, Neel did make statements that cut against the enduring image of the artist as an unmitigated champion of the marginalized and oppressed. "Women and homosexuals have one thing in common," Neel asserted somewhat arbitrarily to journalist Jerry Tallmer in November 1978. "They're lightweight."[64] When contending critically with Neel's life and work, it is exceedingly difficult to reconcile a comment like this with her art, which seems to testify on behalf of women and LGBTQ people. "I say these frivolous reactionary things every so often," Neel explained in this instance, a suggestion that her impulse to provoke occasionally won out over her adherence to what we might call today political correctness.[65]

As curator Helen Molesworth has recently discussed, Neel's sensitivities regarding sexual and gender identity and expression were more pronounced when it came to lesbians, who figure less prominently in her oeuvre than gay men.[66] *Nadya and Nona* (fig. 66), an early painting of two of

Neel's bohemian friends, conveys same-sex female sensuality, but this strange, sapphic moonlit scene casts these "two little tarts," as Neel playfully described them, in a distinctly ominous rather than a sensuous glow.[67] Although one might expect Neel to feel unreserved sisterhood with other accomplished, convention-bucking women regardless of their sexual orientation, differences in identity and desire could occasionally prove to be gulfs too wide to bridge. Thus, the artist articulated several distinctly anti-lesbian sentiments, ranging from her attributing her move to Spanish Harlem in 1938 to the prevalence of lesbians in Greenwich Village to her perception of the pervasive faddishness of lesbianism in the women's liberation movement. "I'm almost ashamed of not being lesbian," Neel asserted in a tongue-in-cheek manner to her audience at the New School for Social Research in 1978, adding, "but I don't think my sons would like it."[68]

Exactly how and to what degree Neel's negative attitudes regarding lesbians register in her imagery is difficult to determine, but a subtle index of her relative distance from gay women is the fact that she depicted Kate Millett (fig. 29), Adrienne Rich (p. 174), and Mary Garrard (fig. 67) on paid commission and not entirely on her own volition, as was her usual practice.[69] Moreover, accounts of her sittings with Rich and Garrard reflect tension, with the artist confronting both women about their sexuality. "I drove Adrienne Rich crazy," Neel recalled, before going on to

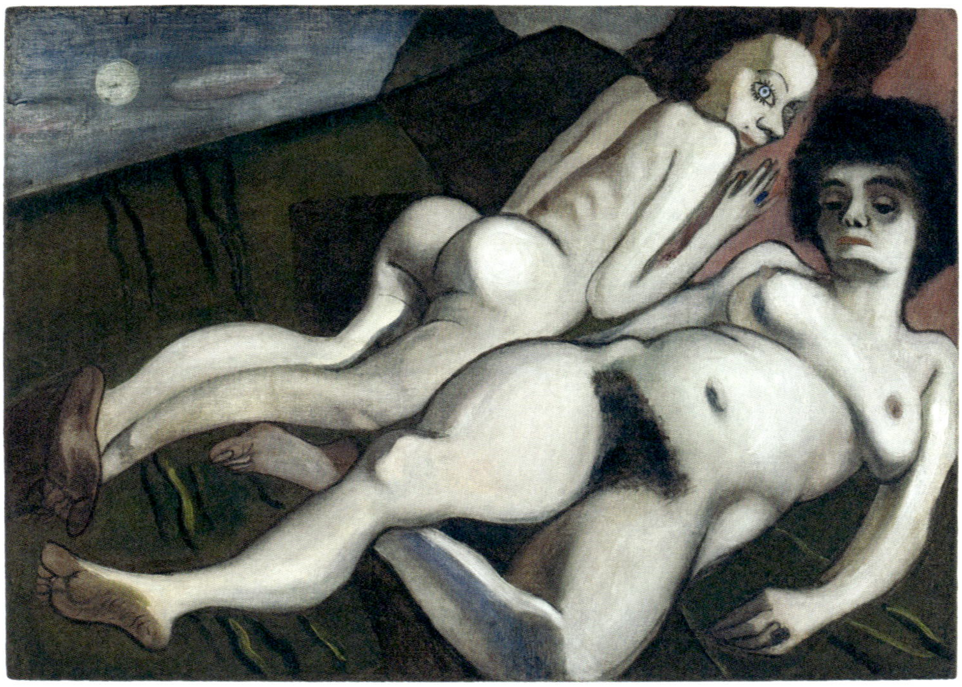

FIG. 66 *Nadya and Nona*, 1933. Oil on canvas, 26 × 35 1/2 in. (66 × 90.2 cm). Private collection

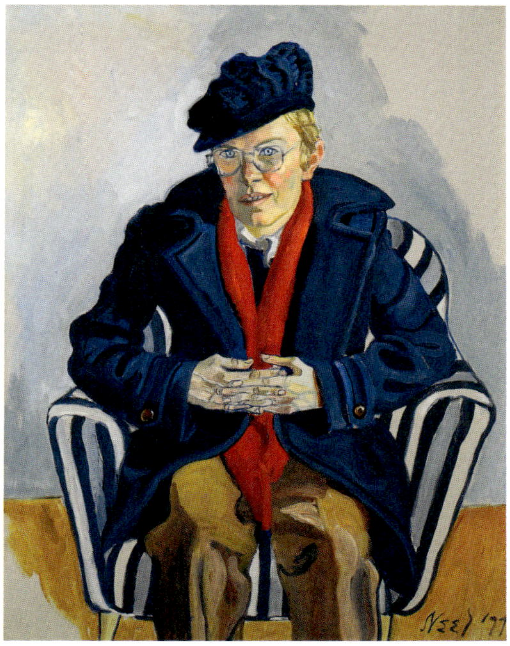

FIG. 67 *Mary Garrard,* 1977. Oil on canvas, 38 3/4 × 29 1/2 in. (98.5 × 75 cm). Collection of Mary Garrard

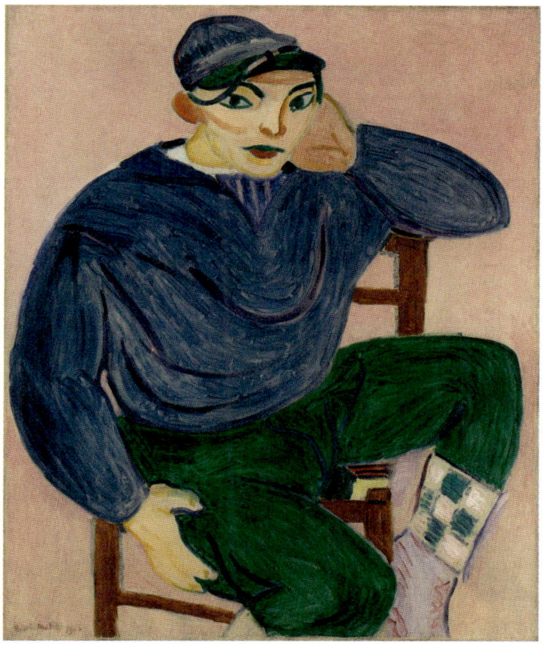

FIG. 68 Henri Matisse (French, 1869–1954). *Young Sailor II,* 1906. Oil on canvas, 40 × 32 3/4 in. (101.6 × 83.2 cm). The Metropolitan Museum of Art, New York, Jacques and Natasha Gelman Collection, 1998 (1999.366.41)

invoke a derogatory term for gay women. "I said, 'I never did want to be a muff diver,' . . . and I could feel her freeze in front of me."[70] Garrard endured a similar experience: "Early in the first sitting, Alice asked me if I were a lesbian . . . and it made me quite uneasy."[71]

Perhaps some of Garrard's expressed uneasiness in response to Neel's bold inquiry comes through in her closed body language and defensively clasped hands in her portrait.[72] Buried in her overcoat, scarf, and hat, the art historian looks much like she did when she came in from outside. As Garrard recalled of her sitting, the painter suggested this wardrobe scenario. The resulting androgyny becomes all the more pronounced when compared to Neel's drawing of Garrard for the same sitting (p. 174), in which the scholar appears more at ease in a fashionable and form-fitting sweater and slacks.[73] Thus, the final painting, which departs so markedly from the drawing, seems to locate Garrard's lesbianism in ambiguity with regard to gender, an inverse of the artist's painterly feminization of Warhol. As Garrard herself has explained, the quasi-masculine quality of Neel's portrait recalls aspects of Henri Matisse's *Young Sailor II* of 1906 (fig. 68): "My navy blue pea coat and cap would have summoned up Matisse's famous painting for the art-history-savvy Neel, and—style aside—the analogy is striking. She probably considered it relevant on several levels, cross-gendered allusions being the foremost."[74]

However complicated and sometimes contradictory her attitudes about them could be on occasion, LGBTQ people offered Neel irresistible opportunities as potential sitters, another marginalized segment of society to which she was drawn. In addition and in hindsight,

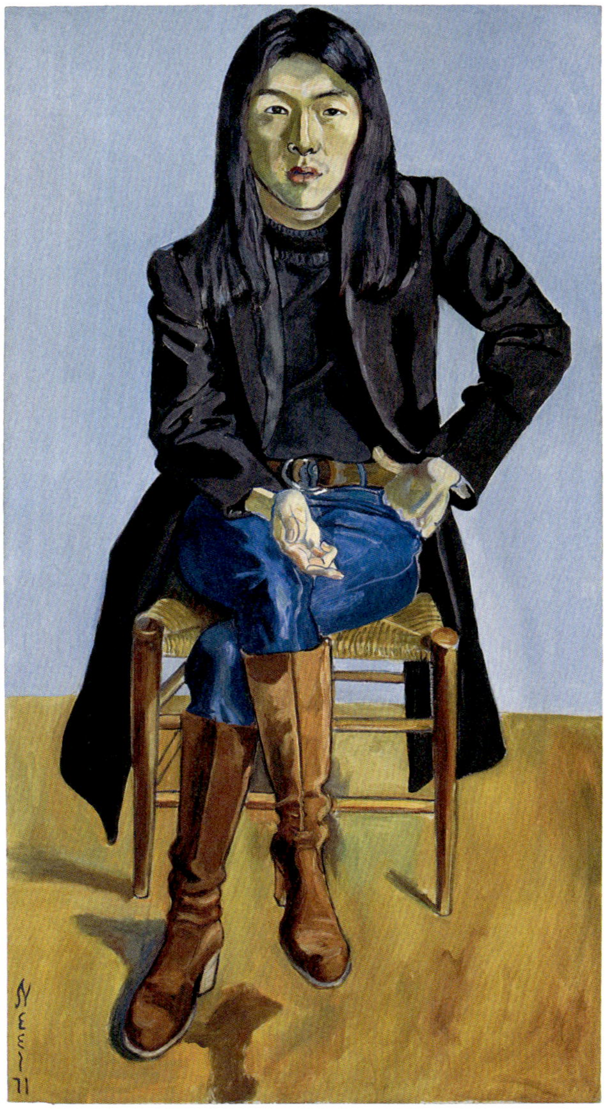

FIG. 69 *Ron Kajiwara*, 1971. Oil on canvas, 67 7/8 × 35 1/8 in. (172.4 × 89.2 cm). Estate of Alice Neel

her artistic disposition to play "hide and seek" with ideas seems well suited to portraying sexual minorities who, despite increased visibility and political agency over the course of the century, understood personally what it meant to have to hide, to deflect, and, thereby, to rely often on codes to embody identity and desire. Even so, the range of LGBTQ subjects Neel painted—from the seemingly lonely and afflicted Lazare to the openly loving, well-adjusted Hendricks and Buczak—could be seen to trace the relative increasing acceptance and decreasing stigmatization and decriminalization of queer individuals throughout her lifetime.

Neel liked to think that by painting portraits she was, in fact, painting history, and she did so in more ways than one. While she died without realizing as much, her portraits of the 1970s recorded a generation of young gay men just before it would be devastated by disease. In addition to Brian Buczak, AIDS would claim several of Neel's sitters, including Dennis Florio, Roger Jacoby, Ron Kajiwara (fig. 69), Robbie Tillotson (p. 181), and Ritta Redd. The parents of

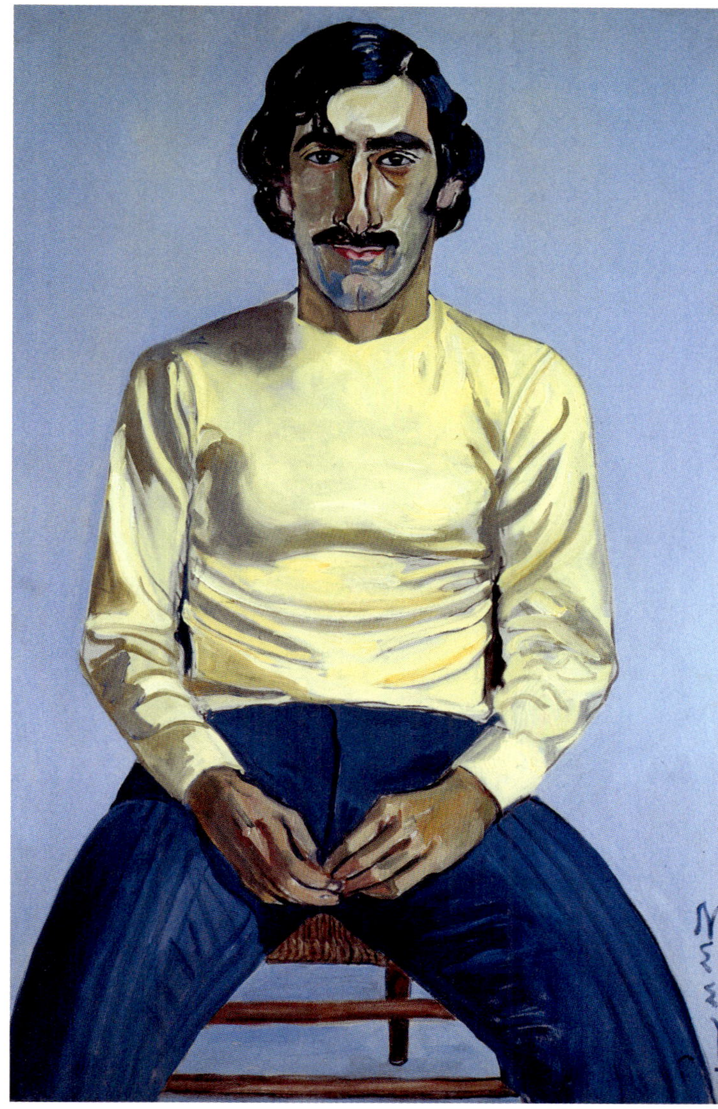

FIG. 70 *Robert Avedis Hagopian*, 1971. Oil on canvas, 46 × 29 3/4 in. (116.8 × 75.6 cm). Fine Arts Museums of San Francisco, Gift of Richard H. and Beatrice Hagopian in memory of their son, Robert (1993.17)

pianist Robert Avedis Hagopian (fig. 70) gave the portrait Neel painted of their son, who also succumbed to AIDS, to the Fine Arts Museums of San Francisco in his memory. Given Neel's innate understanding of life's inexplicable cruelties, one can easily imagine, had she lived a bit longer, her facile and fearless brush taking the disease head-on, capturing the gaunt faces and withering bodies, the frightful but colorful Kaposi sarcoma lesions, and the overwhelming misery and impending loss.

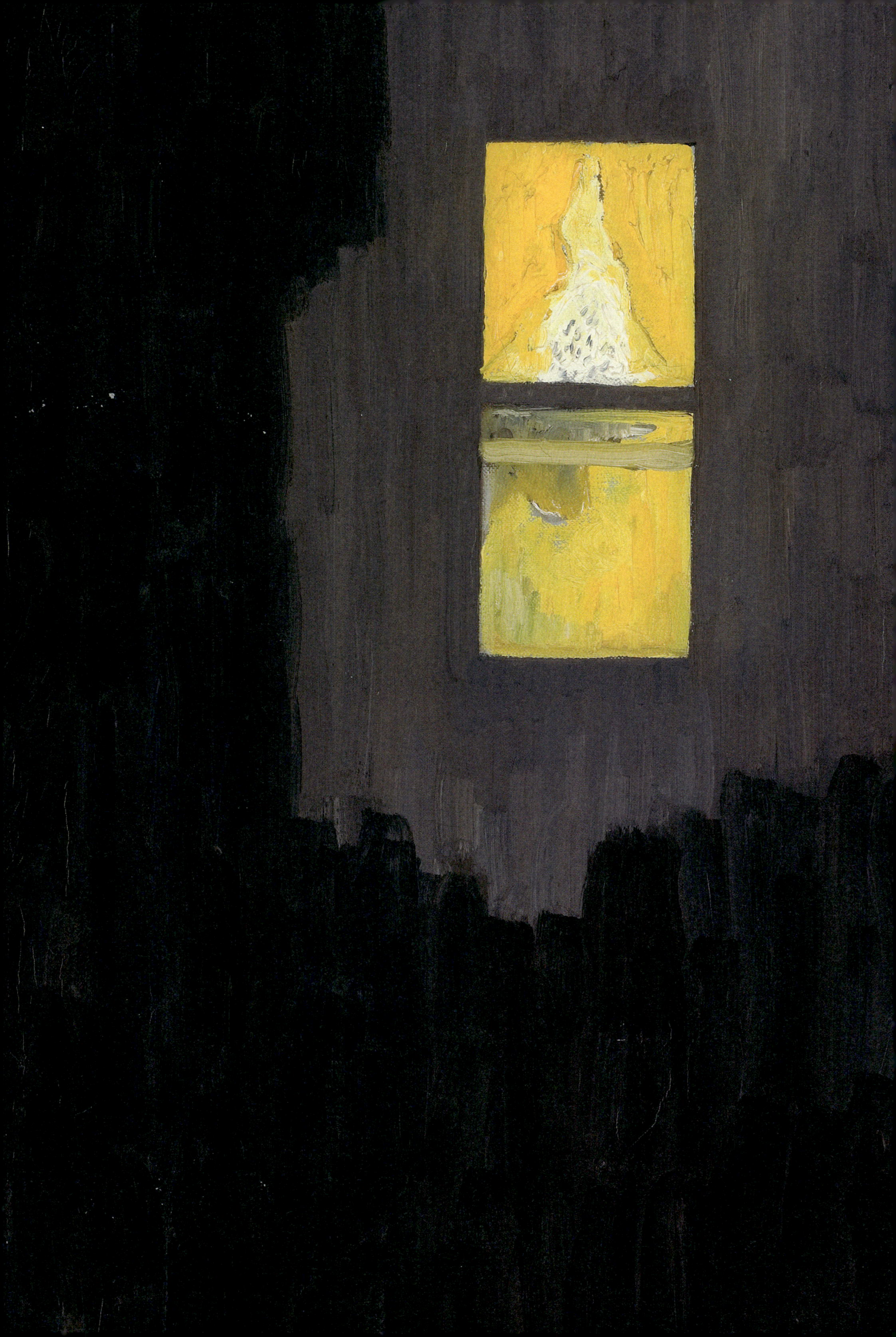

# ALICE NEEL'S "GOOD ABSTRACT QUALITIES"

**JULIA BRYAN-WILSON**

Few painters in the history of twentieth-century American art are as firmly associated with their commitments to expressive figuration as Alice Neel. She is rightly famous for her carefully considered portraits, and as this book demonstrates, her ideology of art-making was grounded in a belief that the human form was a primary conduit of social meaning. By the 1940s and 1950s, her seemingly tight tether to the realm of representation defied some of the most influential American modern art criticism of the day, criticism molded by the context of the Cold War that heralded abstraction as the only advanced artistic practice and decried realisms—of any type, including the Social Realism of the 1930s in the United States or Stalinist Socialist Realism in the USSR—as old-fashioned and regressive, or, worse, reactionary.[1]

Yet to position her work in terms of a clear rejection of early and midcentury modernist nonobjective art is too simple, as she moved nimbly on her canvases between abstracting and legibly depicting. Neel was both a painter of recognizable nouns—people, places, things—as well as an artist of prodigious imagination who reveled in technical experimentation, deploying verbs such as schematizing, simplifying, flattening, distorting, and estranging. She made familiar objects and faces unfamiliar, using her own brand of abstraction to swim decidedly against the prevailing tides of masculinist formalism to enact her own hybrid vision of painting. Accounting for Neel's capacious embrace of elements of abstraction throughout her figurative work helps undo the false binary of "abstract versus representational" that has hindered traditional art historical accounts and has contributed to the relegation of women and artists of color—whose work might not so neatly fit into categories falsely assumed to be discrete—to the margins.

In this essay, I build on Mira Schor's formative article "Some Notes on Women and Abstraction and a Curious Case History: Alice Neel as a Great Abstract Painter" to highlight Neel's feminist innovations around form that obviate hard distinctions between figurative and nonfigurative.[2] As Schor convincingly puts forward, often what is most interesting about a Neel portrait such as *Two Girls, Spanish Harlem* of 1959 (p. 135) is "what is in surplus to that representational content: the completely abstract painterly strokes of pink and gray that swirl around the two girls."[3] While Schor focuses on the backgrounds of Neel's painted portraits, I expand on her premise to examine a handful of works that more resolutely bleed into abstraction—those that appear to engage directly with its terms and result in images that hover at the edges of visual comprehension or narrative coherence. In doing so, I argue that the artist's unique aesthetic language positions her as central to a lineage of minoritized women and artists of color in the twentieth century who seized on *abstracting* as a critical and political process.

Detail of *Night*, 1959 (p. 225)

## "GOOD ABSTRACT QUALITIES"

"I don't think there is any great painting that doesn't have good abstract qualities," Neel plainly stated toward the end of her life.[4] This acknowledgment flies directly in the face of previous statements in which she minced no words regarding her disdain for abstract art, including this 1950 scorcher, written during the peak of Abstract Expressionism's institutional ascendancy: "I am against abstract and non-objective art because such art shows a hatred of human beings. It is an attempt to eliminate people from art, and as such is bound to fail."[5] Yet in a tape-recorded interview conducted by realist artist Werner Groshans in the 1970s, Neel laid out a nuanced understanding of the history of twentieth-century painting in which her previous scorn has shifted, perhaps softened by the passage of time. Such remarks may also serve as a reminder of the abstracting elements she herself had integrated in her work since the late 1920s.

To the surprise of her interviewer, Neel expresses admiration for the strict neoplastic geometries of Dutch artist Piet Mondrian. "I used to realize that Mondrian would make . . . great book covers. But then I saw a retrospective of Mondrian, and the paintings are better than their reproductions," she comments.[6] When Groshans pushes back on her respect for Mondrian and objects to his elimination of subject matter from his compositions, Neel dismisses the idea that Mondrian's grids are free from reference, contending that there is social meaning latent in or haunting his abstractions. Surely one could approach Neel's art using a parallel tactic, asserting the importance of abstracting procedures throughout her figurative work.

Tracing an arc of affinity between the seemingly decorative "book covers" of Mondrian and her own process of painting in which she rigorously composed her canvases using a gridded system to define its different arenas, Neel explains in the interview, "One of my greatest joys is dividing up a canvas before I paint." Comparing Mondrian's *Broadway Boogie Woogie* of 1942–43 (fig. 71) with Neel's *Night* of 1959 (p. 225) reveals how her ostensibly narrative scenes—here, a lit window beckons in the darkness—are replete with structural choices that emphasize formal qualities. Any sense of the solidity of the architecture of the building dissolves into loose, shadowy gray and black brushwork. The window itself has two panes, one on top of the other, and this elongated rectangular orientation echoes that of the canvas itself. This is a composition for the sake of composition, a conversation written in paint about paint. With its luminous yellow shapes positioned just to the right of the center of the canvas, *Night* revels in the contrast between the defined lines of the window and the murky space within; lace curtains (maybe) and a human head (maybe) are suggested with expertly placed white squiggles and an evocative half circle, but they never resolve into pictorial clarity.

Neel grasps how the optically vibrating works of Mondrian, such as his *Broadway Boogie Woogie*, not only are richly textured when seen in person but also carry with them vestiges of content beyond their surfaces that speak to the dynamic welter of urban life—in this case, the pulsations of New York streets and the enlivening rhythms of boogie-woogie, which is, significantly, an African American musical and dance style related to swing and the blues. Indeed, poet and scholar Fred Moten theorizes that late Mondrian, with its explicit invocation of Black jazz and

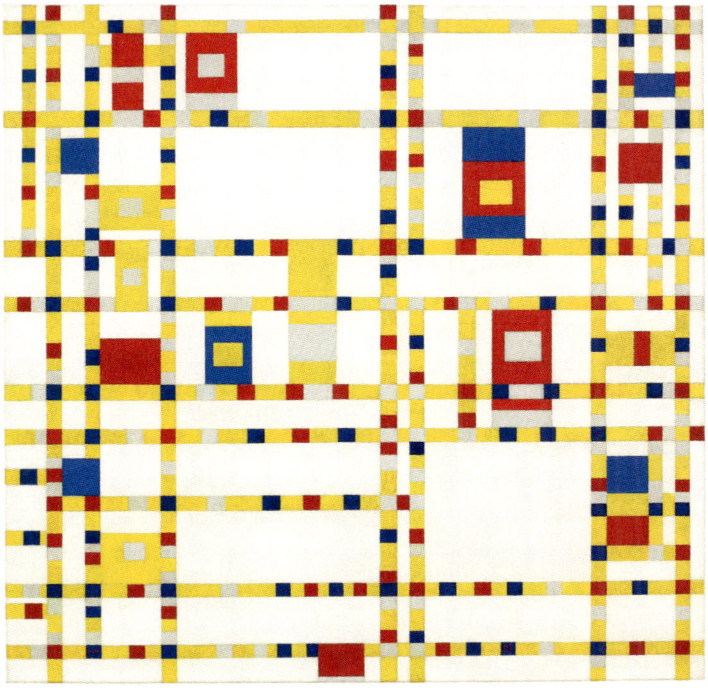

FIG. 71 Piet Mondrian (Dutch, 1872–1944). *Broadway Boogie Woogie*, 1942–43. Oil on canvas, 50 × 50 in. (127 × 127 cm). Museum of Modern Art, New York, Given anonymously (73.1943)

social life, delivers "a scene of forms as well as a thing within the black community of things."[7] Additionally, placing Mondrian's painting next to Neel's cityscape reveals how both were inspired by the energetic, multiple, and intersecting white/dominant and non-white/minoritarian cultures of New York, which they experienced in different ways—Mondrian, a newly arrived white European male immigrant escaping the chaos of World War II; Neel, a white woman fleeing US bourgeois conventions who called Spanish Harlem home at the time. Neel's work, like Mondrian's, was consistently animated by her proximity to racialized Blackness and Brownness, not least her intimacies with family members, neighbors, friends, and acquaintances of color whose visages she paid profound homage to with her specific, detailed portraits.

In *Night*, Neel plays with the spatial ambiguities of the building's facade; the rectangles simultaneously float up against the foreground and appear punched out of the darkness, receding into its inky field. This compositional play with space appears in Neel's earlier cityscapes as well, including *Harlem River at Sedgwick Avenue* of 1928 (p. 117), in which she amasses an array of forms to conjure a sense of place; as with many of her images, the paint and brushwork bear the visible traces of her laborious and tactile work. Such evident handiwork and a physical engagement with her materials further fuels a political reading of Neel's abstraction as she insists upon revealing her artistic efforts. Here, crowded elements jostle for the viewer's attention, demonstrating the artist's persistent deployment of methods of abstracting as she highlights her use of bold line and thickly applied impasto. The canvas refuses to settle on a singular focal point; dark swaths of painting at the top and bottom of the canvas suggest somewhat dematerialized registers of earth and sky while a stubbornly solid cloud of steam from a faintly decipherable boat stands out against the rest of the work's relative flatness with looming dimensionality.

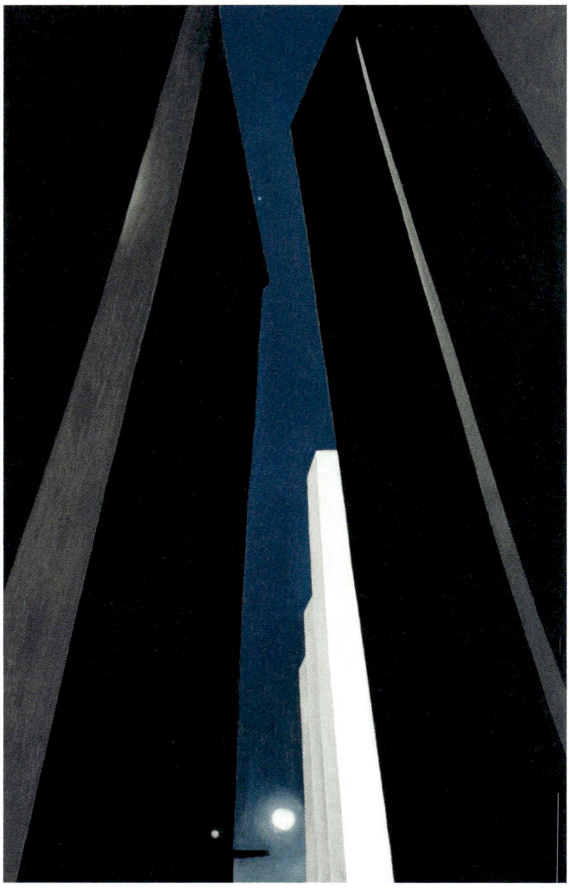

FIG. 72 Georgia O'Keeffe (American, 1887–1986). *City Night*, 1926. Oil on canvas, 48 × 30 in. (121.92 × 76.2 cm). Minneapolis Institute of Art, Gift of funds from the Regis Corporation, Mr. and Mrs. W. John Driscoll, the Beim Foundation, the Larsen Fund, and by public subscription (80.28)

In a related vein, Georgia O'Keeffe—another woman artist whose prescient work mingled references to the known world and a painterly vocabulary of abstracting—turned to the city in the 1920s. In her *City Night* of 1926 (fig. 72), part of a series of more than twenty canvases depicting New York skyscrapers, O'Keeffe pares down and streamlines a cluster of towering blocks, rendering them into a series of trapezoids in contrasting tones of black, silvery gray, and crisp white. In later years, O'Keeffe became pigeonholed for her sensual flowers and her organic renditions of the so-called feminine natural world, but these earlier stark, graphic compositions demonstrate her keen interest in urbanization, modernization, and the metropolis in the grip of rapid development.[8] The emphasis on mechanization and the built environment within many of Neel's landscapes, including *Central Park* of 1959 (p. 134), which portrays a human-made environment designed to look natural, lays bare the entanglement between humans and modern technology, an entanglement that she embraced as she envisioned her practice as one inextricably connected to the economics and politics of the time. An avowed Marxist, she refused ideologies of artistic purity or the supposed autonomy of art, and instead understood her work as complexly imbricated in the changing social, economic, and cultural circumstances of the moment, writing,

"I believe in art as history. The swirl of the era is what you're in and what you paint."[9] And though precisely *how* such a swirling era might be best captured not only through subject matter but also via form was a matter of considerable debate among left-leaning artistic circles, Neel bravely forged her own path.

A focus on elements that exceed a work's apparent content or move beyond its ready readability leads to a reconsideration of the overly policed boundaries between abstraction and representation. During their lifetimes, neither Neel nor O'Keeffe was granted enough credit for their major contributions to modernist vocabularies that mingled representation with the procedures of abstracting that, following Schor, are "in surplus to" the stated subject matter. Sexist criticism of women artists often ignores their manifold achievements, confining them instead within limiting stylistic boxes. In the case of Neel, what was most inventive about her schematic handling was castigated as artistic sloppiness and feminine incompetence. Critic Hilton Kramer (no friend of women's rights), for instance, disparaged what he perceived as her many technical "ineptitudes" and belittled Neel's lack of "the subtleties or strengths of the pictorial medium."[10] He refers to the conception and execution of her paintings as "neurotic"—a term historically associated with irrational, anxious, and high-achieving women—making clear that such scorn, and wider lack of credit, is undeniably gendered.

## HER OWN WORLD

In her interview with Groshans, Neel eschews any doctrinaire or formulaic approach to assessing her art that would seek to contain her creativity, demanding to be recognized for the experimental aspects of her work; as a woman painter stained by her reputation as a "mere" portraitist such acknowledgment was often denied her. "Why can't you let the artist have his own world?," she exclaims (note the male pronoun). "That would be freedom, you know." As discussed, Neel's work suffered in the hands of masculinist high modernist critics (while some, like Kramer, derided her, most ignored her) during decades in which the lines between abstract and representational art were understood as not only hard and fast but also deeply partisan. Indeed, as this quote makes clear, she strove to be accepted for her painterly achievements with pigment and skillful, pioneering handling of materials rather than as a plodding depicter of what she called "frightful shut-in dopey realistic paintings."[11]

Thus, while Neel was refusing the ostensible autonomies of pure abstraction, she was rejecting the strict protocols of realism as well, instead looking for her own hybridization of these two supposedly opposing styles. Over the course of her long career, Neel produced an oeuvre that is more varied than is often acknowledged; she utilized diverse materials, and many of her most experimental images were drawings, watercolors, and pastels, mediums that were quicker to manipulate and cheaper to acquire relative to slow-drying and expensive oil on canvas. Watercolors such as *Bathing in a Furnished Room* of 1927 (p. 142) (which also includes pastel elements) and *Carlos* of 1927 (fig. 73) show the risks she took with vibrant coloration, texture,

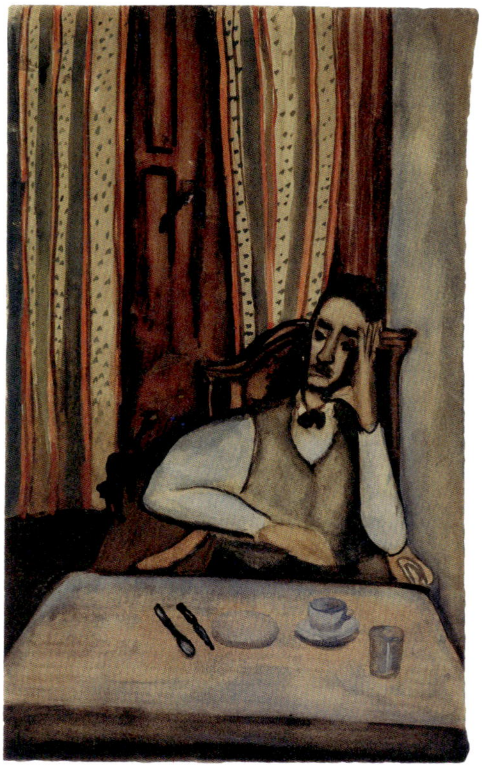

FIG. 73 *Carlos*, 1927. Watercolor on paper, 12 × 7 in. (30.5 × 17.8 cm). Estate of Alice Neel

and eye-catching pattern. The tender pastel *José Asleep* of 1938 (p. 151) demonstrates her dramatic use of negative space; Neel leaves some areas of the paper barely worked as a stand-in for white bedsheets, highlighting the contrast between that blankness and the vivid green-and-red striped pillowcase.

In fact, as these examples illustrate, some of the most interesting "surplus" or abstracted passages of Neel's art are found in her lively depictions of textiles, including curtains, bedclothes, garments, rugs, and upholstery. Though connections between the abstract picture plane and textiles were disavowed in high modernist writing, feminist artists and art historians have long celebrated their similarities (woven canvas, after all, is often the support for a painting).[12] Neel's attentive and detailed handling of the many kinds of domestic textiles that surround us resonate with feminist lineages of the so-called women's work of weaving and quilting. Using small brush-strokes to assemble a form and piecing small bits of fabric together to sew a blanket are similar procedures of patchwork and aggregation. Neel's rendering of the pillowcase that becomes like another character in *José Asleep* and the dotted curtains featured in *Carlos* also resonate with the techniques used by groundbreaking African American abstract painter Alma Thomas, whose dazzling surfaces in works such as *Red Roses Sonata* of 1972 (fig. 74) are composed of short blocks of saturated colors and whose patterned bands have the quality of a textile even if they do not literally refer to textiles. Thomas turned to abstracting not only for its capacity to convey

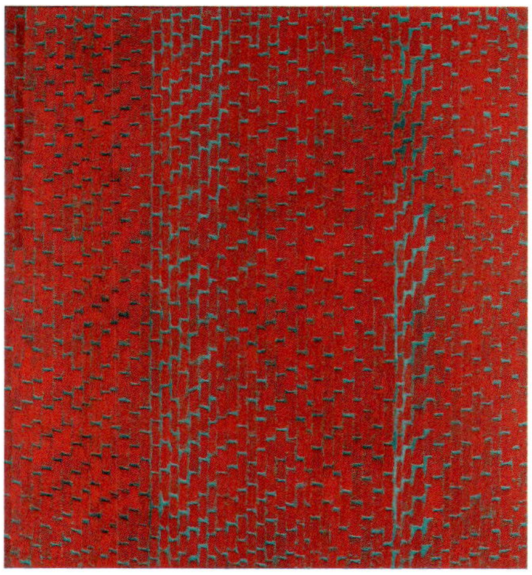

FIG. 74 Alma Thomas (American, 1891–1978). *Red Roses Sonata*, 1972. Metropolitan Museum of Art, New York, Gift of Longview Foundation Inc., in memory of Audrey Stern Hess, 1976 (1976.94)

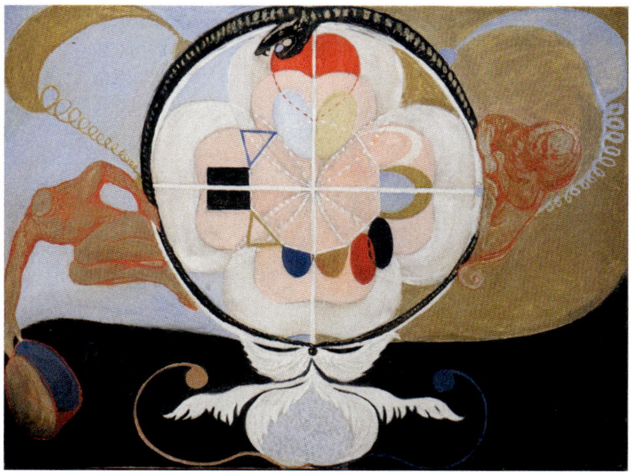

FIG. 75 Hilma af Klint (Swedish, 1862–1944). *Group VI, Evolution, no. 13*, 1908. Oil on canvas, 39 × 51 in. (99 × 129.5 cm). Courtesy Hilma af Klint Foundation, Stockholm

rhythm (the title *Red Roses Sonata* gestures to the influence of music in her work) but also because it unbound her from burdensome, tired expectations around "representing" her experiences as a Black woman.[13] As art historian Kobena Mercer has pointed out, for artists of color around the globe, abstract art can be a crucial way to speak back to ways in which non-white populations have been violently massed together, deindividualized, stereotyped, and "abstracted."[14]

Like Thomas, Neel wanted to be taken seriously as a creator of her "own world," and her flouting of the boundaries between abstraction and figuration was a crucial component of this singular vision. In this, she is akin to other women artists from the twentieth century, including Swedish painter Hilma af Klint, who also embarked on the project of world-making in their art and took liberally from many artistic traditions while inventing their own course. In works such as *Group VI, Evolution, no. 13*, of 1908 (fig. 75), af Klint freely intermingles abstract circular motifs and direct reference to human and animal figures. This indeterminacy and disregard for the supposedly sacrosanct membrane between abstract and nonabstract is key to an entirely revised feminist genealogy of twentieth-century art, one in which Neel prominently features. Though it is unlikely that Neel knew of af Klint's work (which has only recently been popularized), the comparison helps establish that Neel is not an exceptional outlier but rather part of a long tradition of self-described women whose practices around form and content were mutable.

Further evidence of Neel's permissiveness around style can be found in nonrealistic works such as her quasi-surrealistic watercolor *Addiction* of 1931 (p. 222) and her chilling oil painting *Futility of Effort* of 1930 (p. 185). *Addiction* in particular bears some traits in common with af Klint's work, not only in its whirling petals/pinwheels but also in its invocation of transcendent or altered states of mind.[15] Here, unhinged from any proscription to be faithful to "the real," Neel explores a phantasmatic psychological and emotional realm, in which bodies become boneless, limbs stretch and exaggerate, and chairs defy the laws of gravity. With its near-empty visual field of somber gray, ruptured by a child in a simplified bed, a window—foreshadowing her later work *Night*—and the merest sketch of an adult profile suggested by a few thin strokes, *Futility of Effort* was referred to by Neel as "symbolism I think," a nod perhaps to a more dreamlike use of figuration in the late nineteenth century.[16] But if the adult presence in this painting is abstracted, so too is the child, whose flat, generic features, seen from a strangely elevated perspective, have none of the keenly observed individual characteristics that are usually associated with Neel's images.

## "CAPITALISM USED IMAGES"

Neel was both deploying and rejecting the terms of abstraction in the midst of heated midcentury battles about the political role of form. Critic Clement Greenberg heralded the "superiority of abstract art" in 1940, and his championing of white male Abstract Expressionists like Jackson Pollock perpetuated a myth that there is one singular, teleological thrust to Western art history that leads inexorably to abstraction.[17] In truth, Abstract Expressionism was never a fully consolidated school with a script of hegemonic marching orders—Willem de Kooning's frenetic figures, for instance, and Helen Frankenthaler's allusive, lyrical landscapes like *Western Dream* of 1957 (fig. 76) violate its alleged fealty to iconoclasm. For a painting from that same year, *Sunset, Riverside Drive* (p. 224), Neel likewise utilizes the fluid properties of paint to evoke flow across the canvas, suggesting the melting together of light, flora, water, and horizon.

But it bears repeating that, though she flirted with some of its maneuvers, Neel firmly planted her flag outside the territory of Abstract Expressionism. Moreover, this was a doctrinaire stance, forged via her Marxist allegiances; it is important that her strident statement "against" abstraction appeared in the *Daily Worker*, a Communist publication.[18] Though Greenberg had in the 1930s also identified as a Marxist, some perceived his turn to abstraction as a move away from politics and a betrayal of the more populist strategy of realistic depiction. For many Marxists throughout the middle of the twentieth century, abstraction was seen as an outgrowth of elitist, rarefied, ruling-class mentalities. "It is astonishing to consider the former hostility of most Marxist critics and theoreticians towards abstract art," notes Gerardo Mosquera in a sweeping assessment of the entrenched opprobrium toward nonobjective art across left-leaning circles in Europe, the United States, and Latin America.[19]

And by the 1970s, it was becoming clear that, however polyphonic in practice, Abstract Expressionism as a movement had been used, to quote Eva Cockcroft's 1974 article, as a "weapon of the Cold War," instrumentalized as a vehicle to export optimistic images of US capitalist, democratic freedoms abroad through CIA-sponsored exhibitions in Europe that trumpeted the stylistic liberties available to American artists.[20] In her fruitful conversation with Groshans, Neel also expresses awareness of how Abstract Expressionism was a tool in wider ideological debates. "Capitalism used images without man for its own propaganda," she explains. "But I don't think you can blame the artist really," she adds.[21] Her decision to focus primarily on painting individuals was partly a way to re-center the human in a time of great uncertainty and destruction, in which the abstracting obliterations of the atomic bomb, of world wars, of class struggle, and of dehumanizing capitalism leveled their value. Indeed, according to Marxist theory, the wage labor system itself is one of the ultimate abstractions.

Other Marxist artists in the twentieth century also demonstrated skepticism toward the abstract imperative; in 1932, Mexican artist Diego Rivera declared that the most revolutionary art would reject "art for art's sake" and seize the spirit of the proletariat by conveying readable messages that are "warm and clear and strong."[22] It is significant that Rivera penned this manifesto after mastering a Cubist skill set, one that he attempted to marry with his radical politics, as is evident in his *Zapatista Landscape* of 1915 (fig. 77). In this commanding composition, Rivera utilizes abstracting to generate a wholly fragmented still life that is anchored by a few recognizable elements that assert Mexican identity apart from colonial rule—sombrero, buckle, serape. By the 1930s, Rivera had abandoned this way of working in favor of "warm and clear and strong" murals, grounded in legibility and influenced by figurative traditions within Indigenous art of the Americas that he believed would speak more directly to the workers.

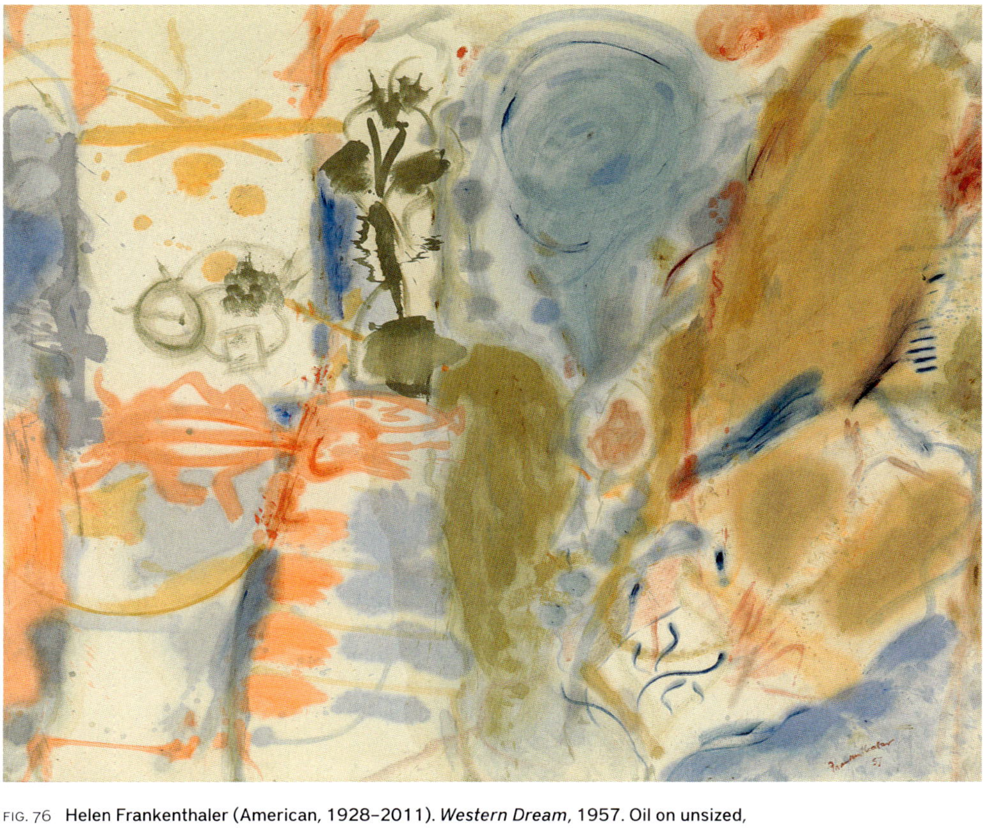

FIG. 76 Helen Frankenthaler (American, 1928–2011). *Western Dream*, 1957. Oil on unsized, unprimed canvas, 70 × 86 in. (177.8 × 218.4 cm). Helen Frankenthaler Foundation

Yet the possibilities of radical style offered up by Rivera's "revolutionary" still life as it trespassed the line between abstraction and representation have been echoed in other images by minoritarian artists. A similar fracturing of space appears in African American artist Romare Bearden's *Feast* of 1969 (fig. 78), in which he uses collage to evoke a festive scene around a table. Here, snippets of photographs of African masks function as surrogates for Black faces, a critique of the overt primitivizing of European Cubism. Though he constructed much of the image via collage with its inherently abstracting tactics, Bearden includes some conventional still life touchstones: a tabletop, bottles, and a yellowish orb that might be a piece of fruit. His mingling of representational forms with abstracted tropes and his integration of African diasporic material culture (like Rivera's defiantly Mexican objects) convey a scene of Black social space and invoke what Moten calls "a black community of things."

For her part, Neel also explored the quiet power of the still life. In her *Still Life with Fruit* of 1940 (p. 152), she embraces a subject that in the past had been seen as one of the lesser genres

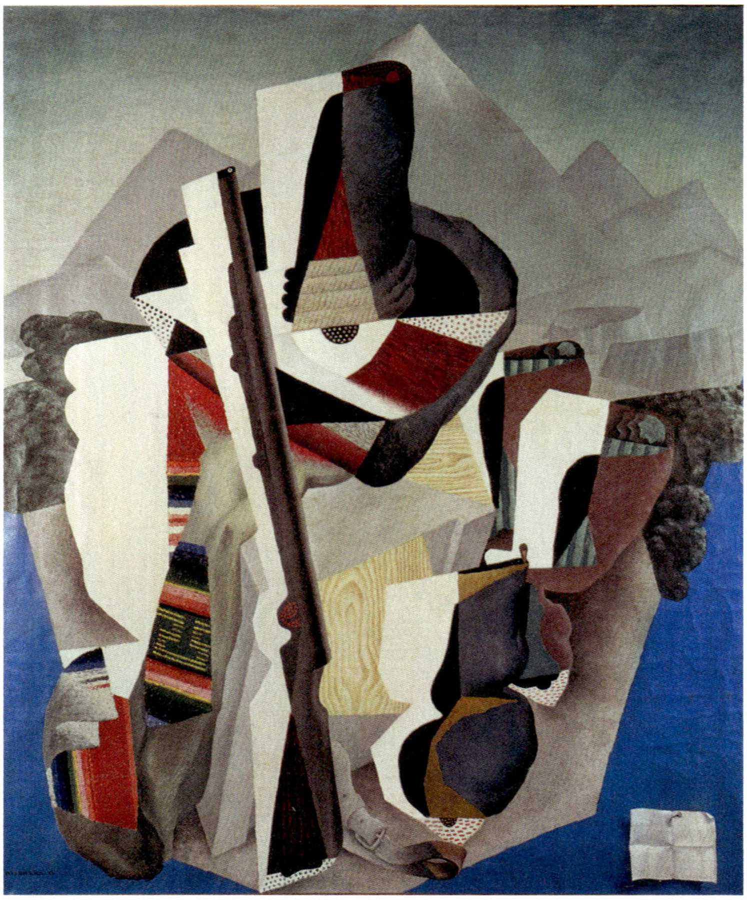

FIG. 77 Diego Rivera (Mexican, 1886–1957). *Zapatista Landscape*, 1915. Oil on canvas, 57 × 49¼ in. (144.7 × 125 cm). Museo Nacional de Arte, INBA, Mexico City

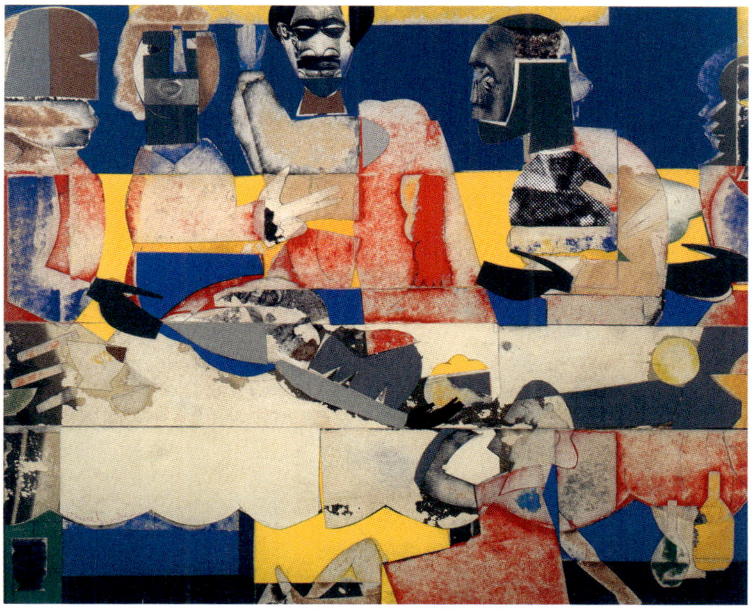

FIG. 78 Romare Bearden (American, 1911–1988). *Feast*, 1969. Collage on plywood, 21 × 25 in. (53.3 × 63.5 cm). Courtesy DC Moore Gallery, New York

within a rigid hierarchy of Western art that positioned epic history painting—almost never the purview of women—at the top. Within her study in solidity and mass, she nestles together six globes in a bowl perched on a table corner next to a brown vessel. Neel later commented that she "always liked this still life for the simplicity of the forms."[23] The earthy palette includes many different rich browns and beiges, tones that appear throughout her oeuvre. (It is tempting to speculate that she had a unique affinity for these pigments due to her conscientious rendering of a range of skin tones across racial difference.) Neel was drawn to the everyday and the mundane, and her focus on seemingly humble subjects and lower genres stood in contrast to Abstract Expressionists' tendencies toward grandiosity.

Schor argued that Neel's abstract "surplus" was part of a distinctly feminist strategy, one that refused to be hemmed in by simplifying categorizations and rebelled against masculinist norms. Placing her art alongside work by such artists as Thomas, Rivera, and Bearden further suggests that Neel's surplus might have been related to the excess or overflow of affective social life that she encountered in her chosen community of racially mixed populations. For Neel, figuration was a political choice, but so too was her formal experimentation that included her tactile manipulation of paint and her persistent penchant for abstracting.

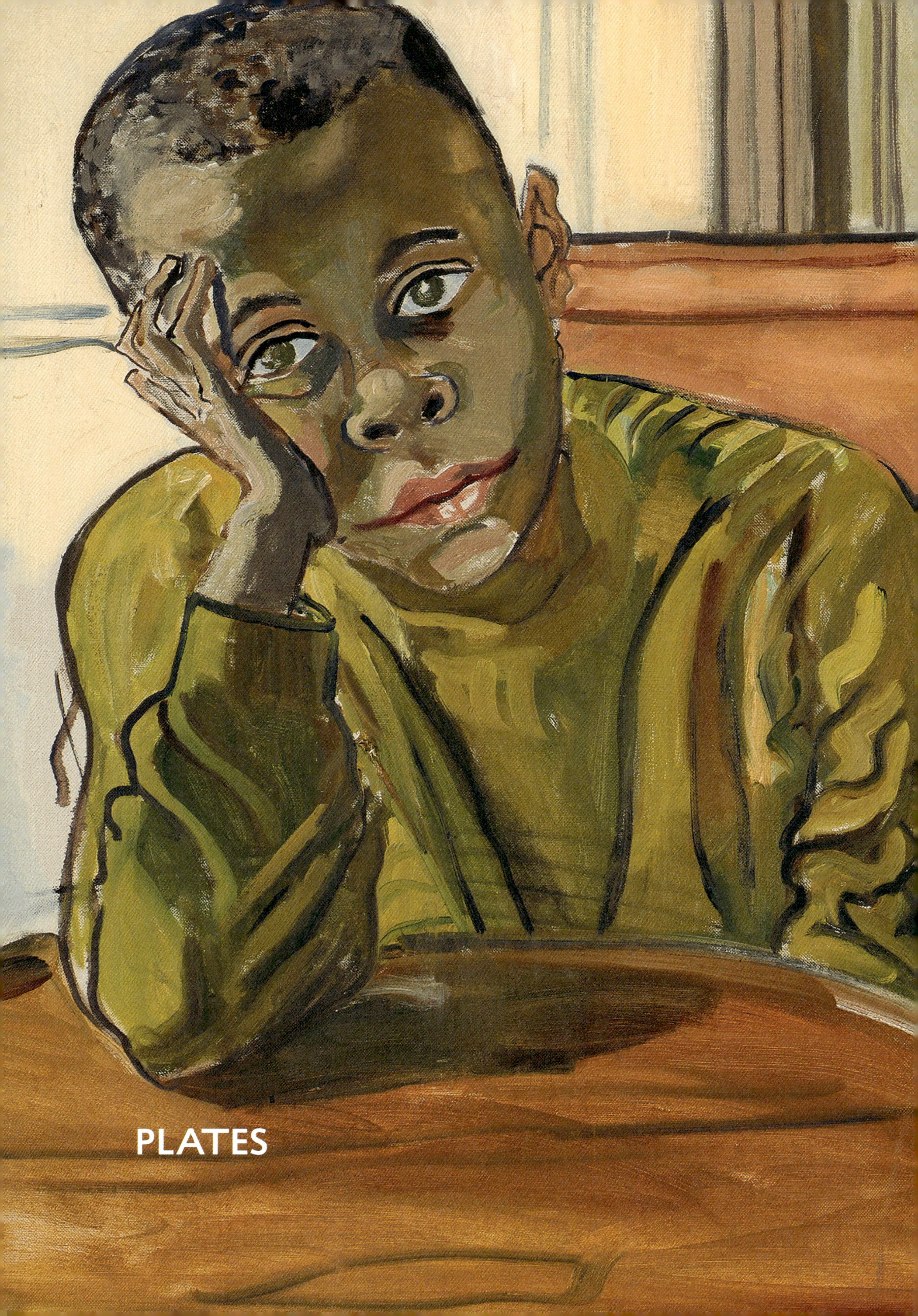

# PLATES

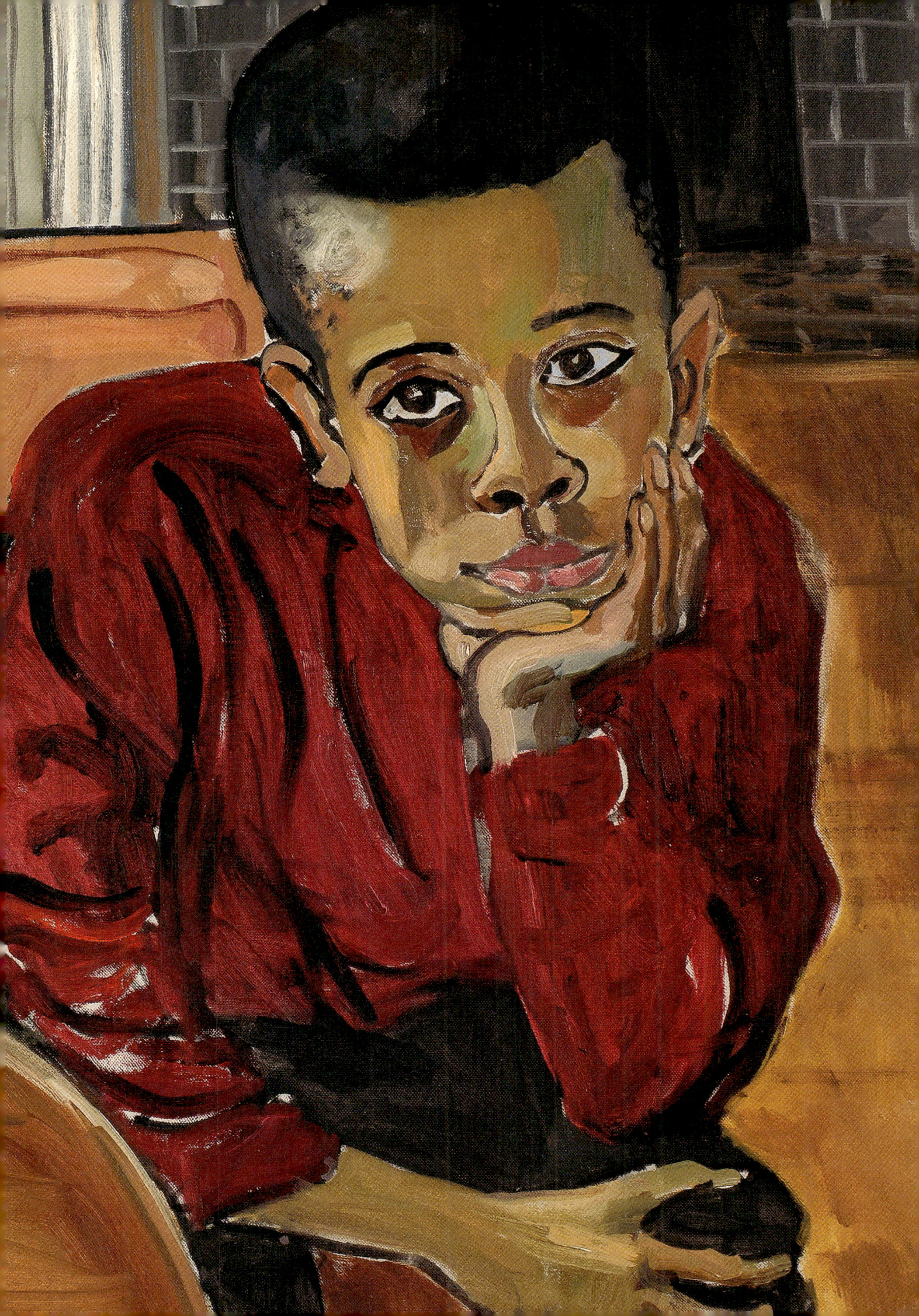

**Harlem River at Sedgwick Avenue** 1928

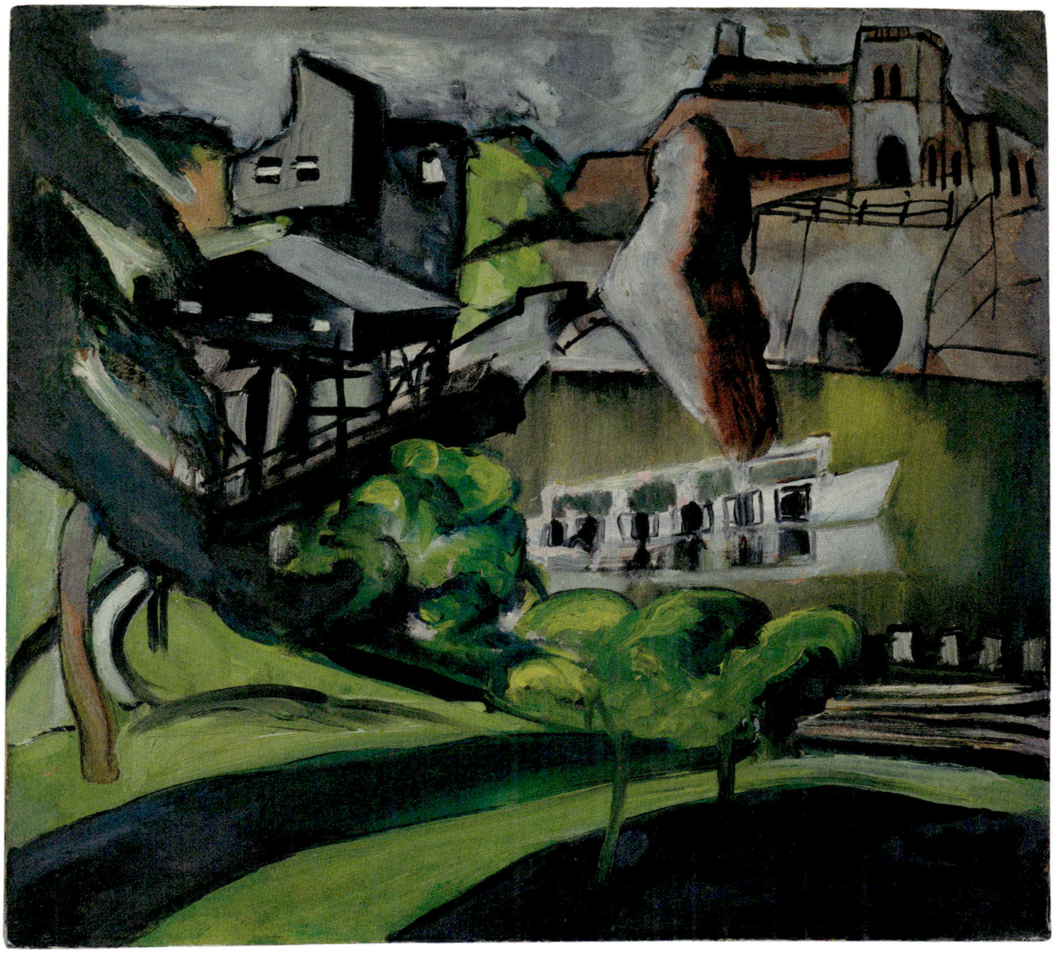

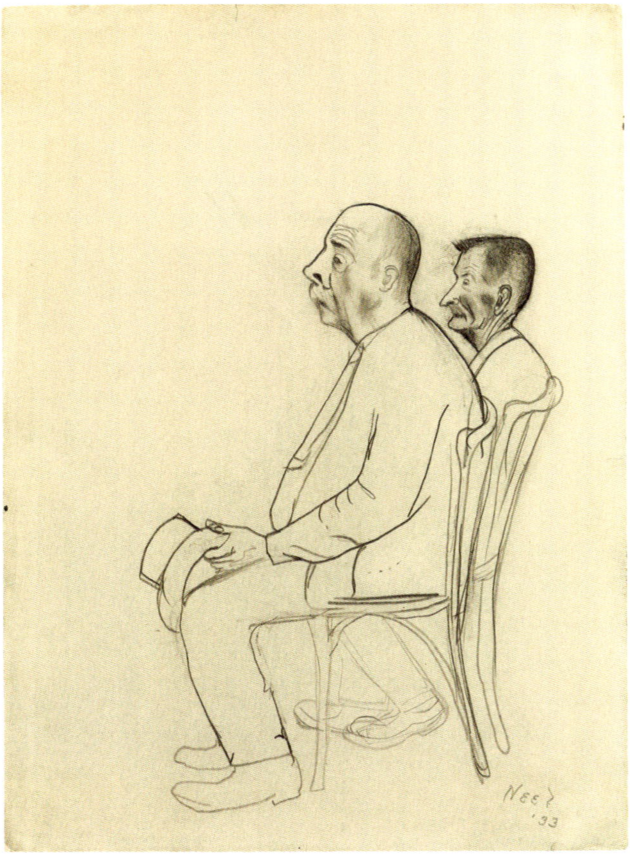


 **Men from Bleecker Street** 1933

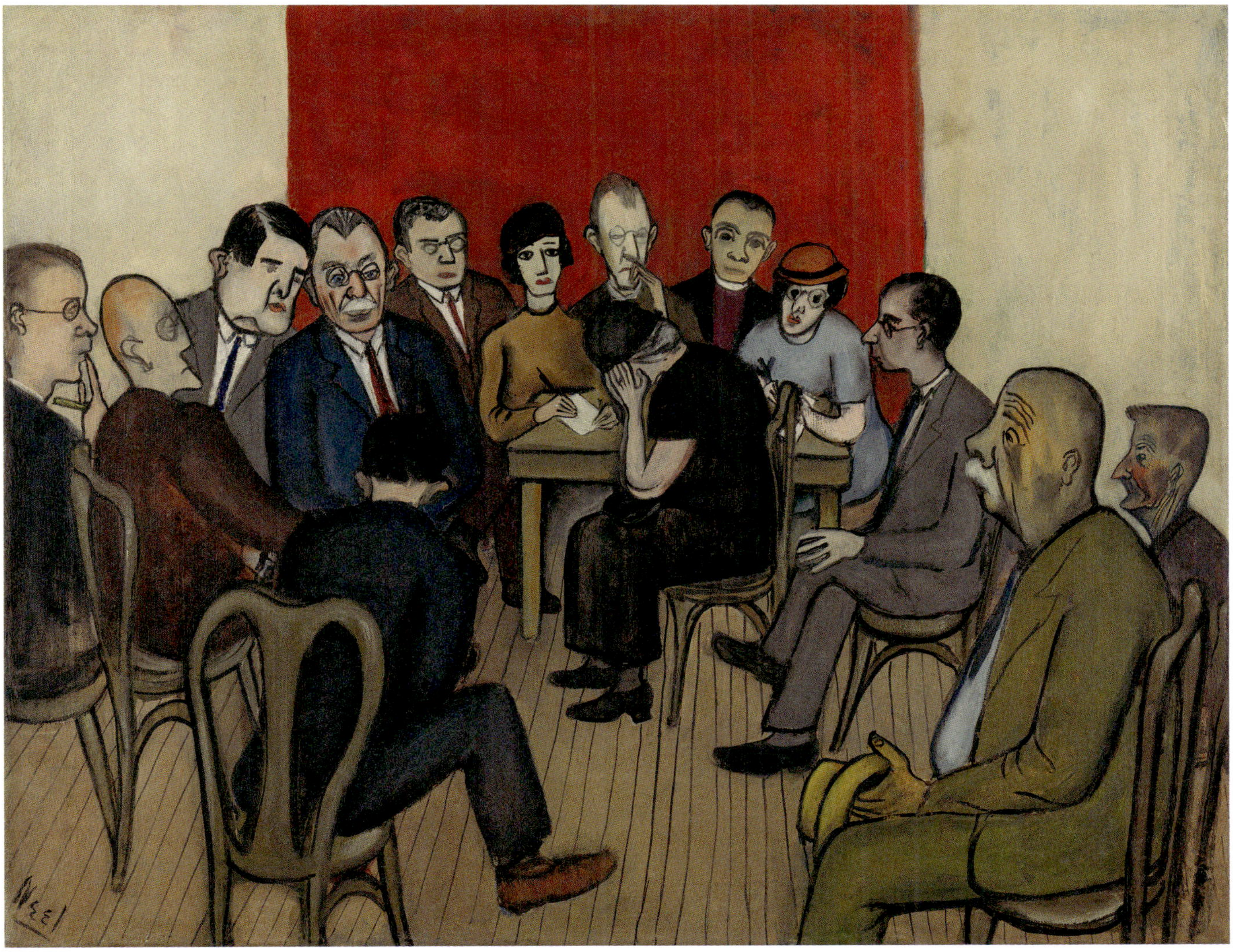

**Investigation of Poverty at the Russell Sage Foundation** 1933

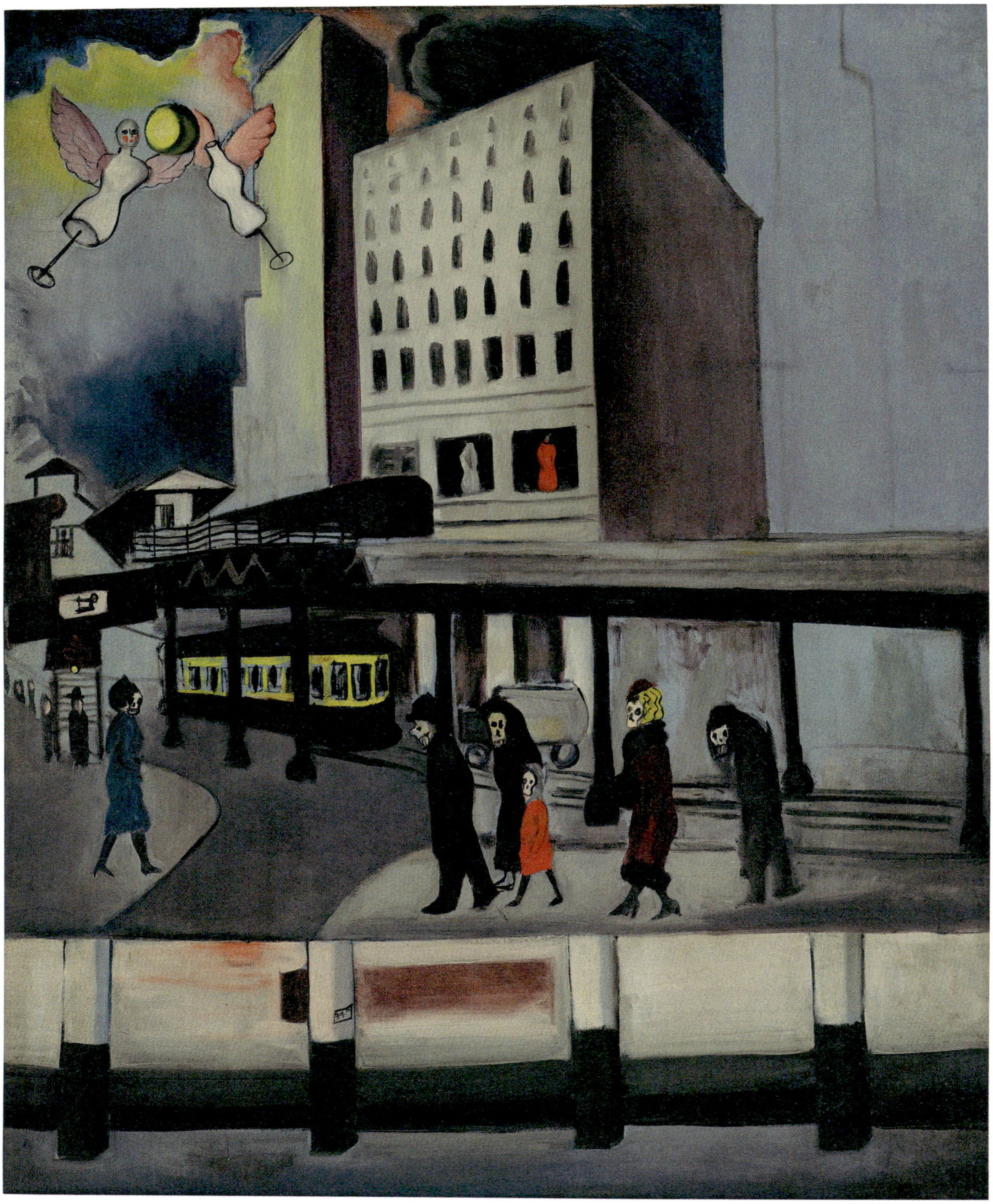

 **Synthesis of New York – The Great Depression** 1933

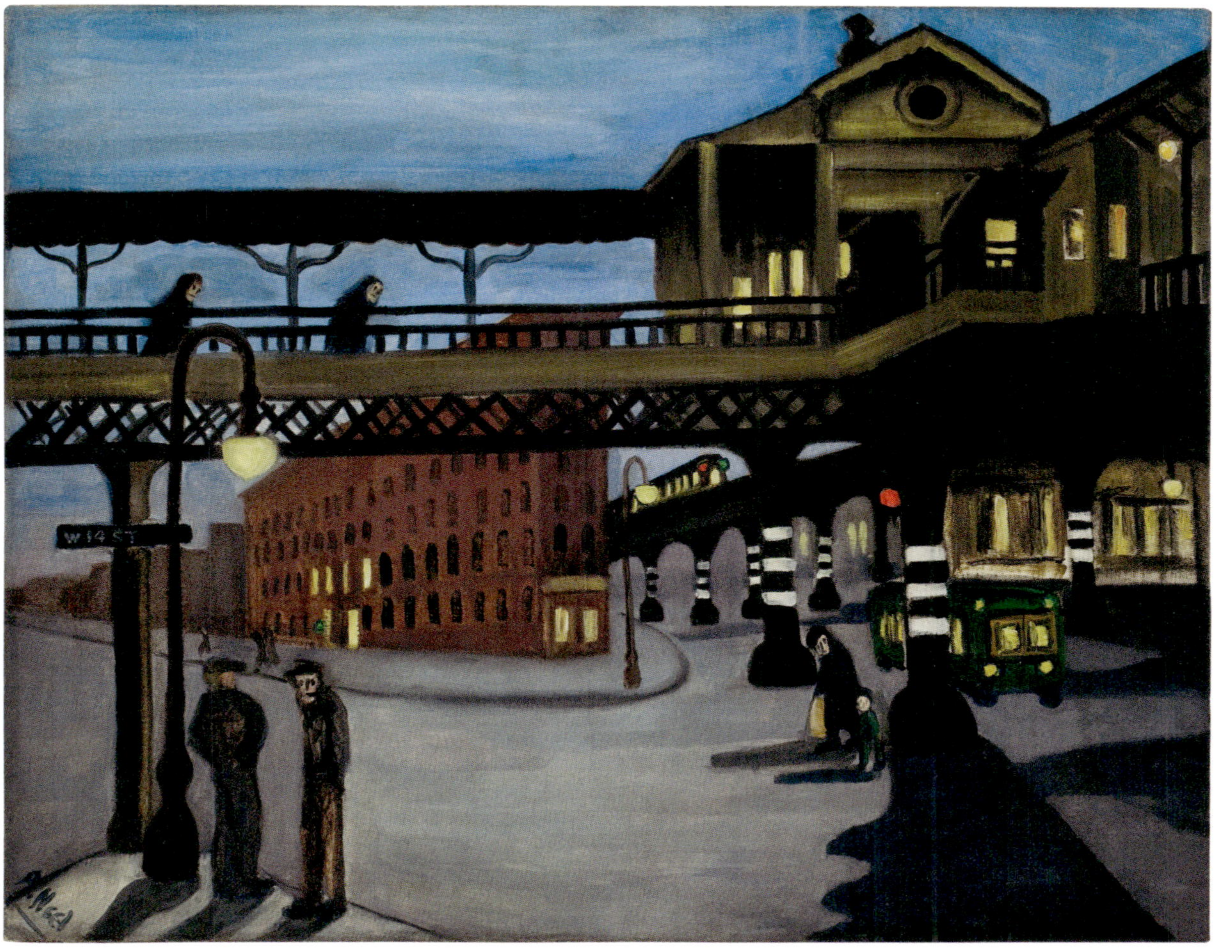


**Ninth Avenue El** 1935

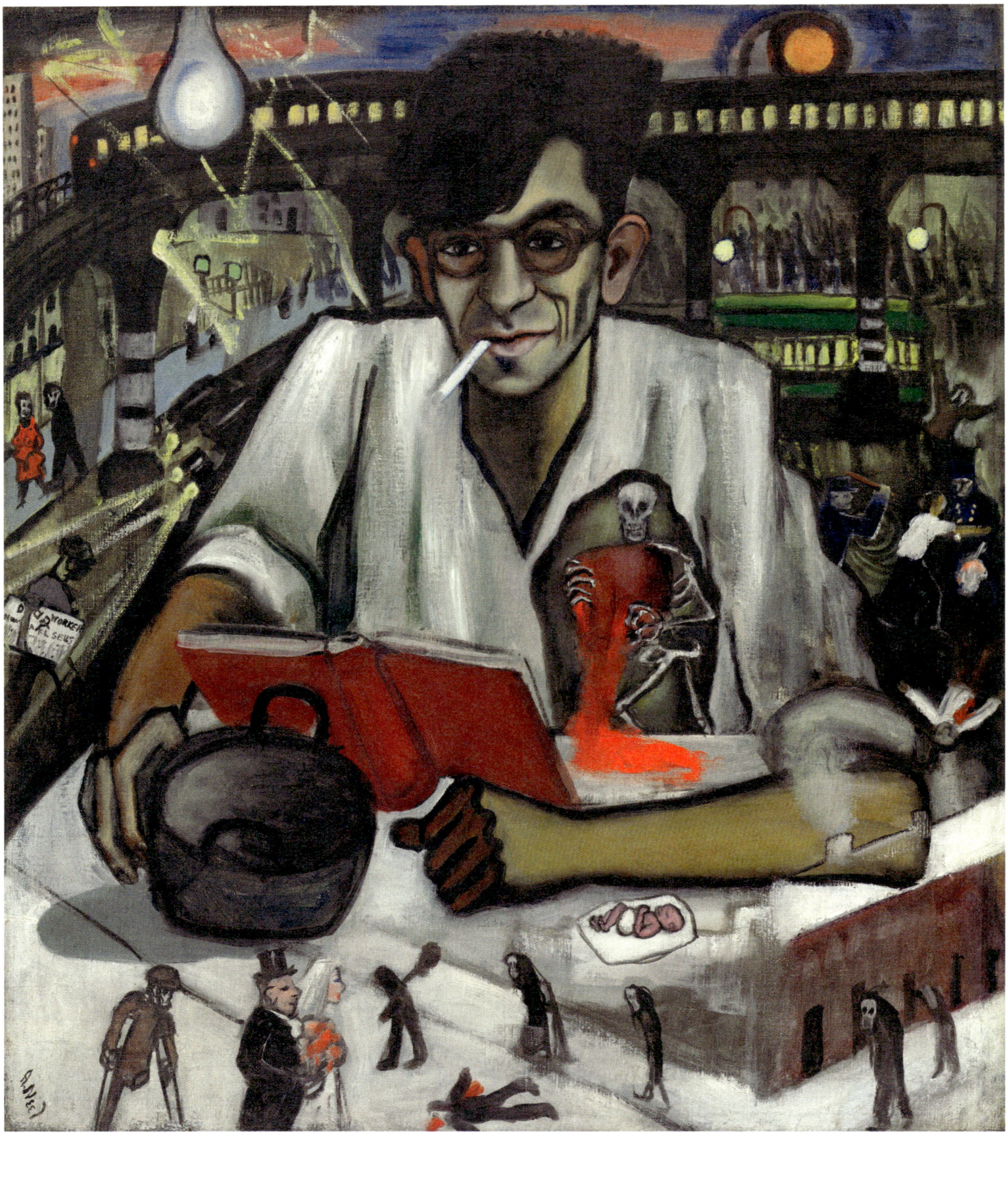

 **Kenneth Fearing** 1935

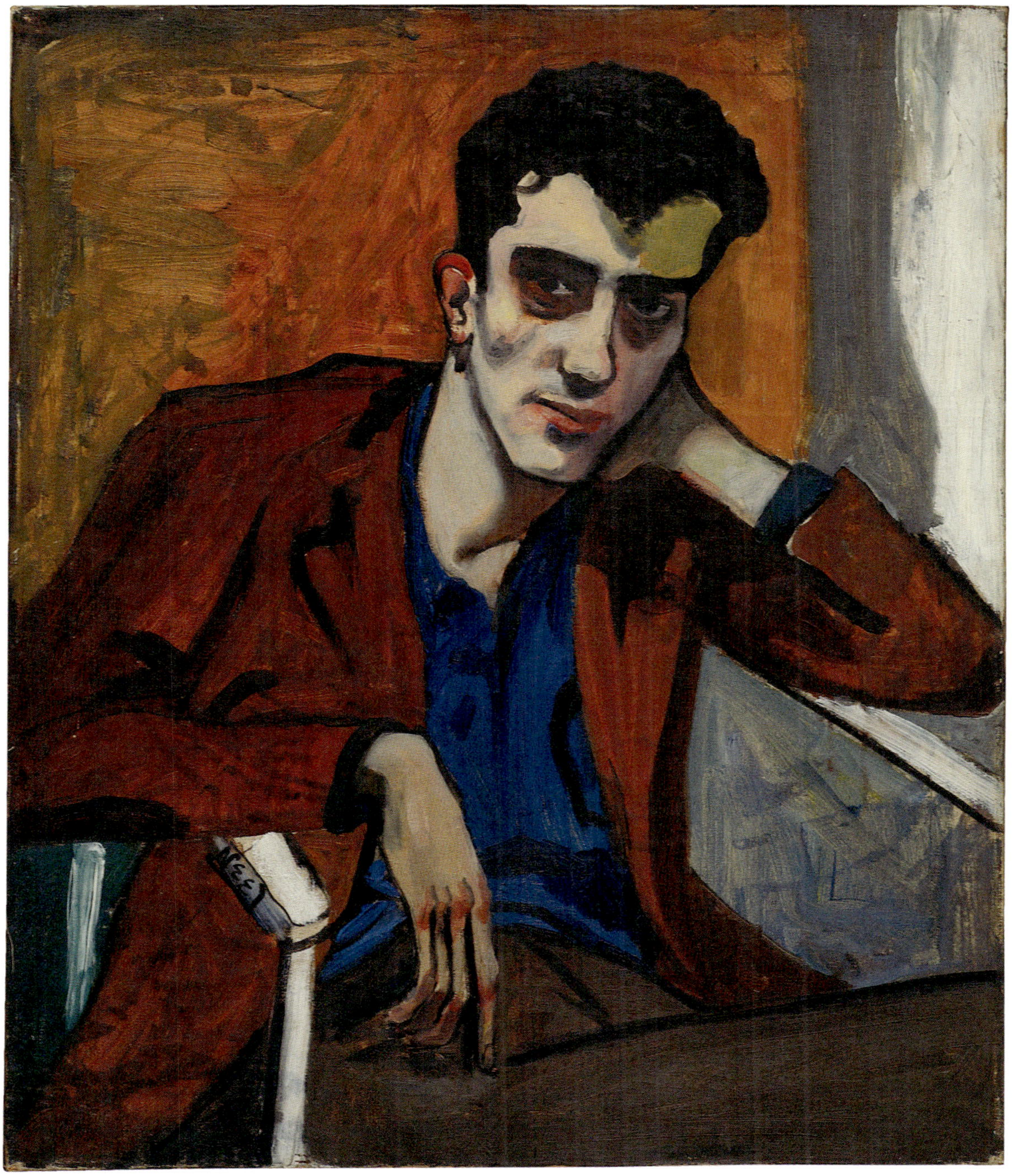

**Dick Bagley** 1946

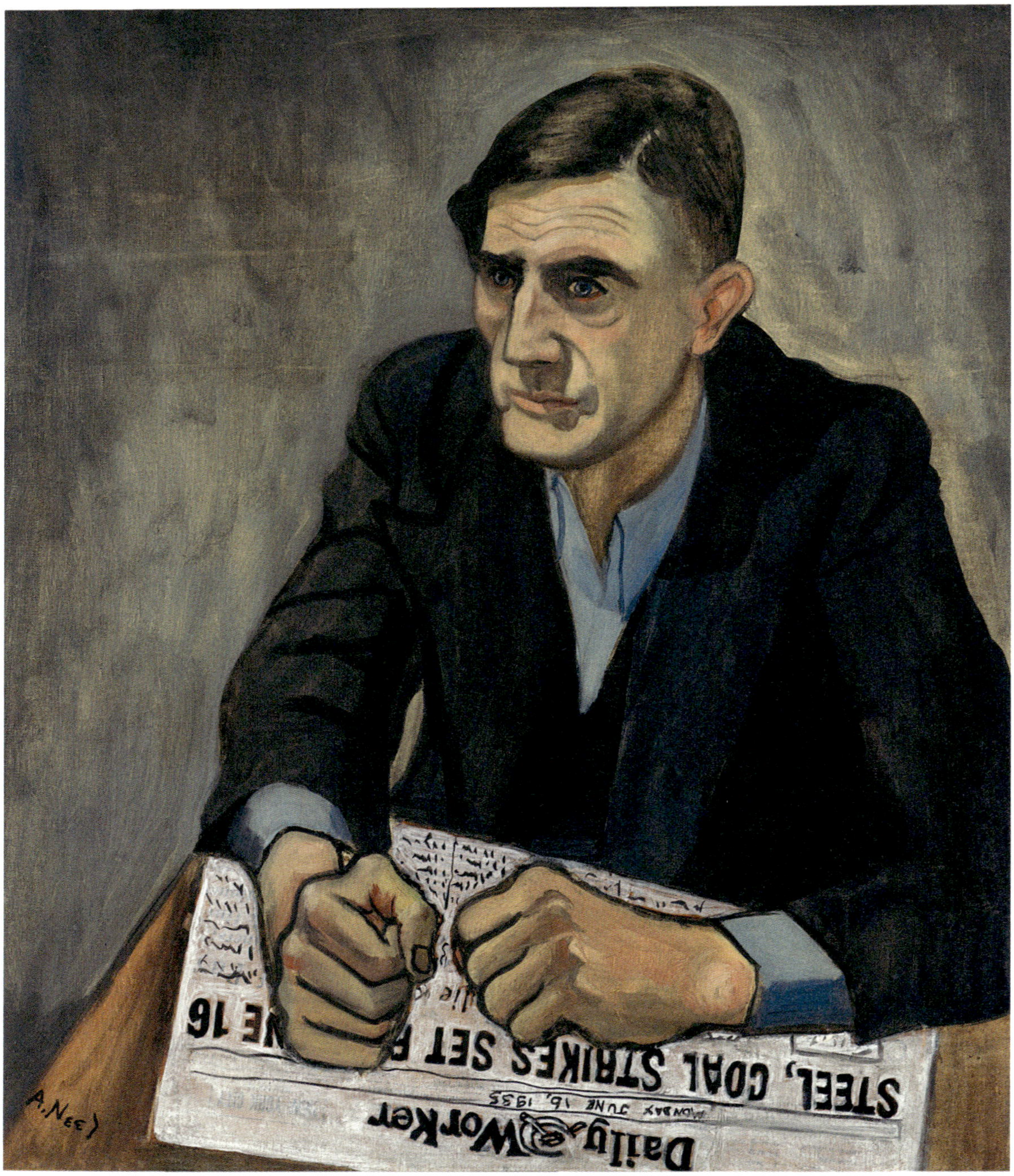




**Pat Whalen** 1935

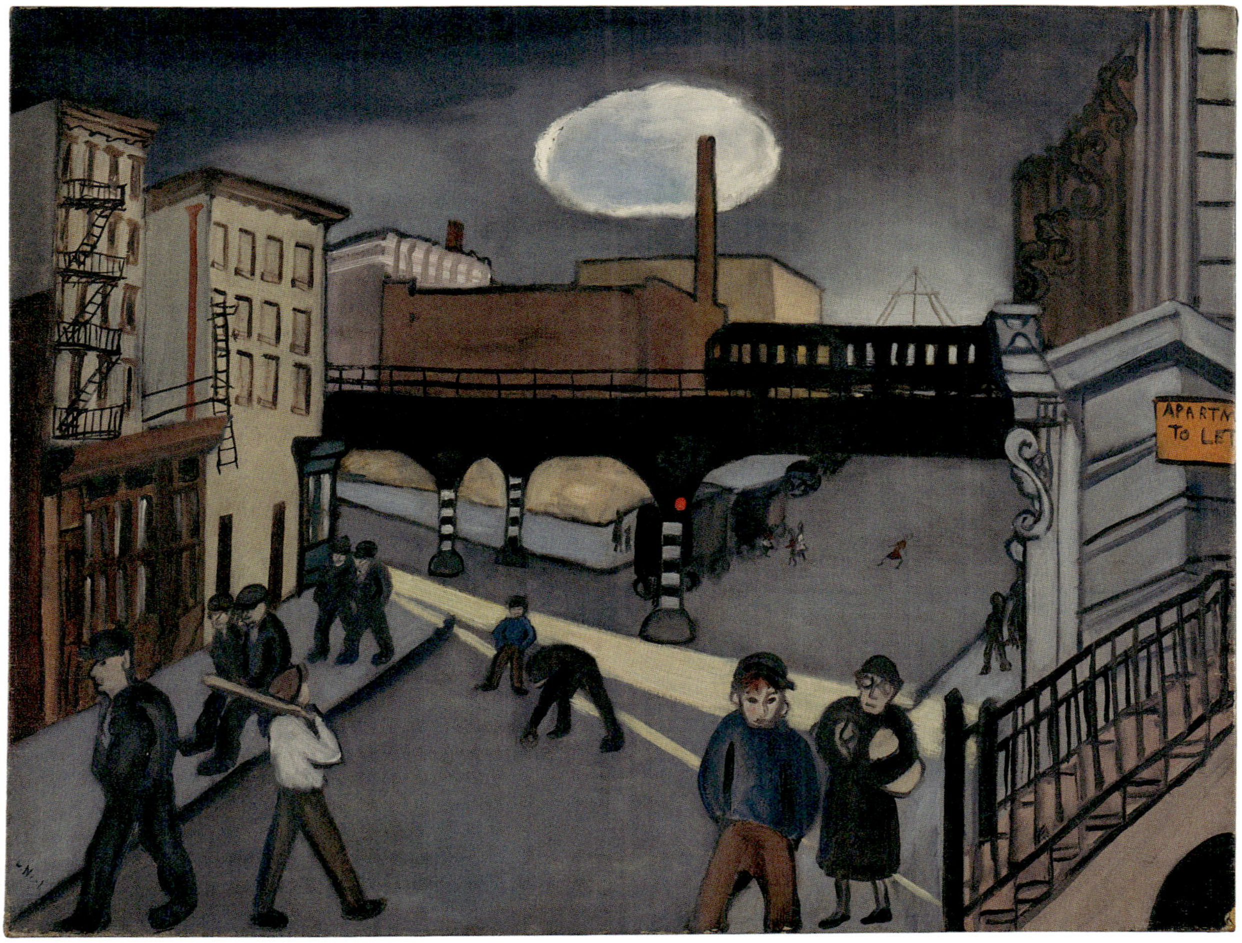


**Longshoremen Returning from Work** 1936

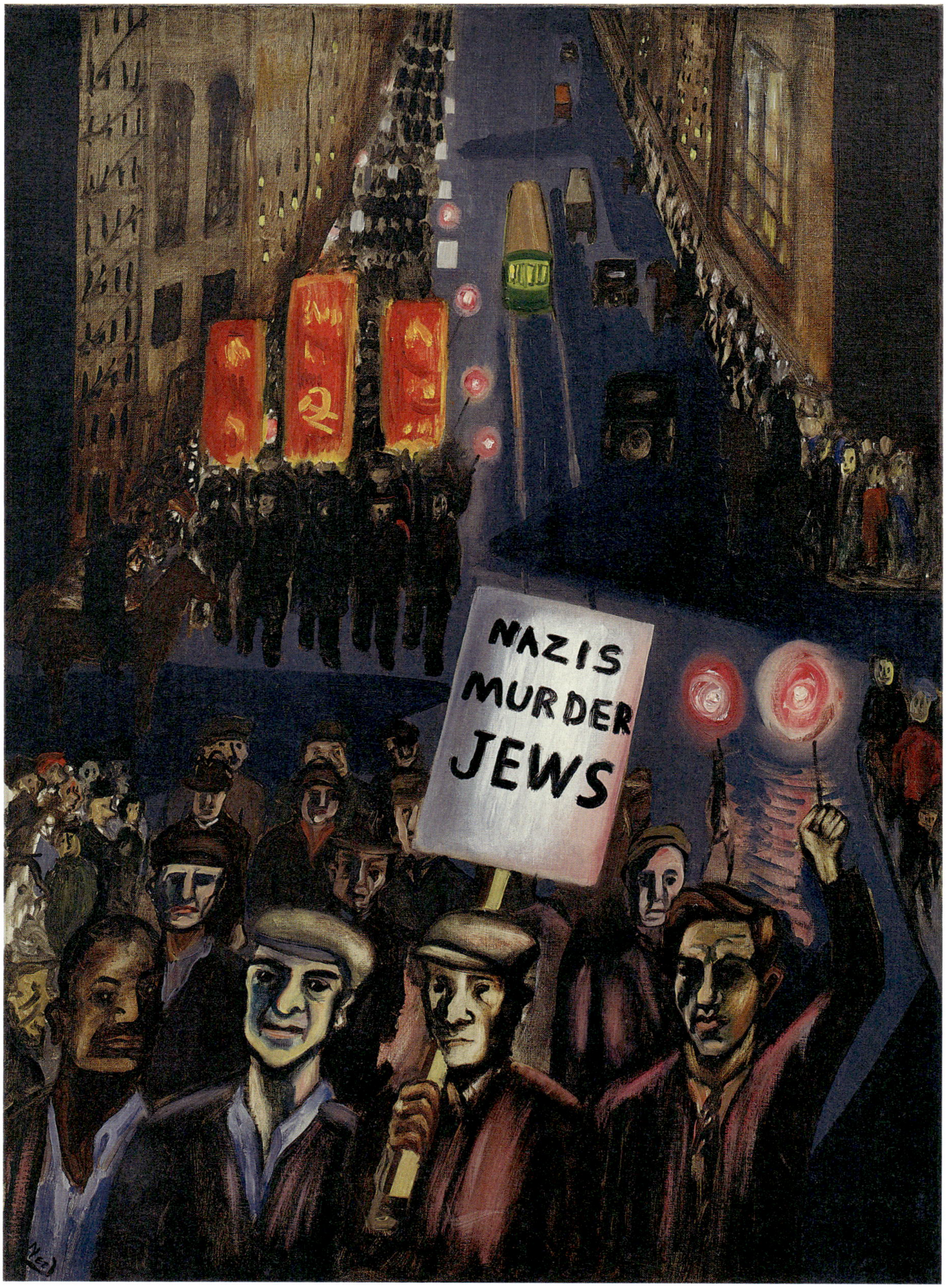


 **Nazis Murder Jews** 1936

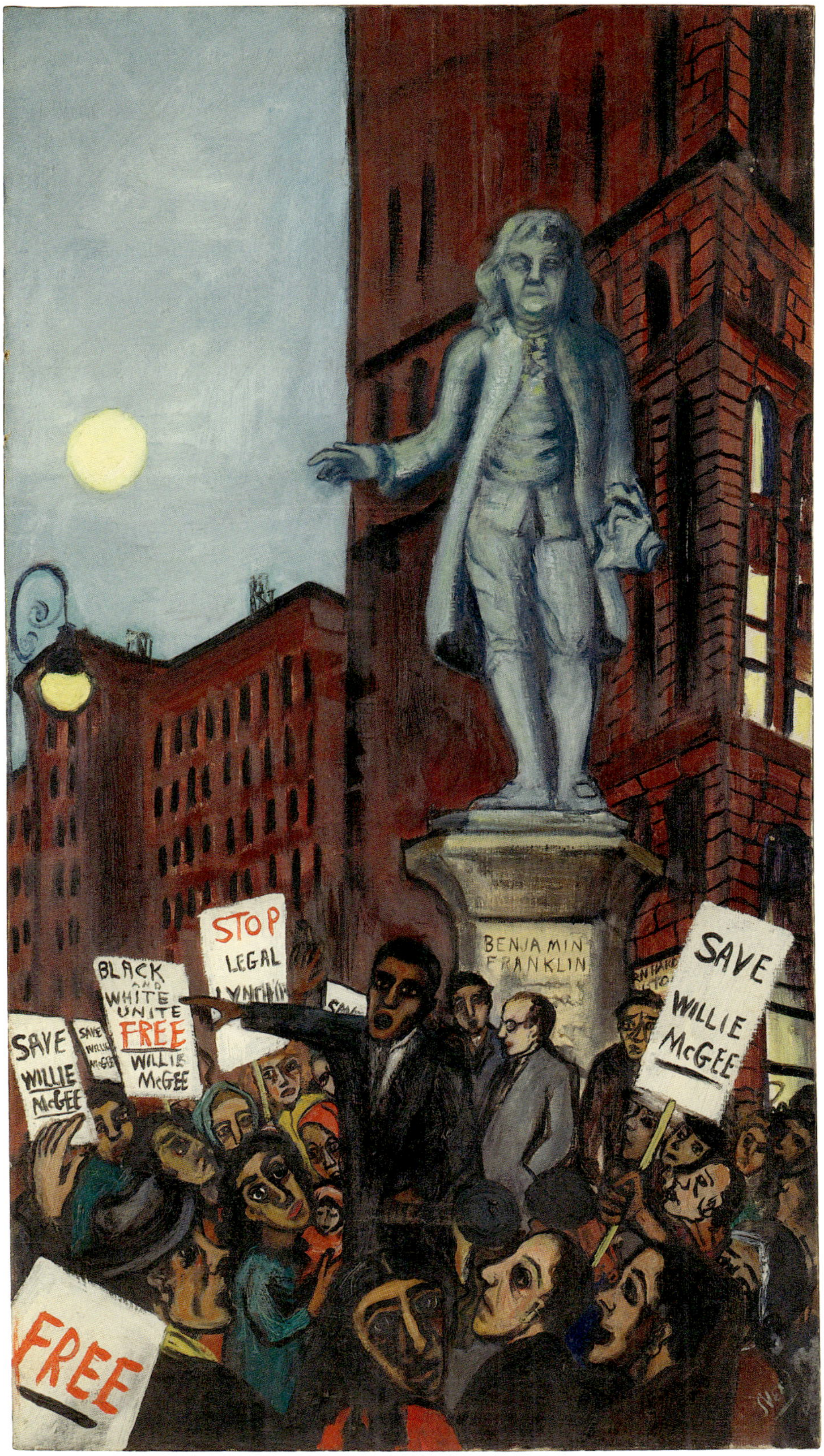


**Save Willie McGee** ca. 1950

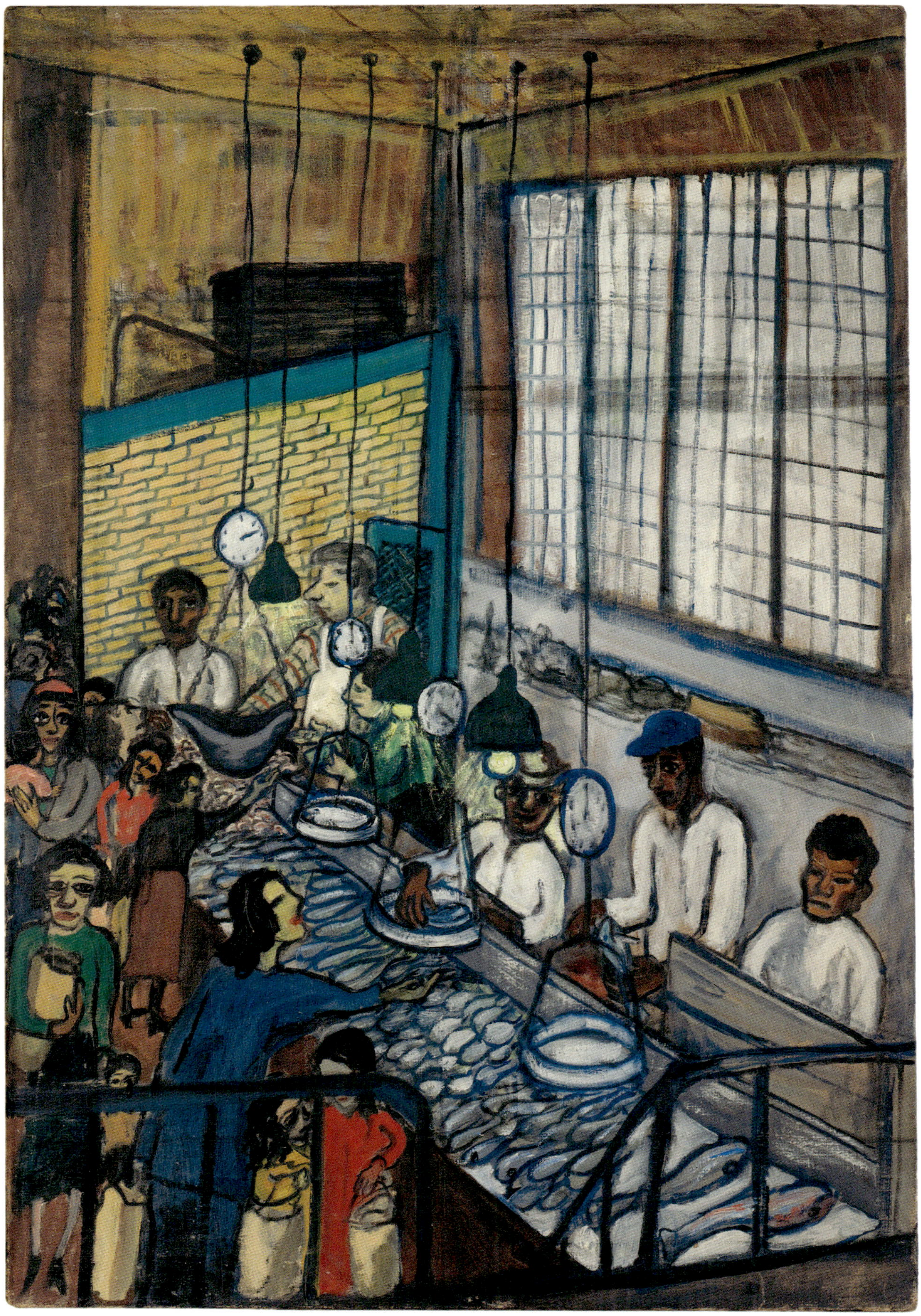

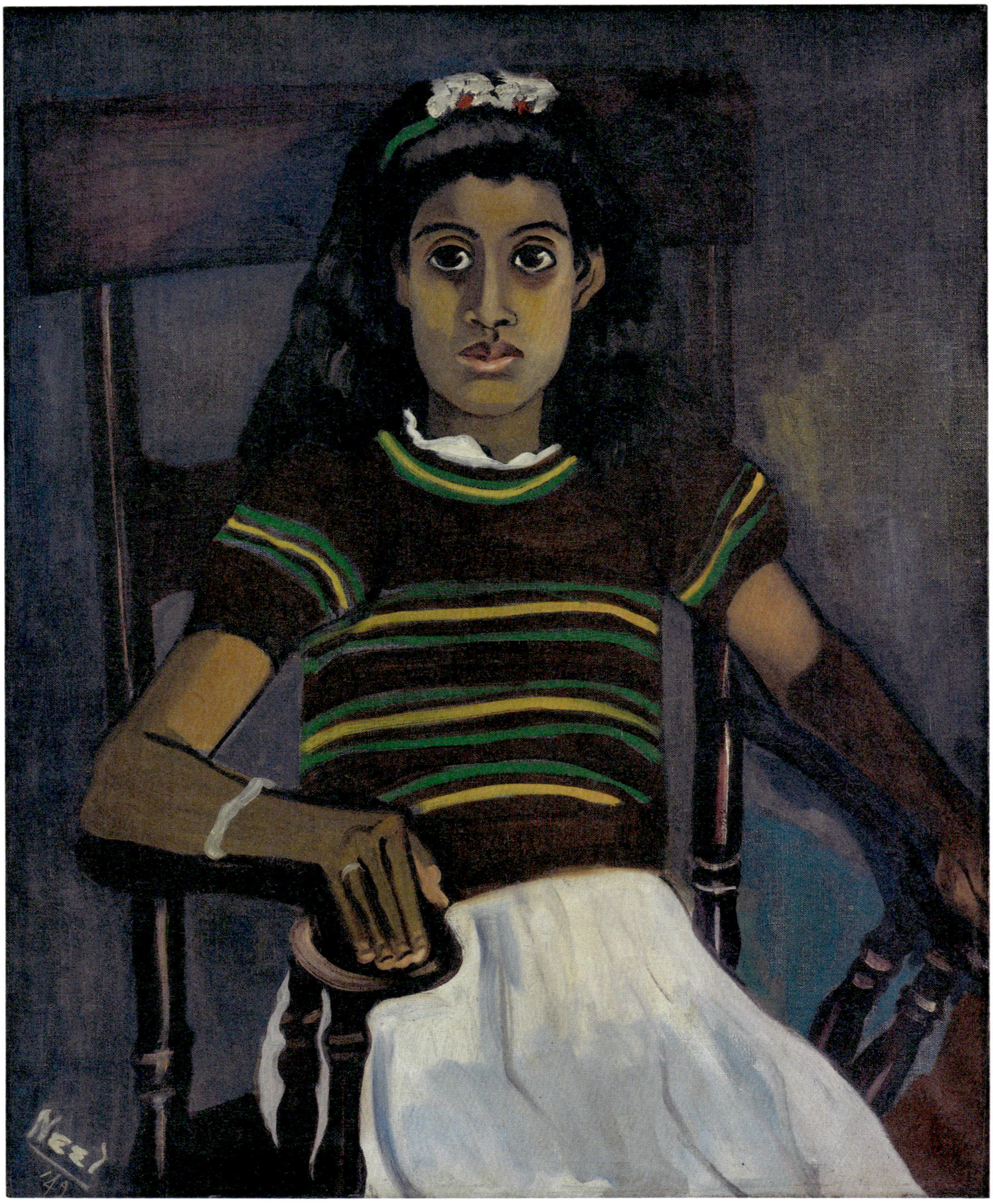

**Puerto Rican Girl on a Chair** 1949

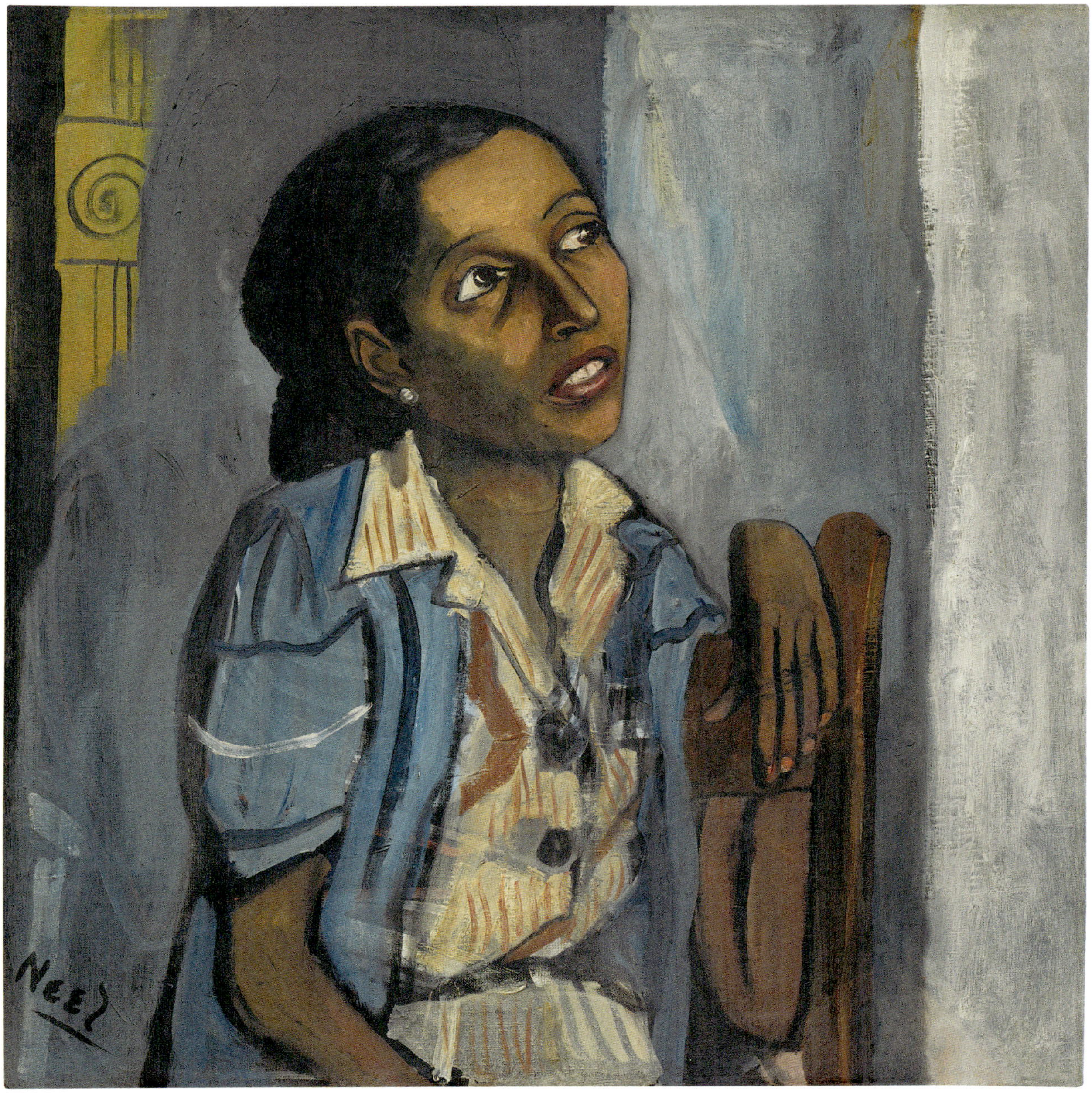


**Mercedes Arroyo** 1952

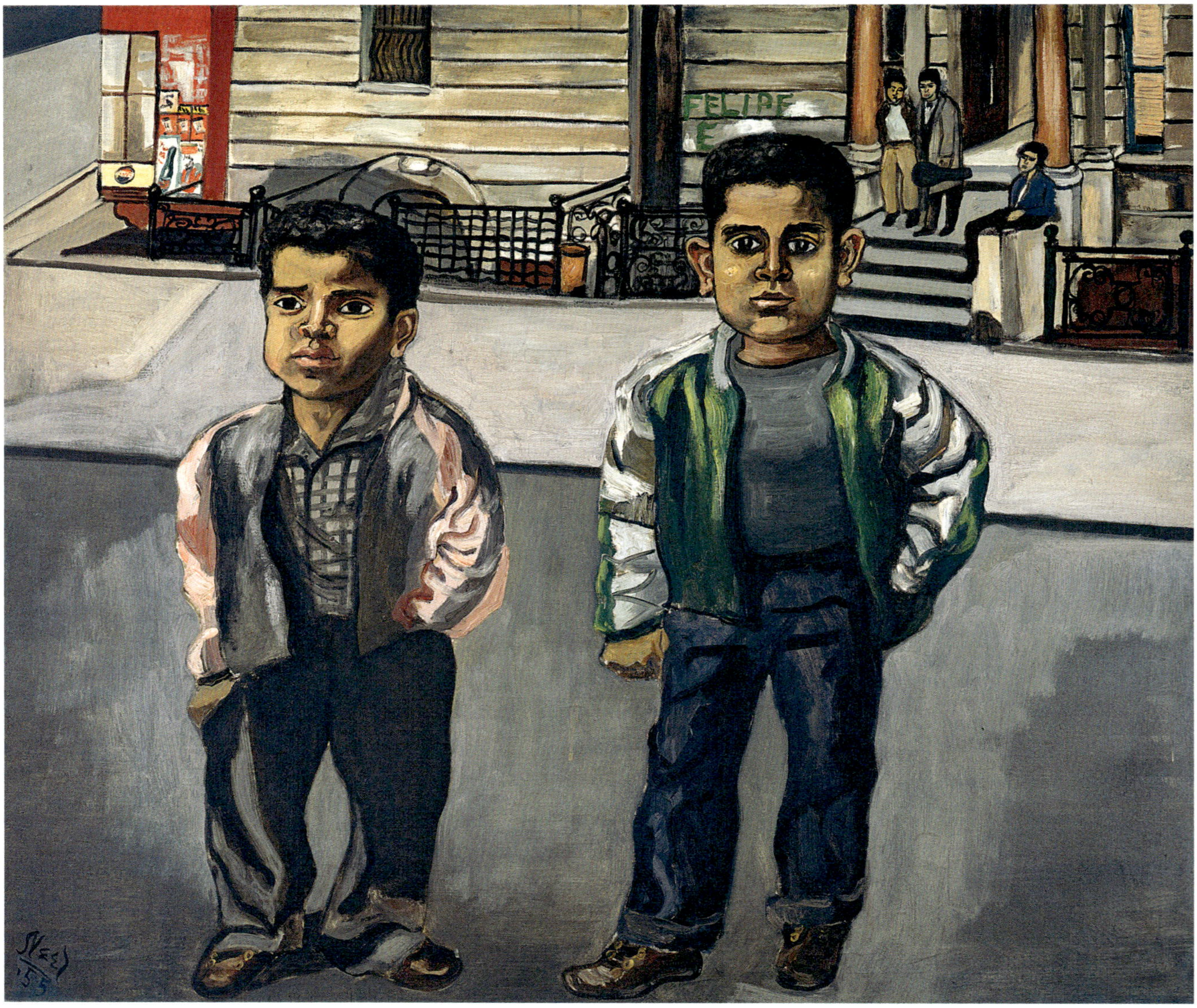




**Dominican Boys on 108th Street** 1955

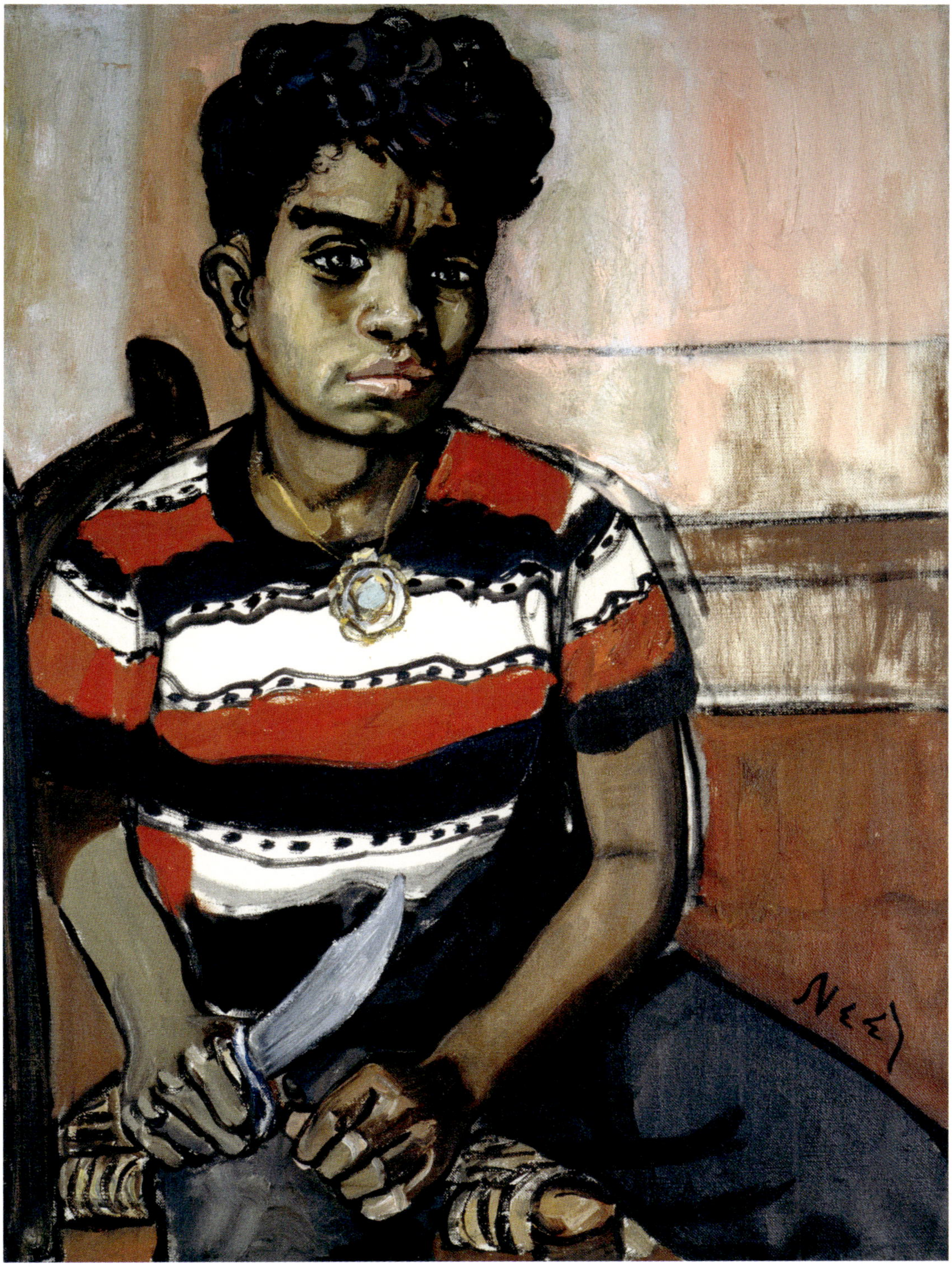


**Georgie Arce No. 2** 1955

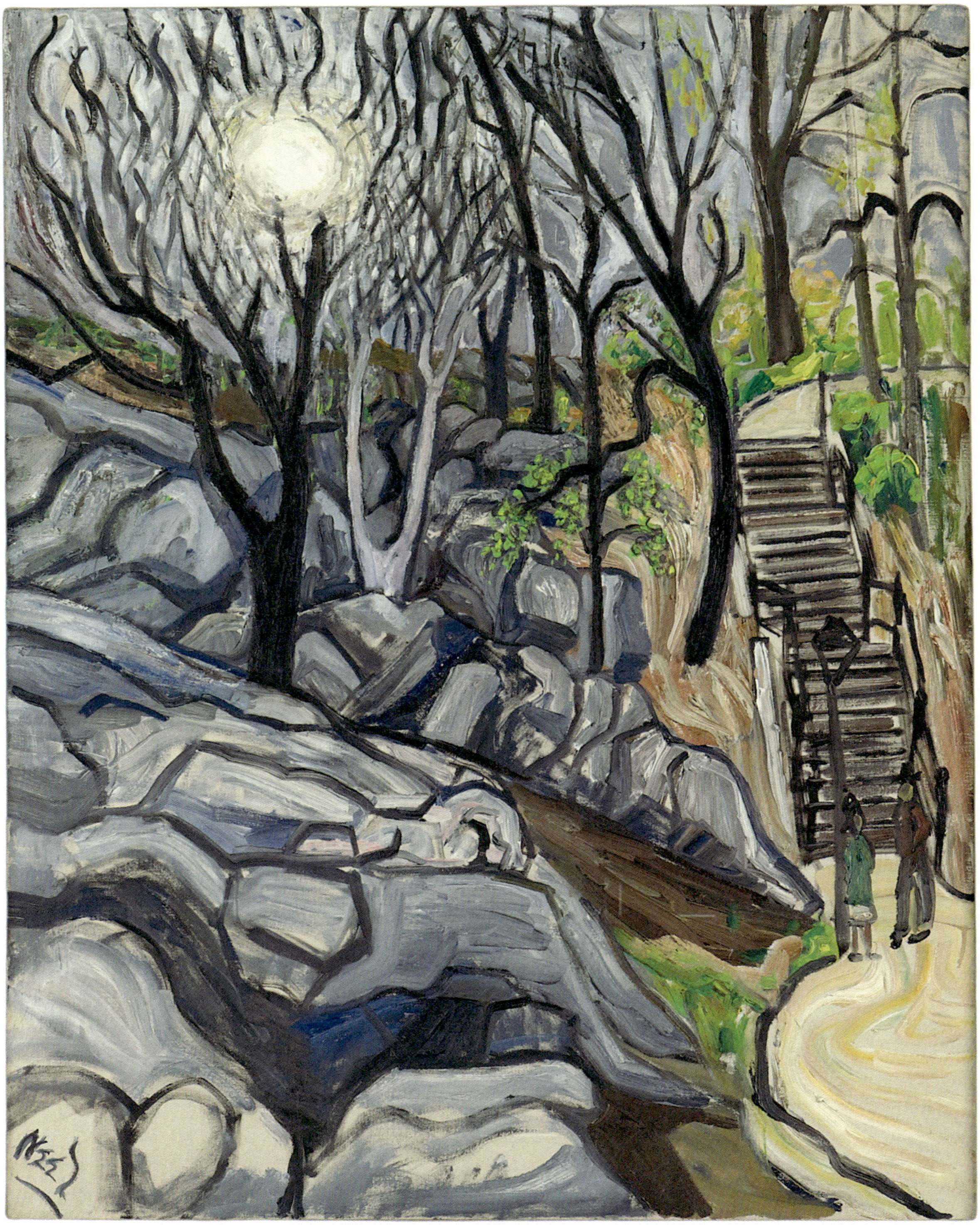

 **Central Park** 1959

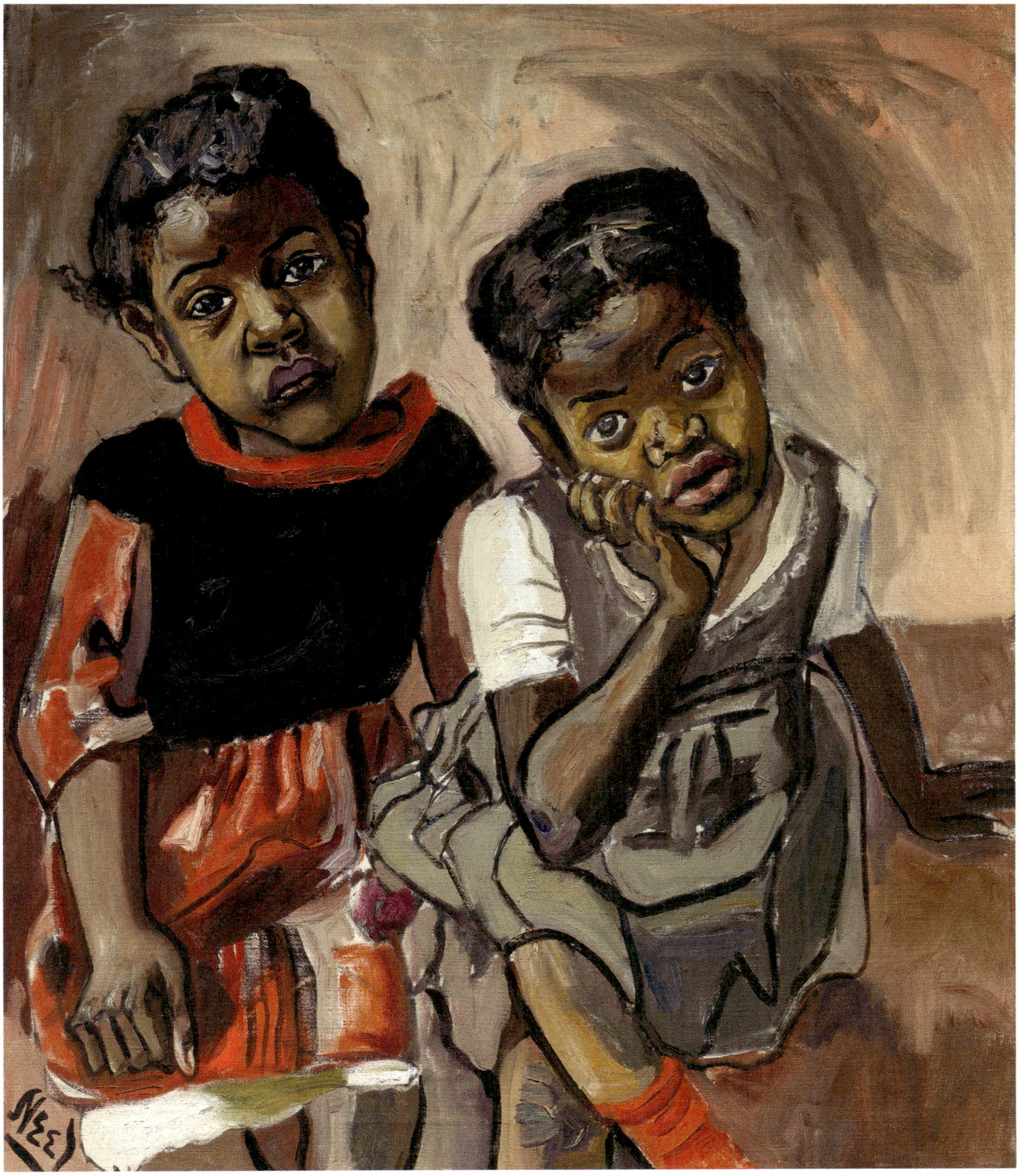


**Two Girls, Spanish Harlem** 1959

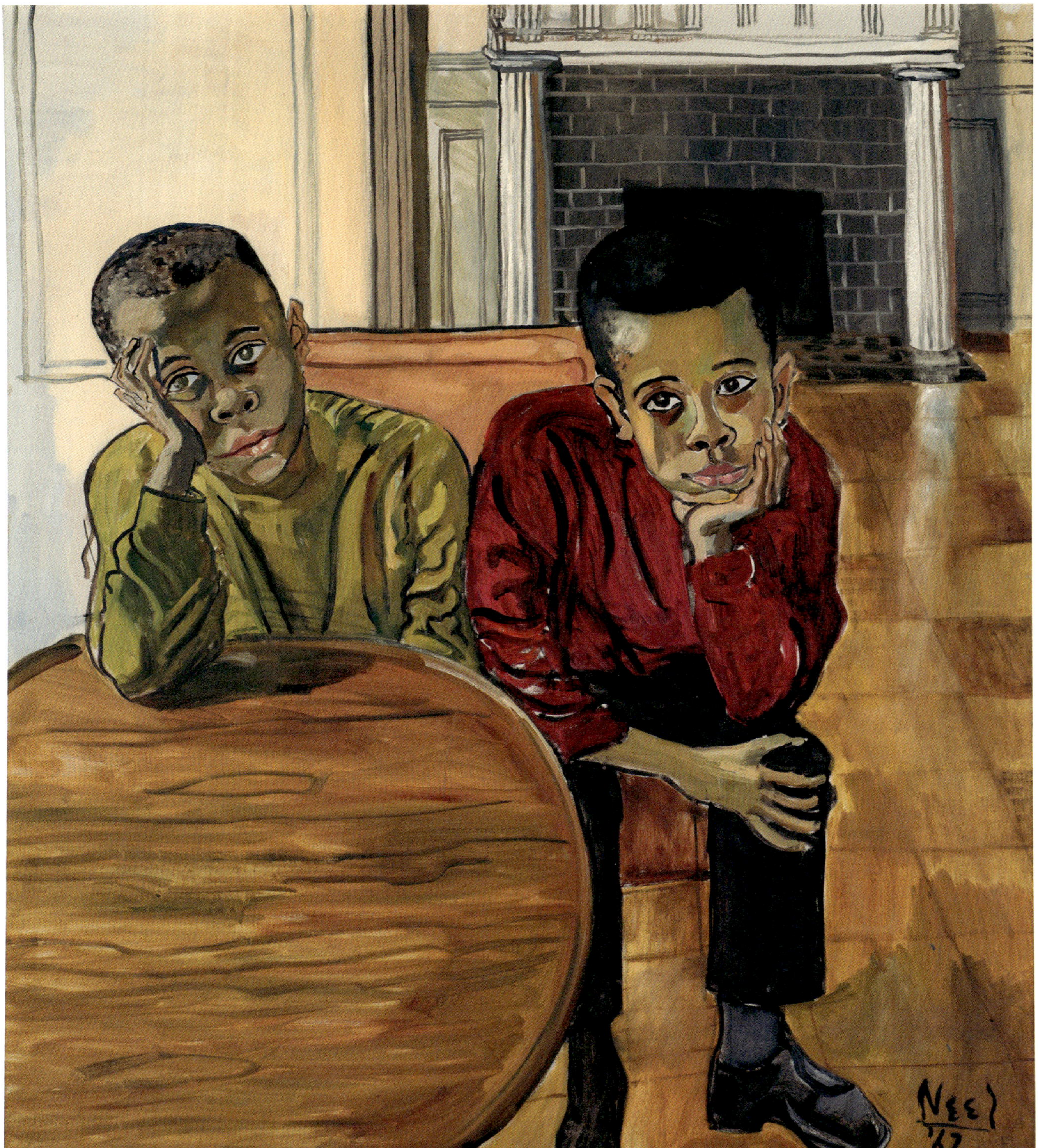




**The Black Boys** 1967

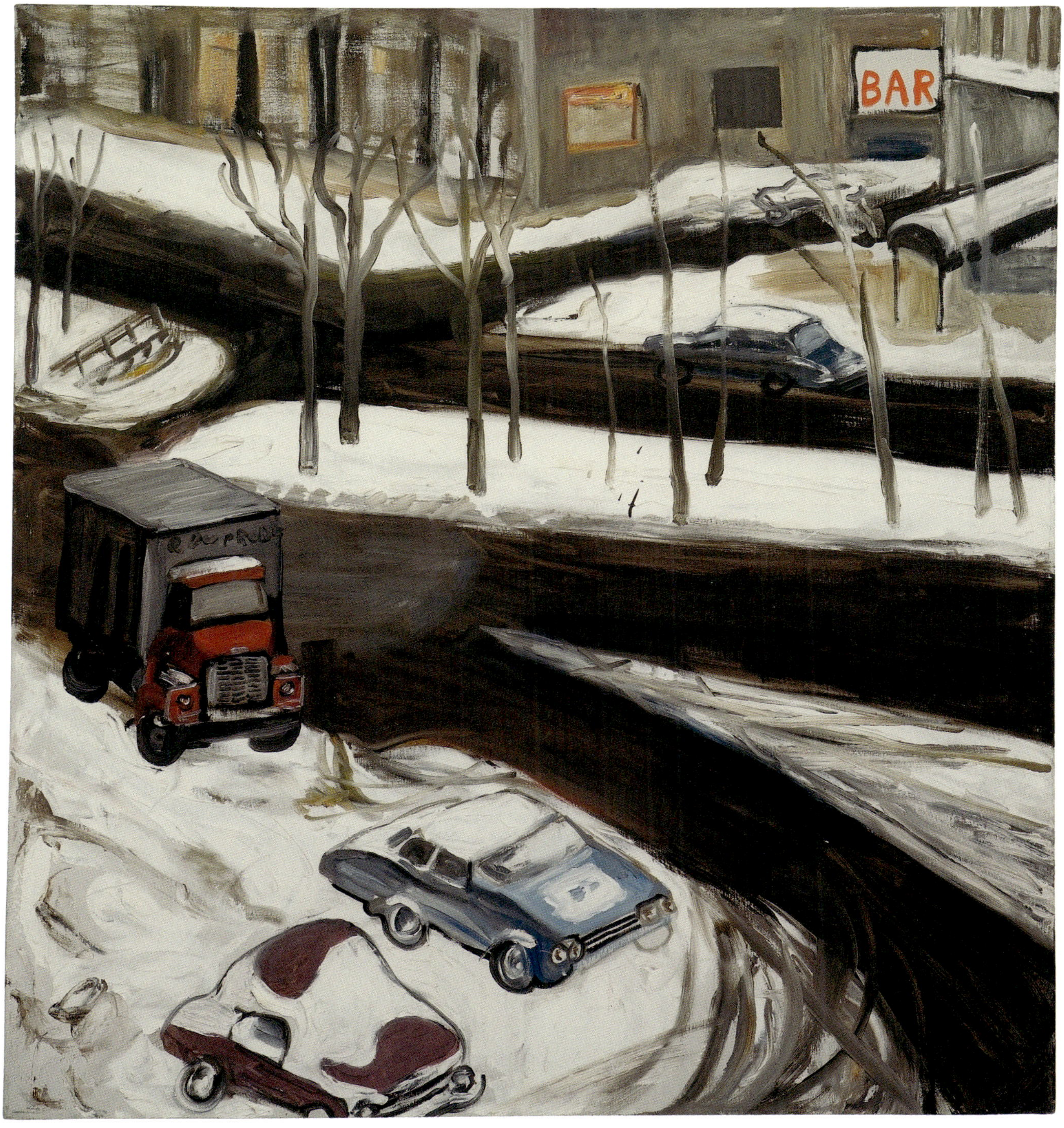


**Cityscape** 1968

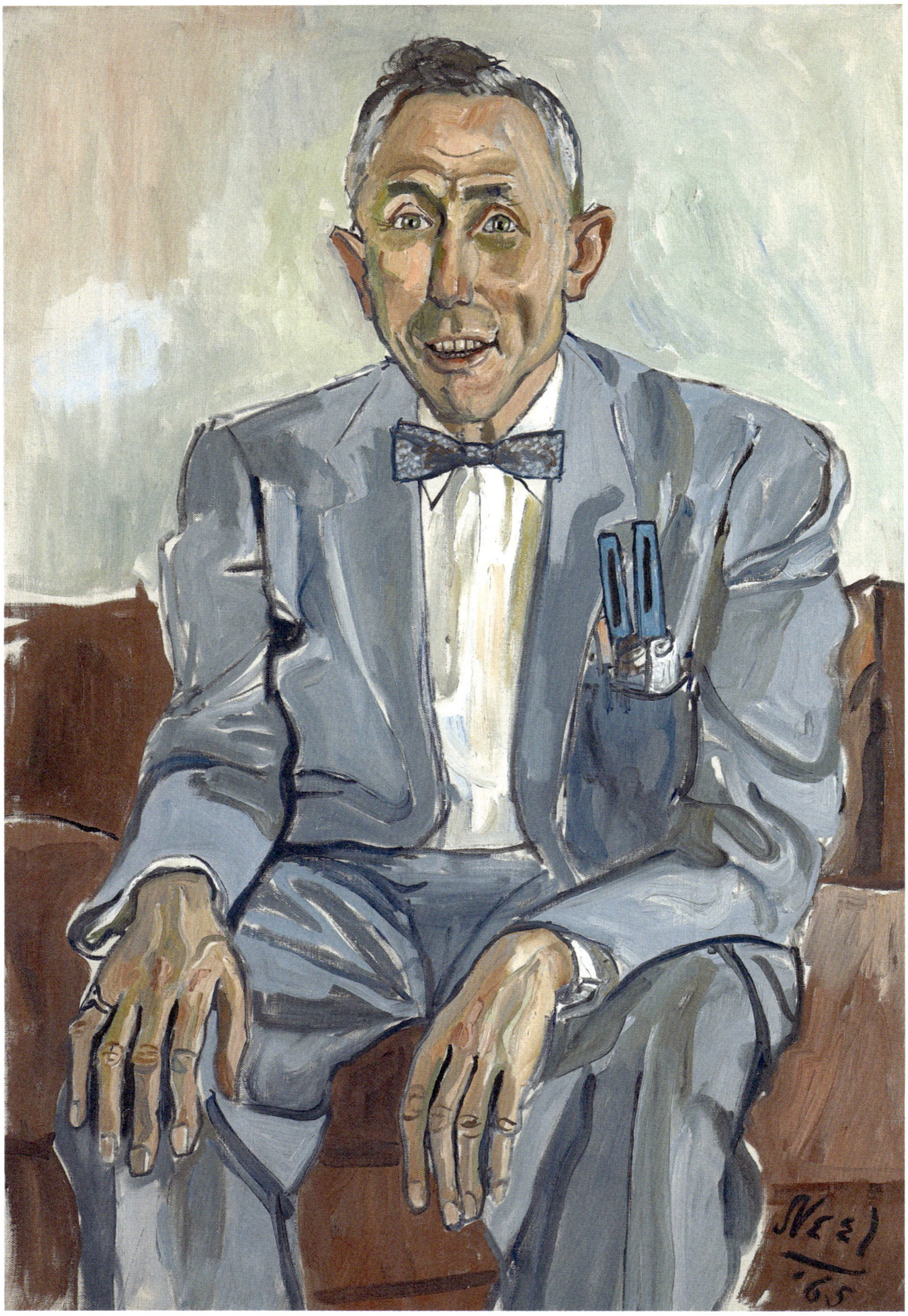




**Fuller Brush Man** 1965

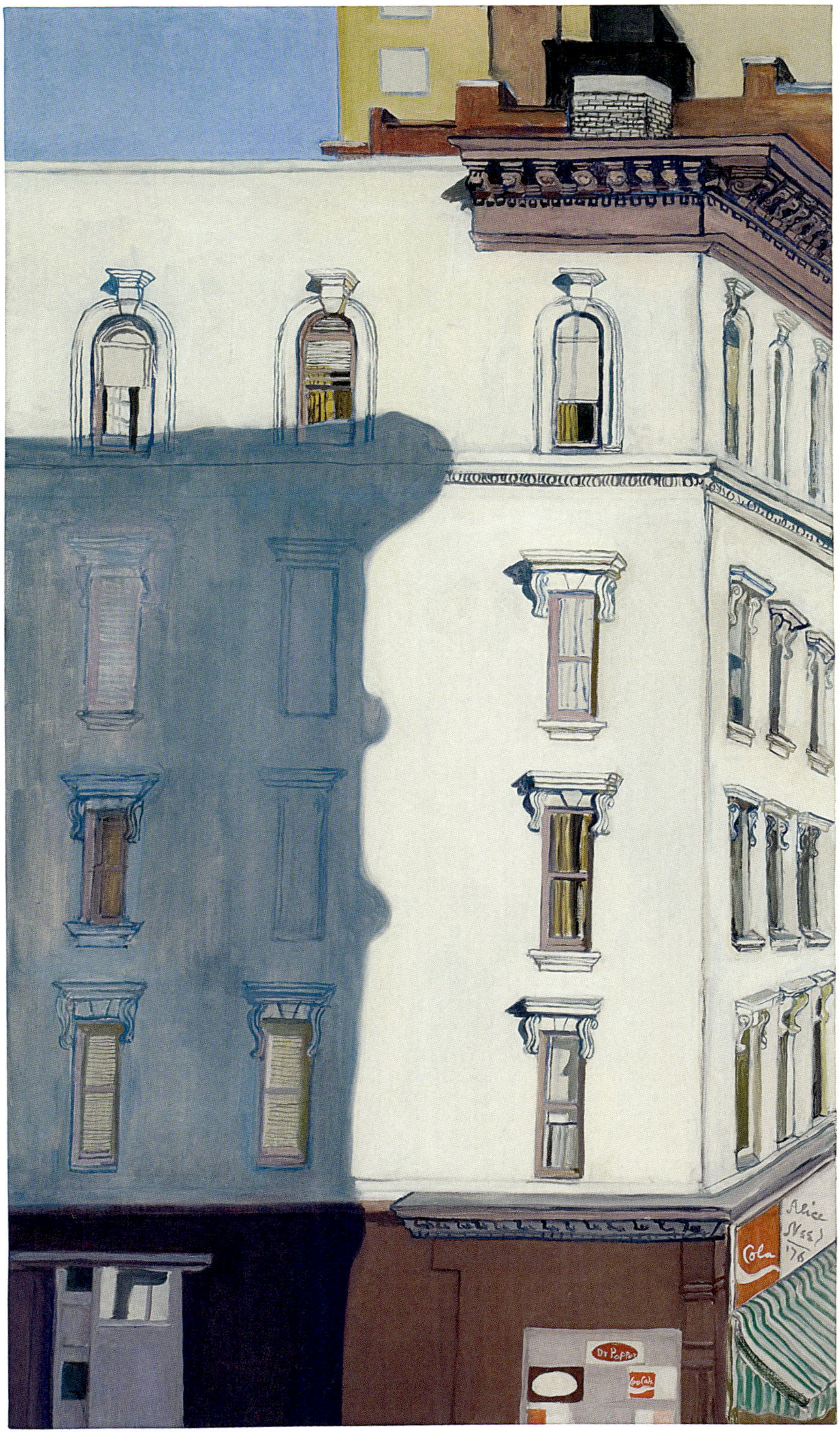


**107th and Broadway** 1976

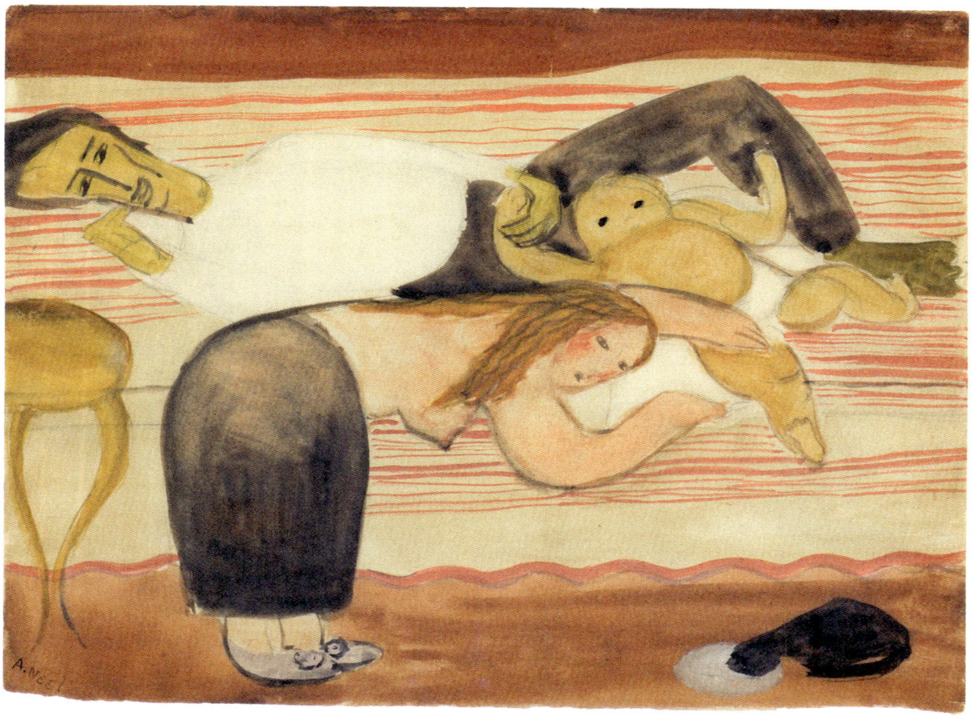



**The Family** 1927

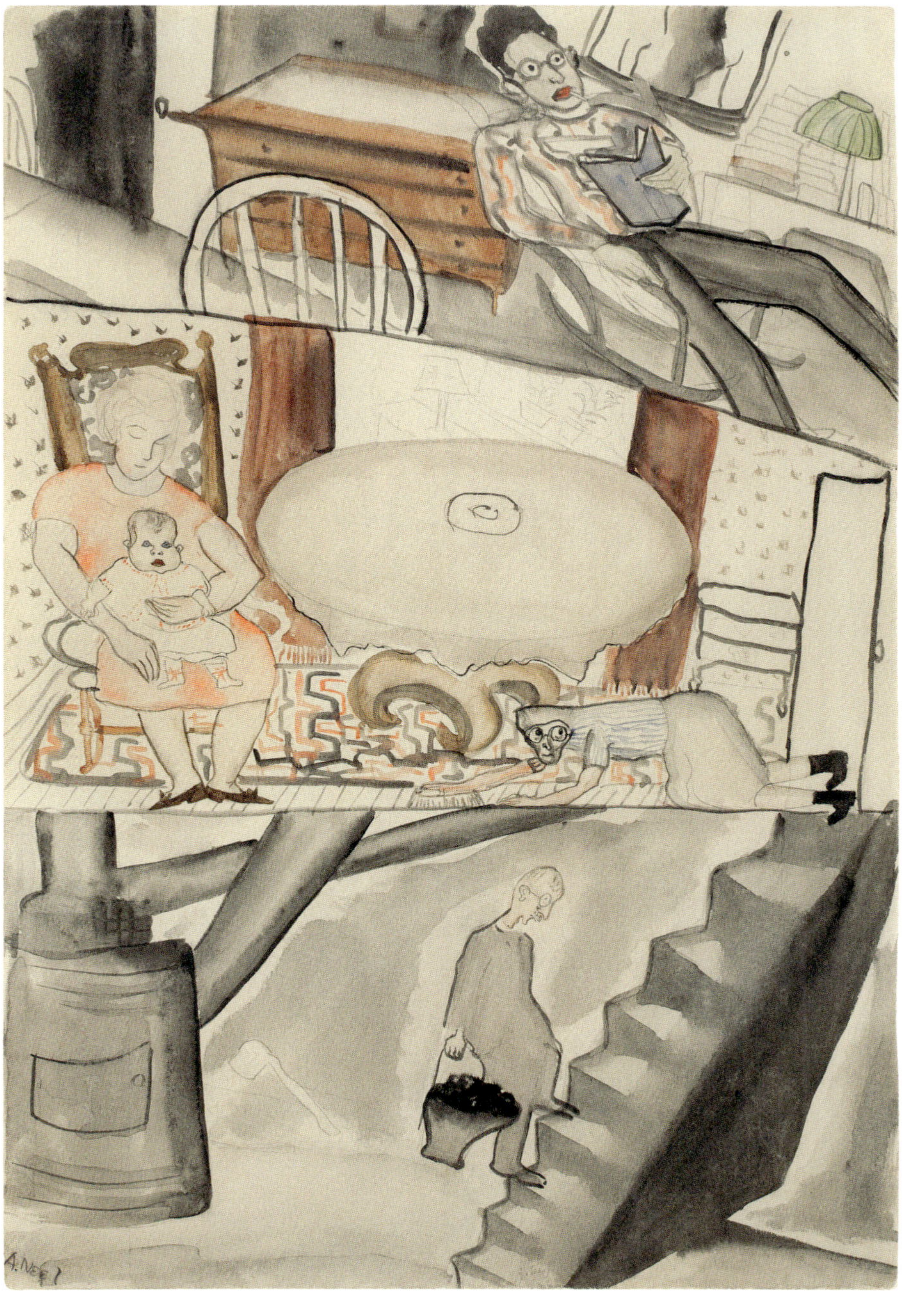

**The Family** 1927

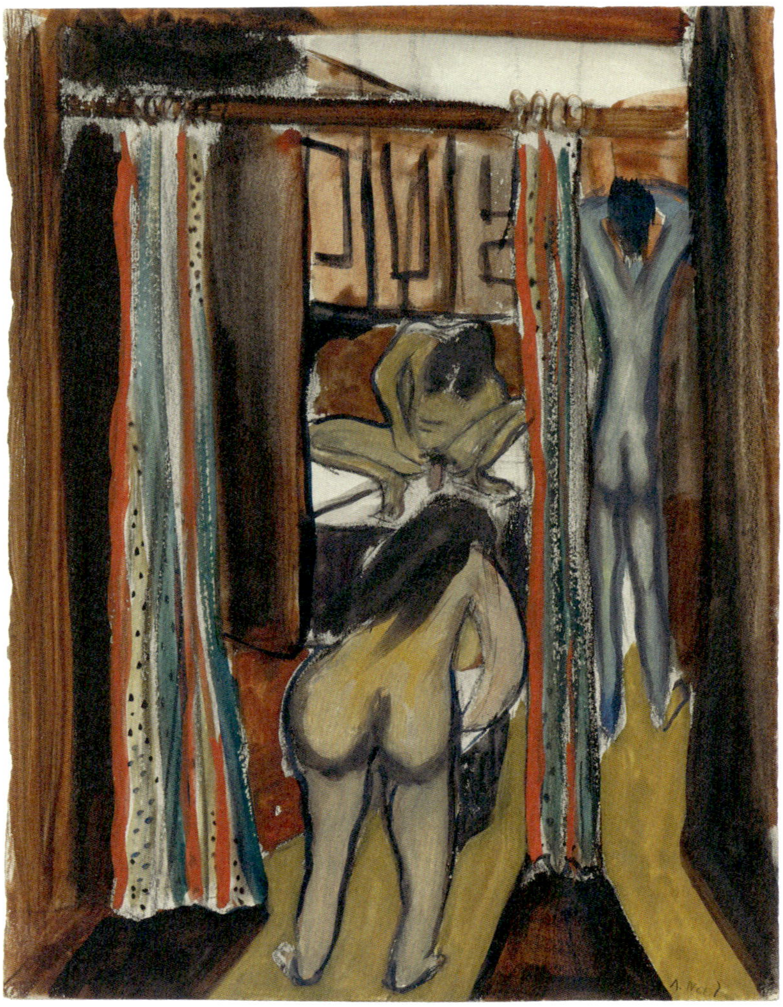



**Bathing in a Furnished Room** 1927

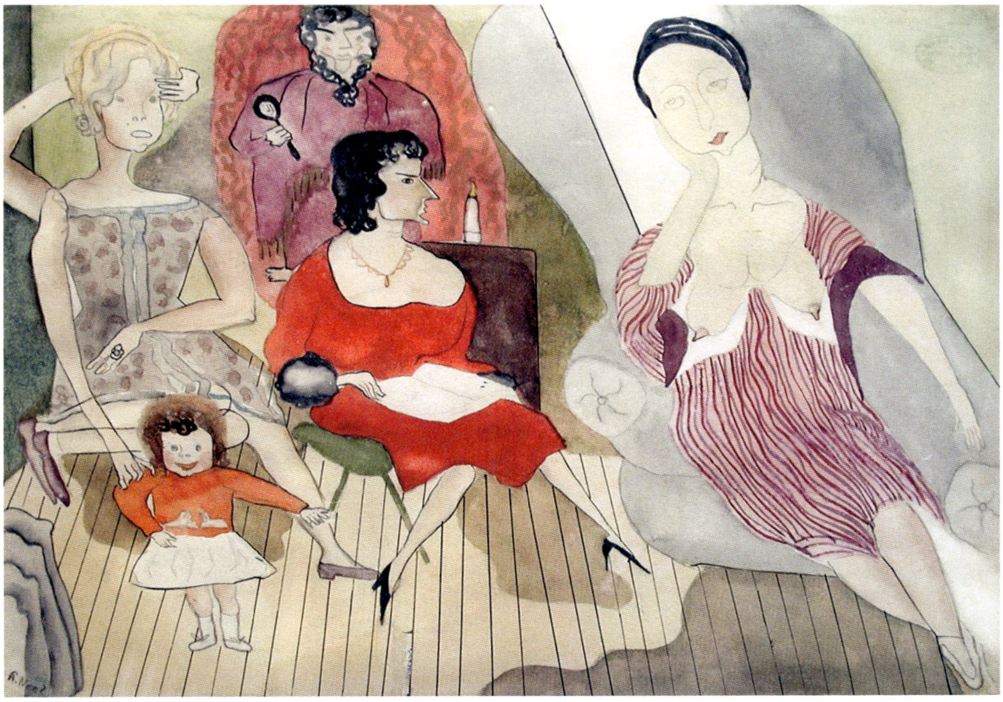

**The Intellectual** 1929

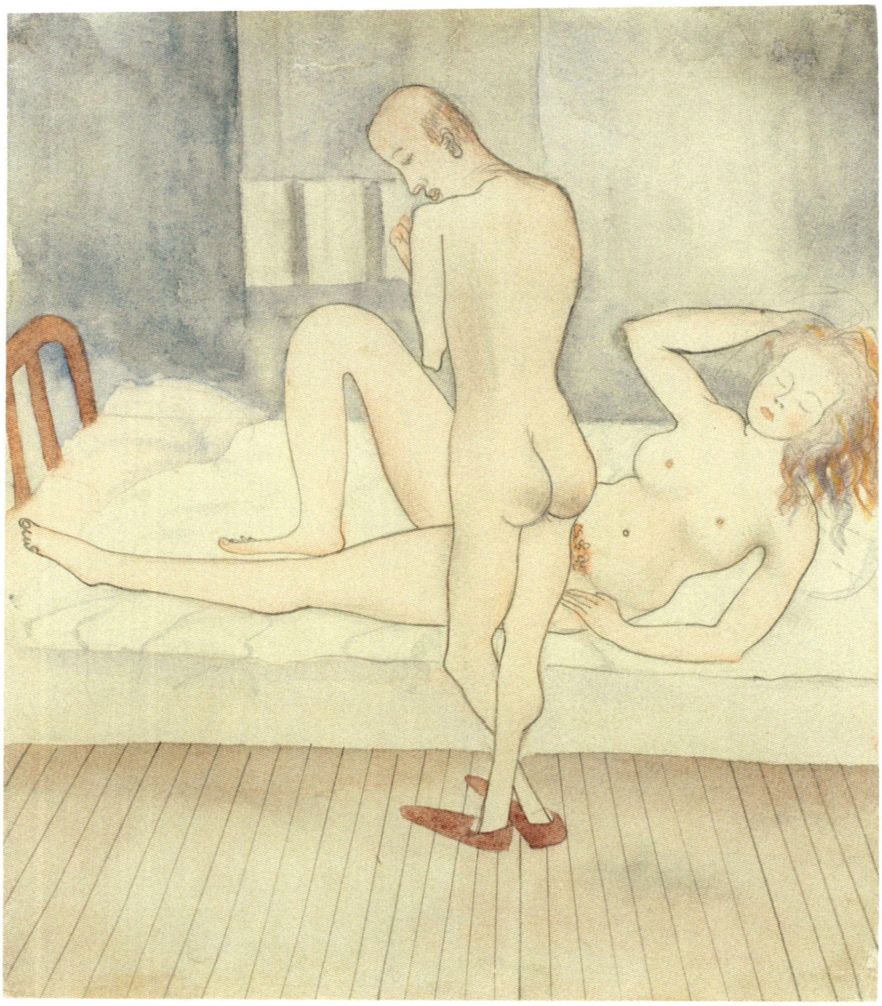



**Alienation** 1935

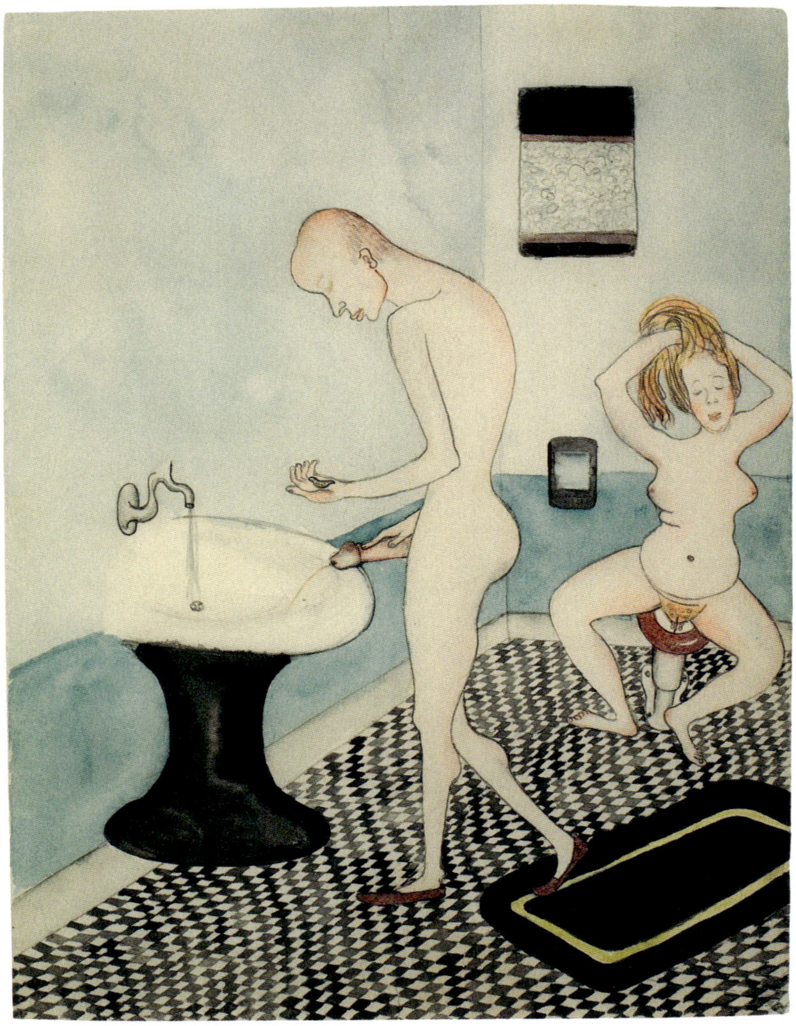

Untitled (Alice Neel and John Rothschild in the Bathroom) 1935

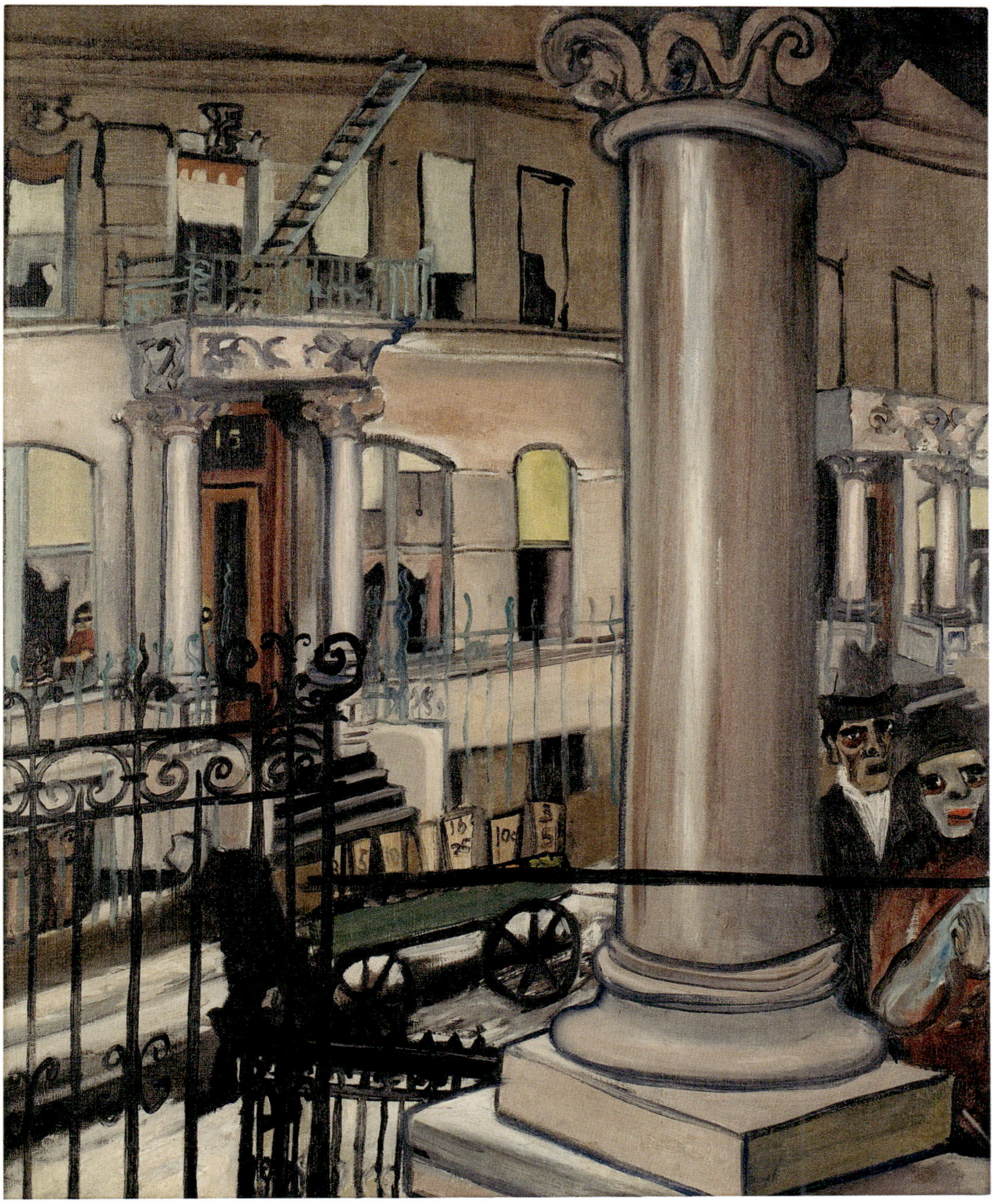

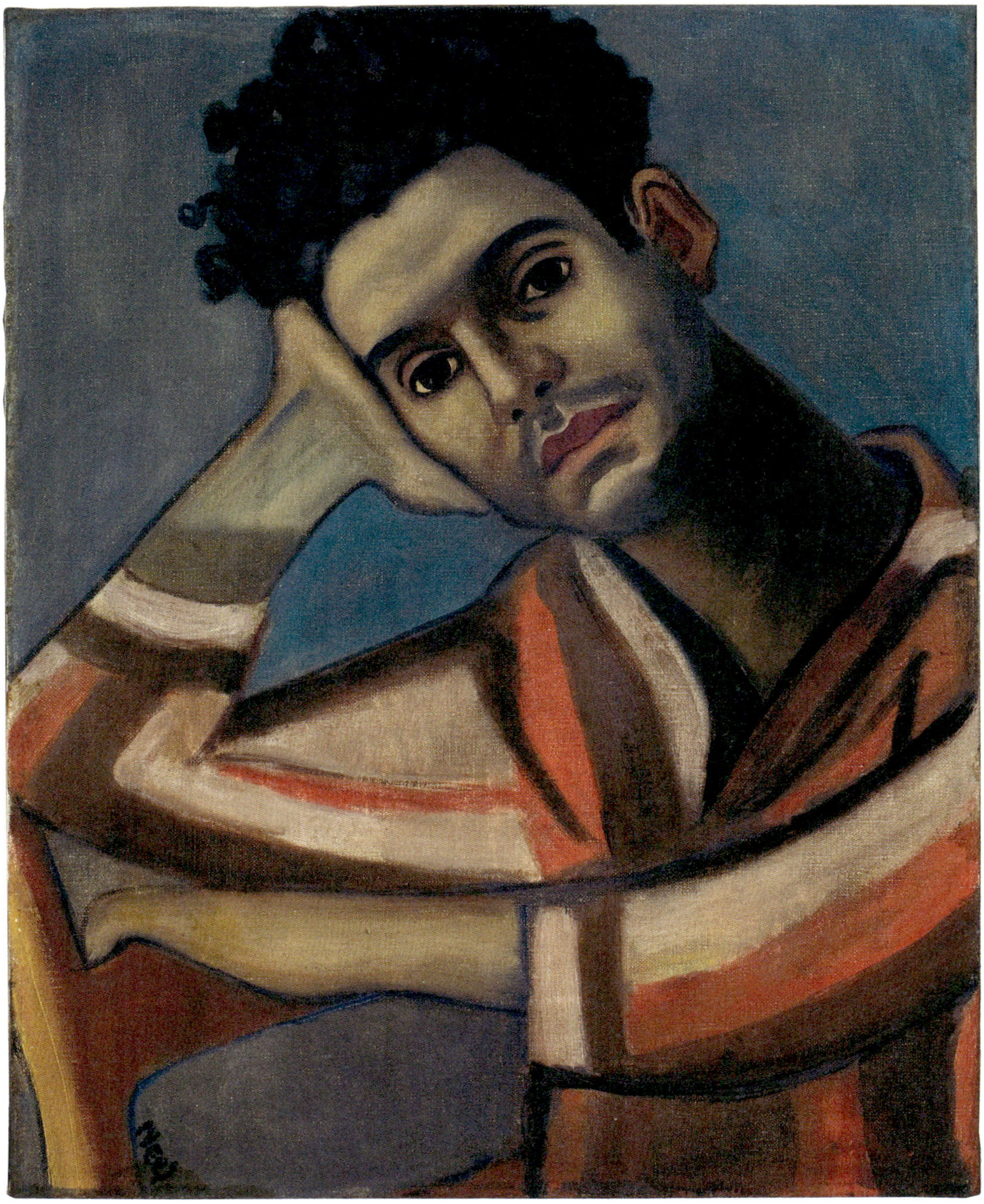



**José** 1936

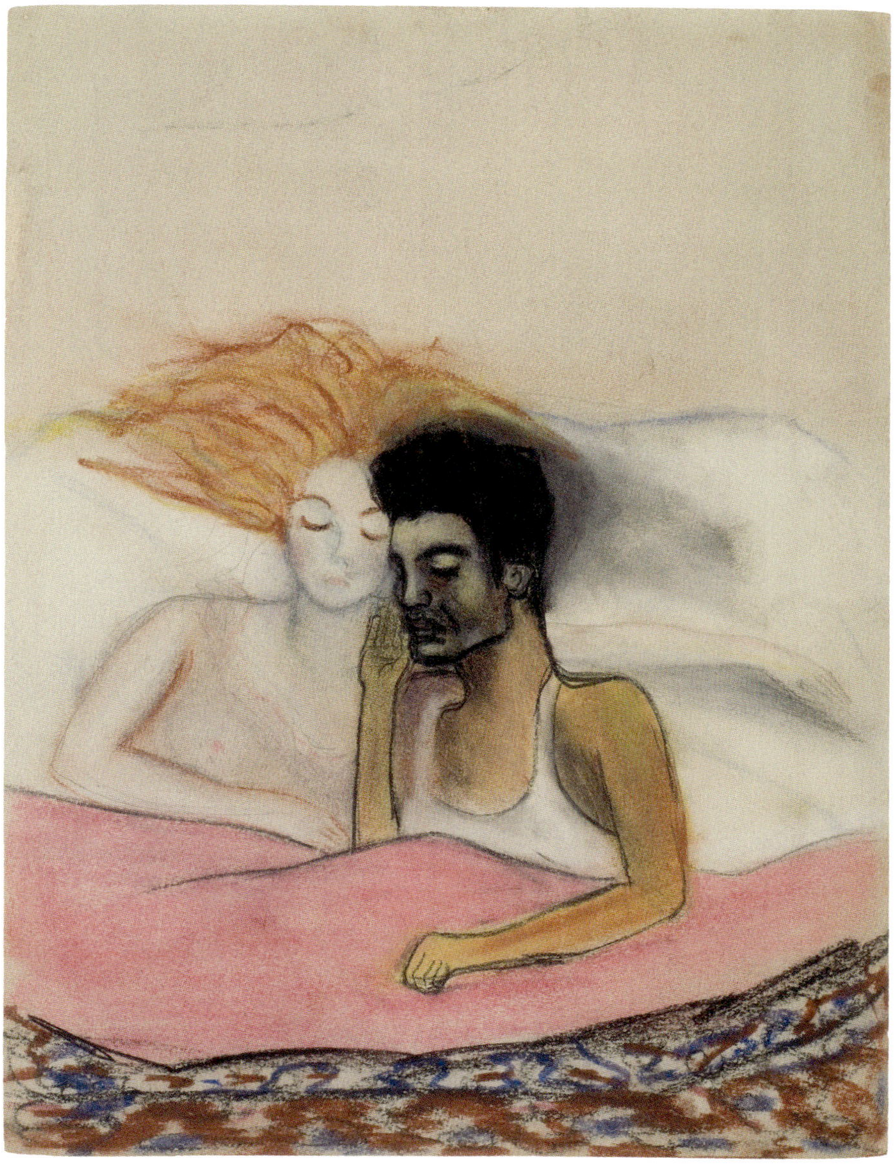

**Alice and José** 1938

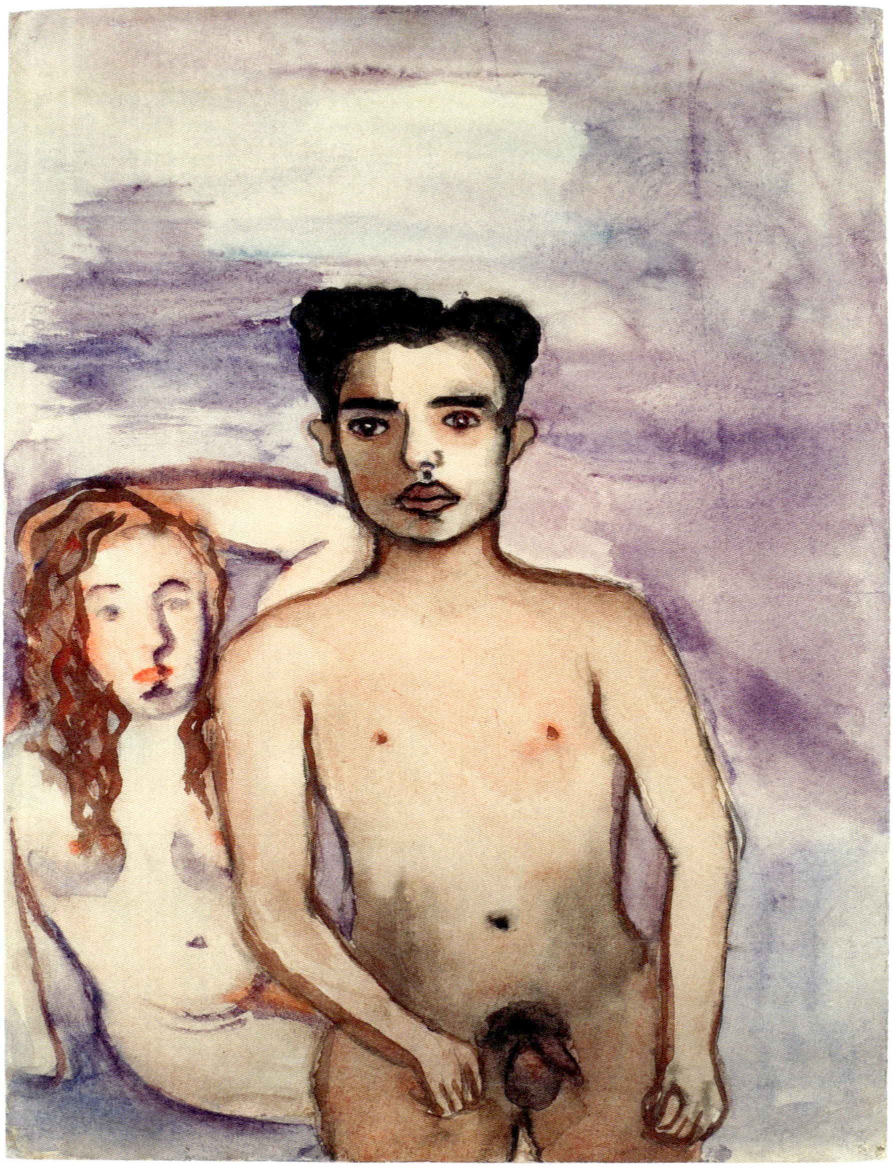

 **Untitled (Alice and José)** ca. 1935

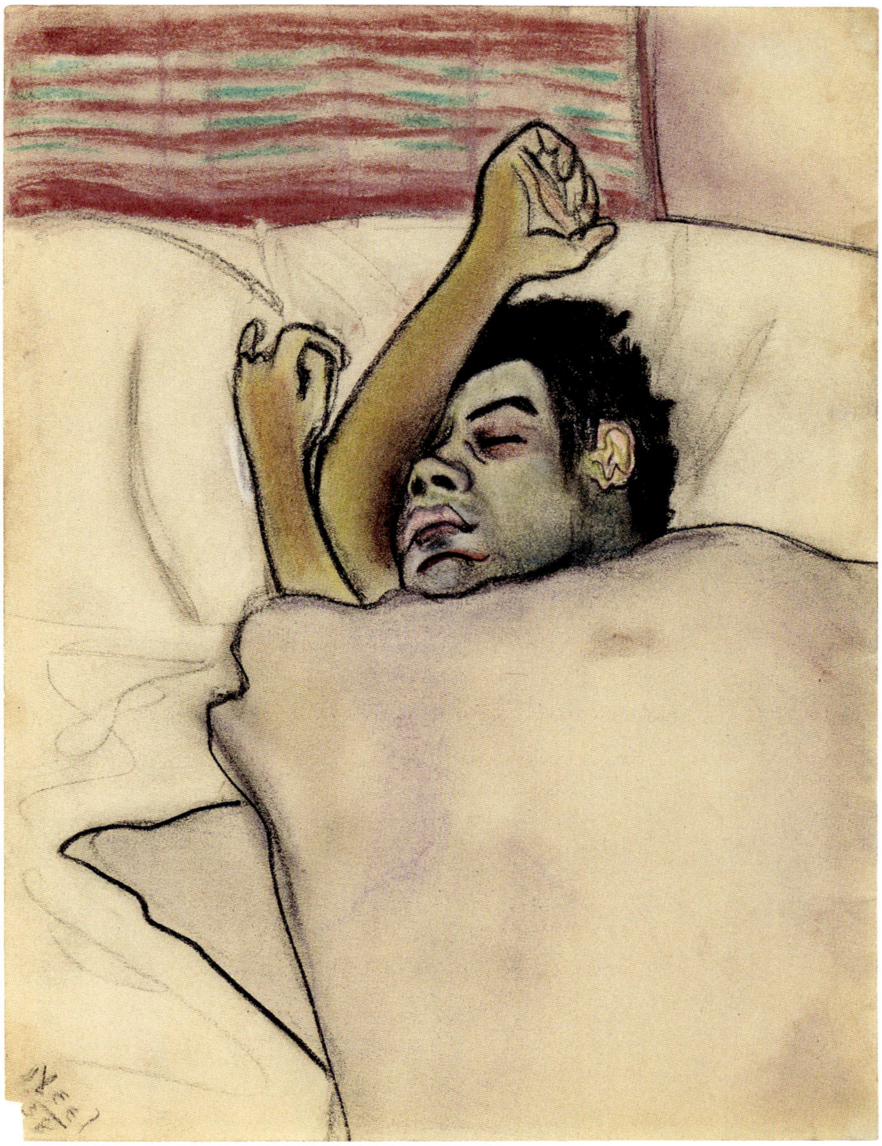

**José Asleep** 1938

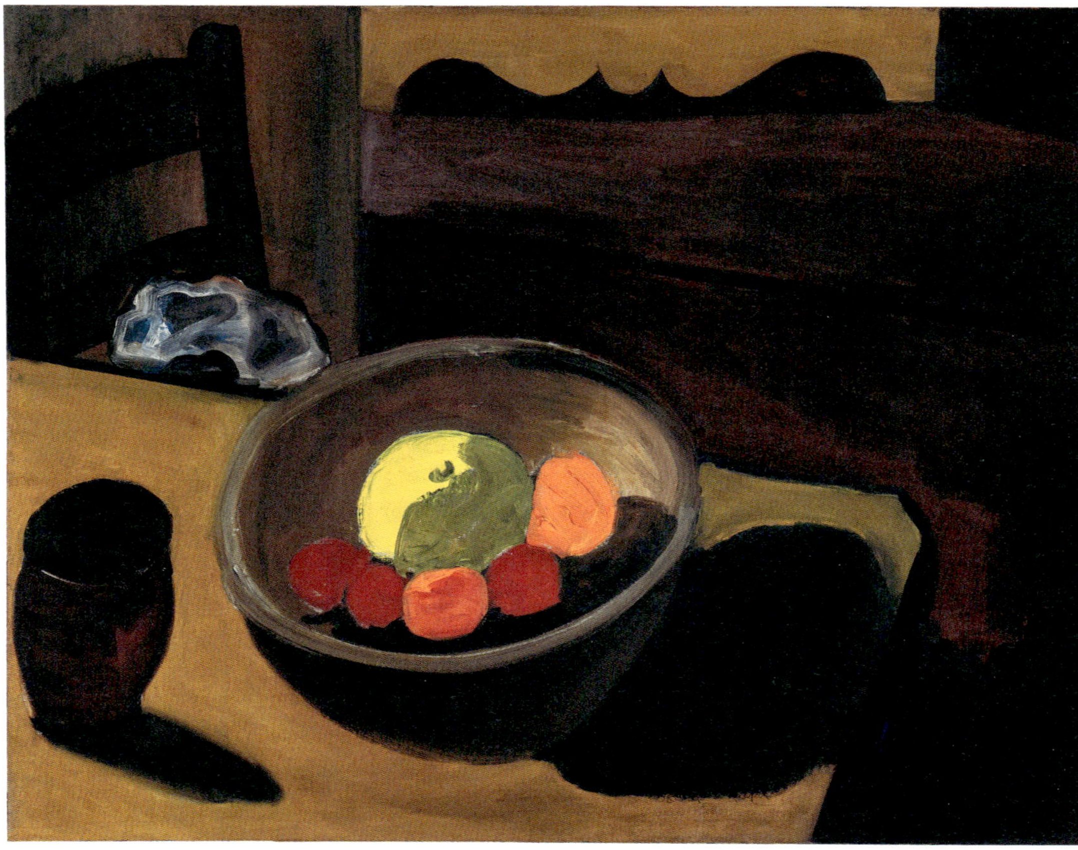

 **Still Life with Fruit** 1940

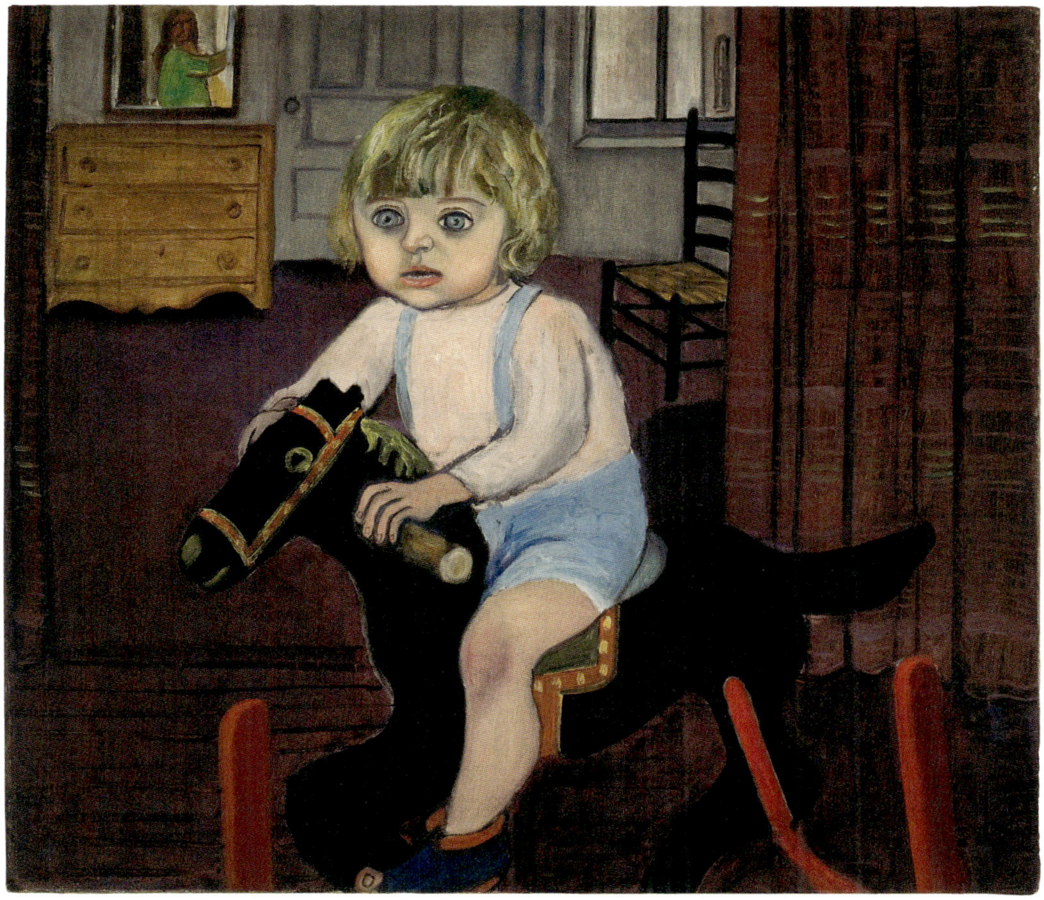

**Hartley on the Rocking Horse** 1943

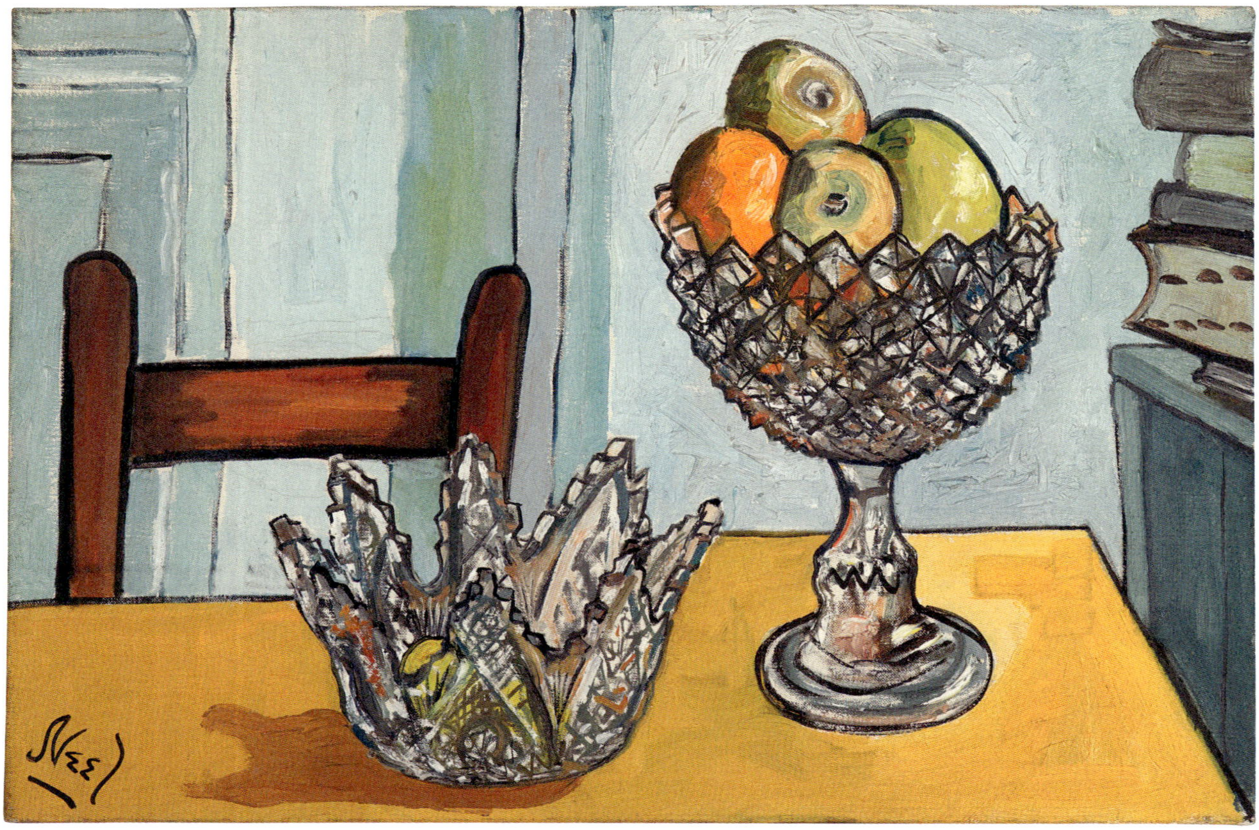



**Cut Glass with Fruit** 1952

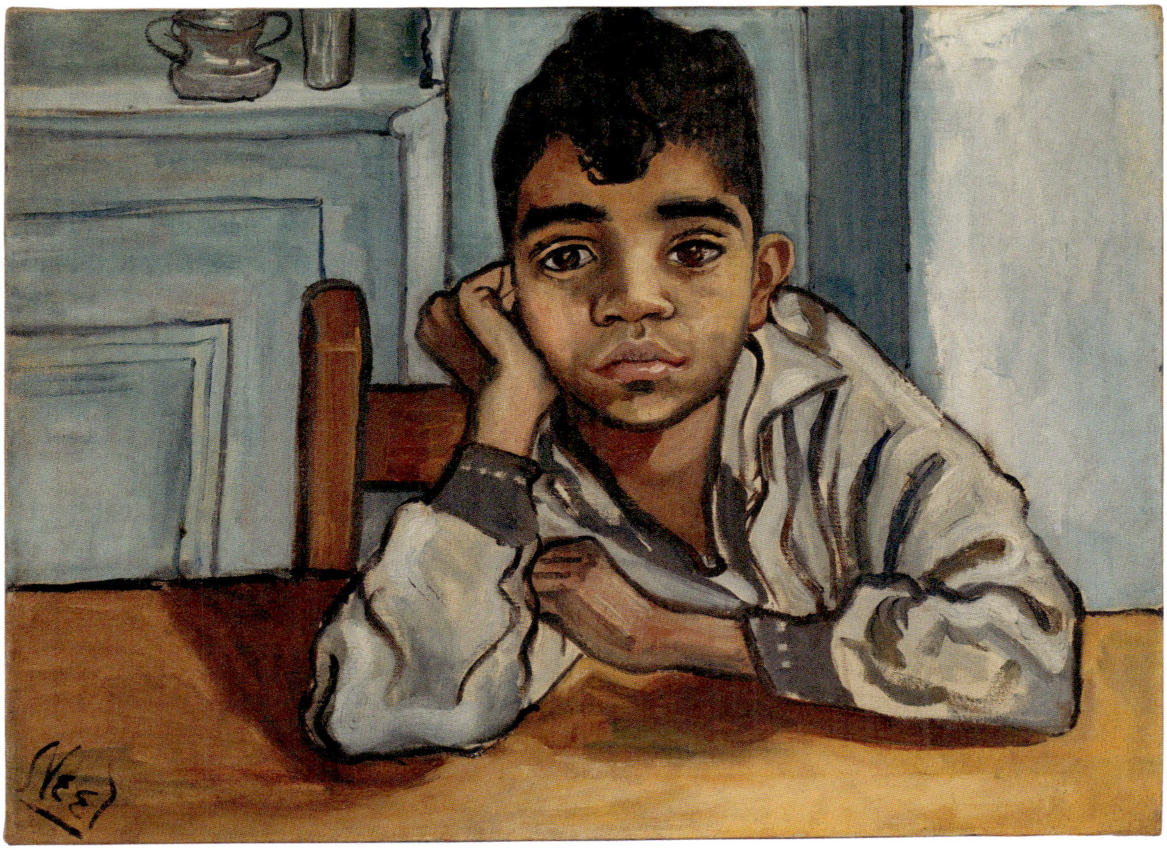

**A Spanish Boy** 1955

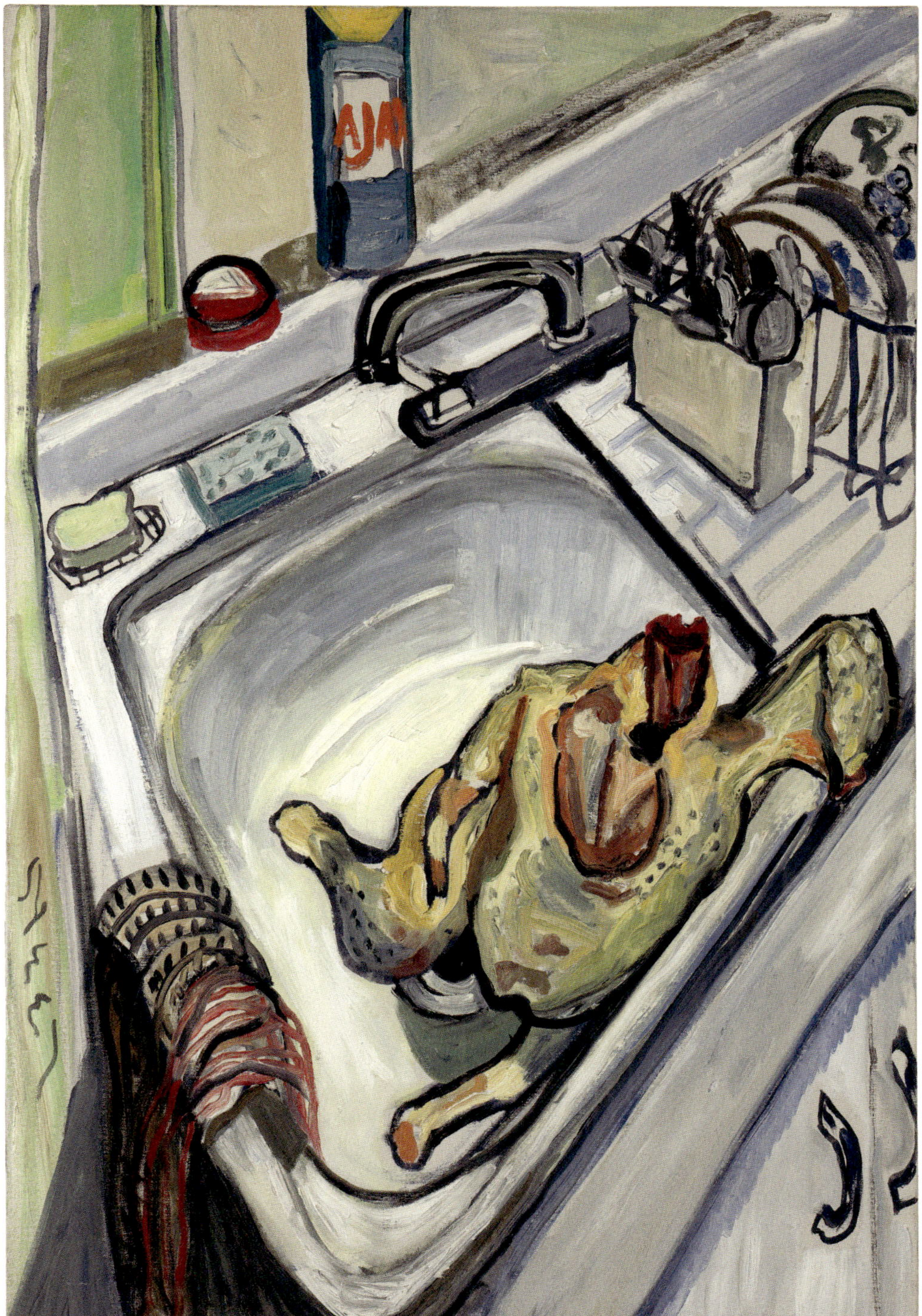

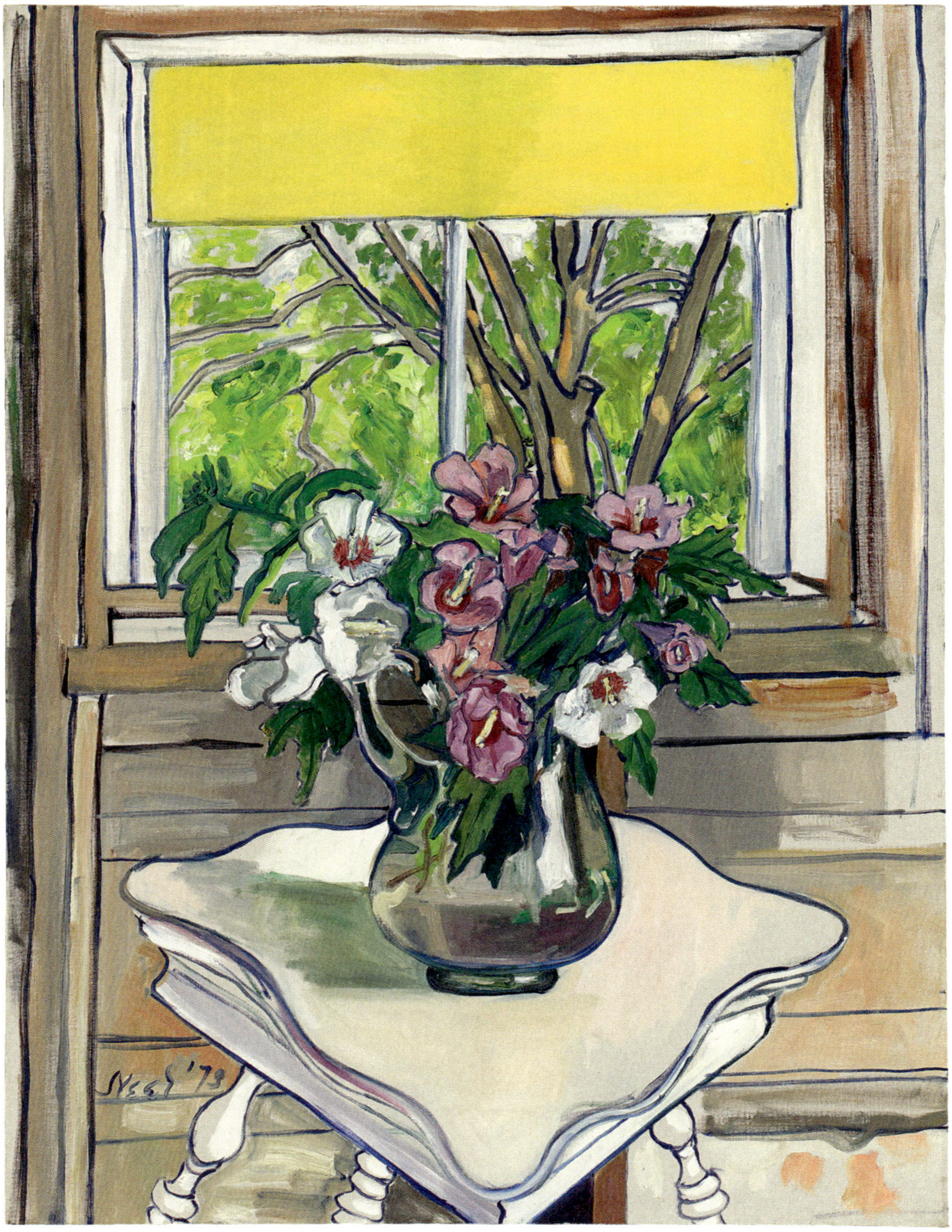

**Still Life, Rose of Sharon** 1973

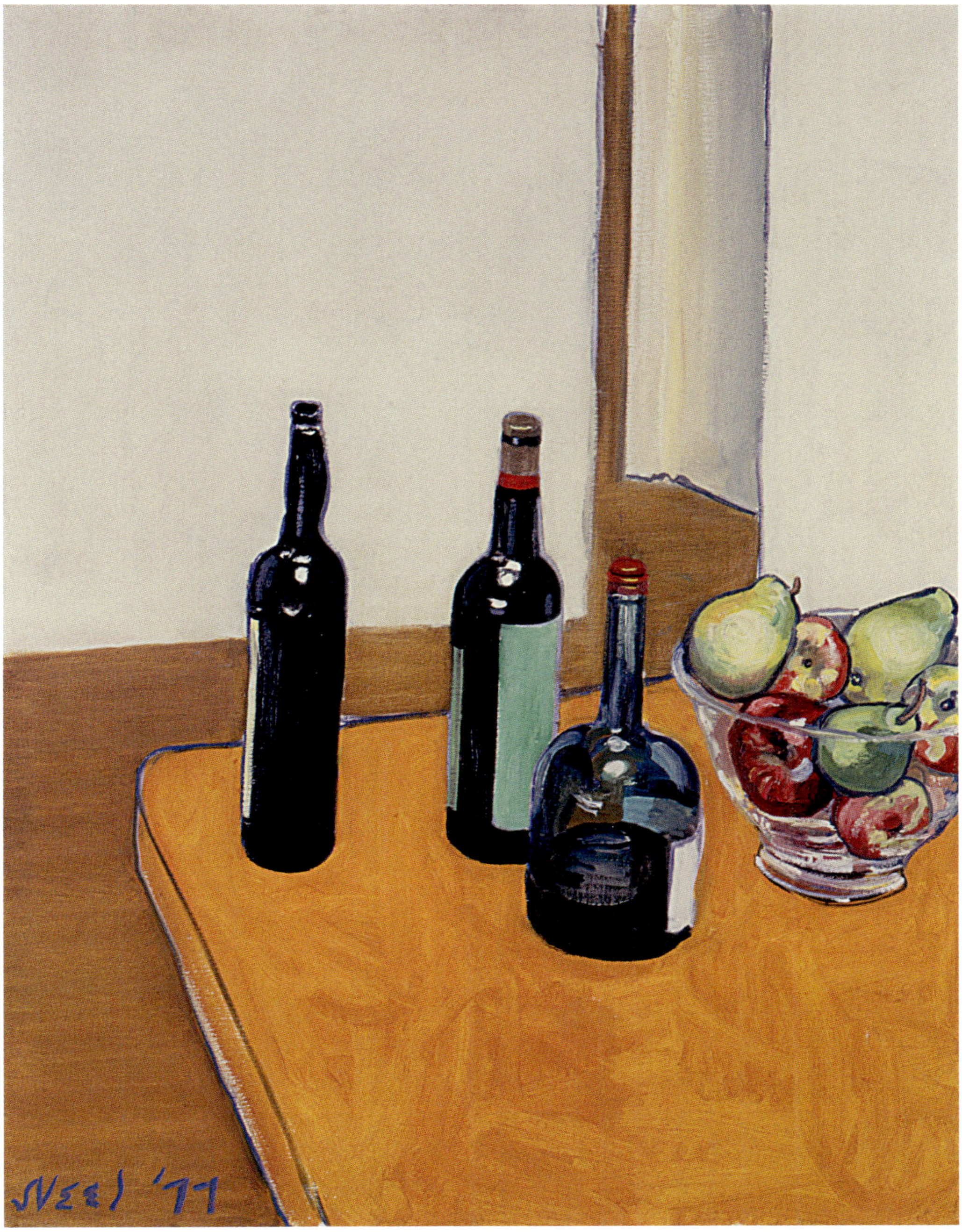

**Black Bottles** 1977

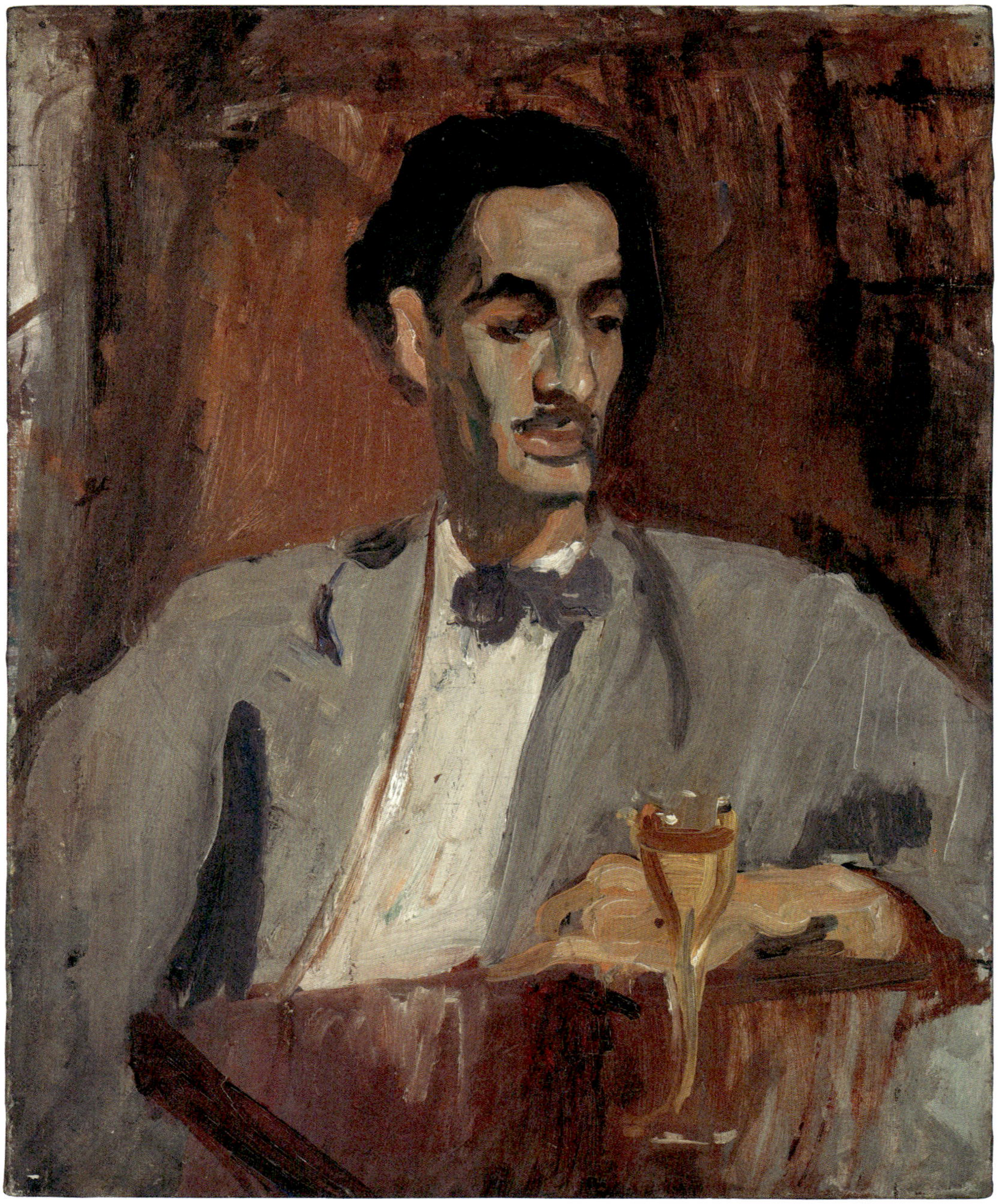

 **Carlos Enríquez** 1926

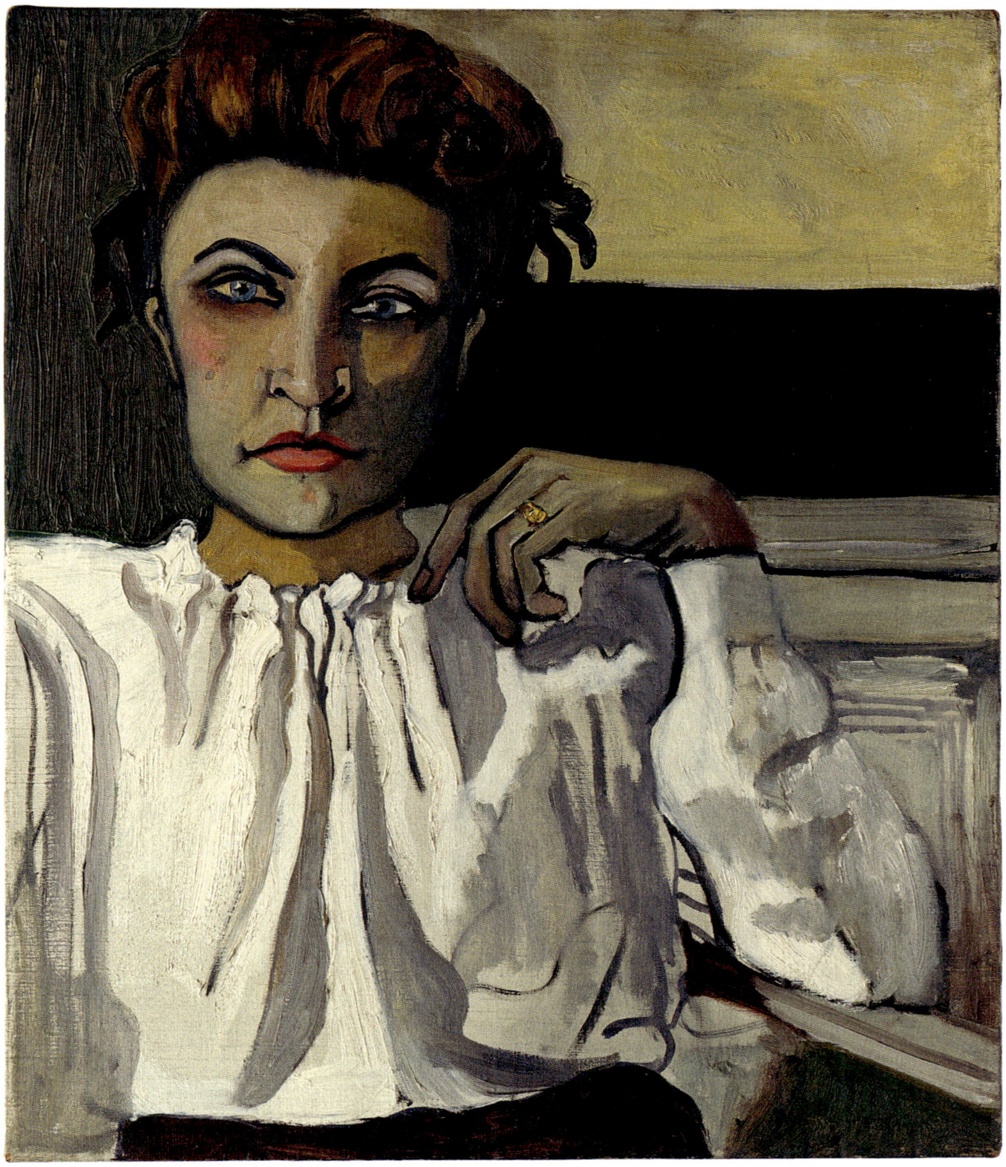

**Elenka** 1936

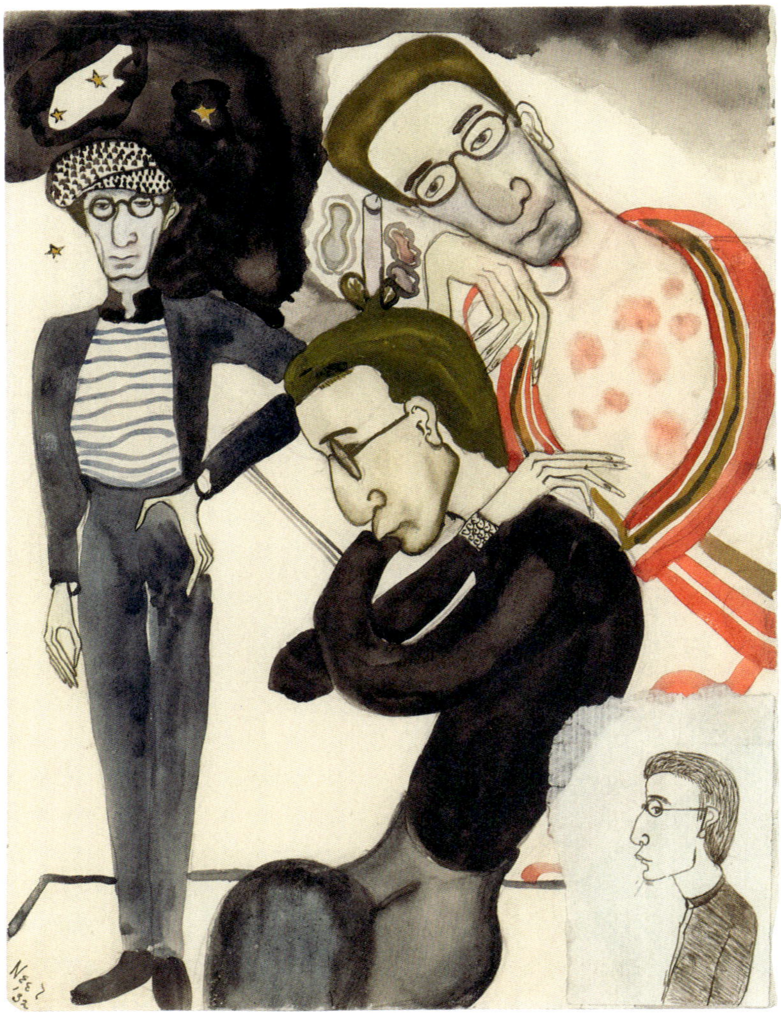

 **Christopher Lazare** 1932

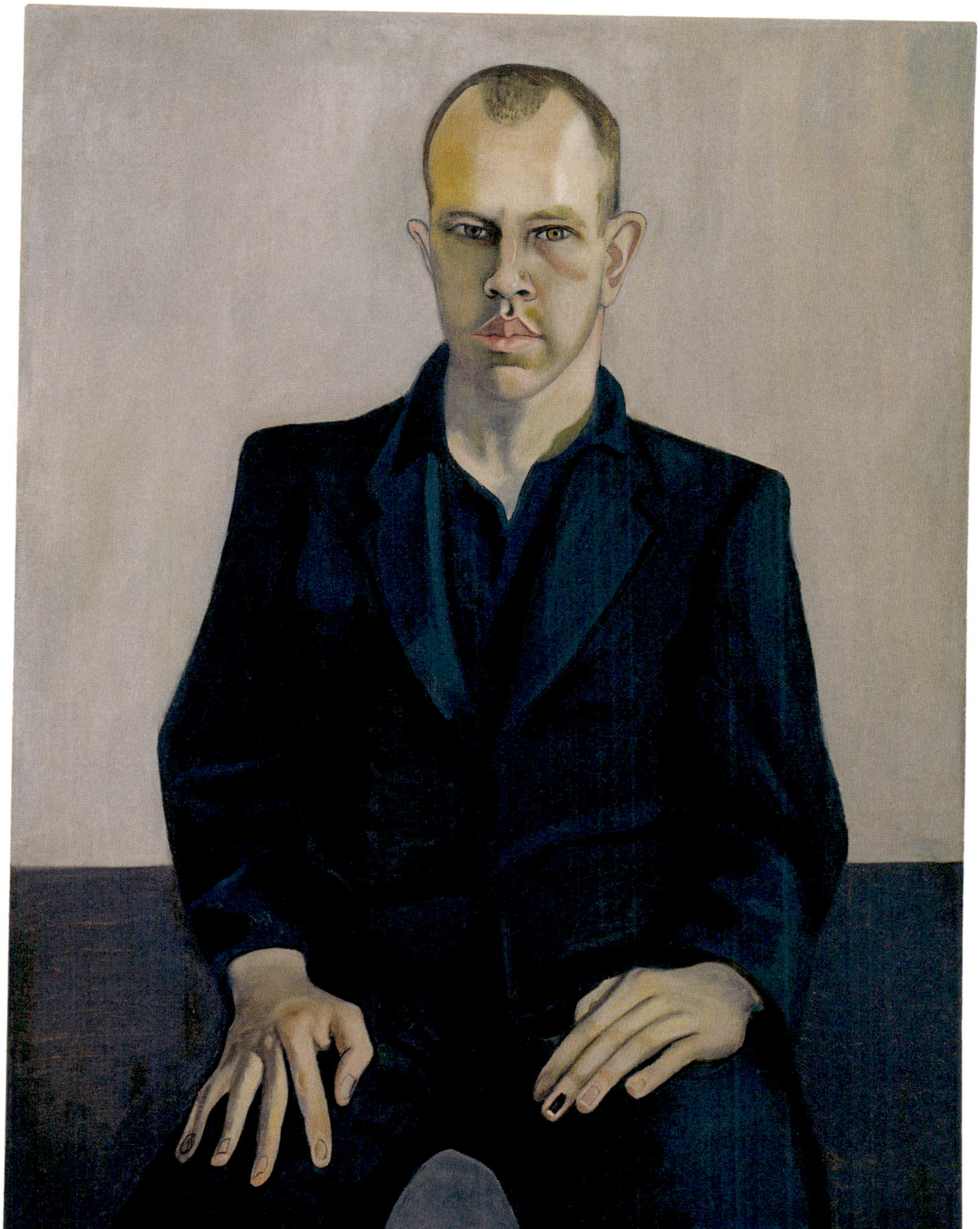

**Max White** 1935

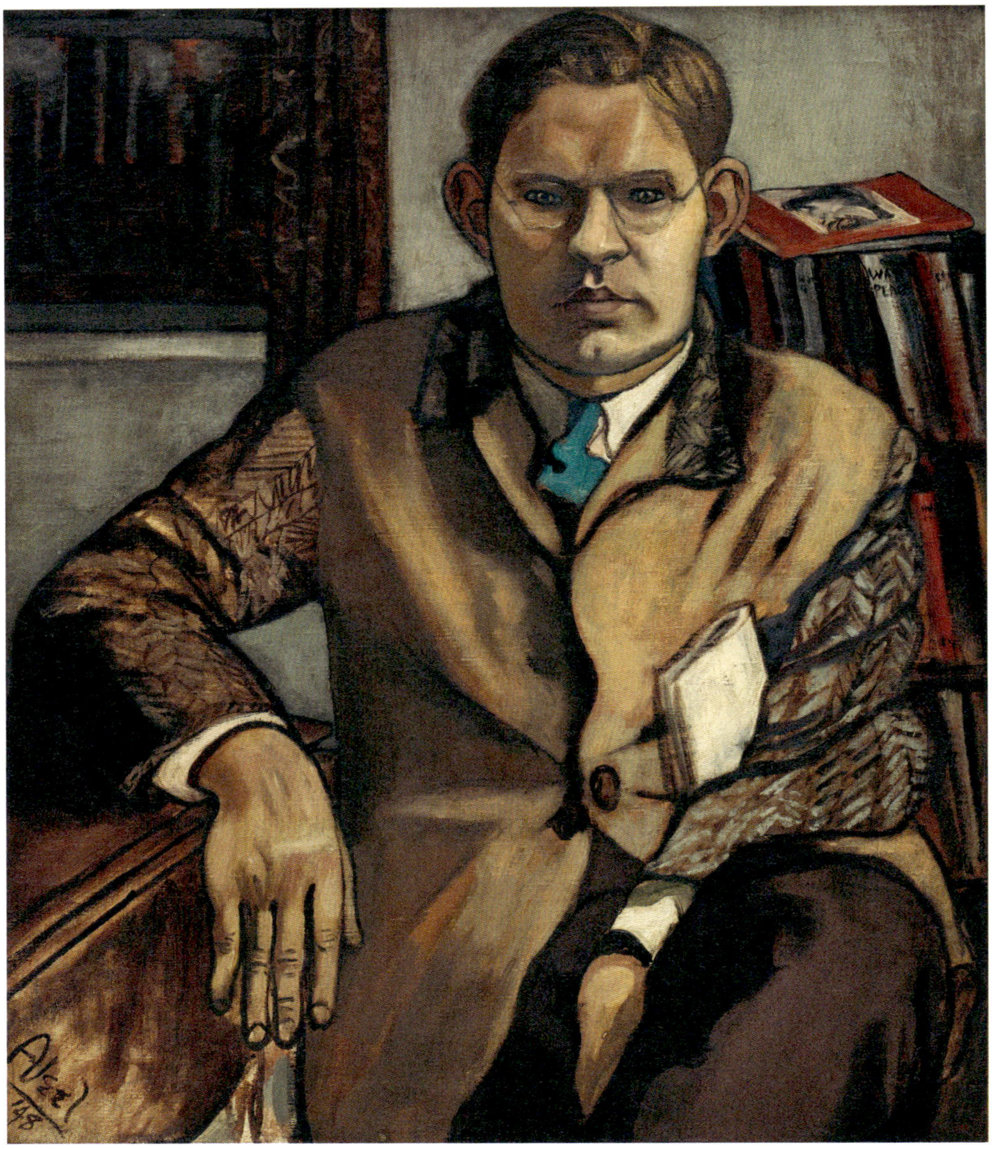

 **Phillip Bonosky** 1948

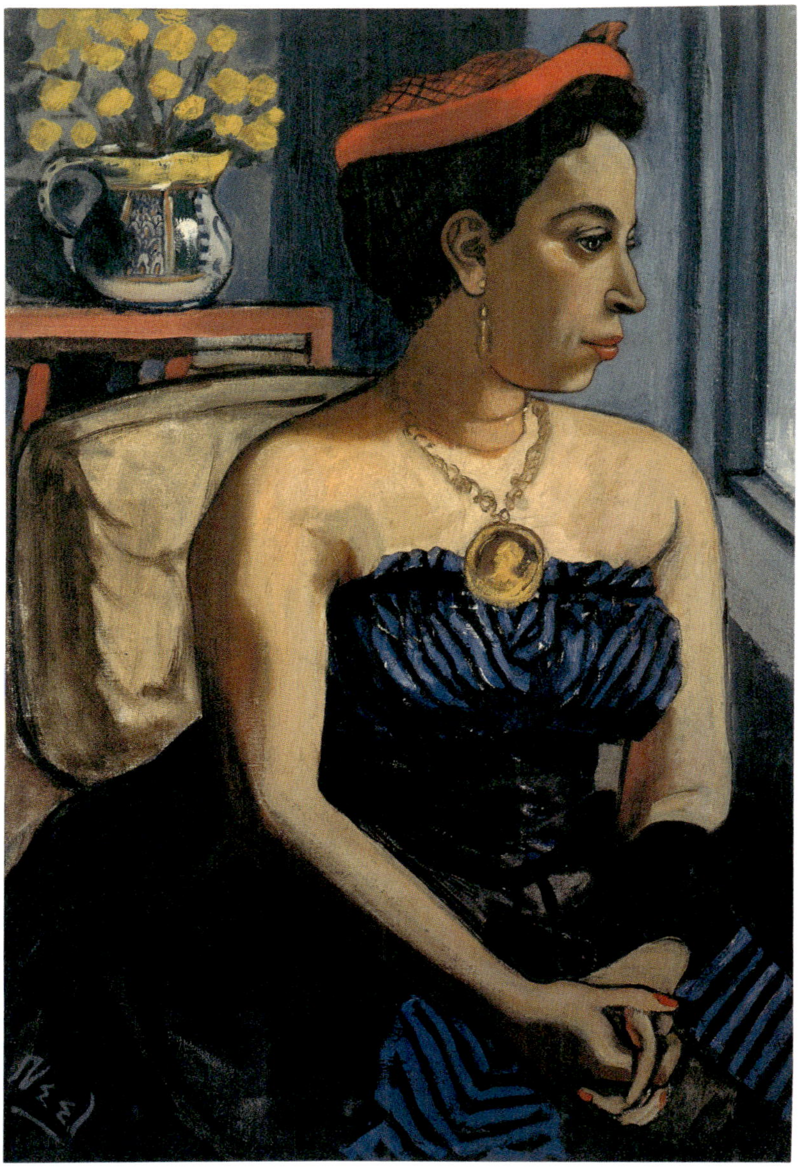

**Alice Childress** 1950

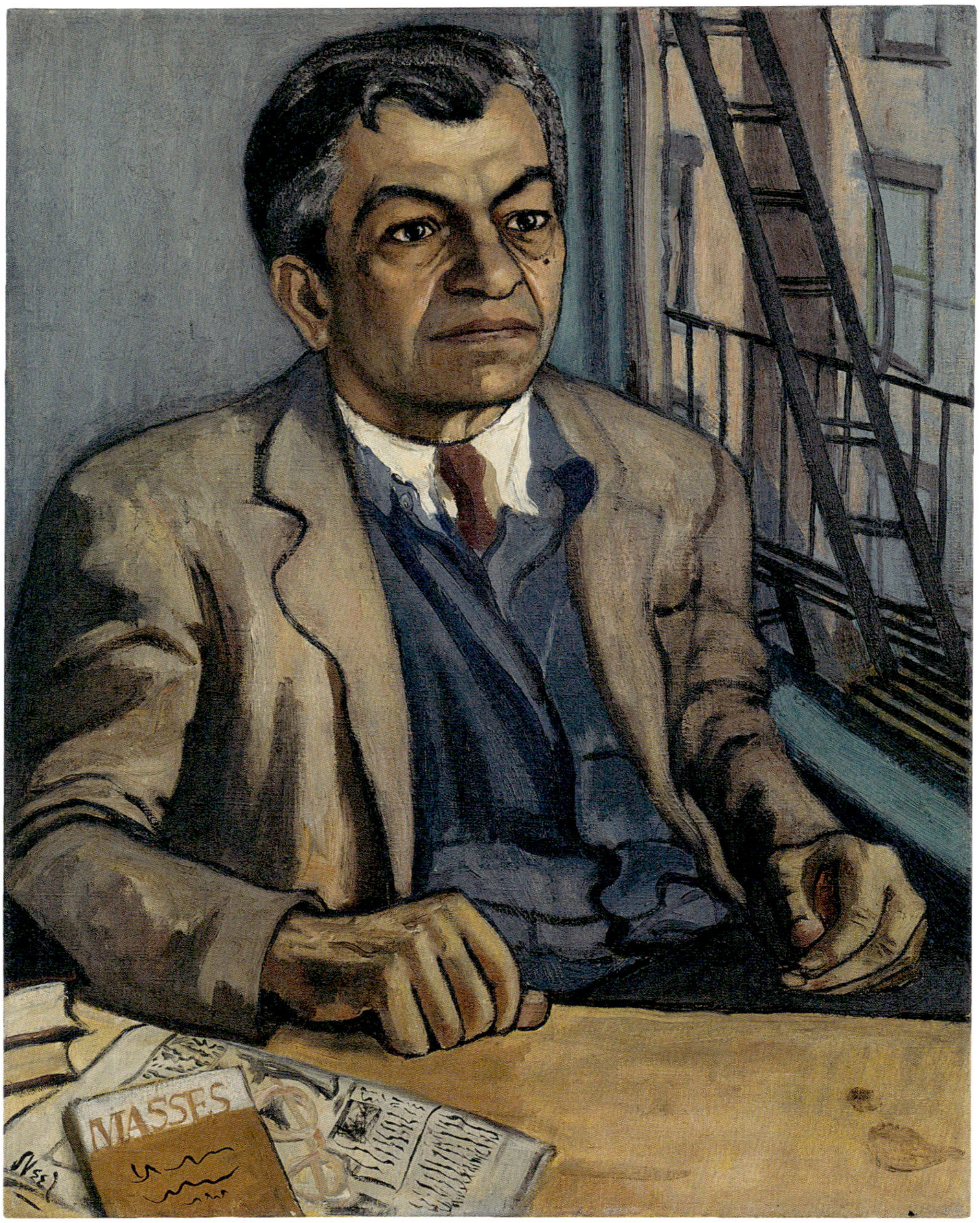


 **Mike Gold** 1952

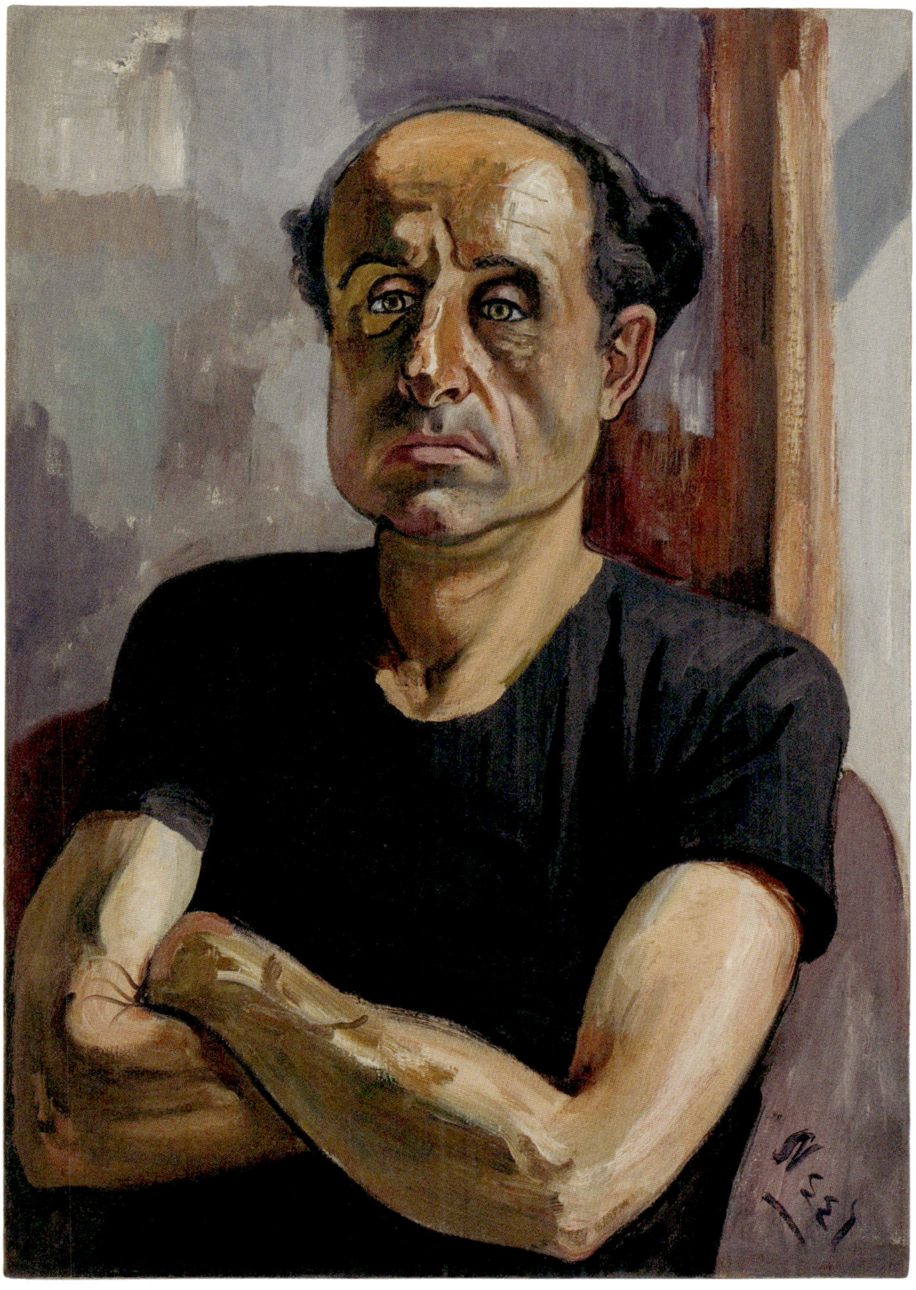

**Sam** 1958

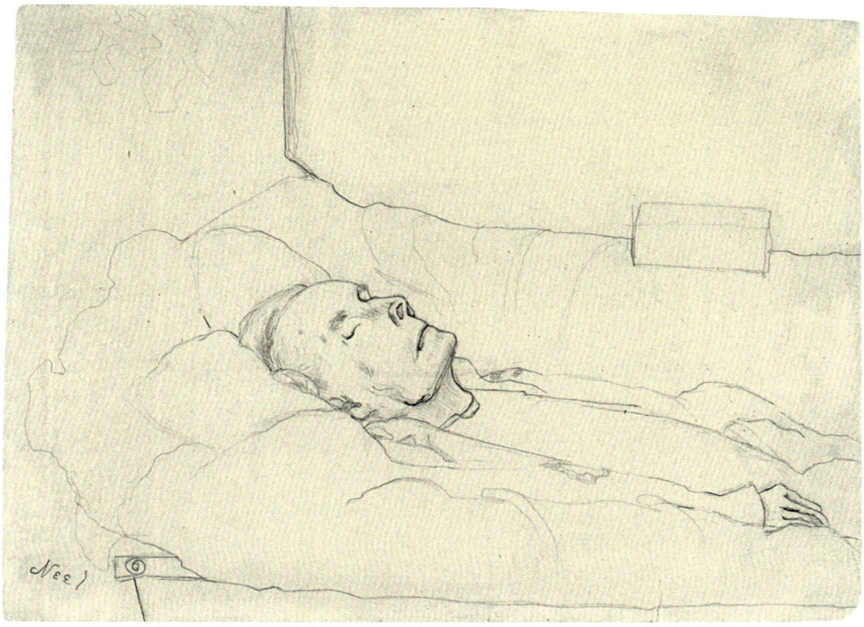


 **Death of Mother Bloor** 1951

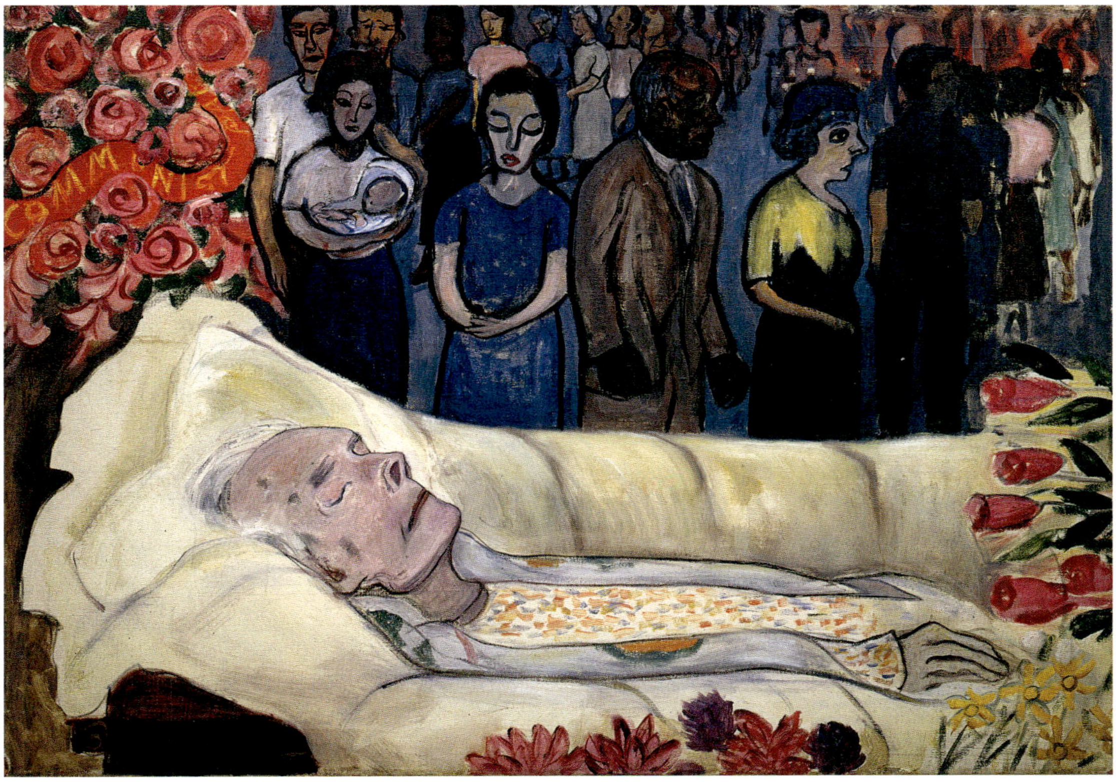

**Death of Mother Bloor** 1951

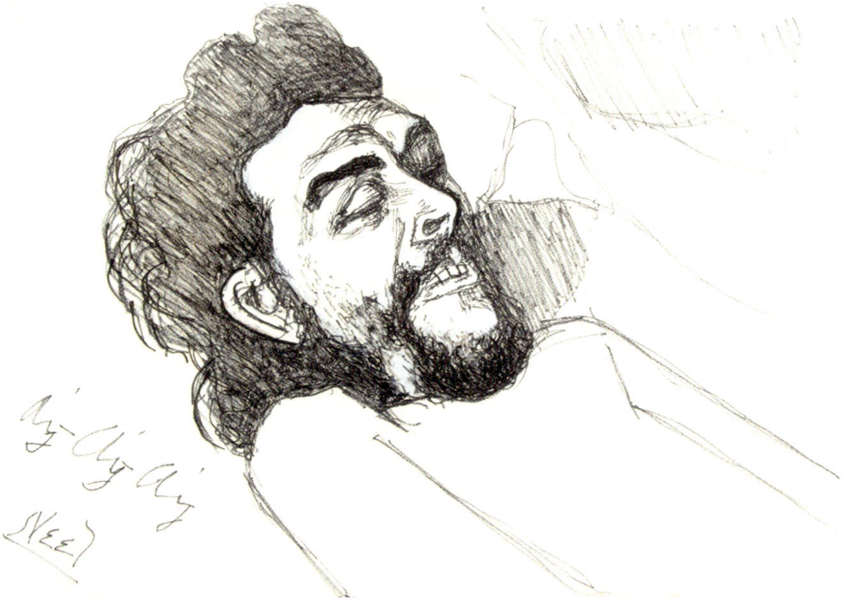




**Ay Ay Ay** 1967

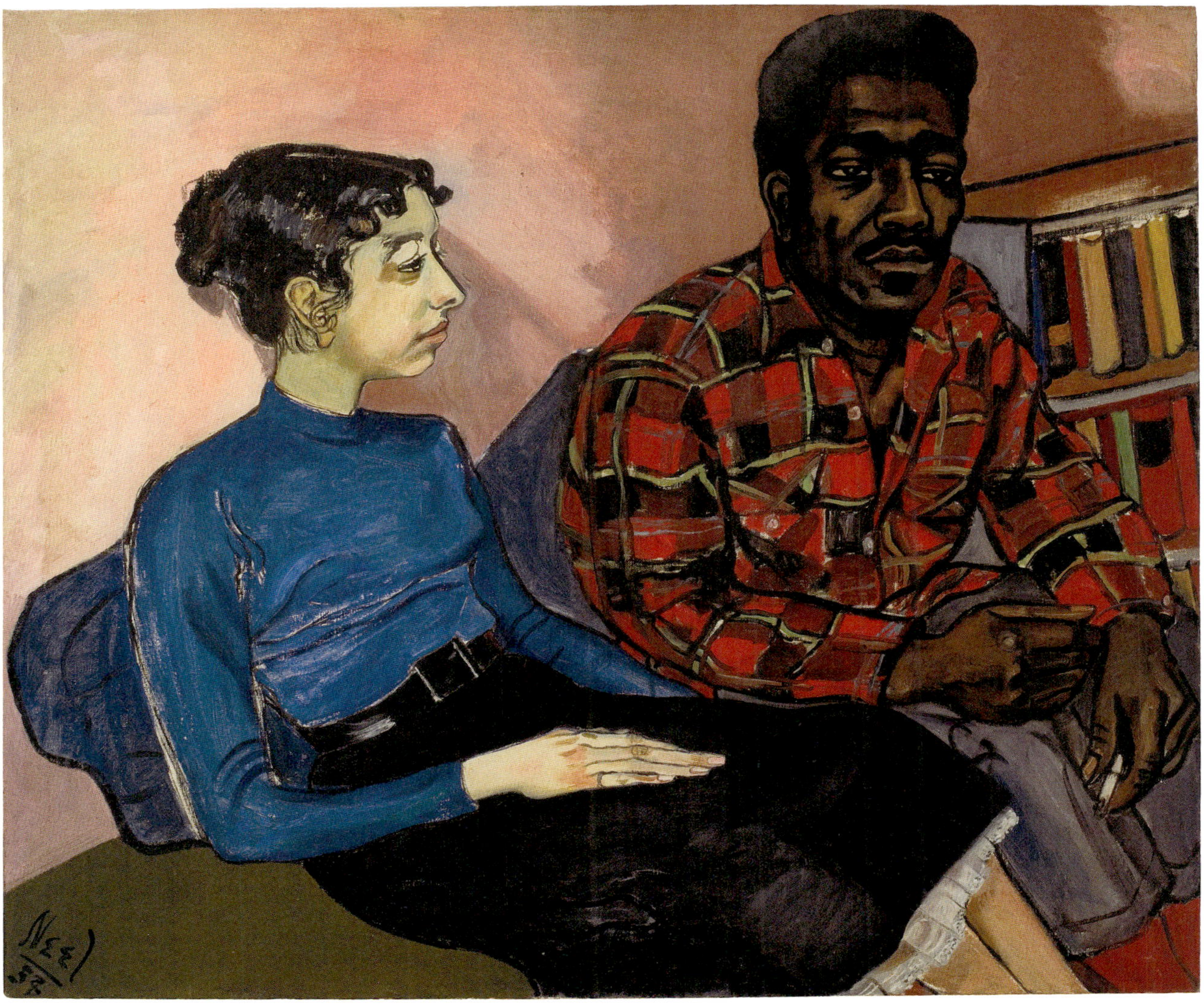

**Rita and Hubert** 1954

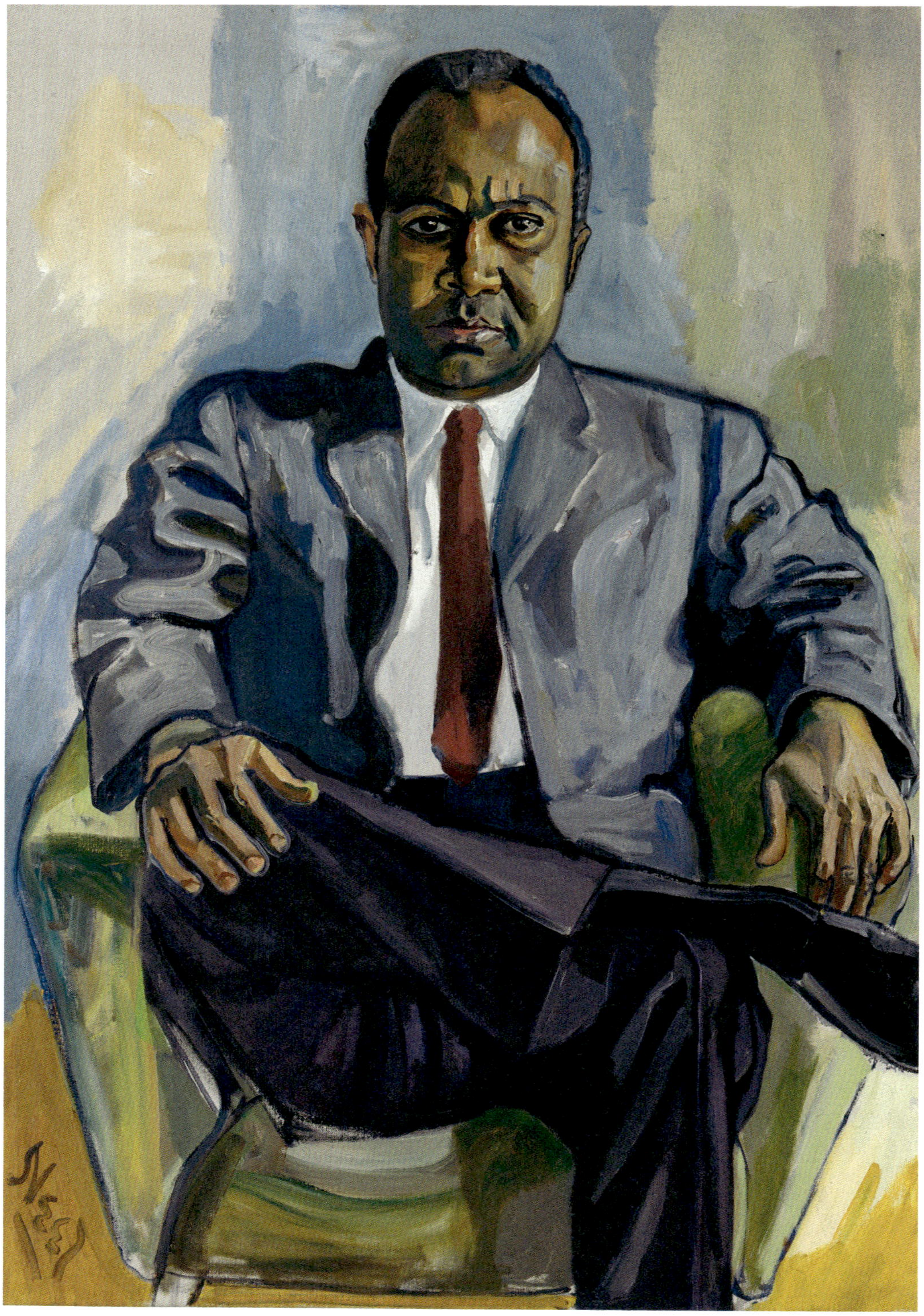



**James Farmer** 1964

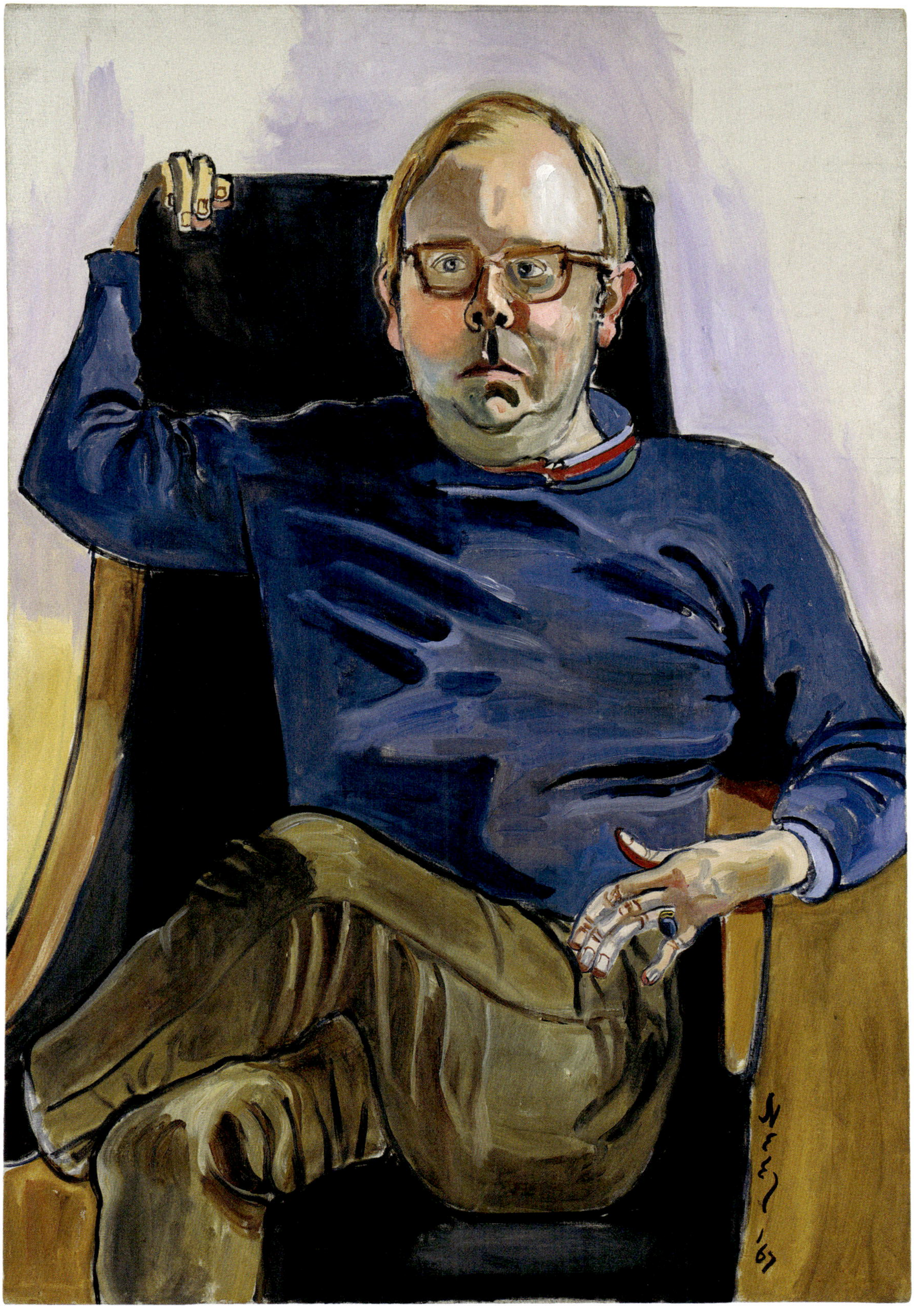


**Henry Geldzahler** 1967

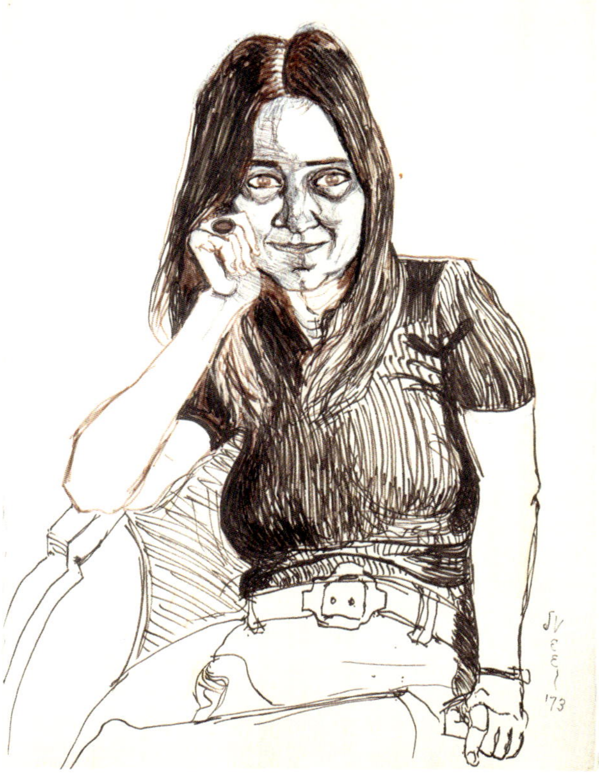


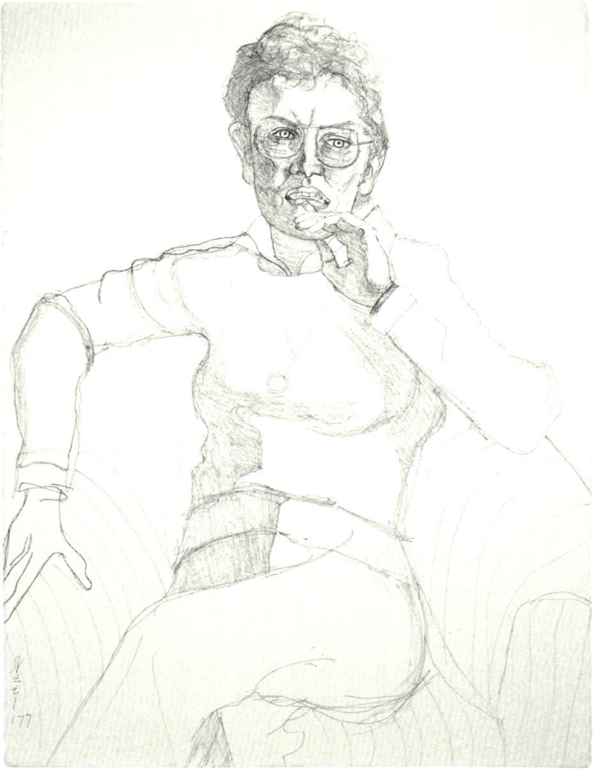




**Adrienne Rich** 1973

**Mary Garrard** 1977

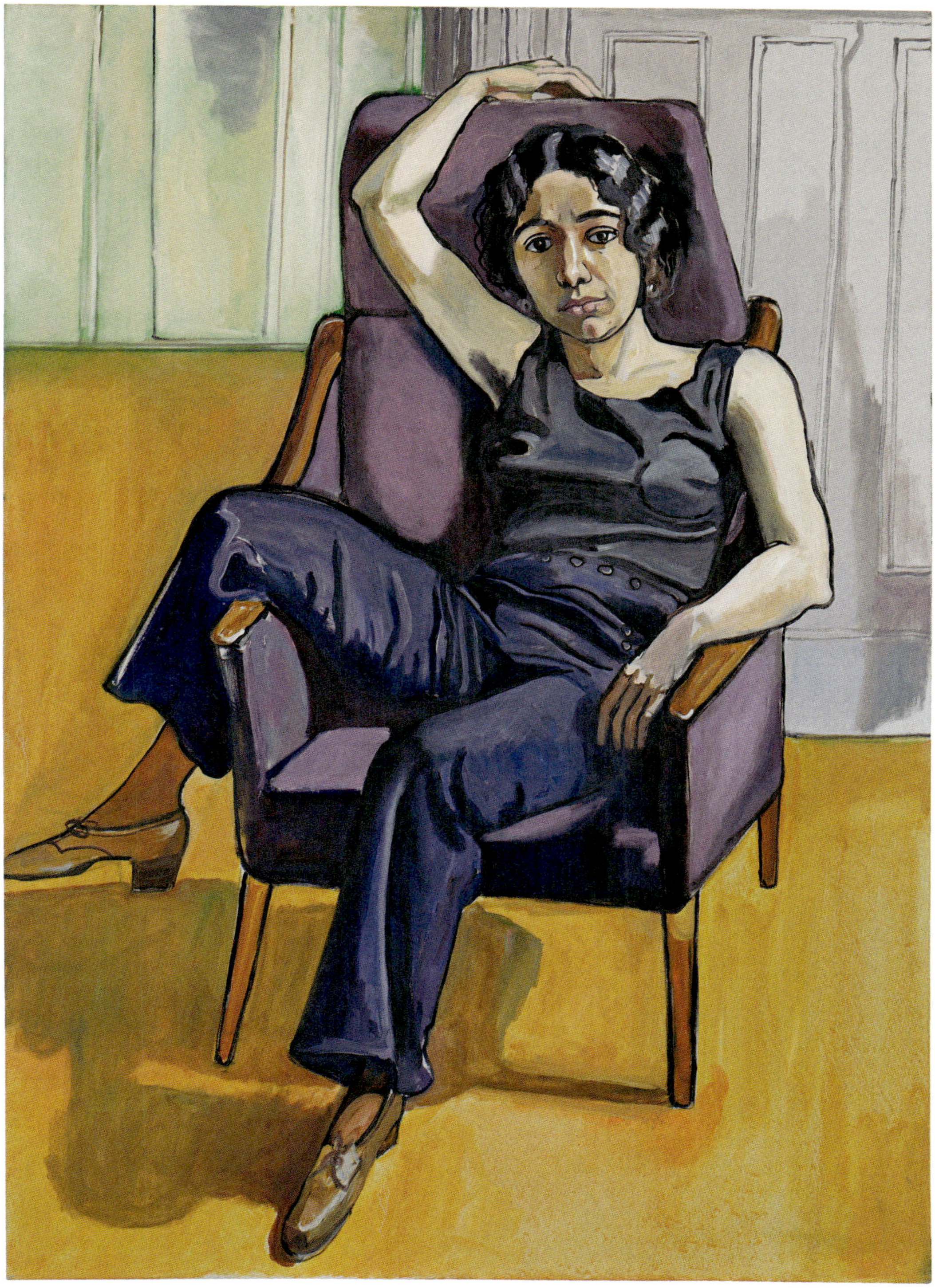

**Marxist Girl (Irene Peslikis)** 1972

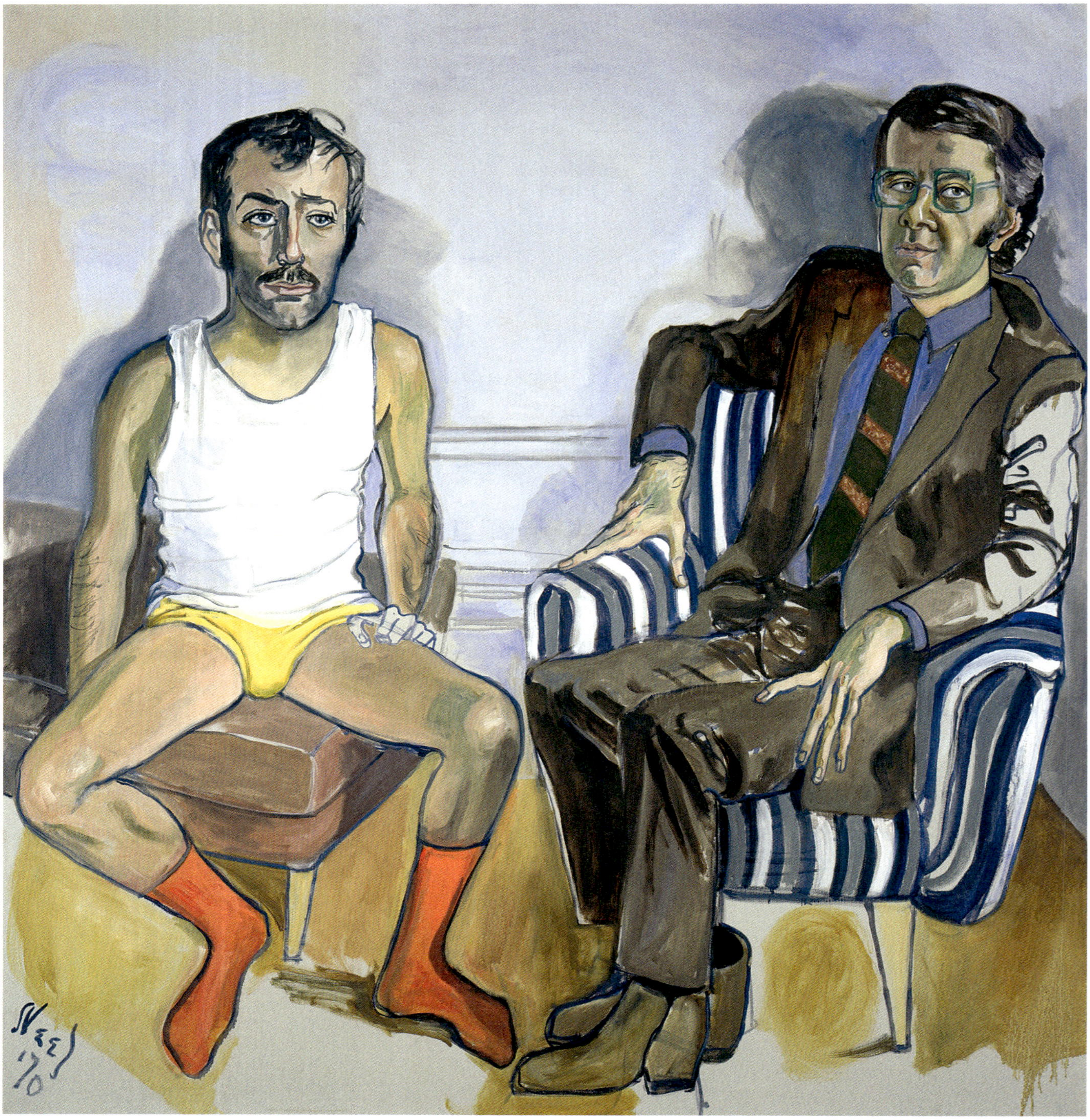



**David Bourdon and Gregory Battcock** 1970

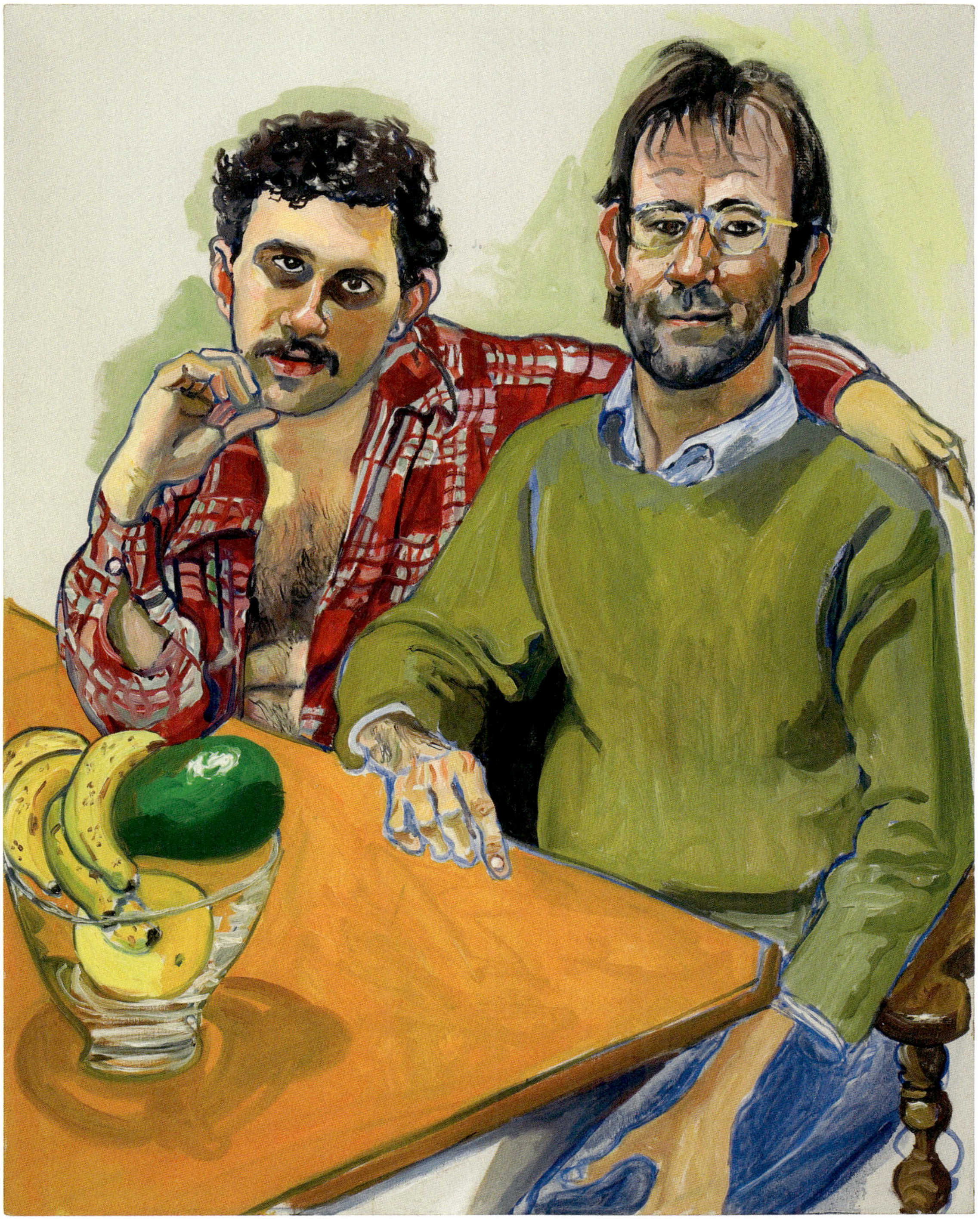

**Geoffrey Hendricks and Brian** 1978

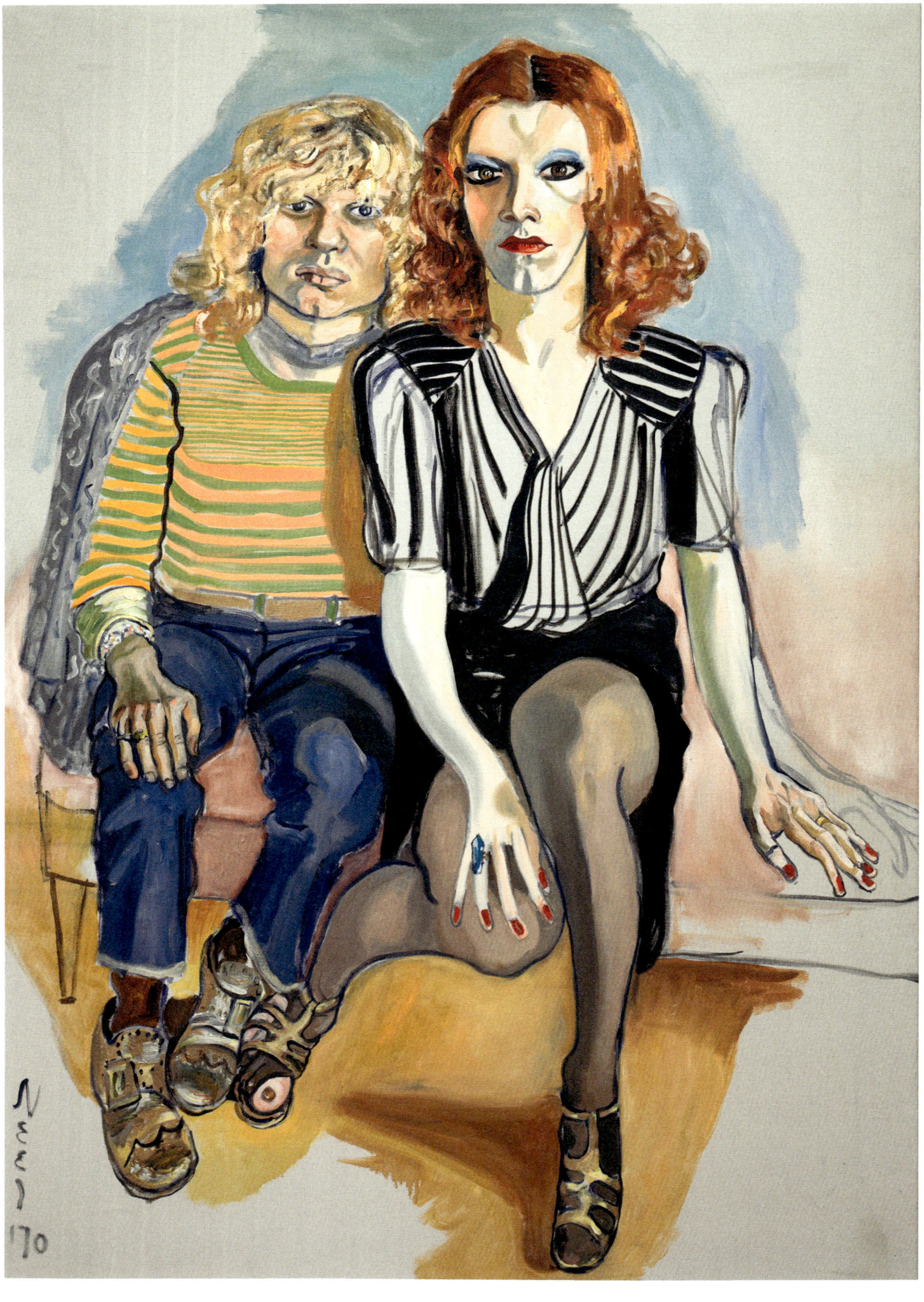
NEEL
'70

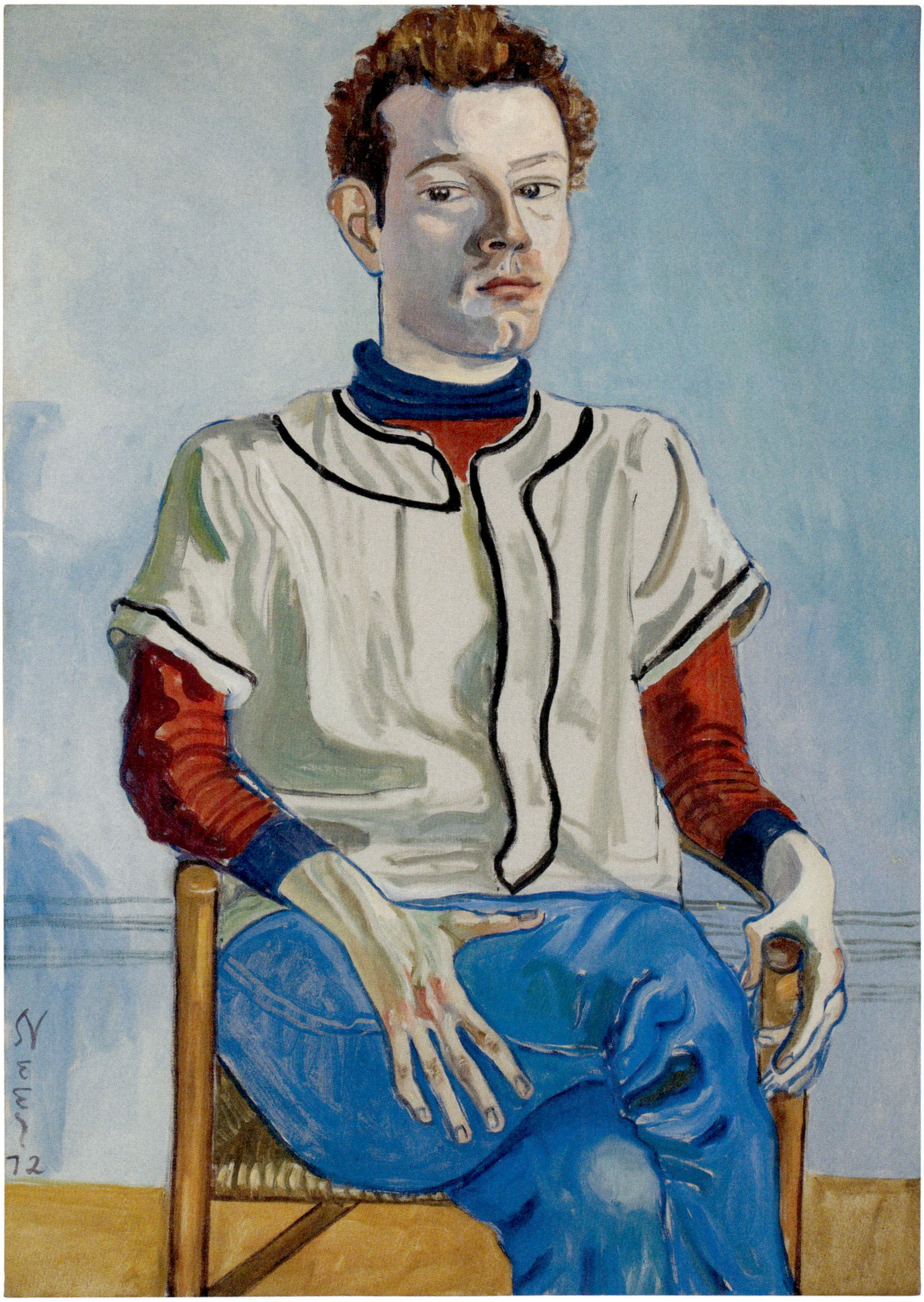

**Jackie Curtis and Ritta Redd** 1970

**Jackie Curtis as a Boy** 1972

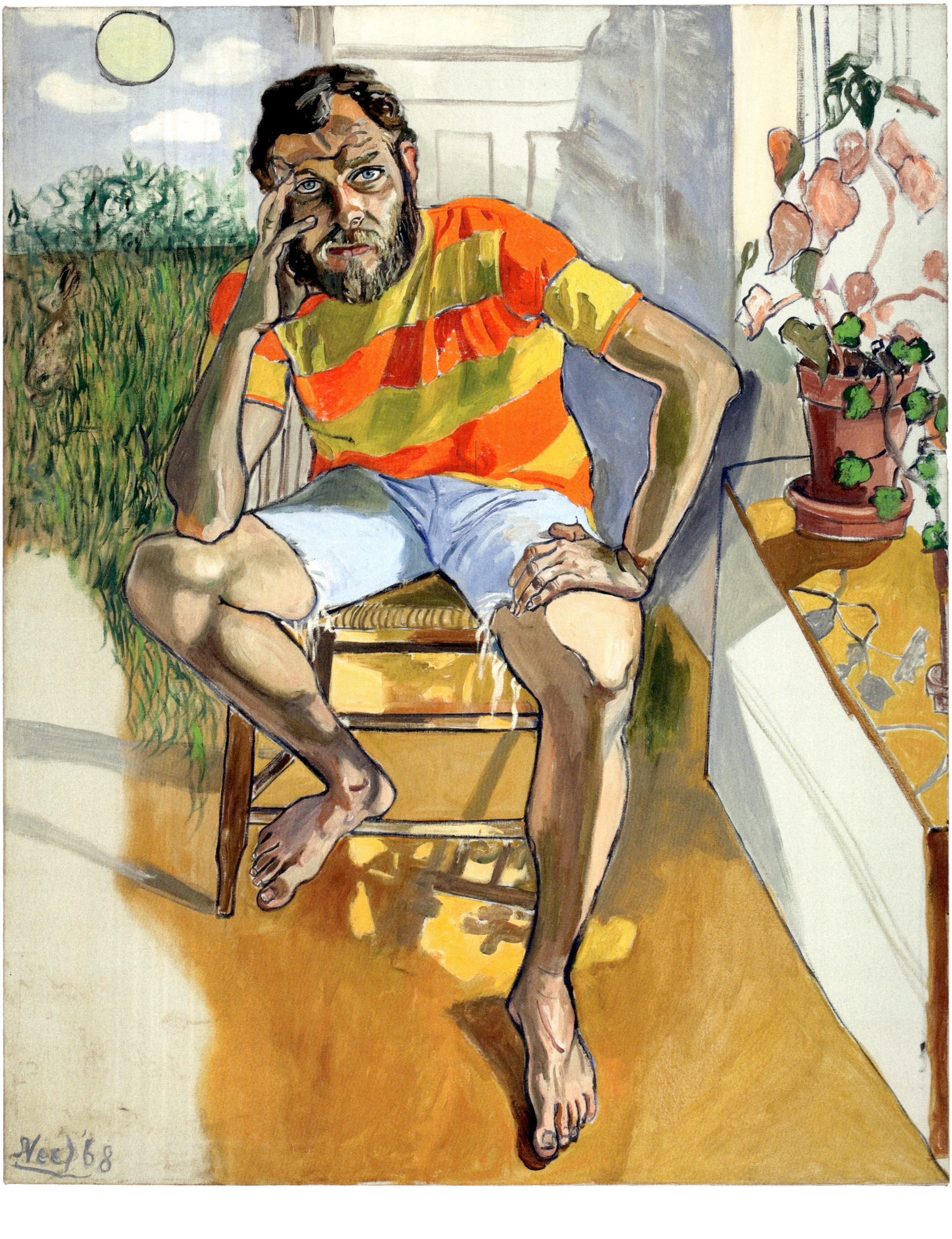
Neel '68

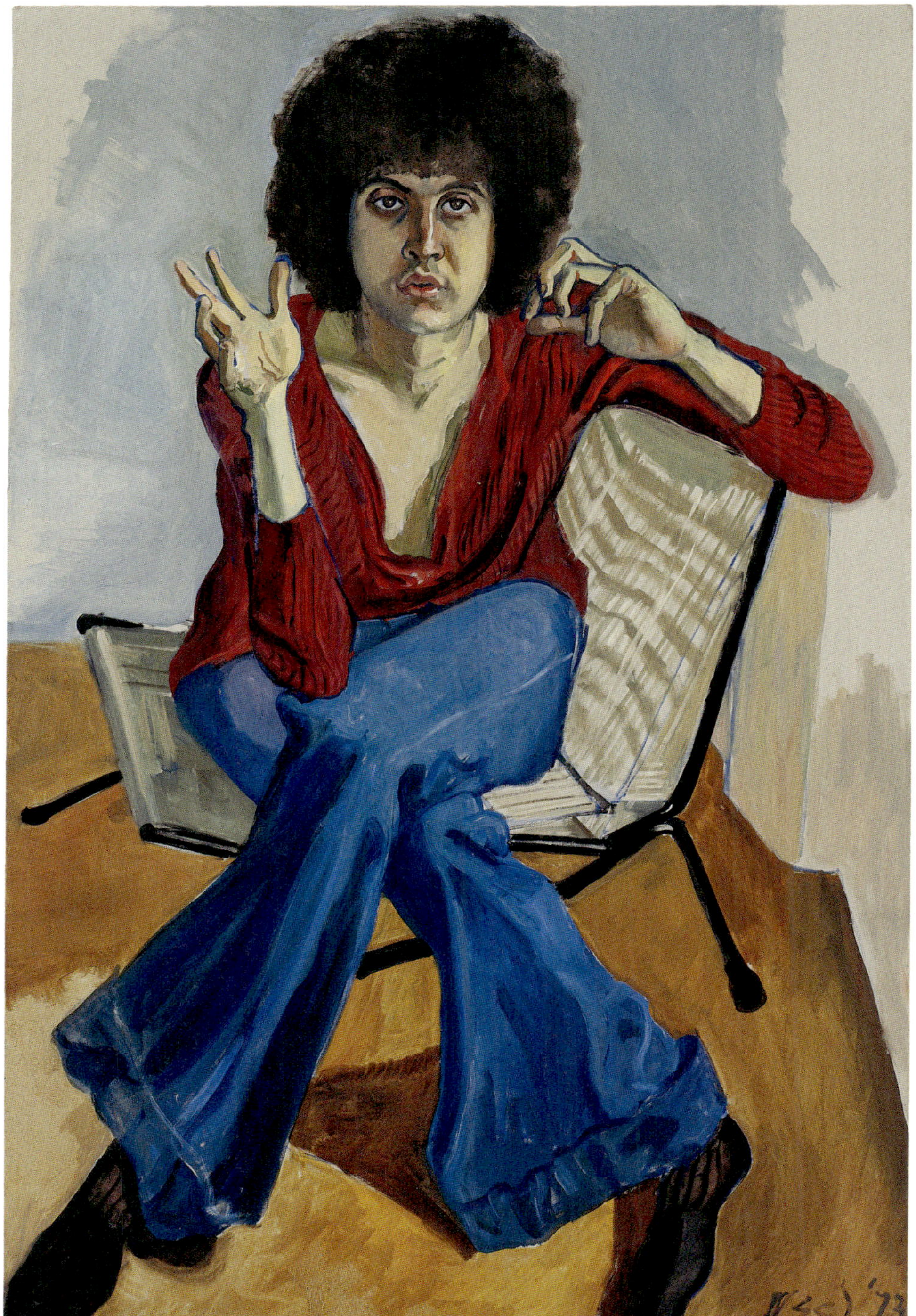

**Richard Gibbs** 1968

**Robbie Tillotson** 1973

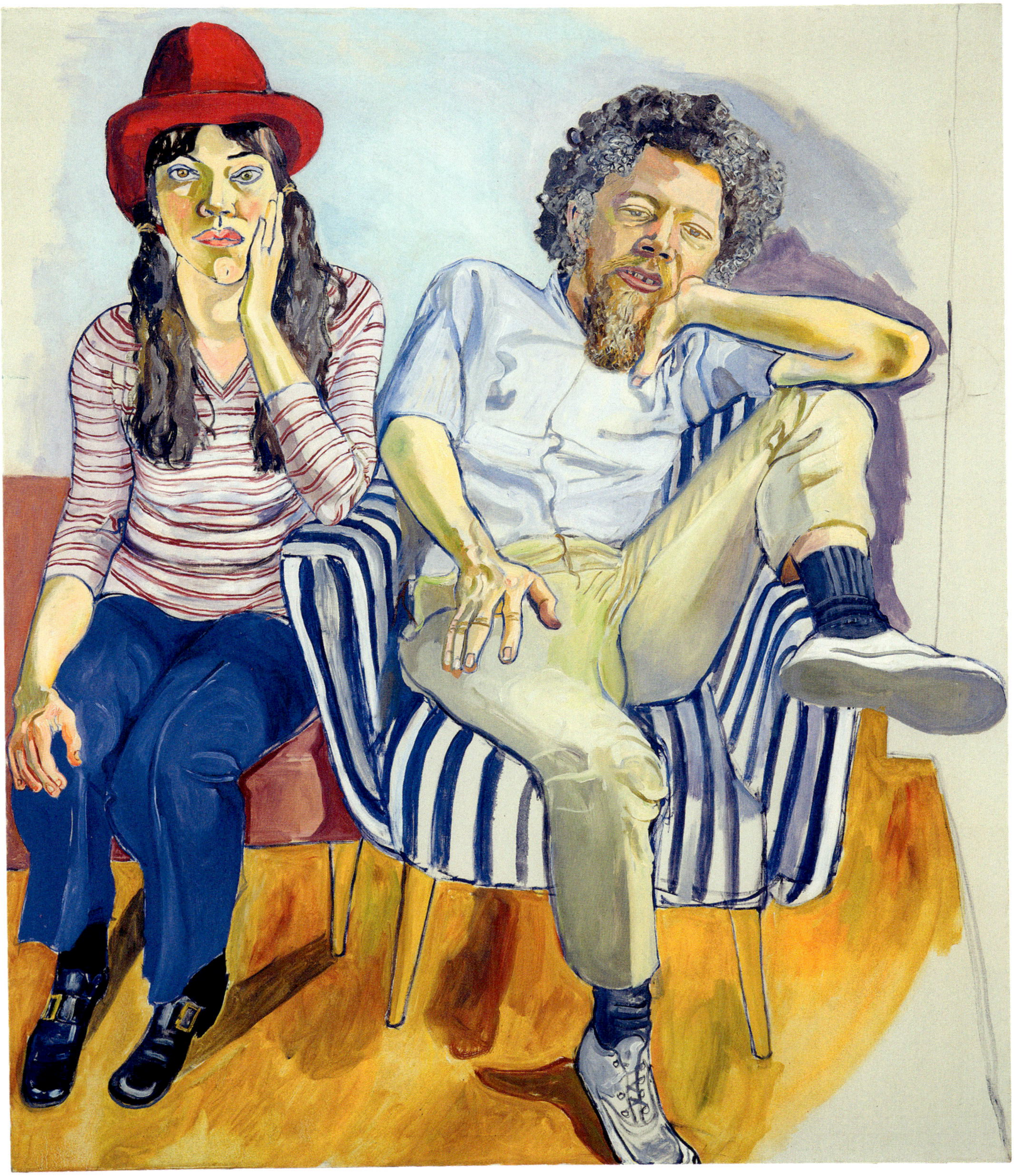

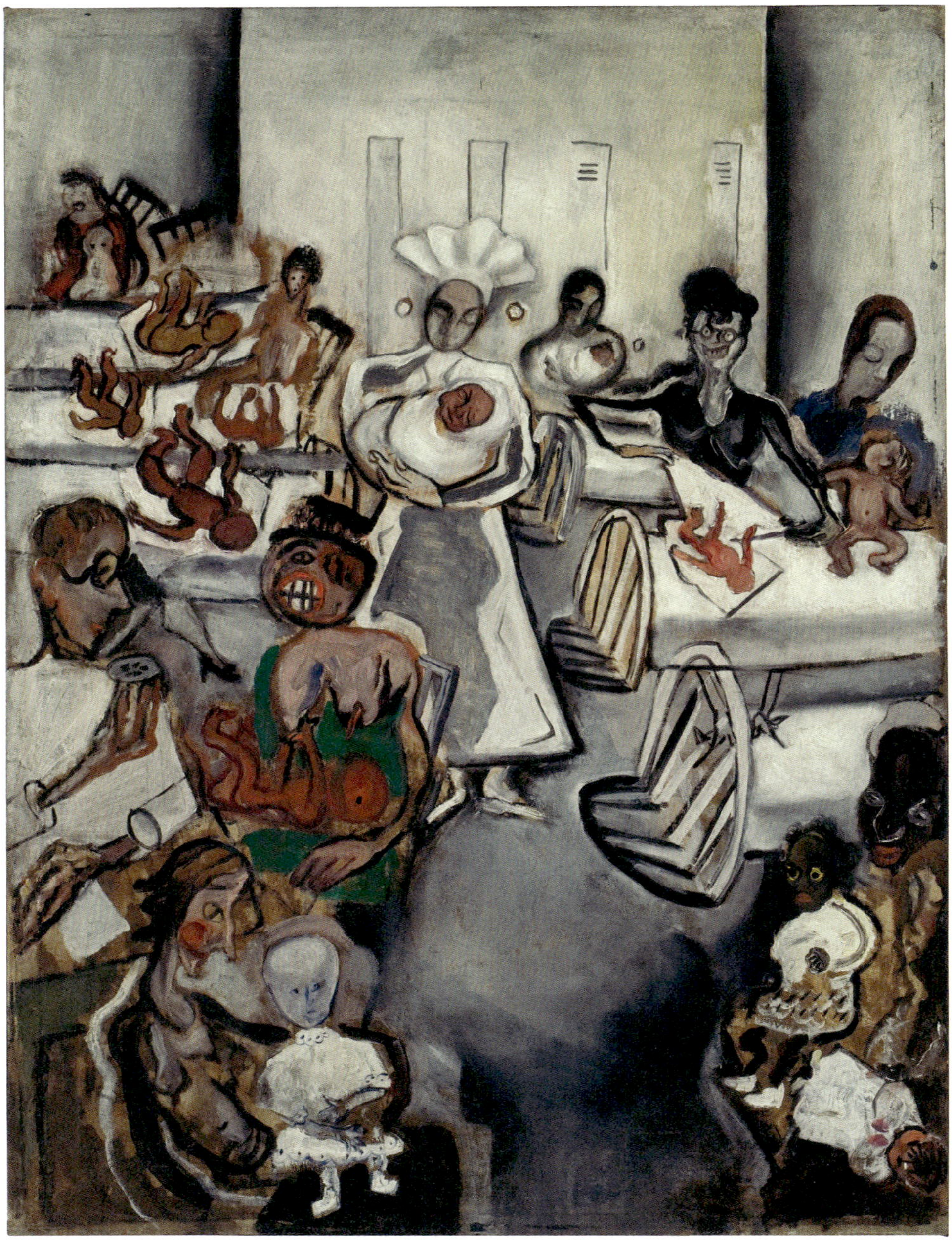

 **Well Baby Clinic** 1928–29

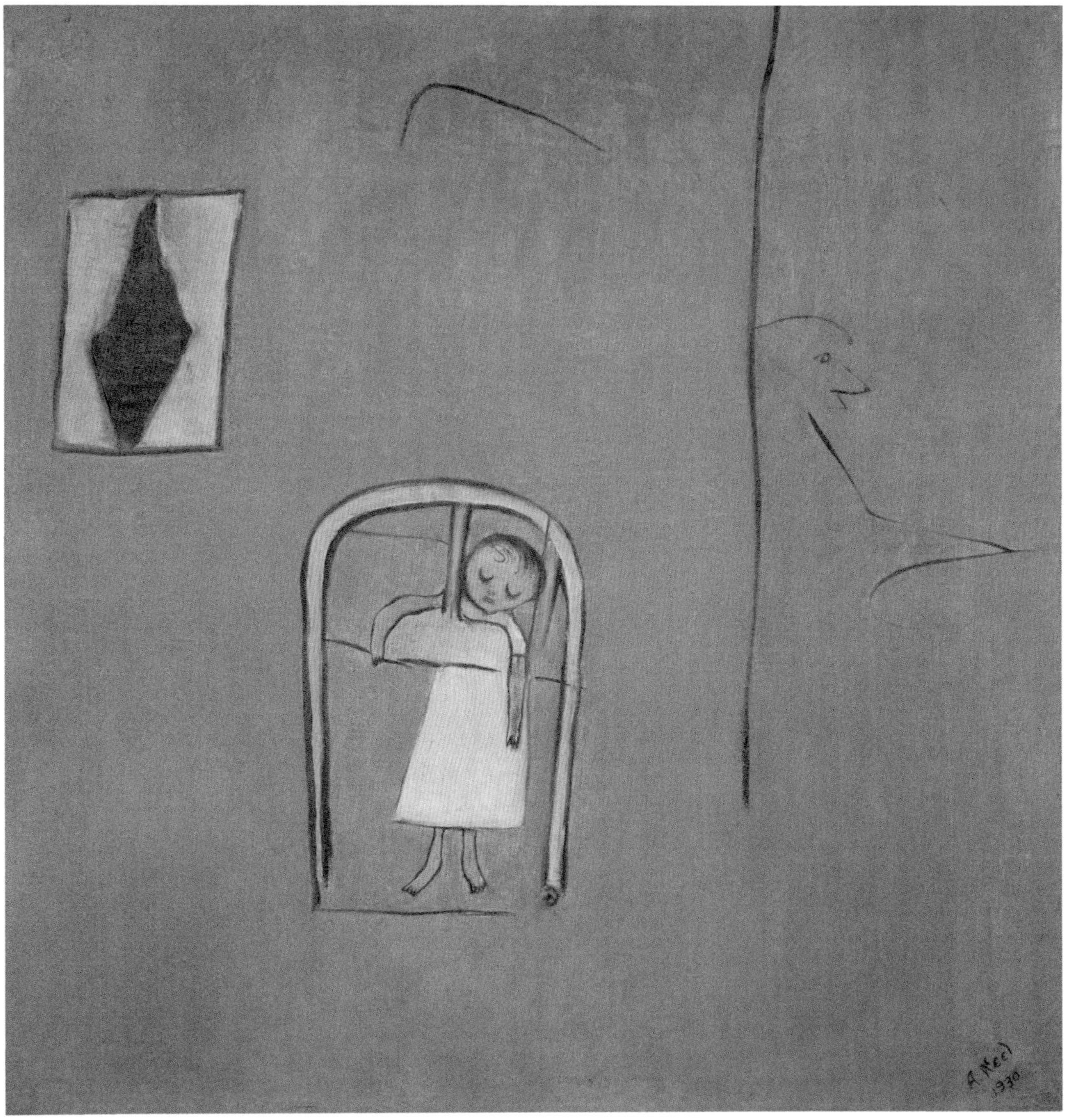

**Futility of Effort** 1930

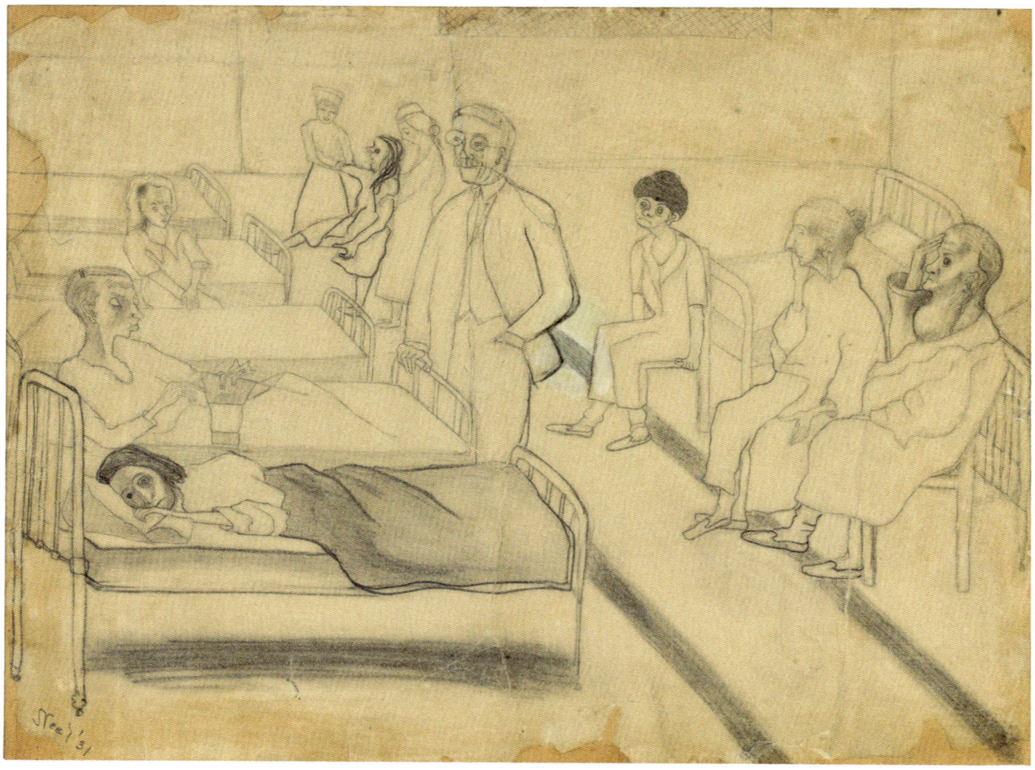

**Suicidal Ward, Philadelphia General Hospital** 1931

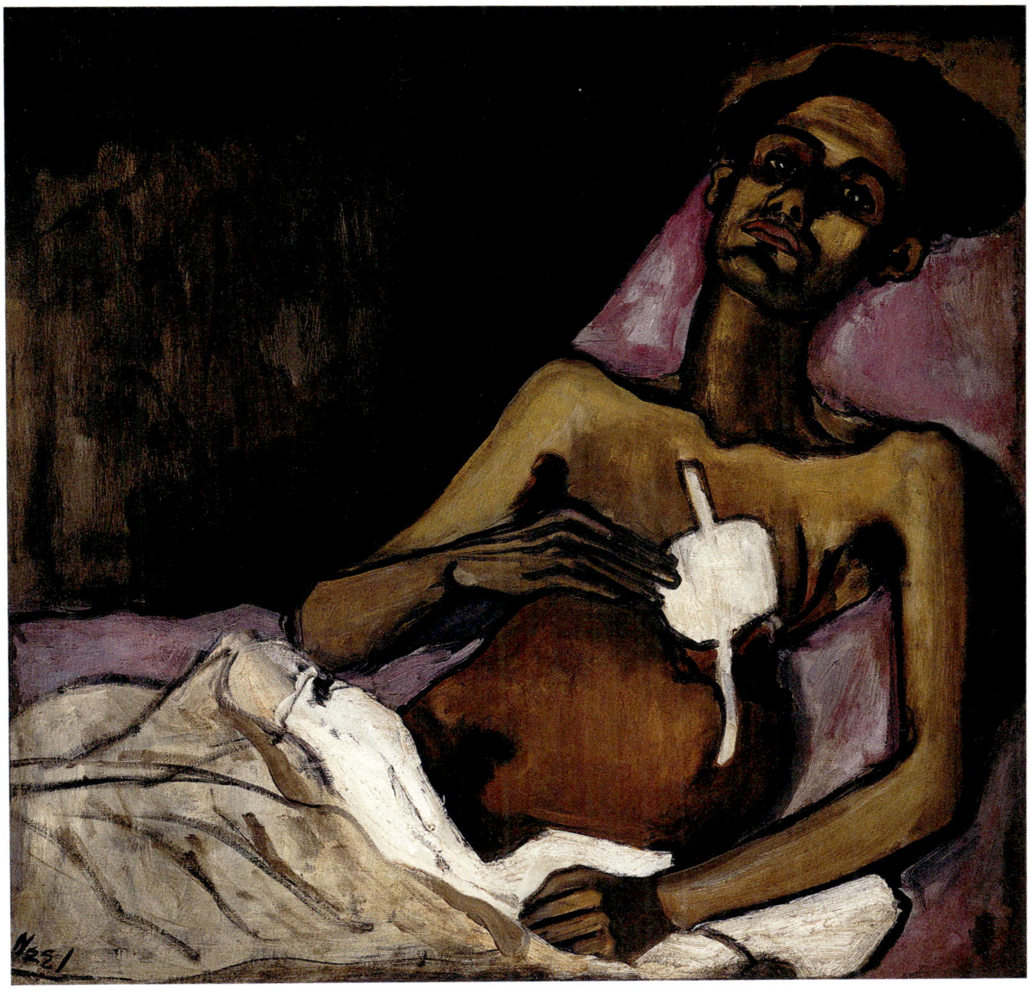

**T.B. Harlem** 1940

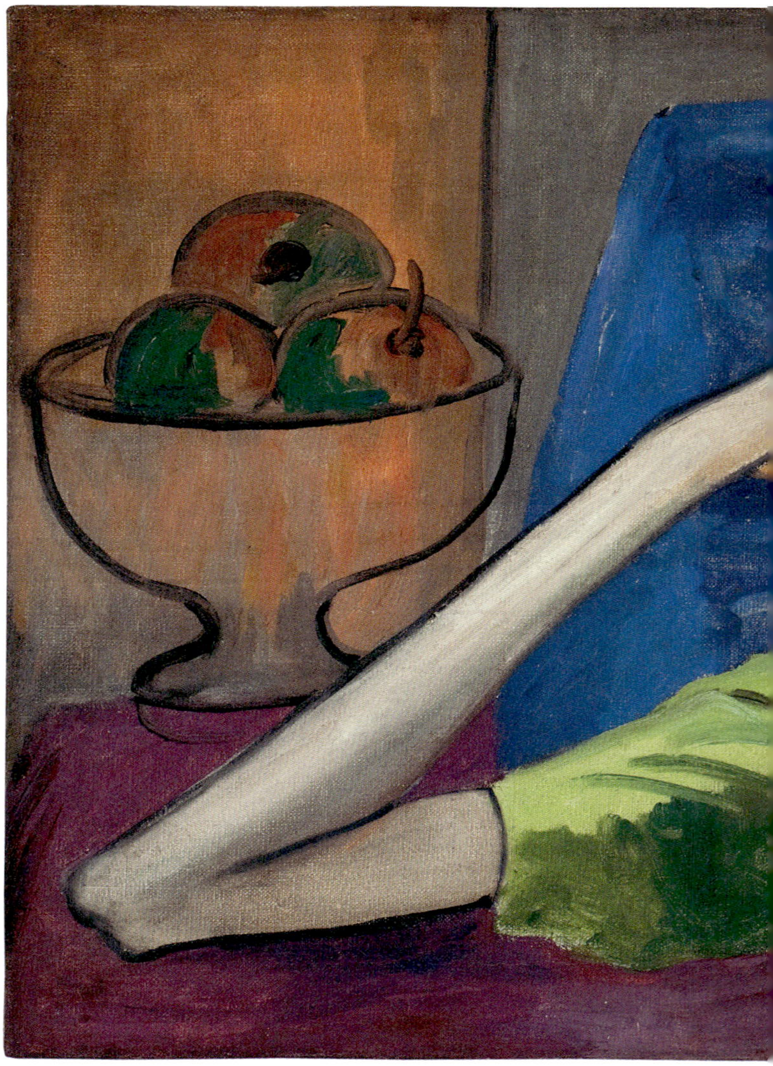

 **Peggy** 1949

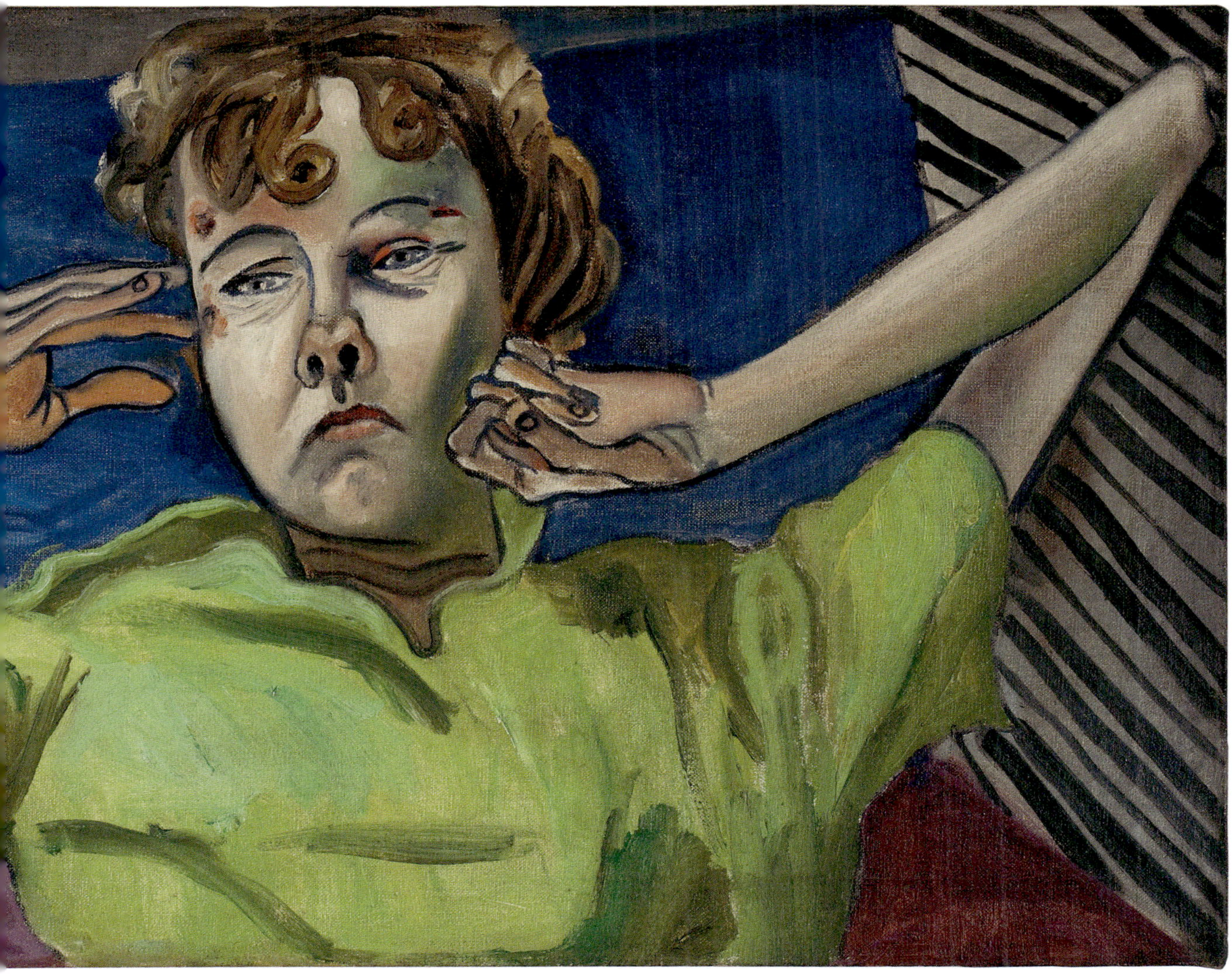

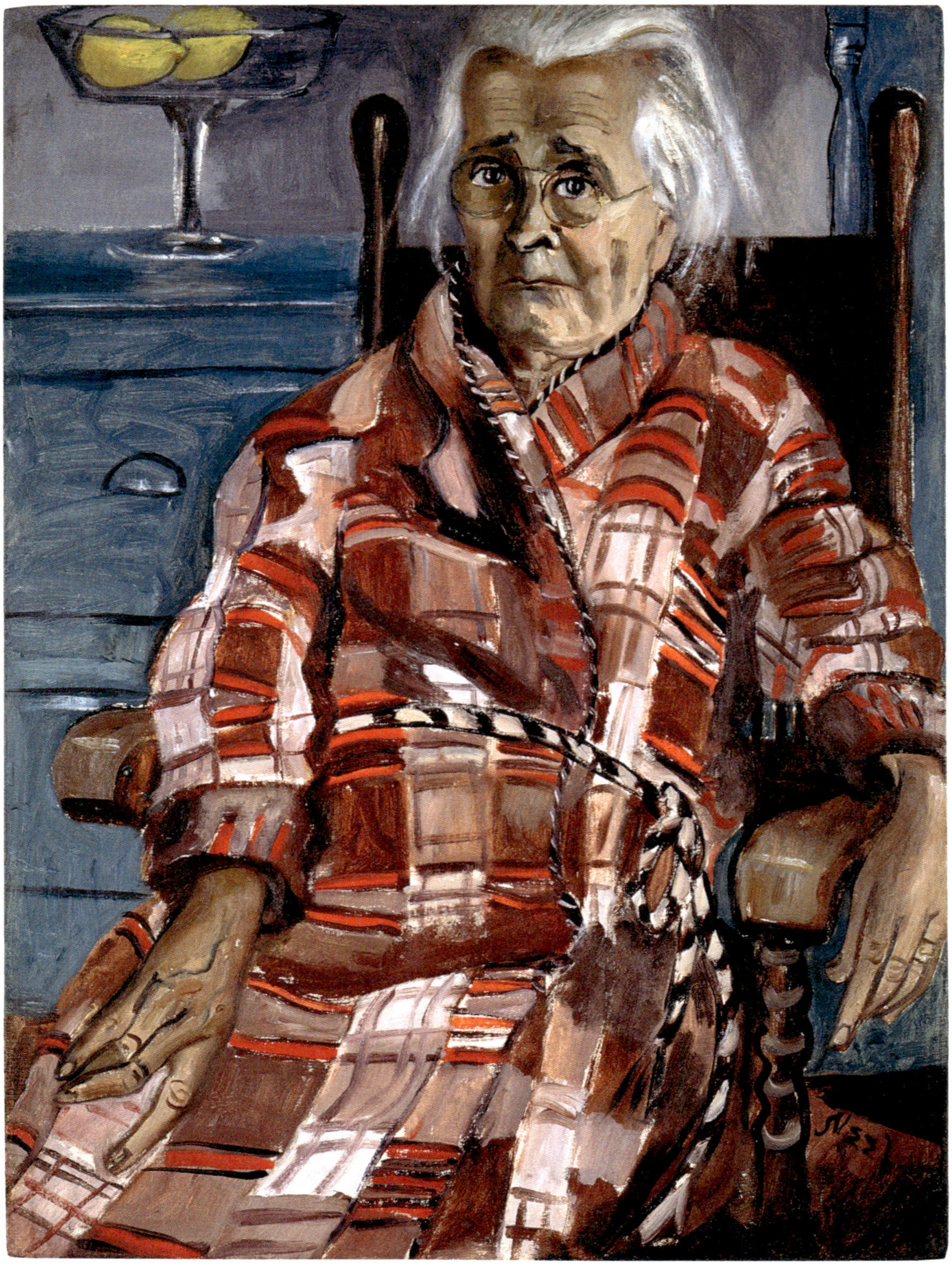

 **Last Sickness** 1953

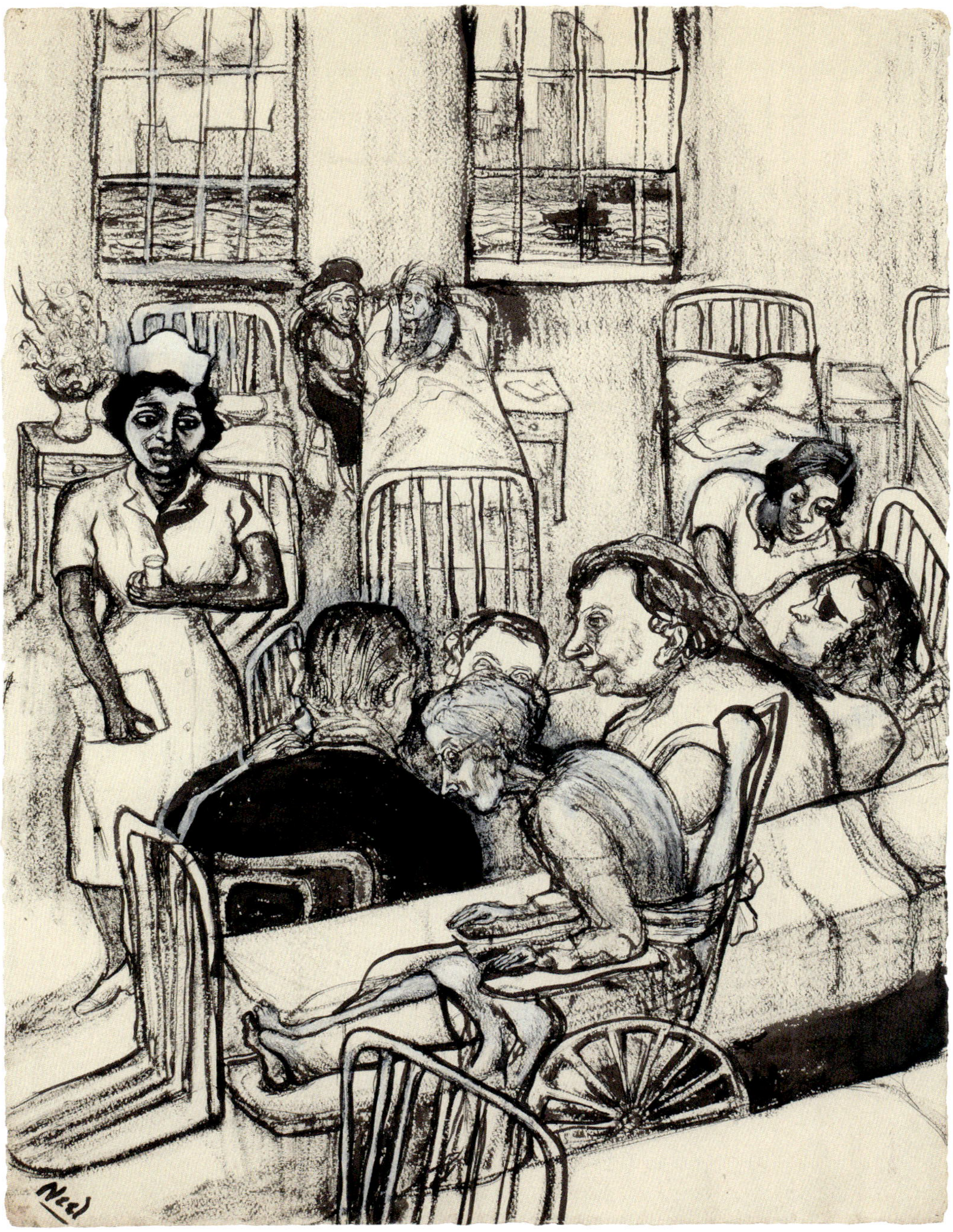


**City Hospital** 1954

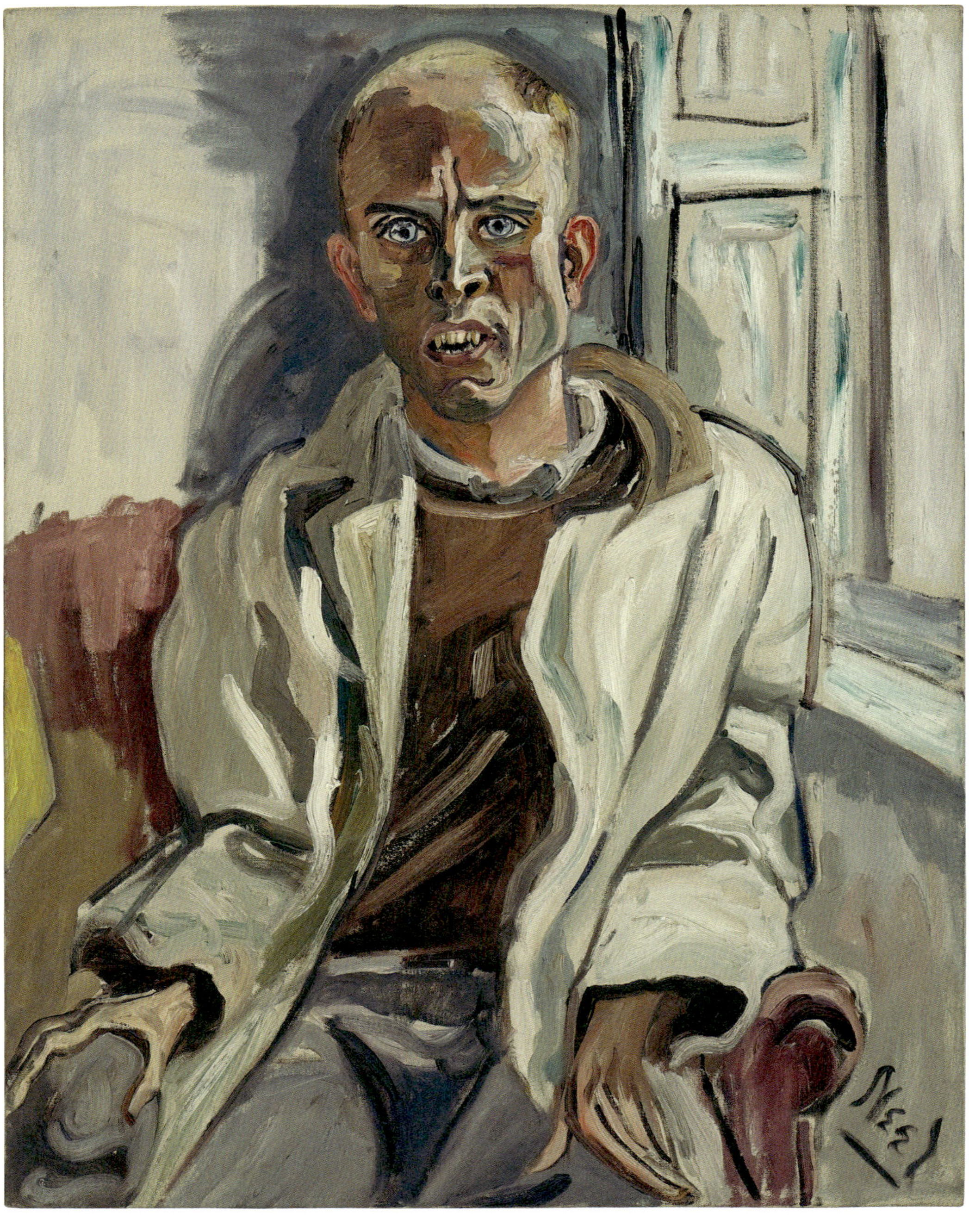



**Randall in Extremis** 1960

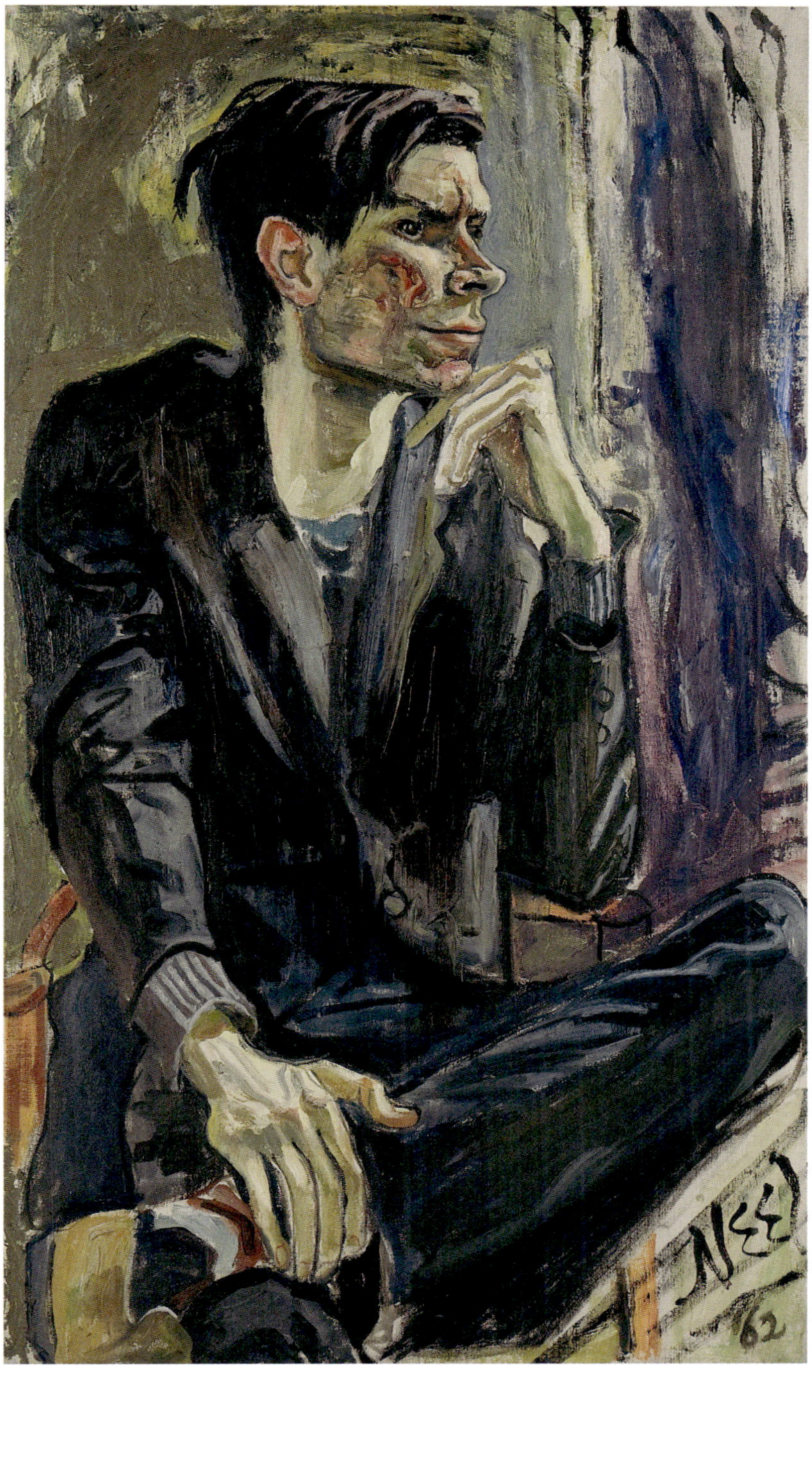

**Robert Smithson** 1962

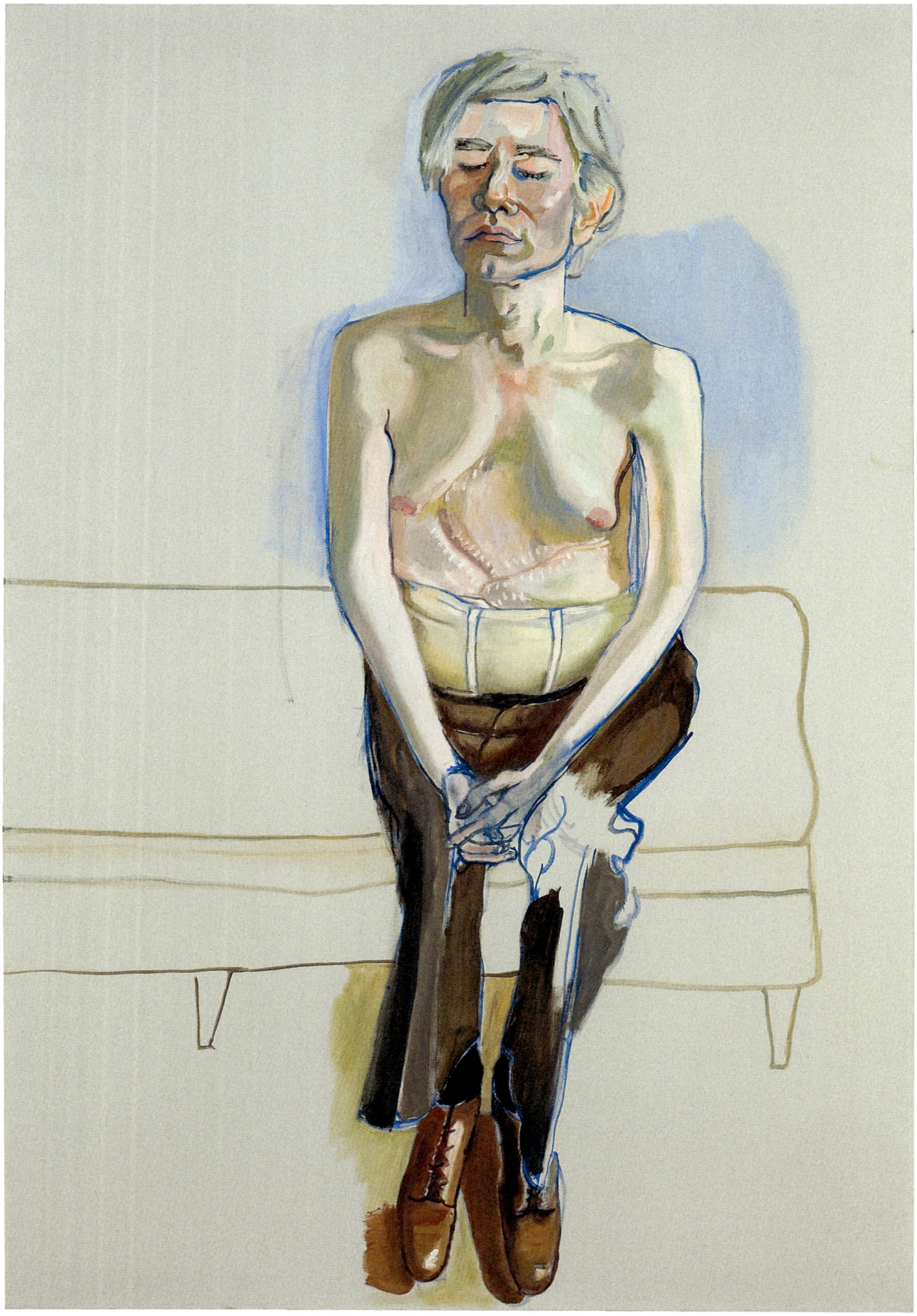



**Andy Warhol** 1970

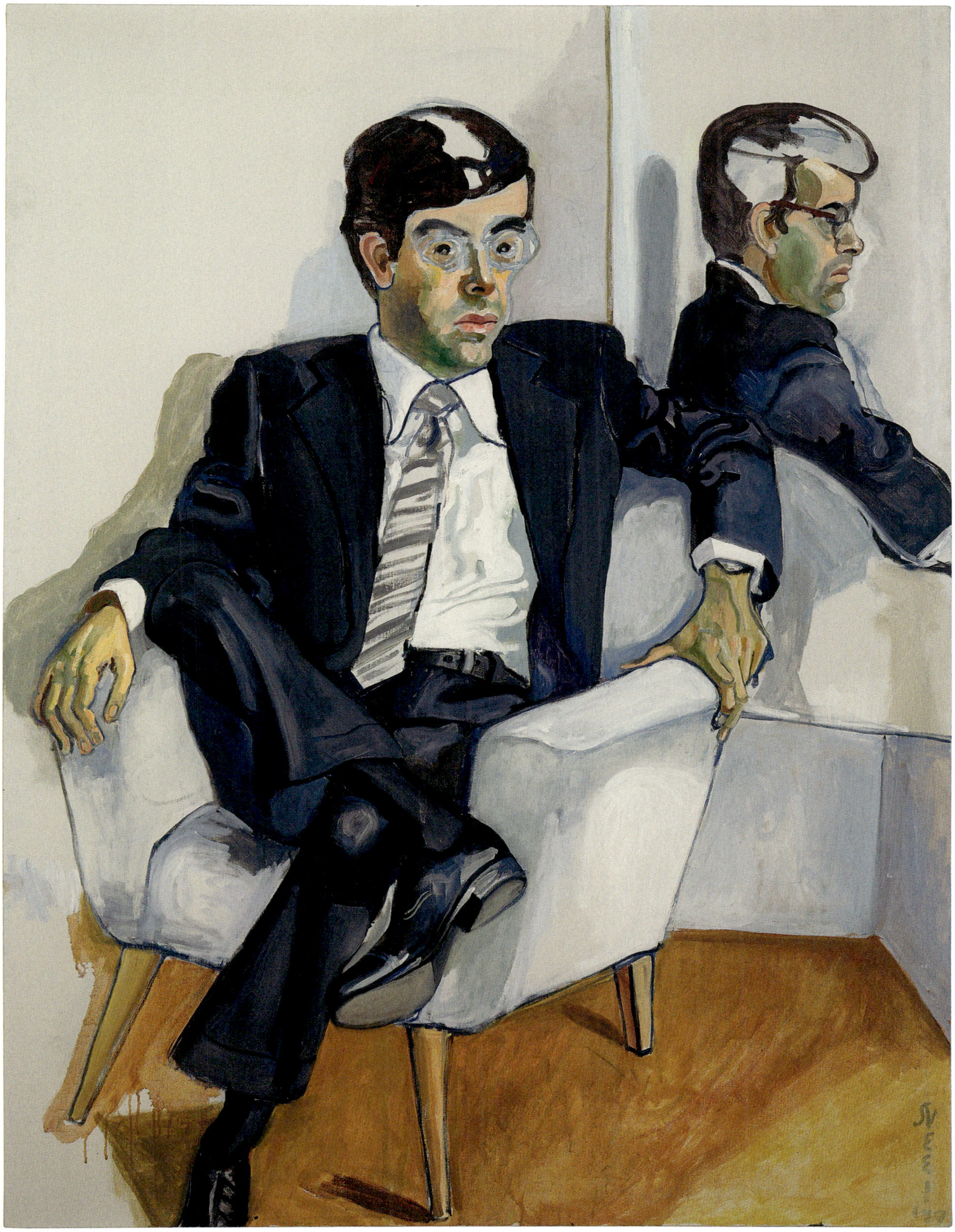

**Richard in the Era of the Corporation** 1978–79

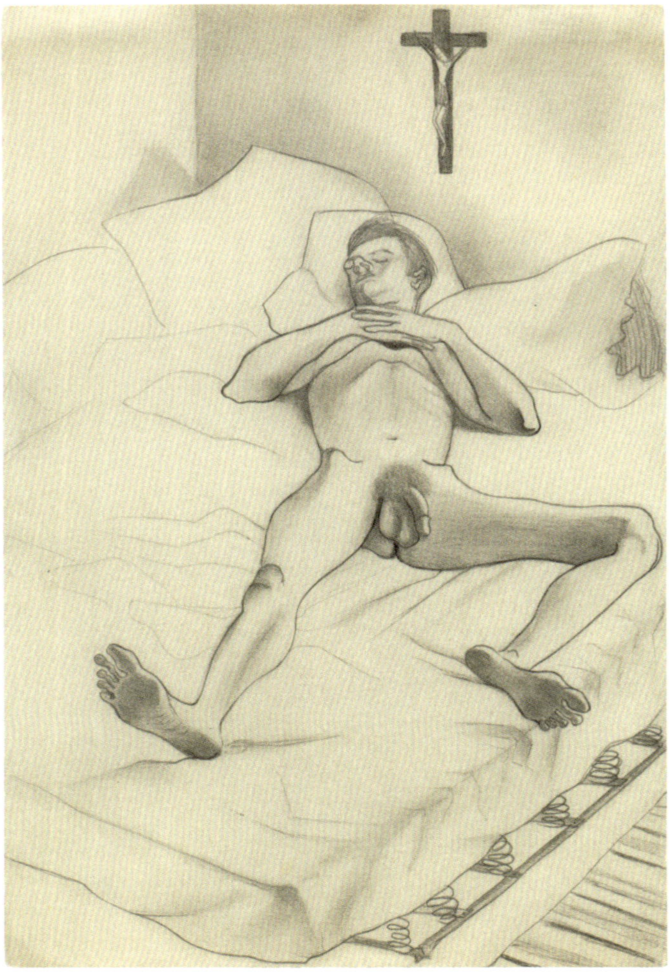

 **Kenneth Doolittle** 1932

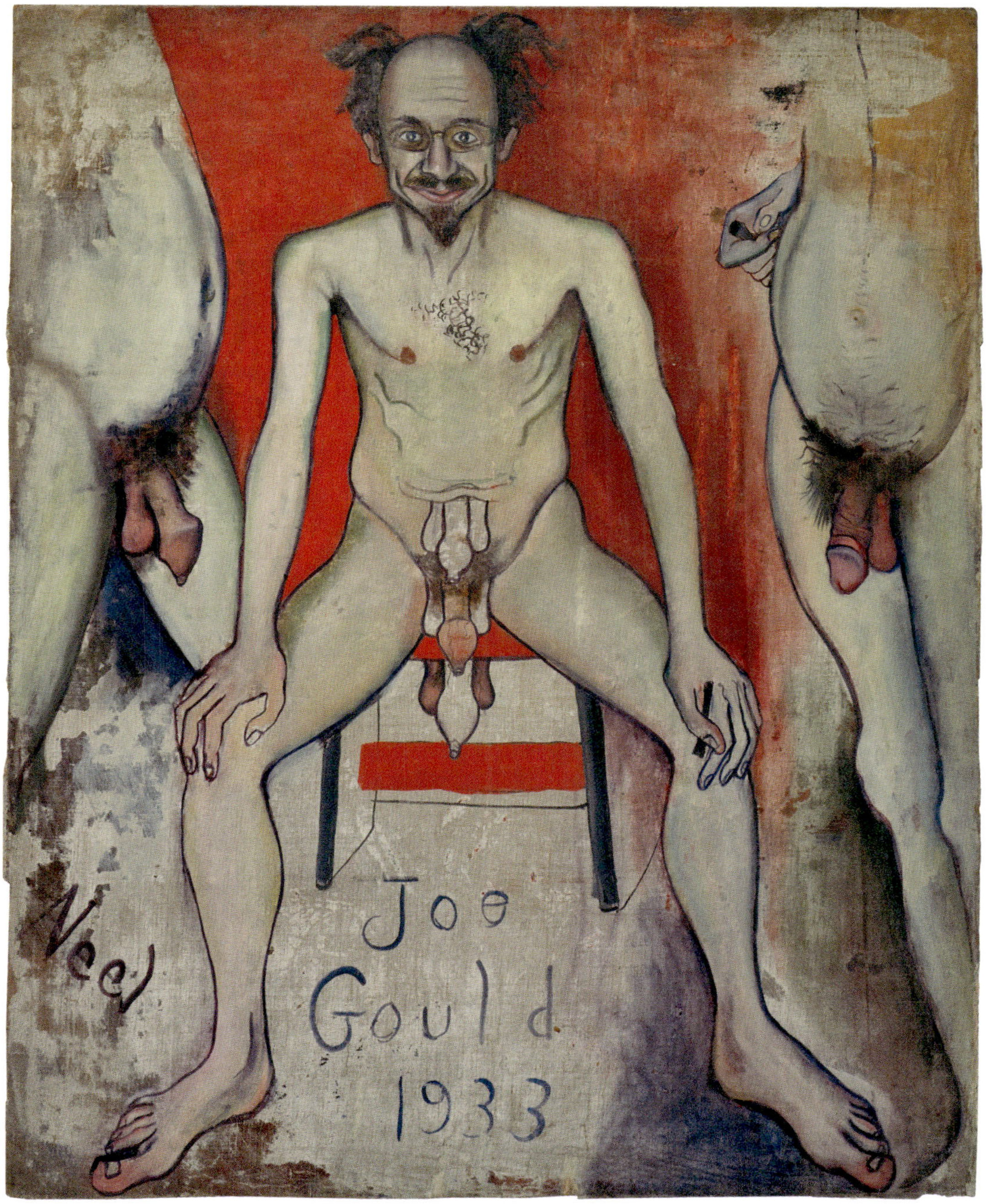


**Joe Gould** 1933

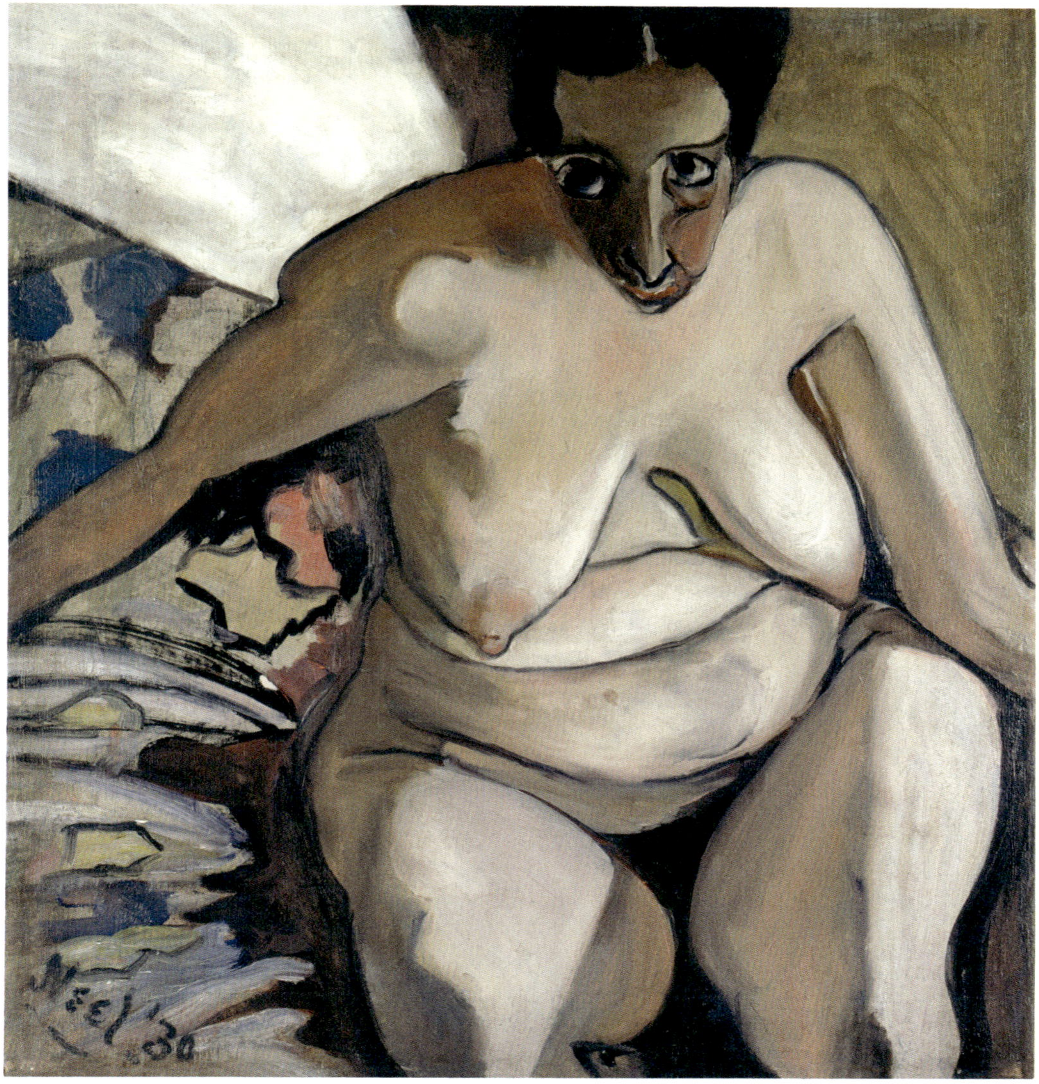




**Ethel Ashton** 1930

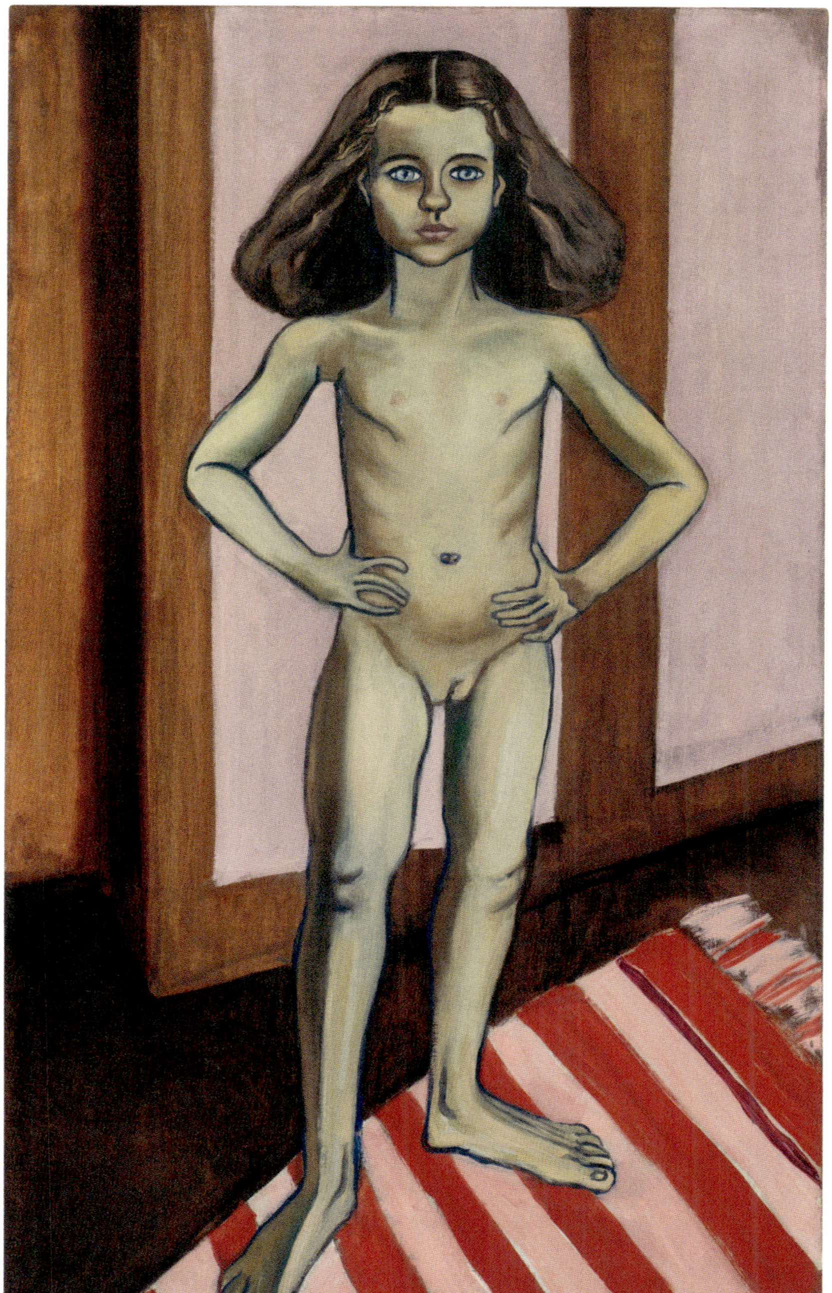

**Isabetta** 1934–35

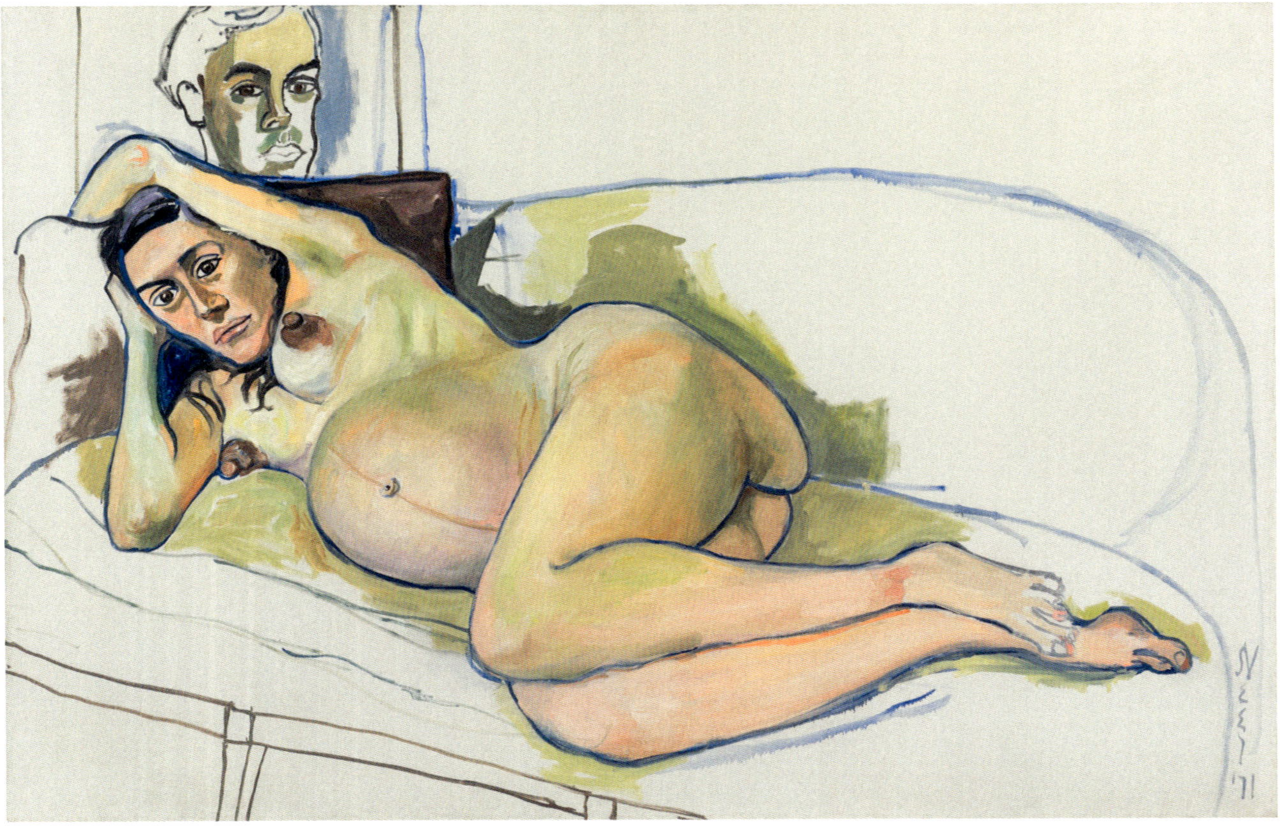

 **Pregnant Woman** 1971

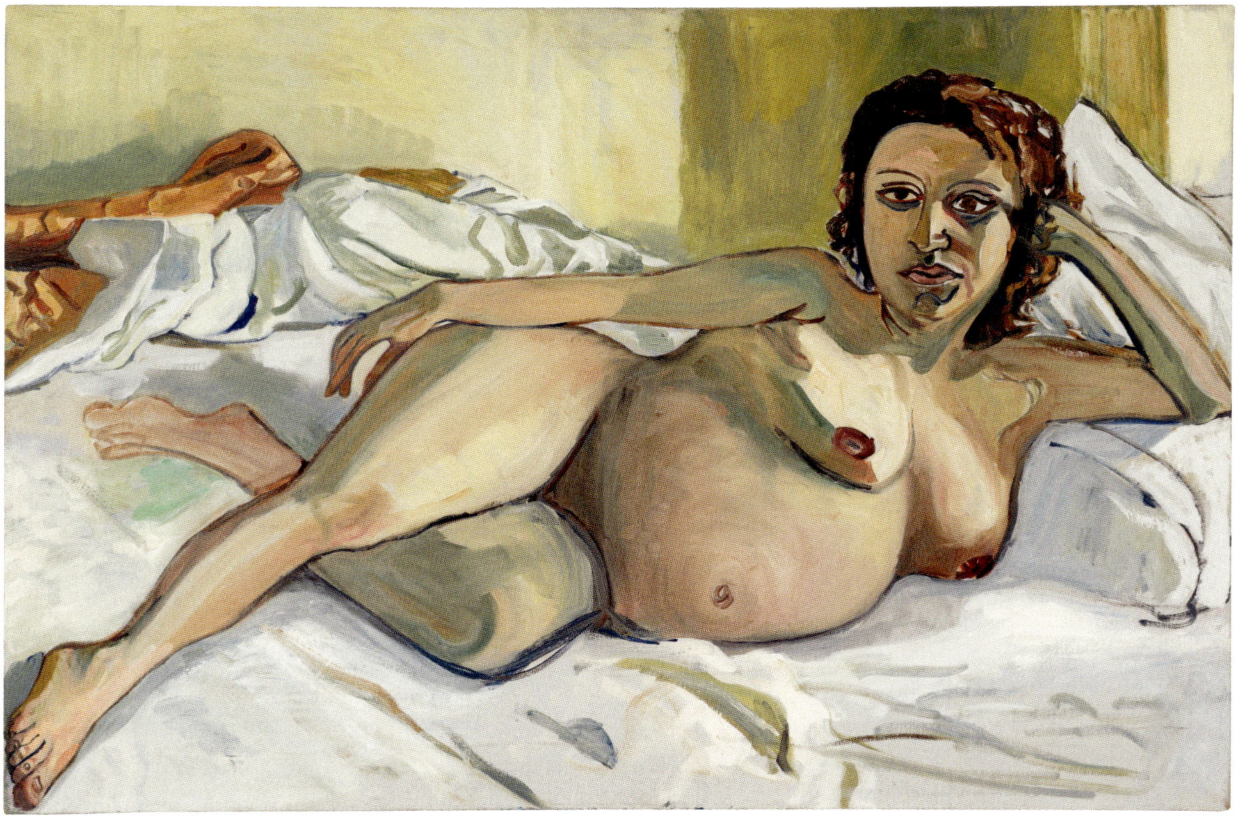

**Pregnant Maria** 1964

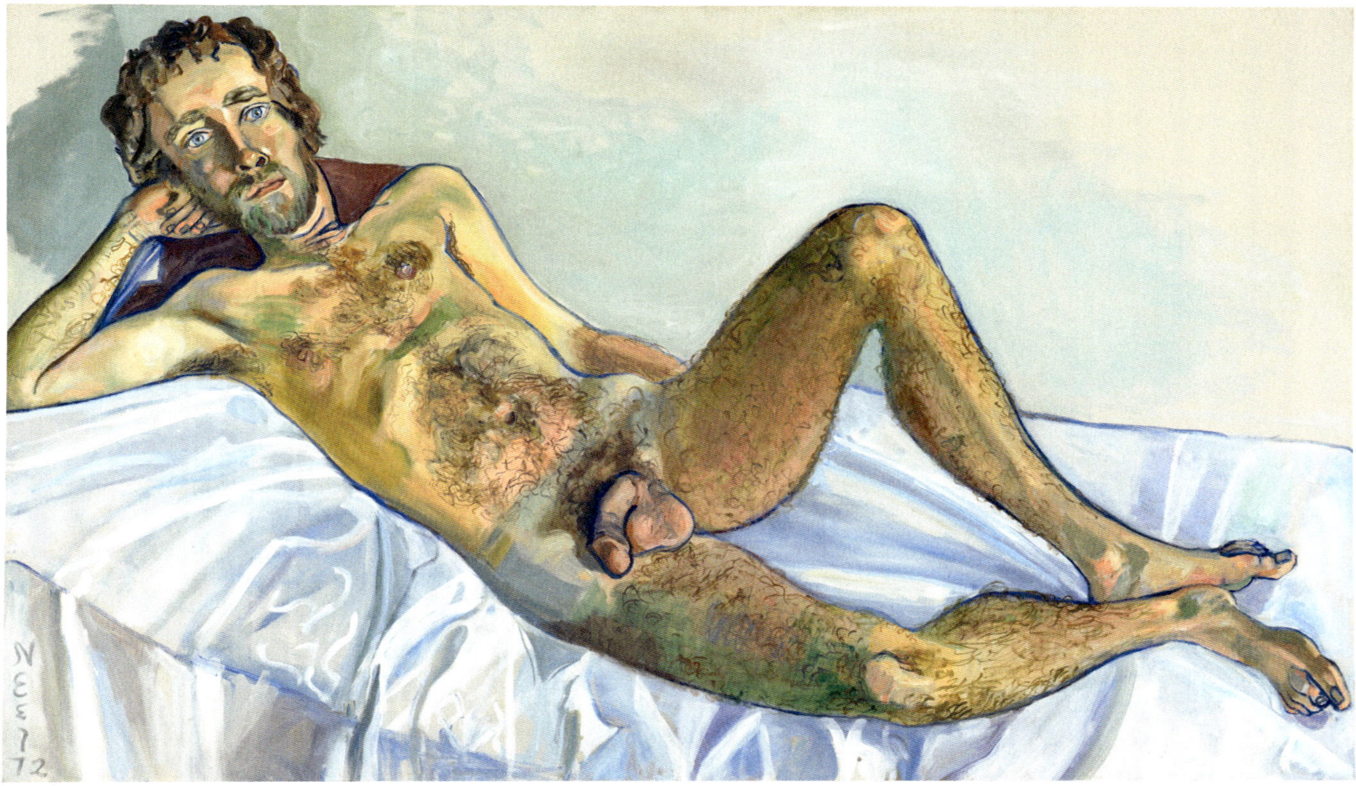




**John Perreault** 1972

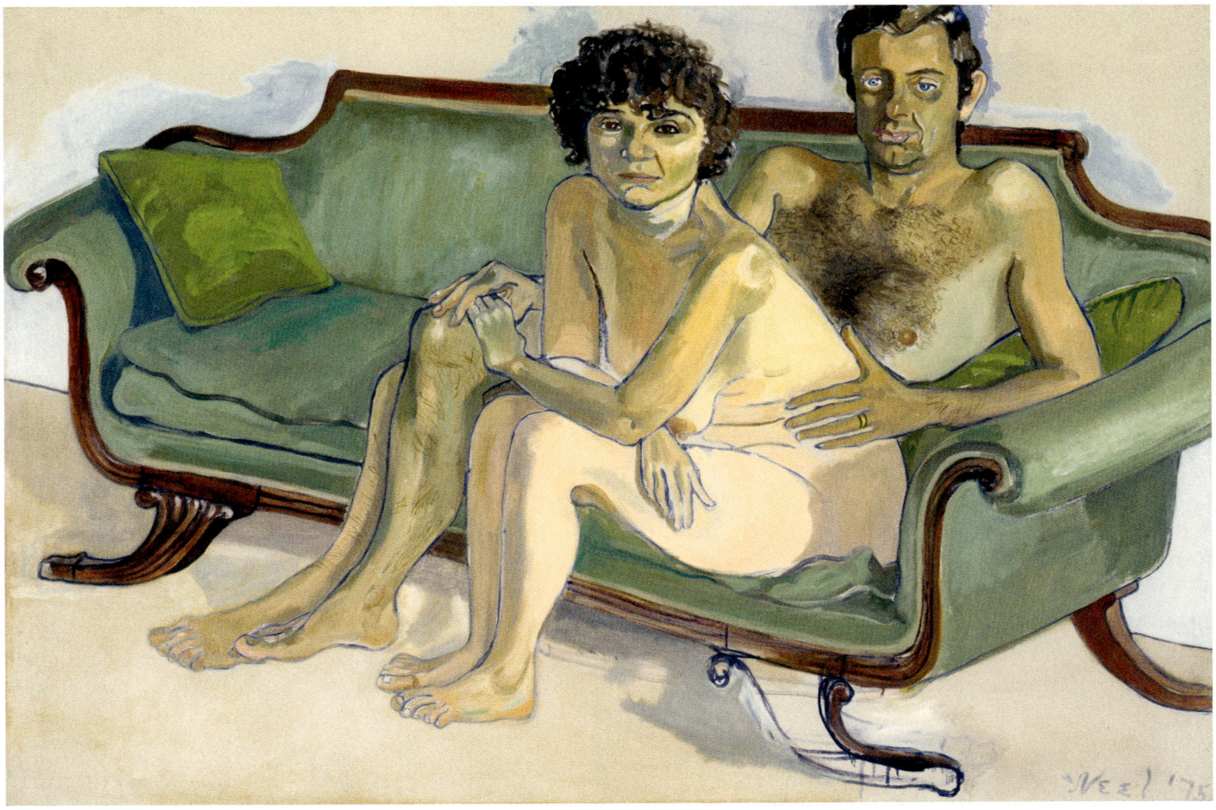


**Cindy Nemser and Chuck** 1975

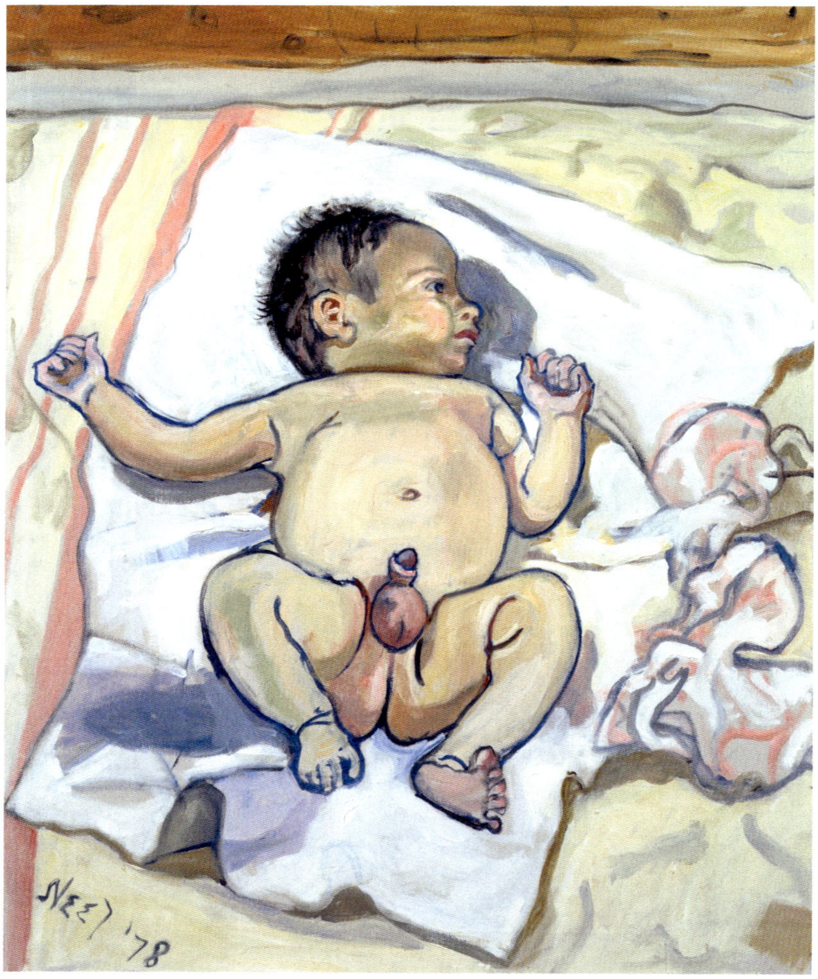




**Andrew** 1978

**Margaret Evans Pregnant** 1978

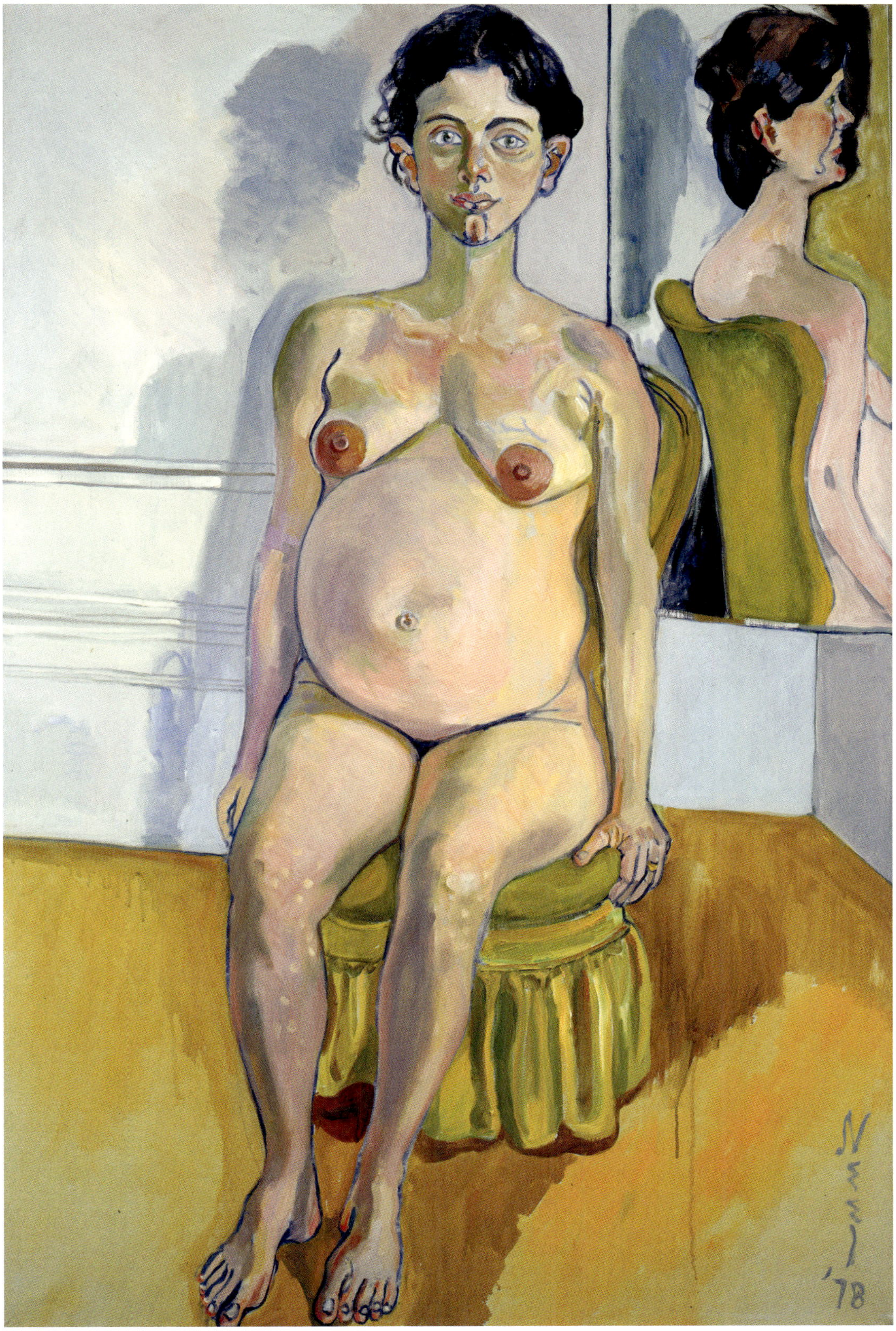
Neel
'78

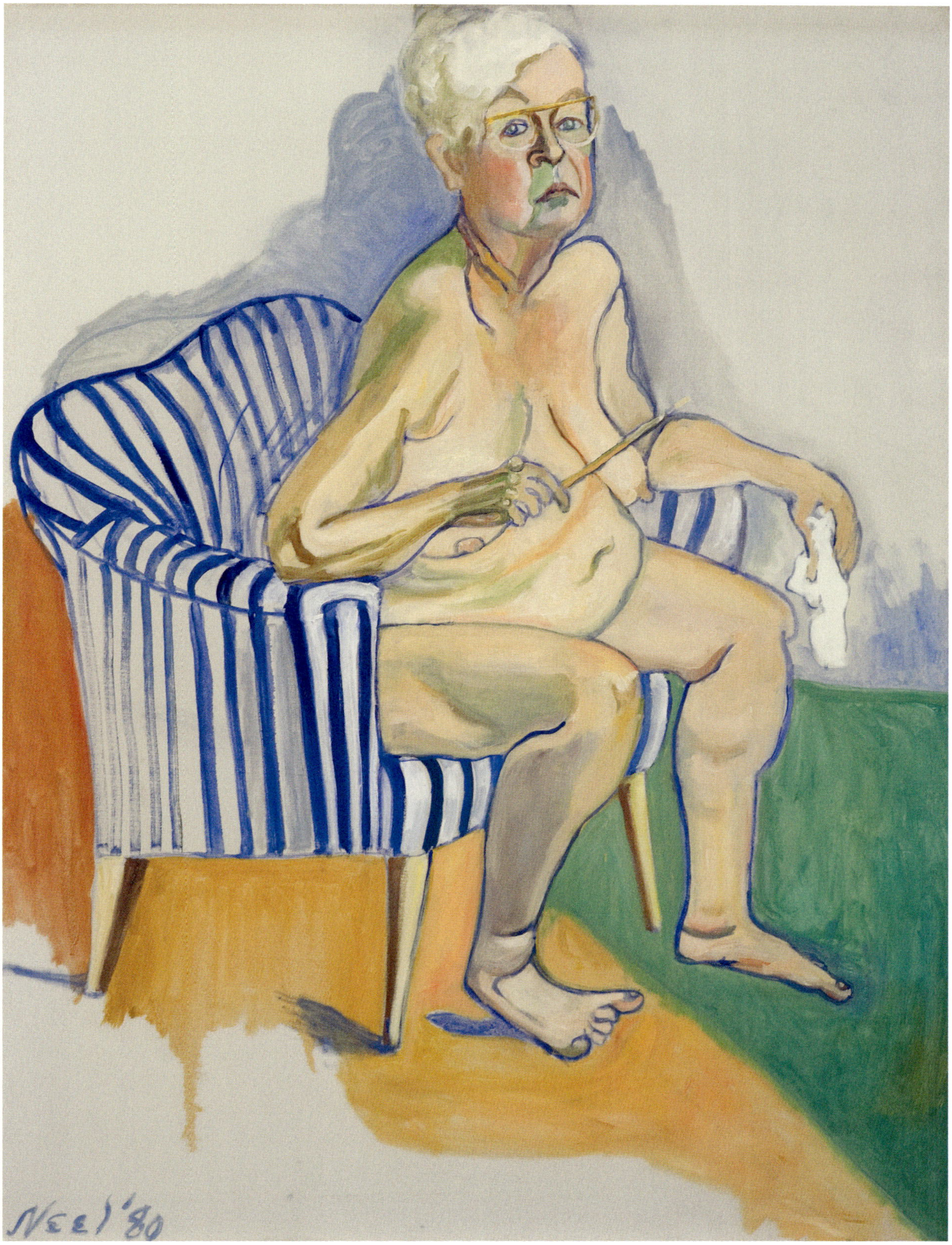
Neel '80

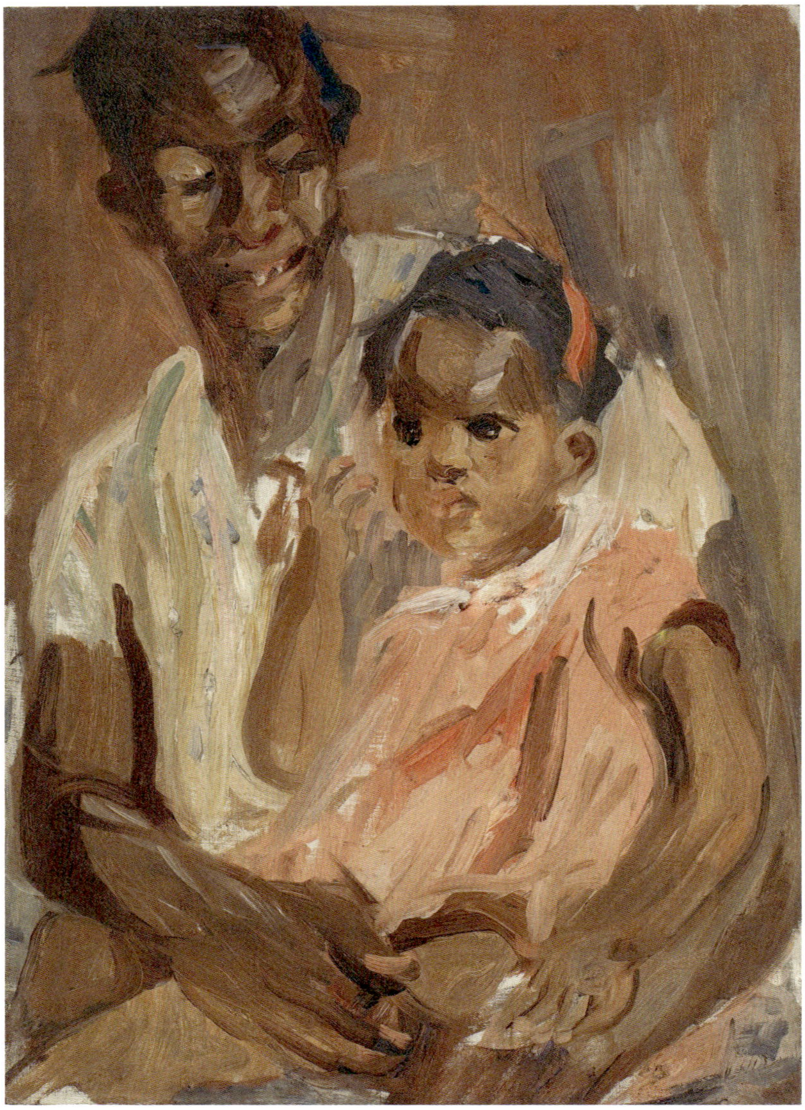

 **Mother and Child, Havana** 1926

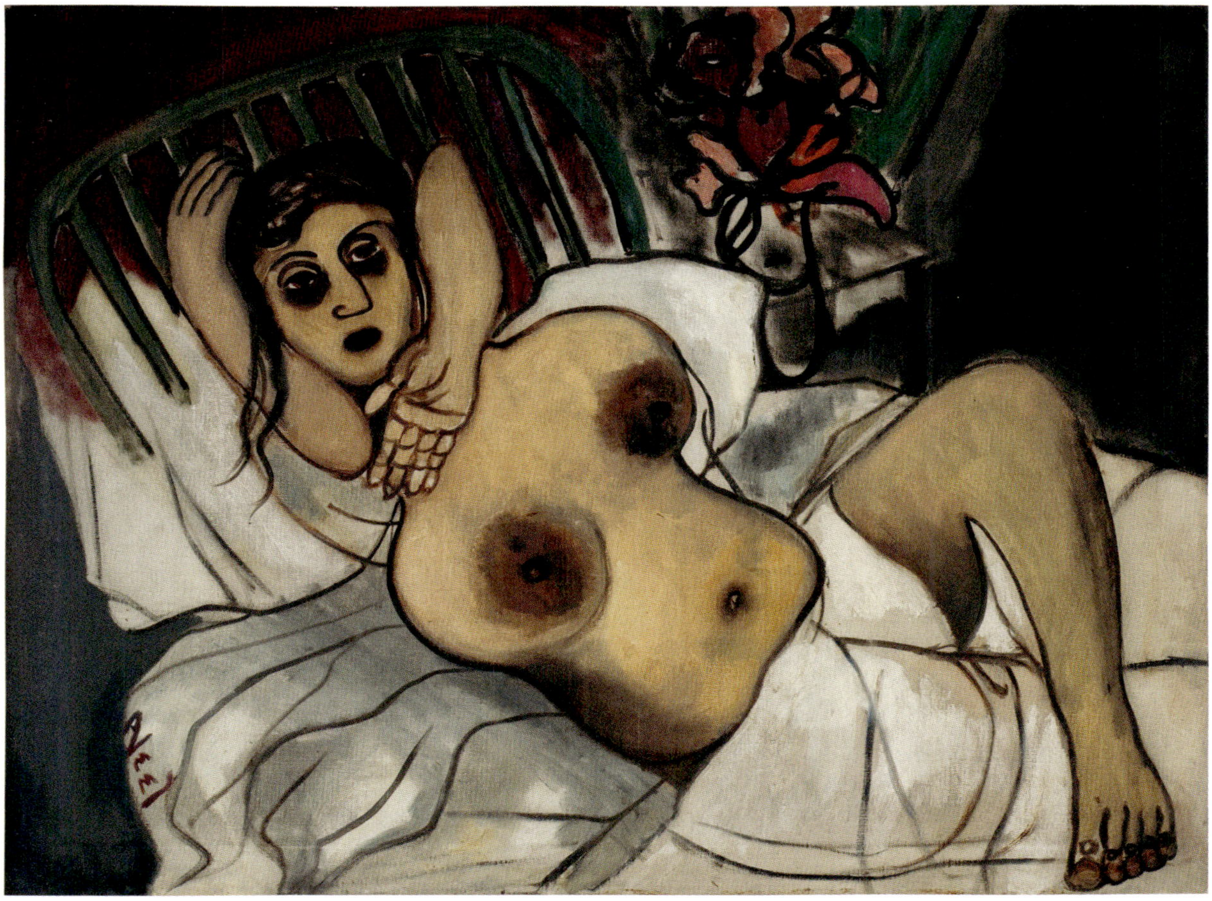

**Childbirth** 1939

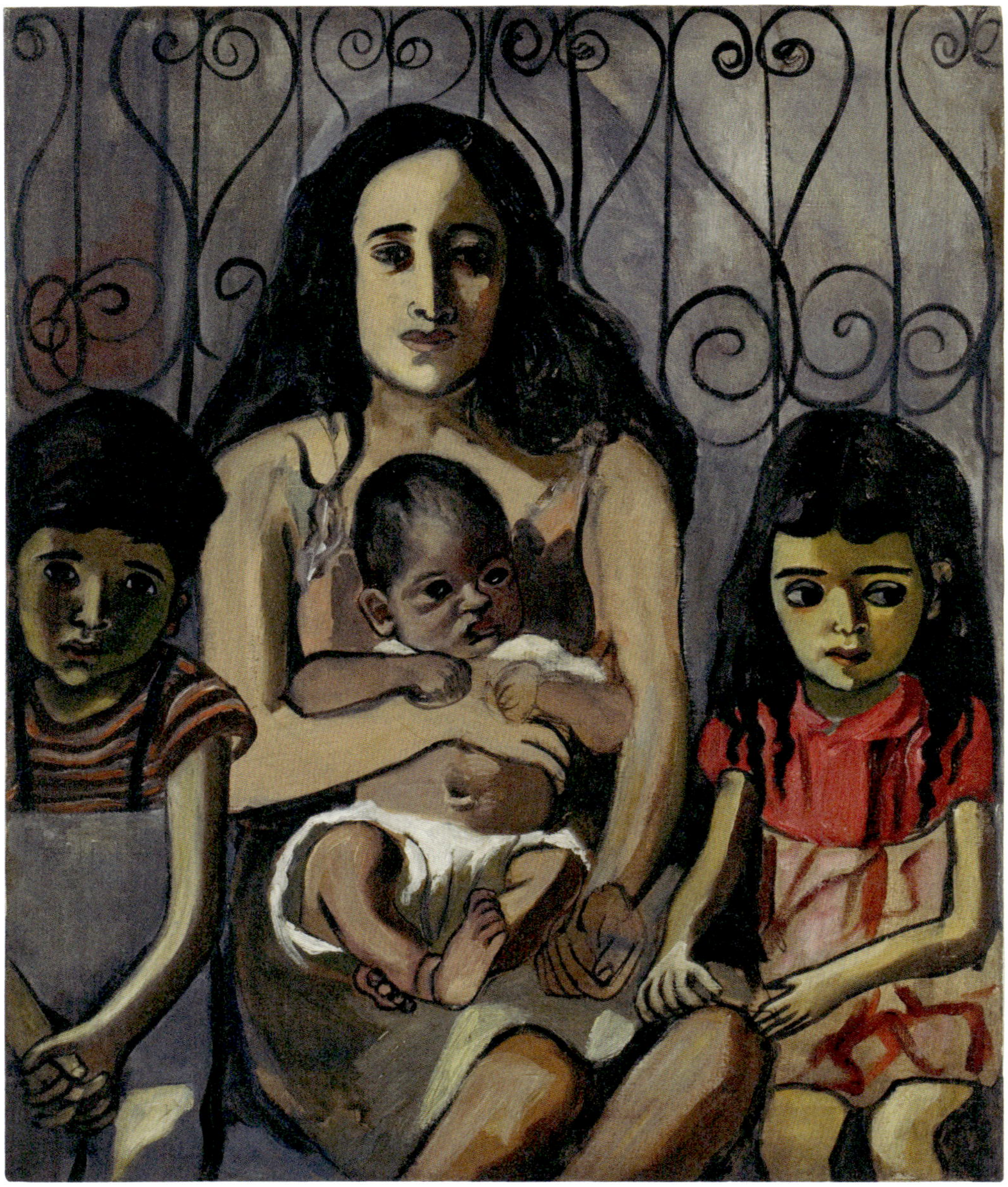

 **The Spanish Family** 1943

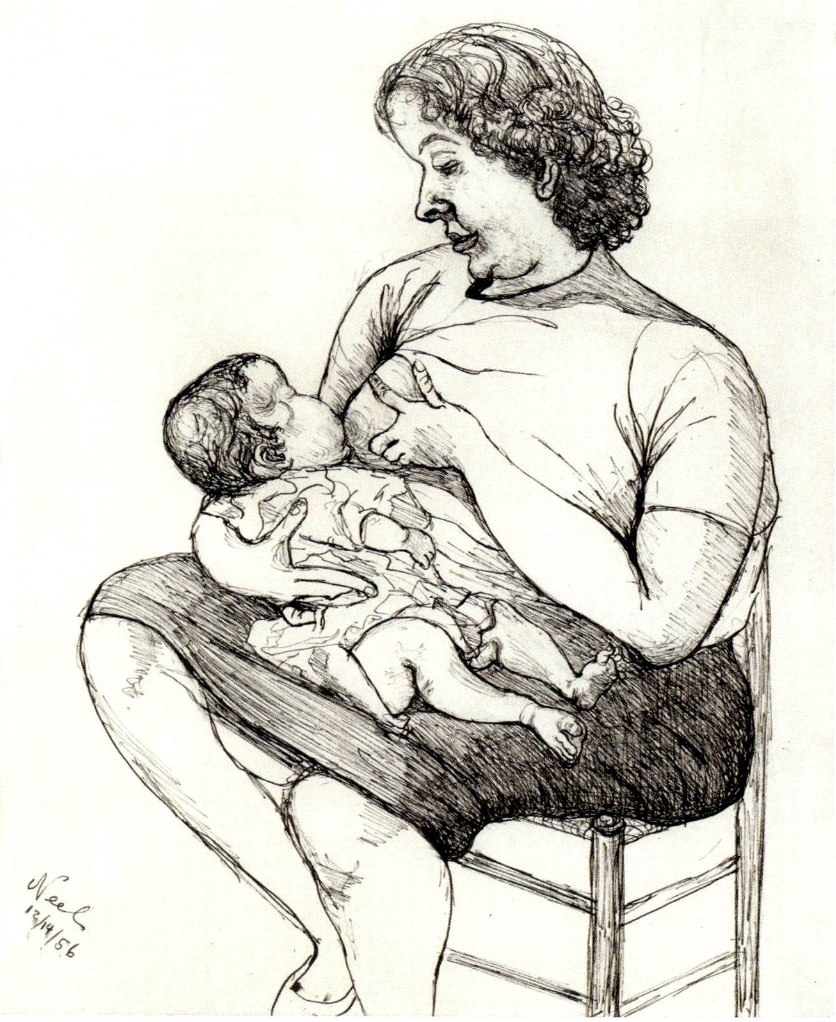


**Mother and Child** 1956

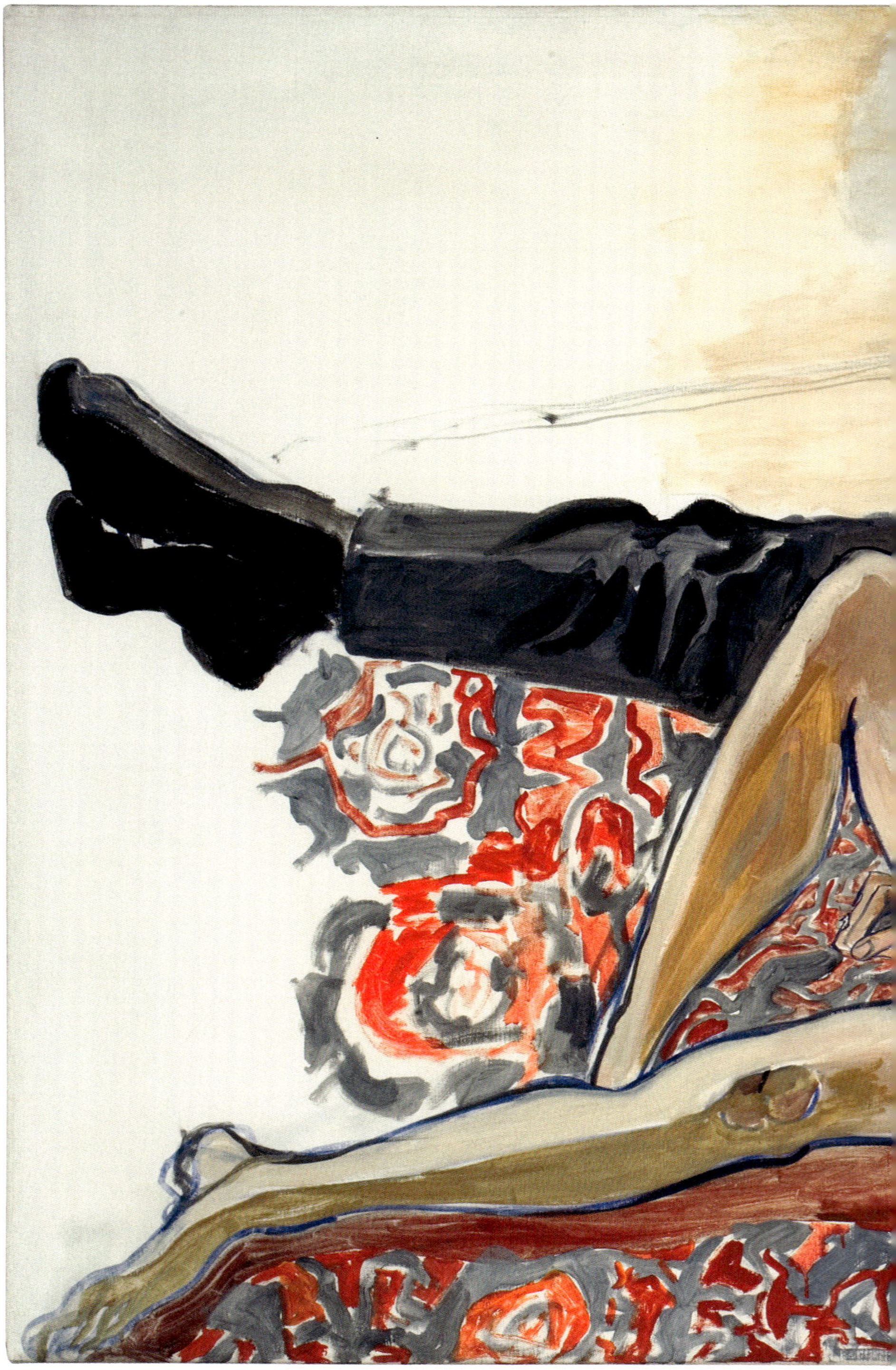

 **Pregnant Julie and Algis** 1967

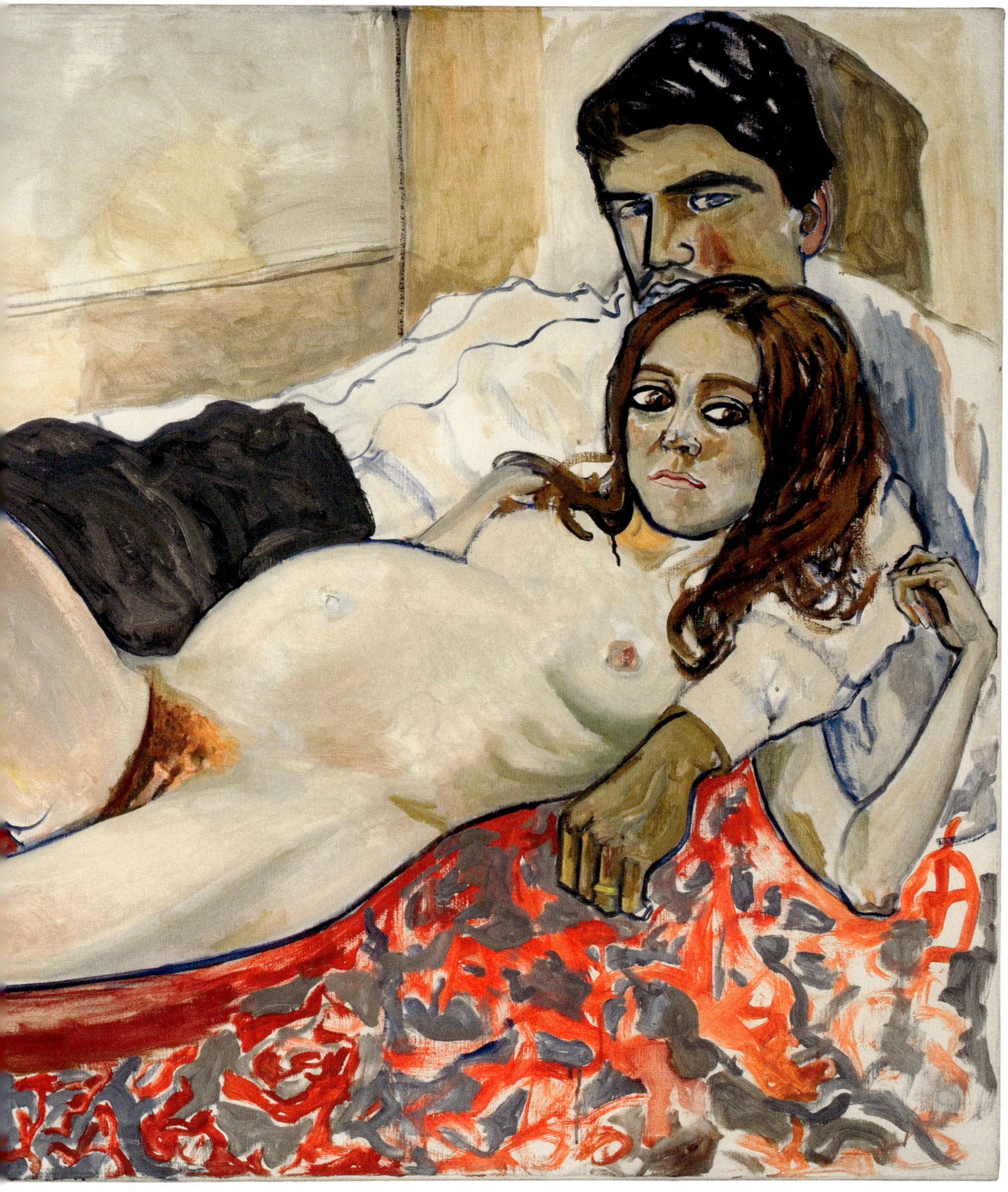

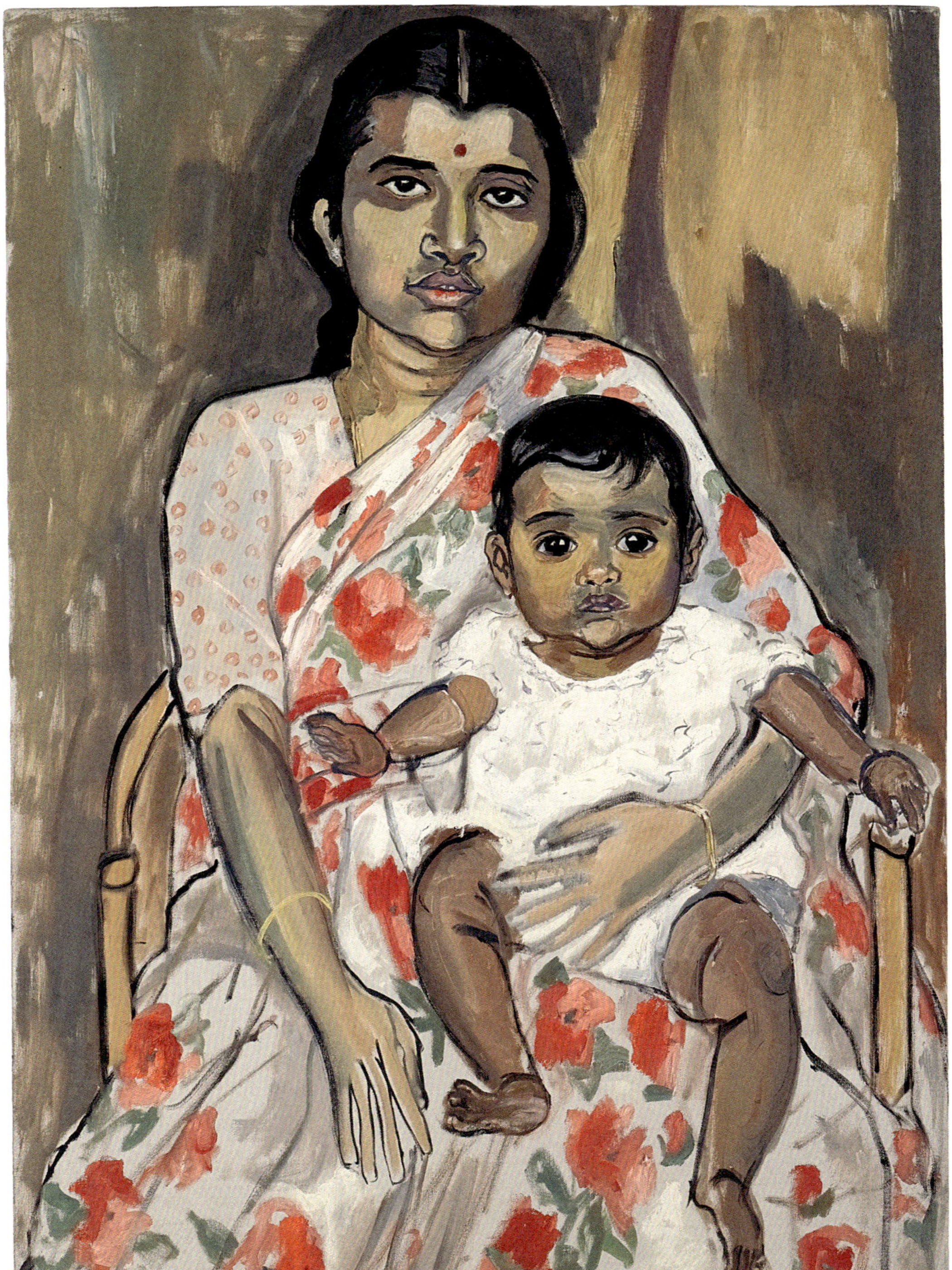

 **Mother and Child** ca. 1962

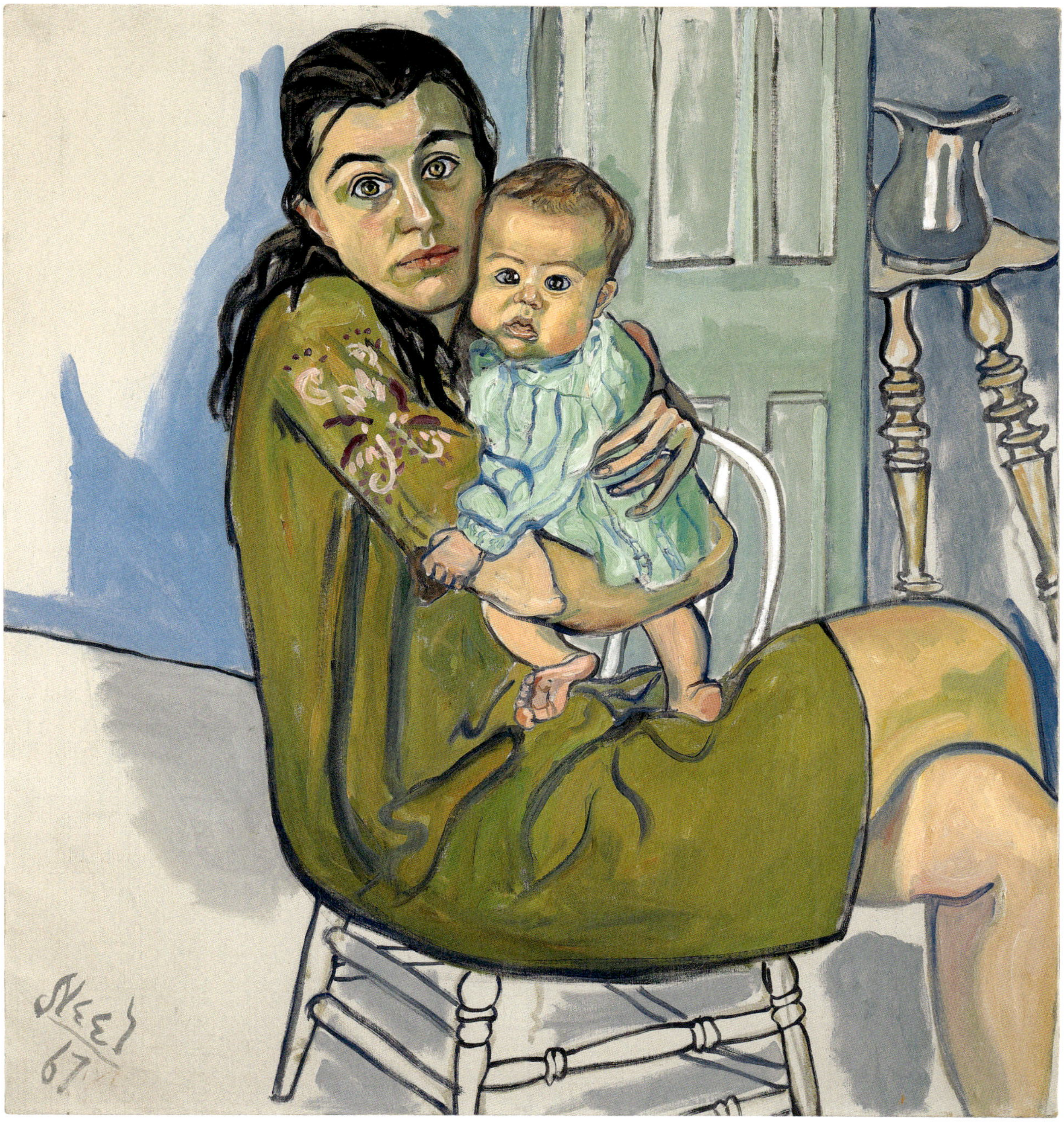

**Nancy and Olivia** 1967

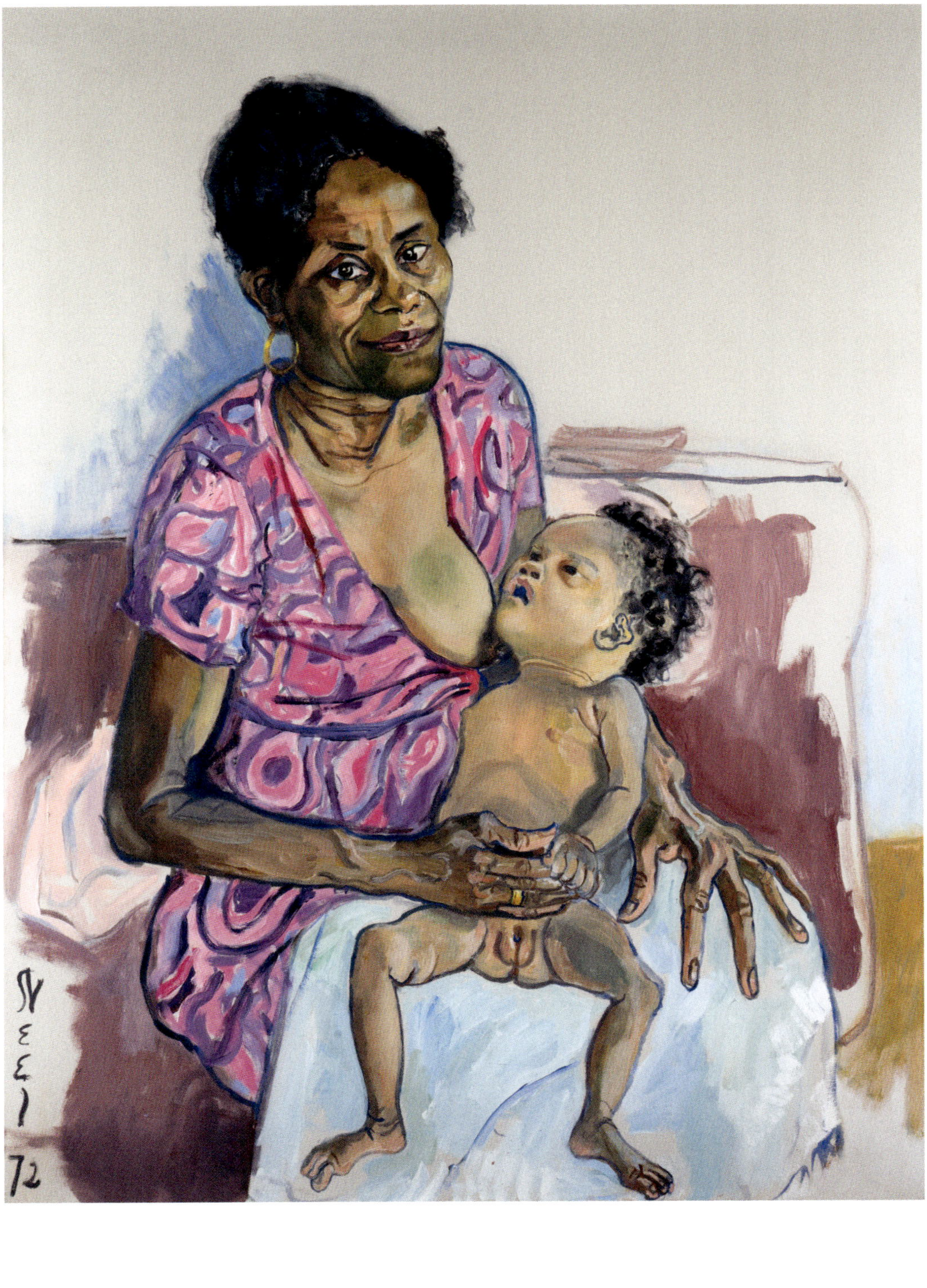
NEEL
72

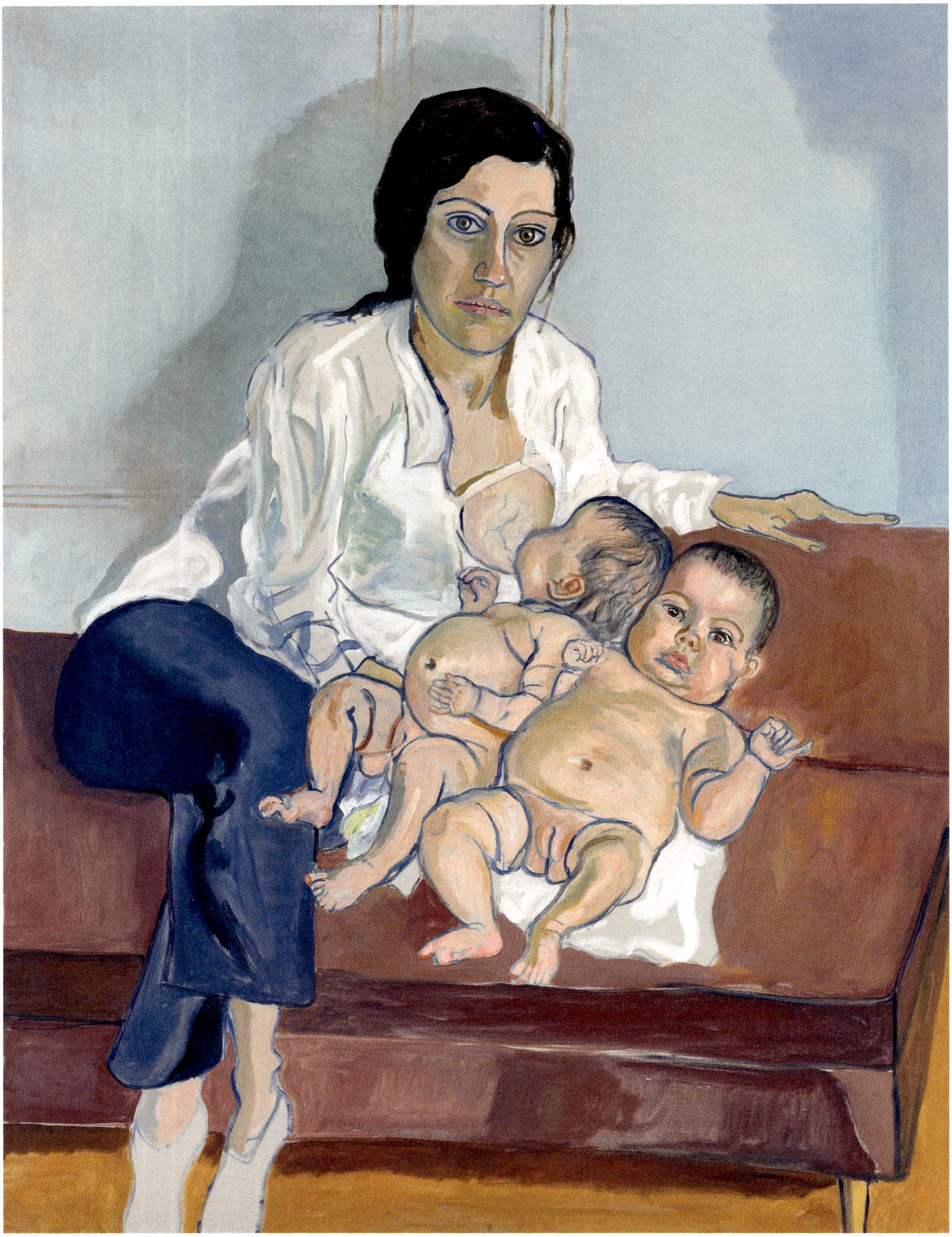



**Nancy and the Twins** 1971

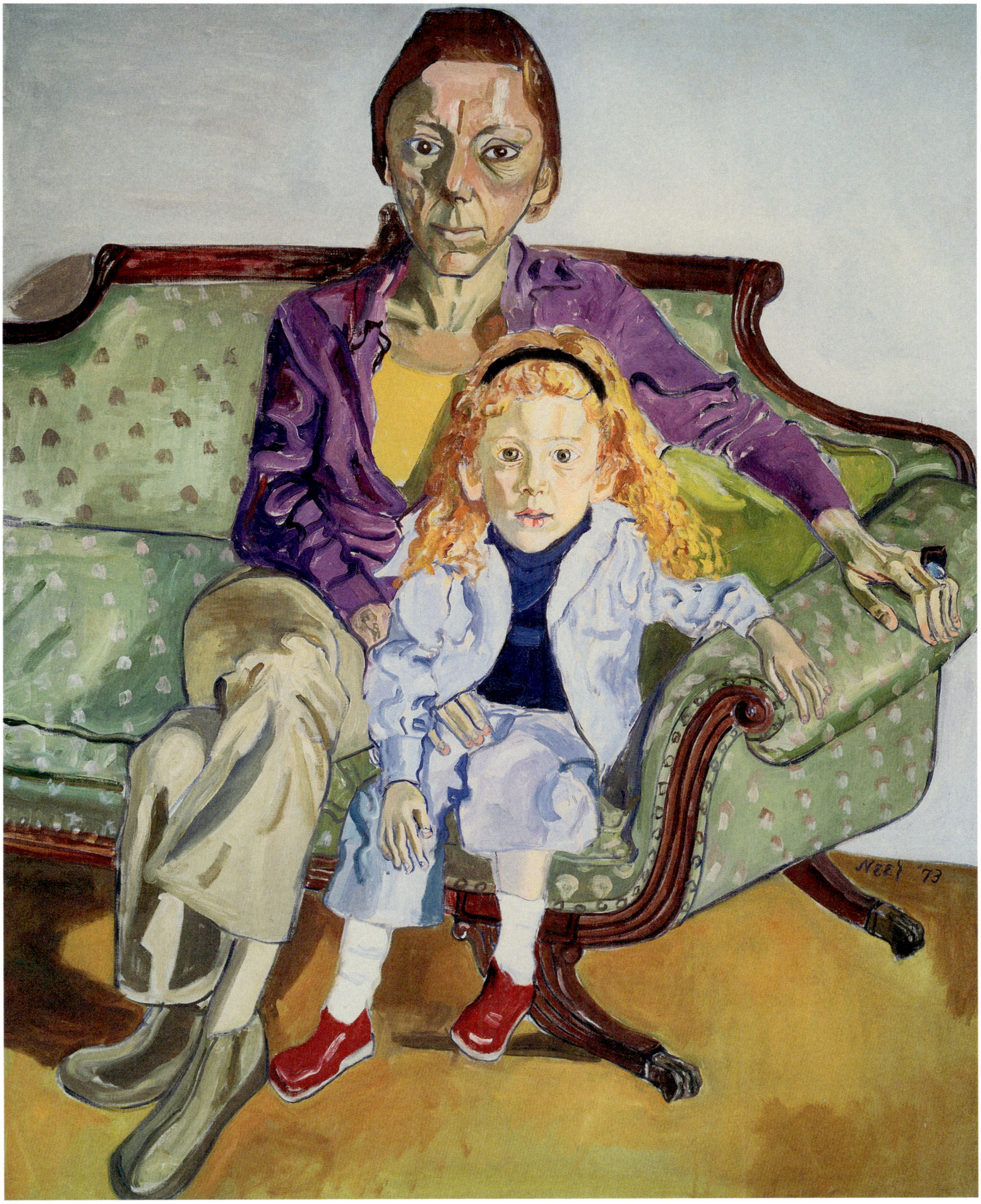


**Linda Nochlin and Daisy** 1973

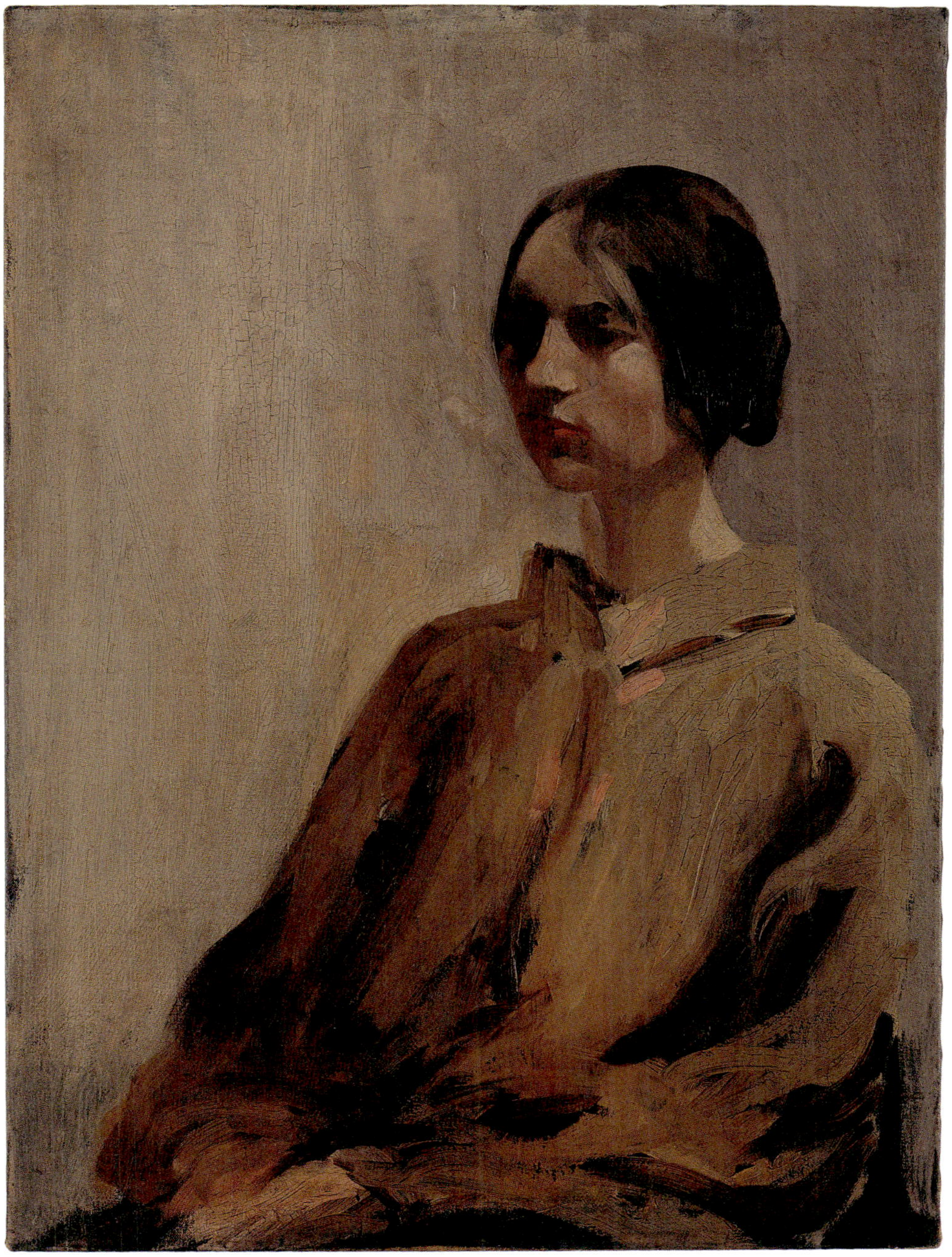

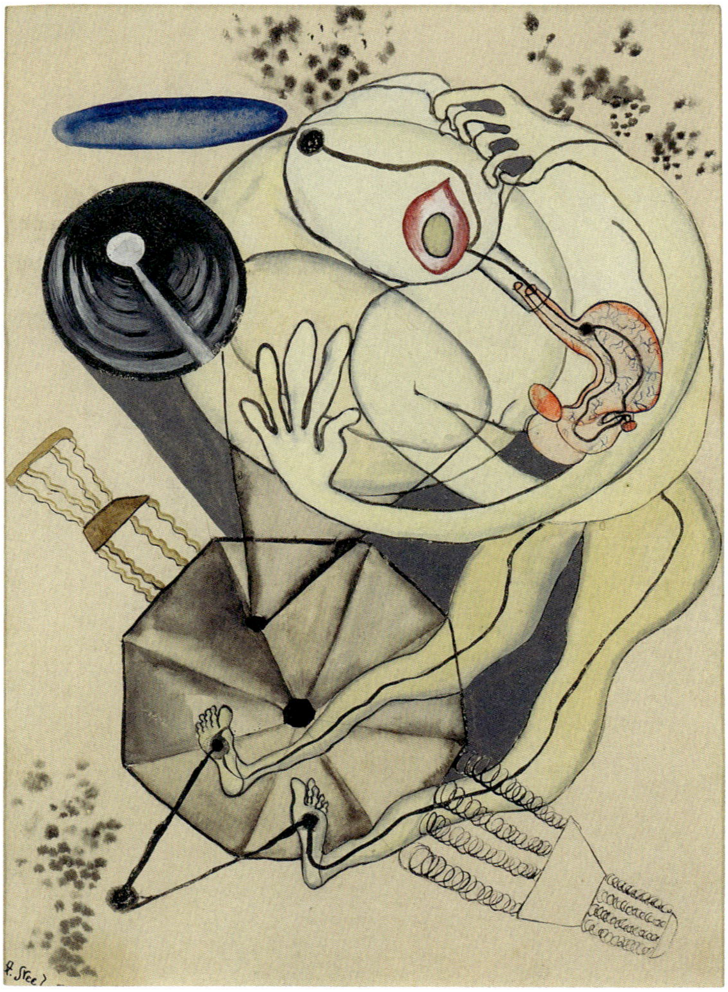


 **Addiction** 1931

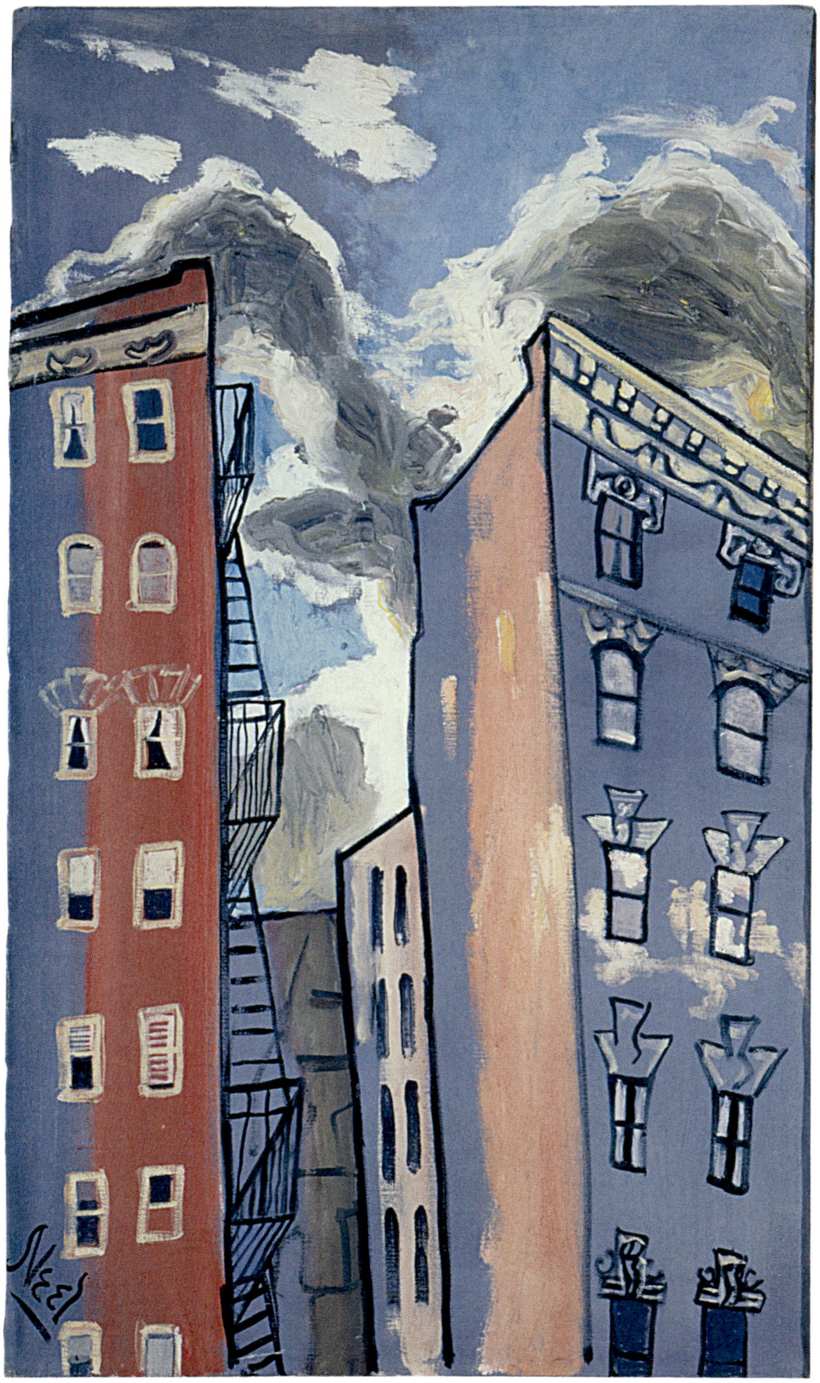


**Sunset in Spanish Harlem** 1958

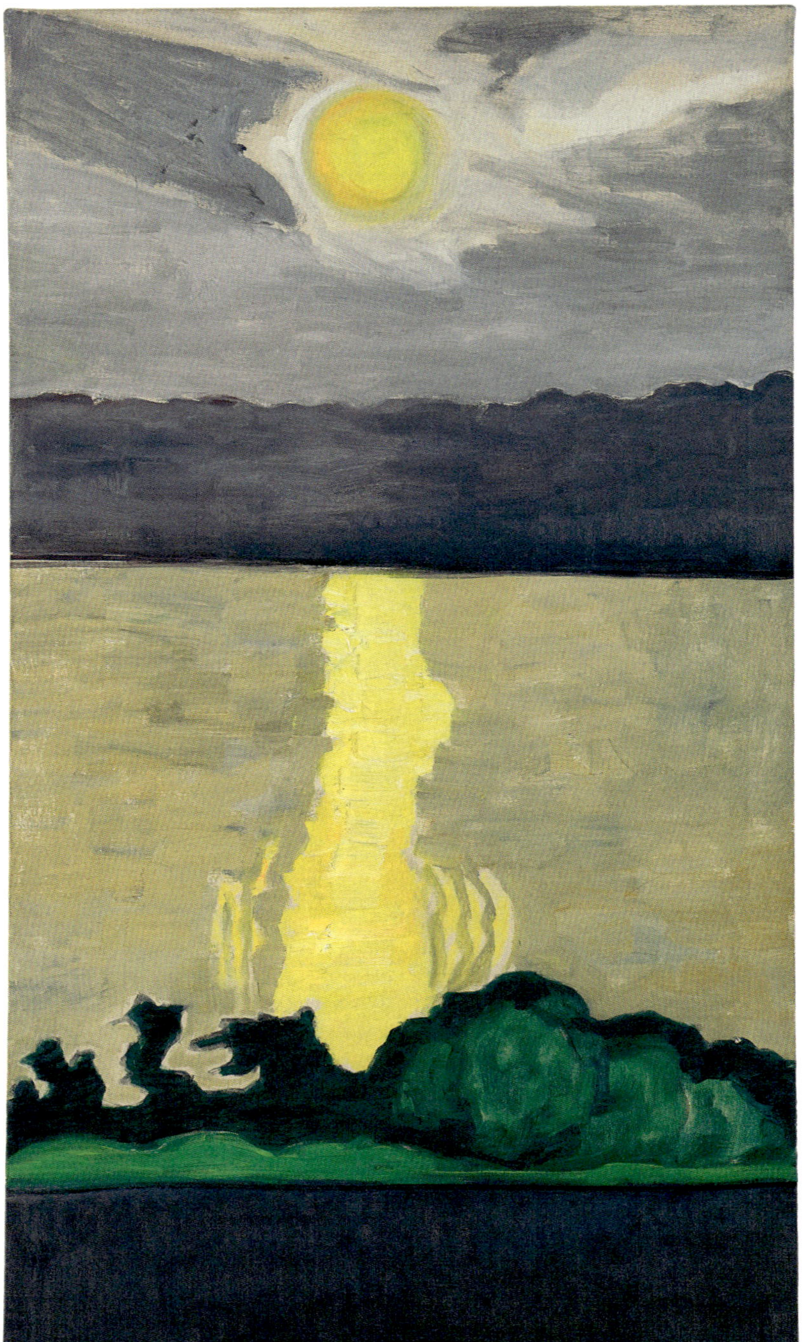

 **Sunset, Riverside Drive** 1957

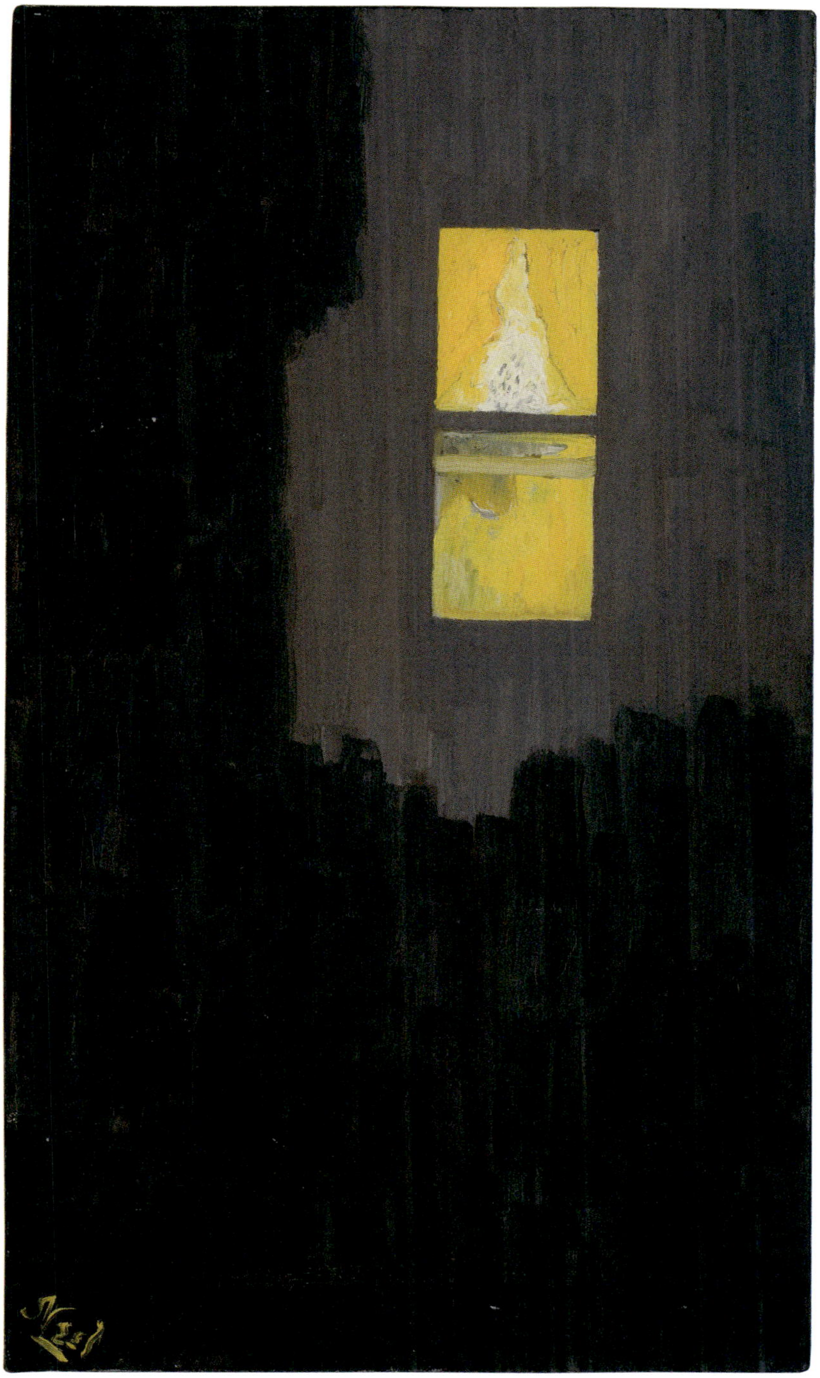

**Night** 1959

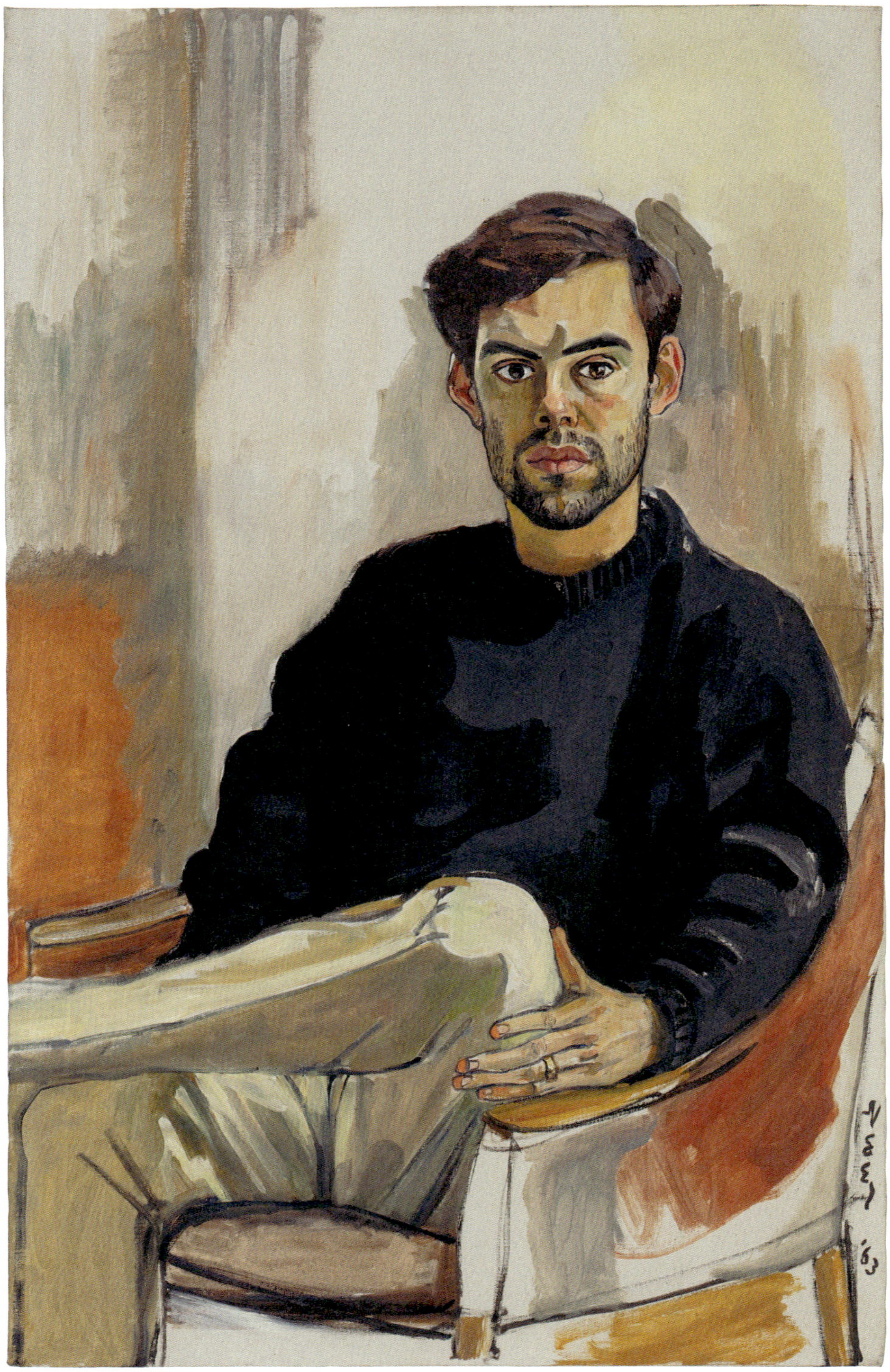



**Richard** 1963

**Black Draftee (James Hunter)** 1965

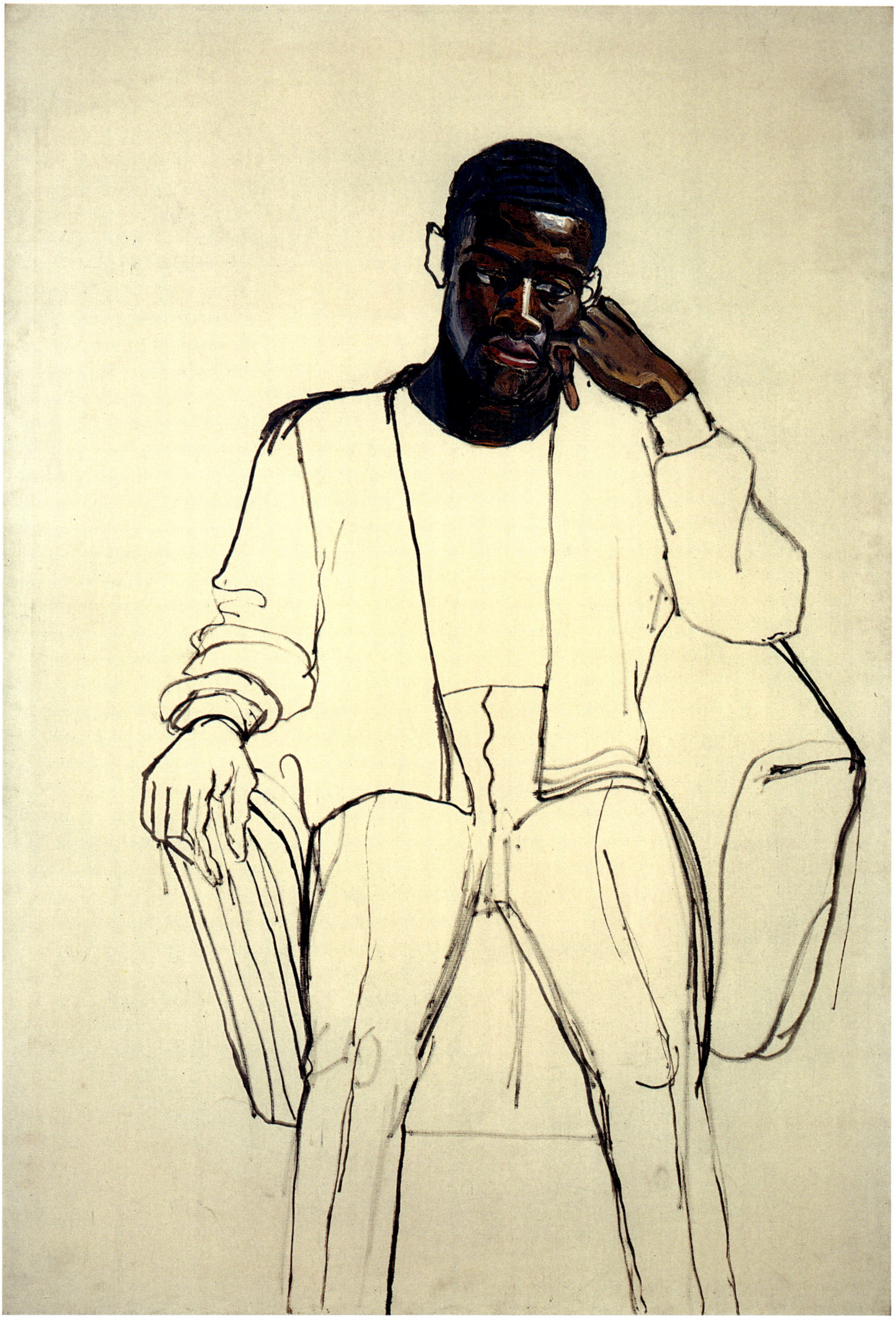

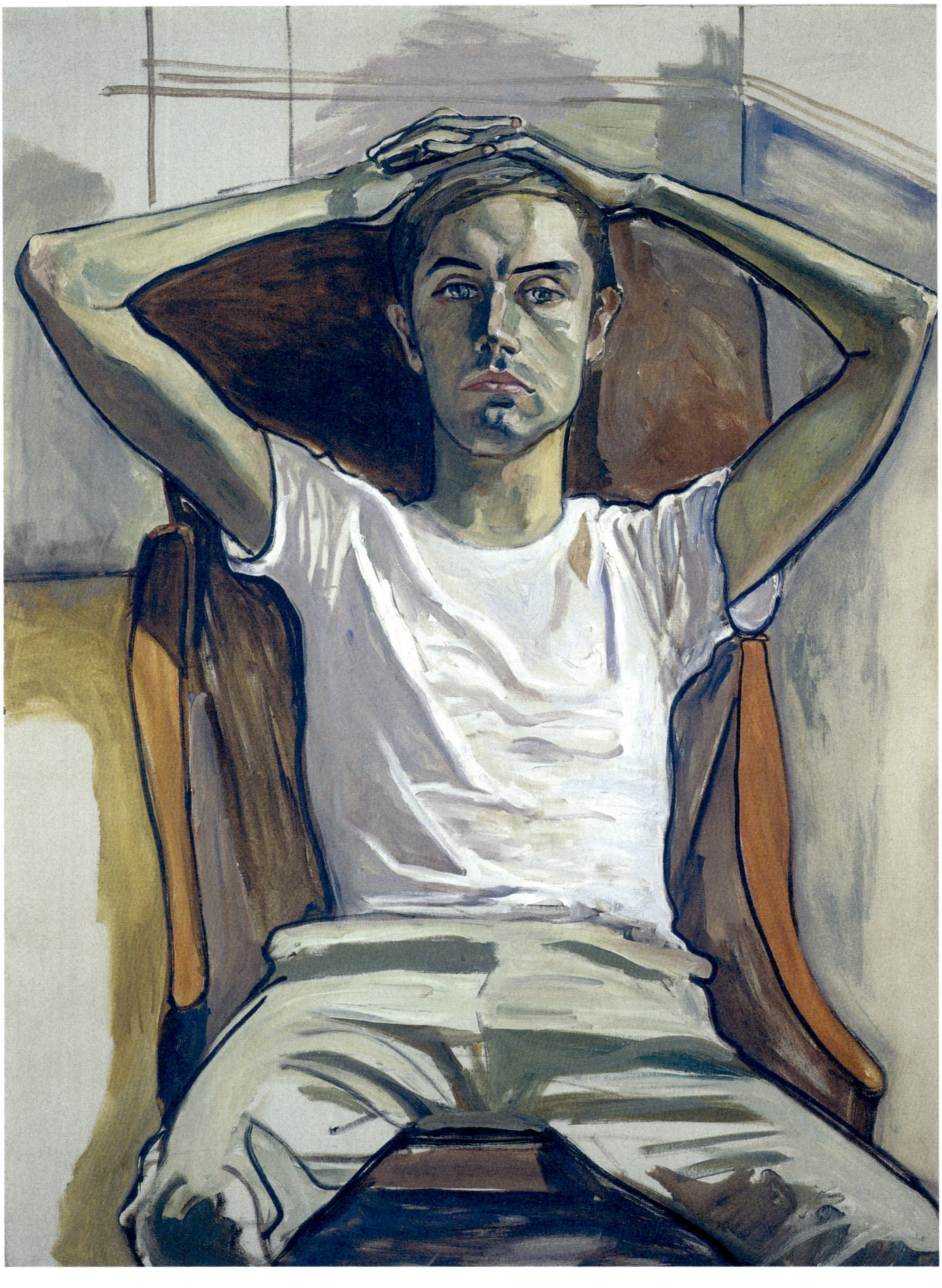

 **Hartley** 1966

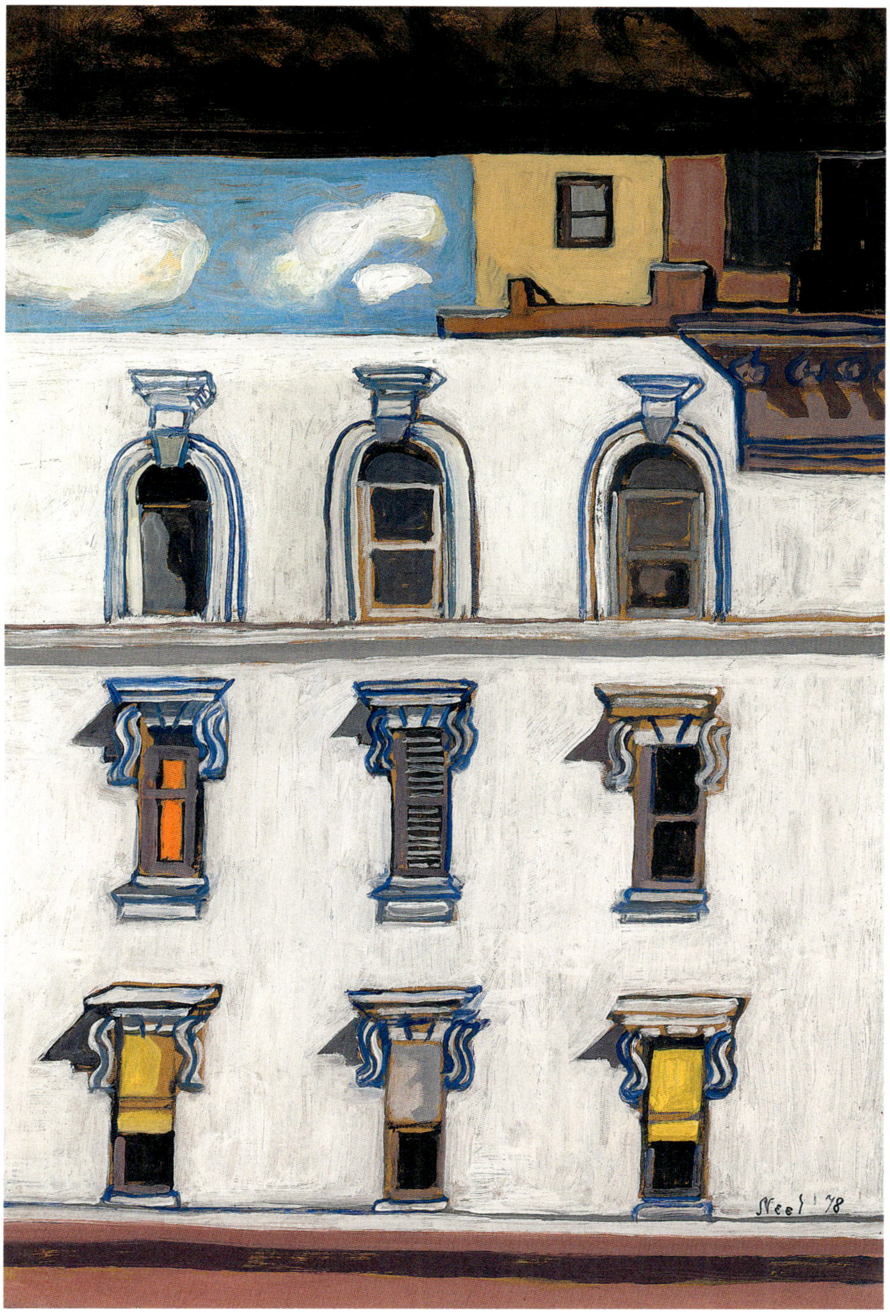


**View from the Artist's Window** 1978

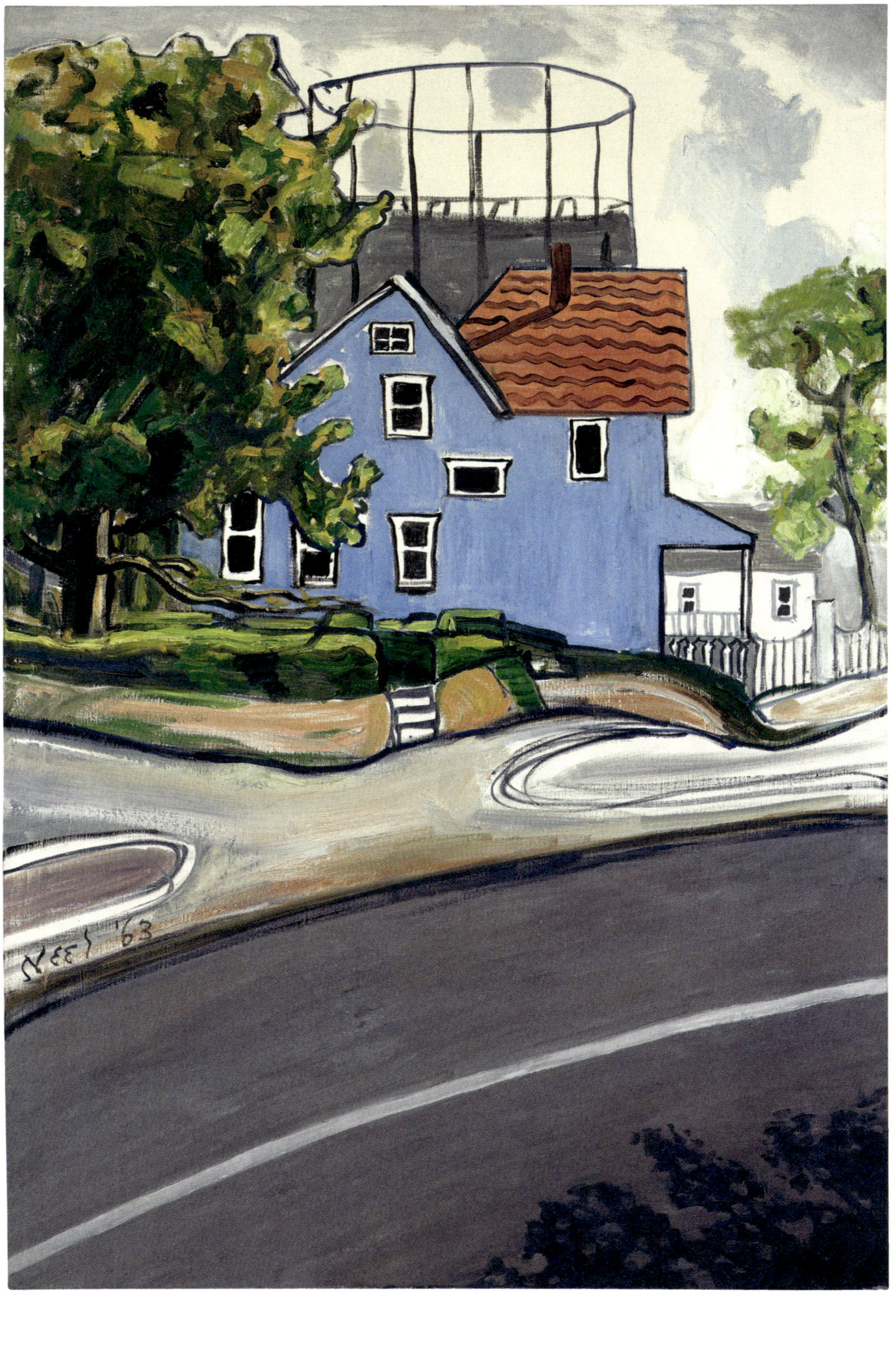

 **Blue House** 1963

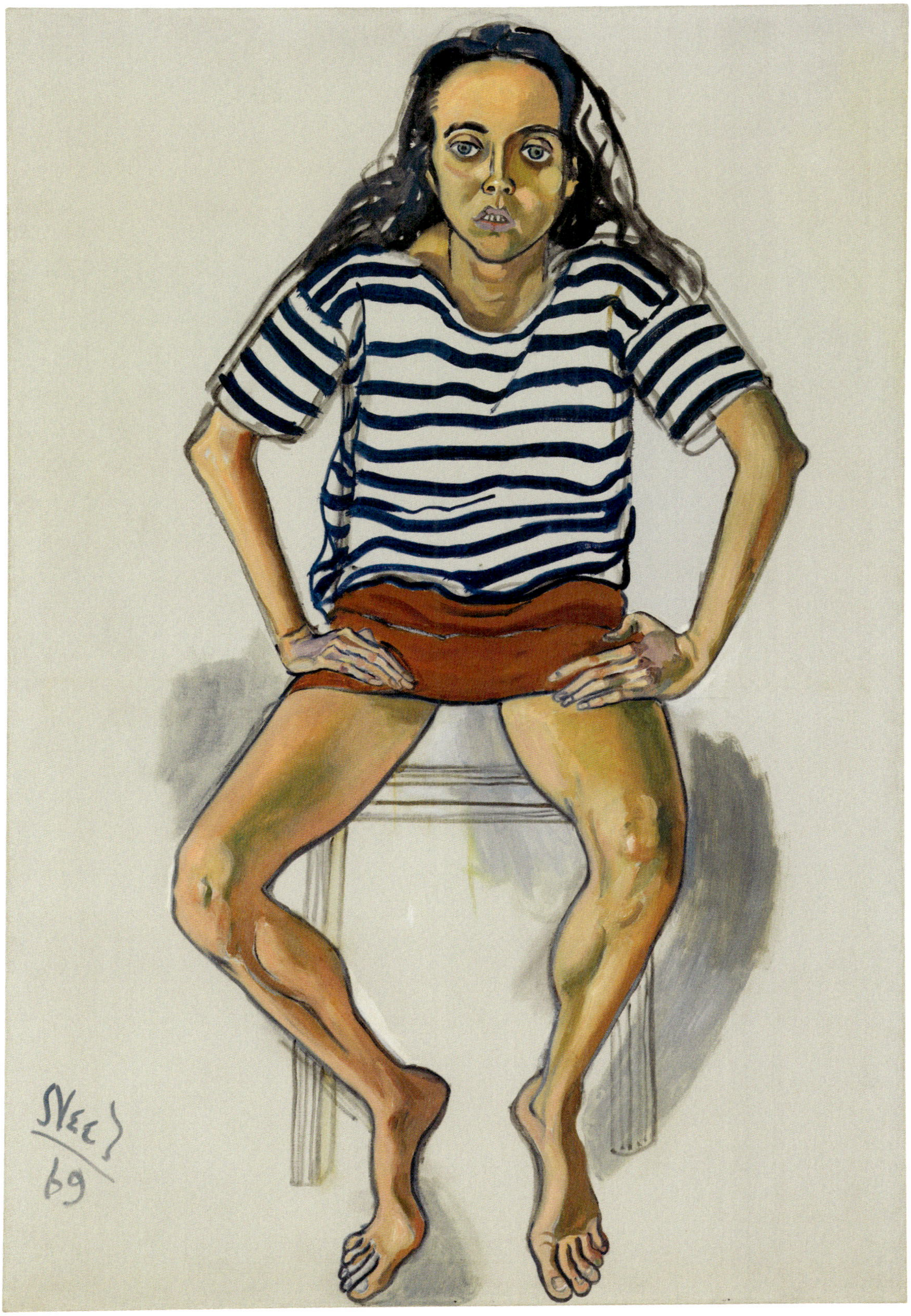


**Ginny in a Striped Shirt** 1969

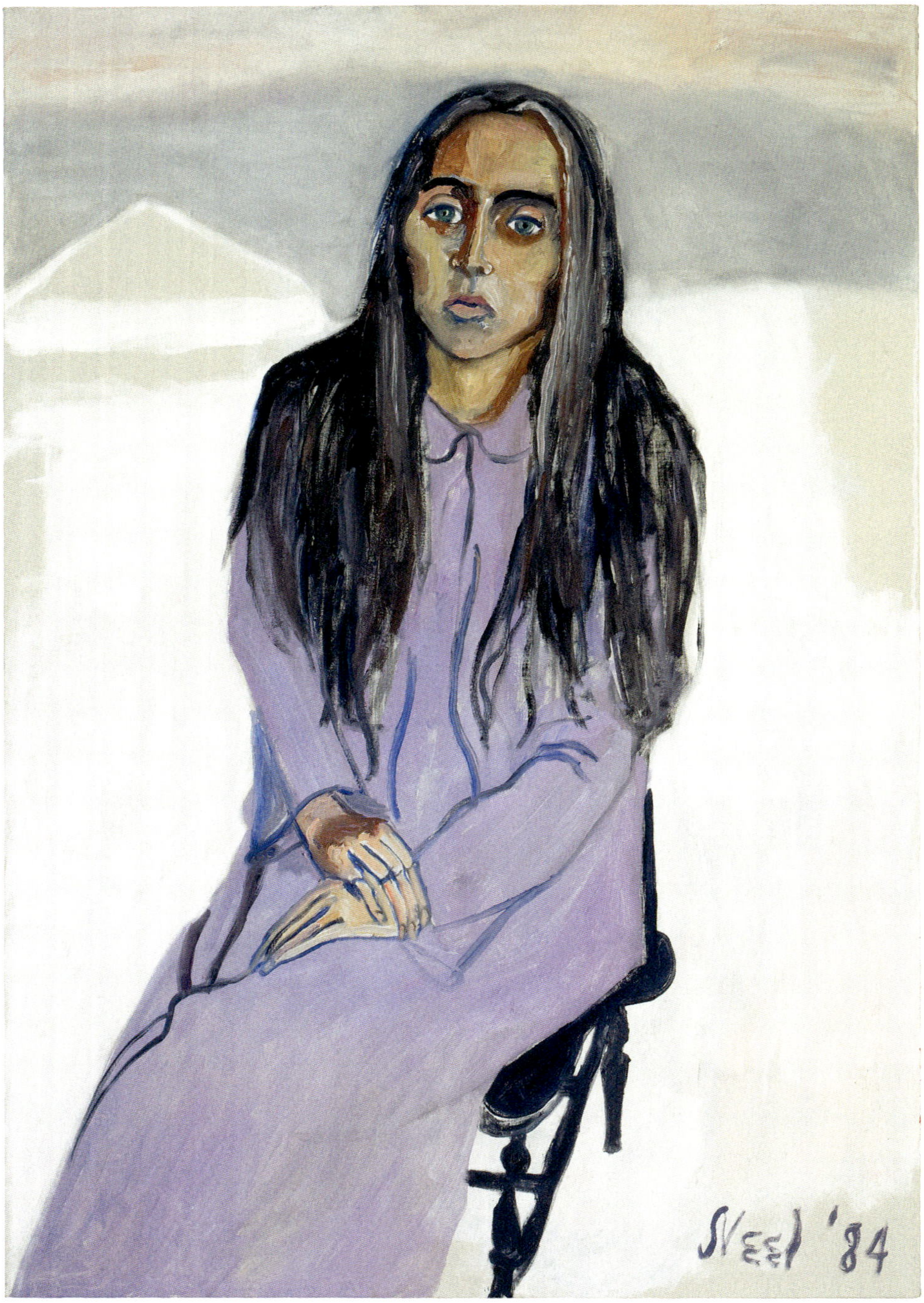


 **Ginny** 1984

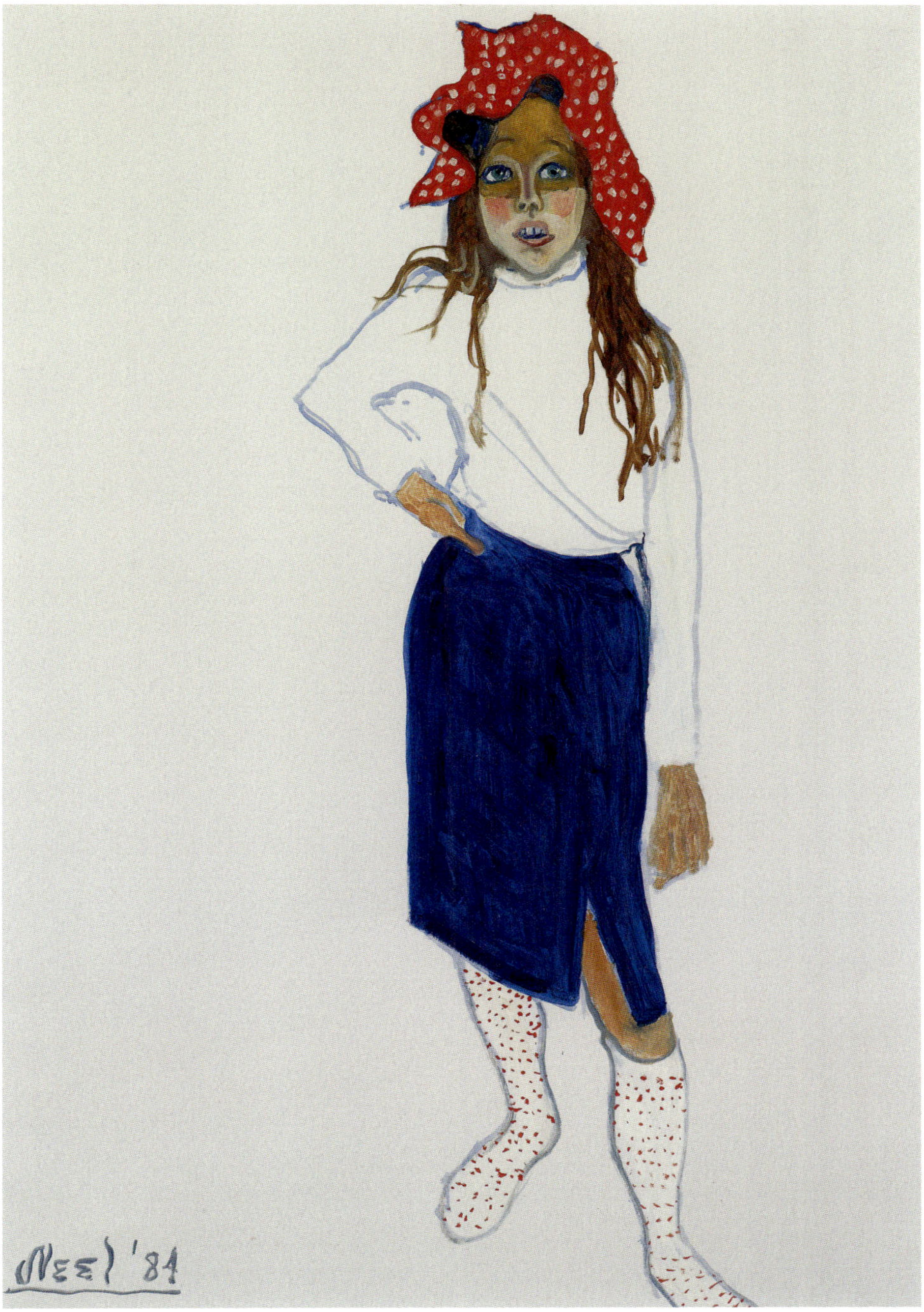


**Elizabeth in a Red Hat** 1984

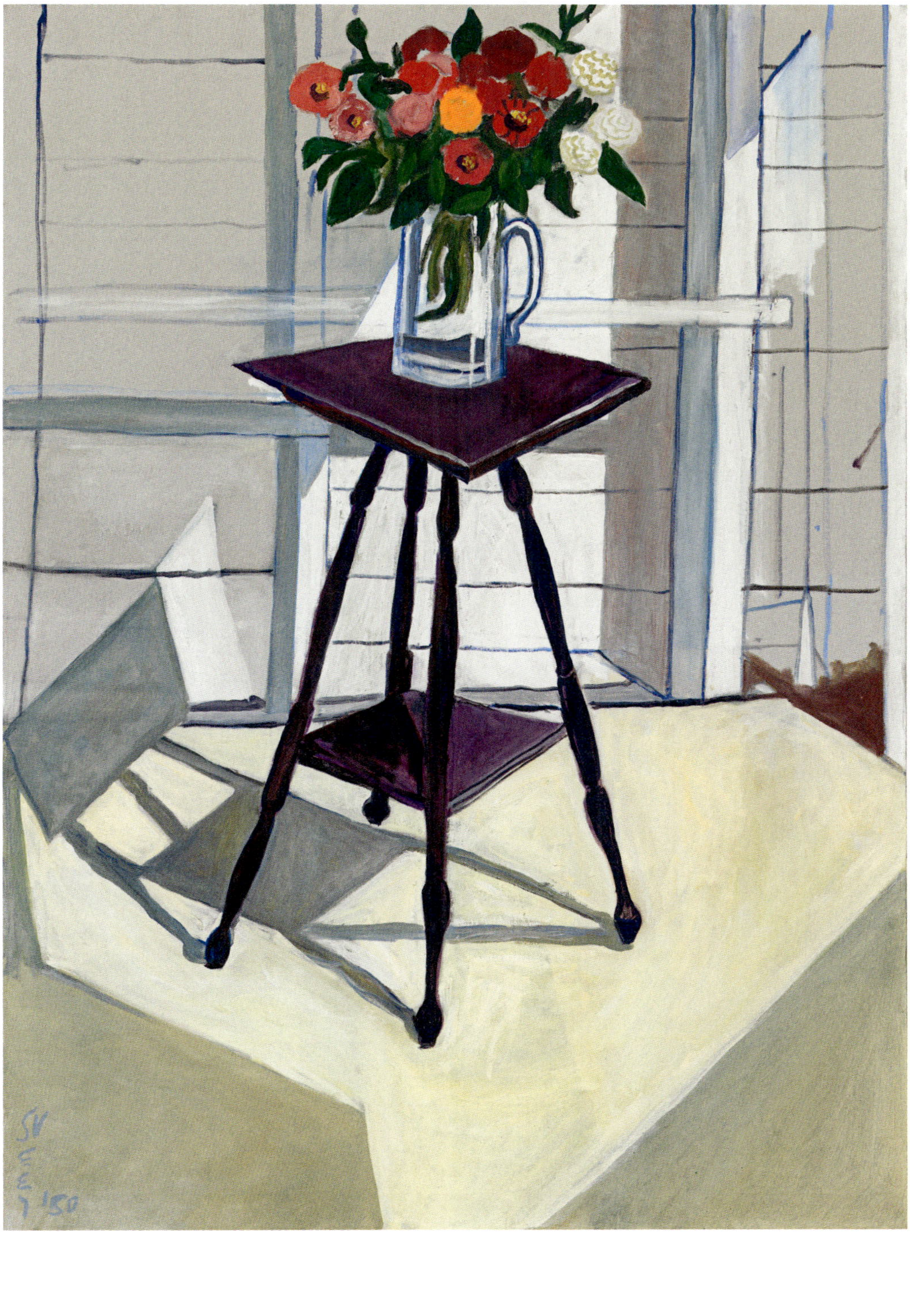

# NOTES

## Anarchic Humanist
### Kelly Baum and Randall Griffey

1. For a full account of Neel's biography, see Phoebe Hoban's indispensable *Alice Neel: The Art of Not Sitting Pretty* (New York: St. Martin's Press, 2010). See also Patricia Hills, *Alice Neel* (New York: Harry N. Abrams, 1983); and Pamela Allara, *Pictures of People: Alice Neel's American Portrait Gallery* (Hanover, N.H.: University Press of New England [for] Brandeis University Press, 1998). On multiple occasions, Neel used the word "humanism" and its variants, "humanist" and "humanistic," to describe her practice. In conversation with Cindy Nemser in the 1970s, Neel said, "I defended human beings from the beginning"; see "Alice Neel," in Nemser, *Art Talk: Conversations with 15 Women Artists* (New York: Icon Editions, 1995), p. 110. Neel told Eleanor Munro, "I never followed any school. I never imitated any artist. I never did any of that. I believe what I am is a humanist"; see Munro, *Originals: American Women Artists* (New York: Simon and Schuster, 1979), p. 128.

2. Mike Gold, "Alice Neel Paints Scenes and Portraits from Life in Harlem," *Daily Worker*, December 27, 1950, p. 11.

3. Alice Neel, interview with Werner and Yetta Groshans, ca. 1980, Werner and Yetta Groshans papers, 1926–1997, Archives of American Art, Smithsonian Institution.

4. Gold, "Alice Neel Paints Scenes and Portraits from Life in Harlem," p. 11.

5. Michael (Mike) Gold, exhibition statement, in *Paintings by Alice Neel, April 23 to May 23*, exh. brochure (New York: New Playwrights Theatre, 1951).

6. "To the word [portrait] clings such a frightful bourgeois taint," Neel said in 1974. "Don't you think, rather, 'pictures of people'? What I do is certainly not what you'd find hanging at the Harvard Club." Piri Halasz, "Alice Neel: 'I have this obsession with life'," *Art News* 73, no. 1 (January 1974), p. 48. See also Allara, *Pictures of People*, p. 16.

7. Hills, *Alice Neel*, pp. 134, 167. Neel reiterated the claim that art is "a form of history" in Wendy Slatkin, "Alice Neel (1900–1984)," in *The Voices of Women Artists* (Englewood Cliffs, N.J.: Prentice Hall, 1993), p. 263.

8. José Ortega y Gasset, *The Dehumanization of Art and Other Essays on Art, Culture, and Literature*, trans. Helene Weyl (Princeton: Princeton University Press, 1968), pp. 26, 38. Ortega's position on modernism is not only reductive but in many cases wildly inaccurate, as he ignores the humanist values that animated so much early twentieth-century abstraction.

9. Slatkin, "Alice Neel (1900–1984)," p. 262.

10. For Neel's relationship with the Communist Party, see ibid., p. 261: "The first time I joined the Communist Party was about 1935. . . . But I was never a good Communist. I hate bureaucracy. Even the meetings used to drive me crazy. . . . But it [the Communist Party] affected my work quite a bit." See also Hoban, *Alice Neel*, p. 118; and Hills, *Alice Neel*, p. 60. According to Andrew Hemingway, Neel likely joined the group in part because it "offered the most sustained critique available of class, racial and sexual inequality"; see Hemingway, *Artists on the Left: American Artists and the Communist Movement, 1926–1956* (New Haven: Yale University Press, 2002), p. 247. Furthermore, participating in the group allowed ambitious, smart women such as Neel to take part in public life more generally—that is, to exercise their political, social, and intellectual muscles—in ways barred to them in mainstream society, which defined gender roles very rigidly, relegating women to the domestic sphere.

11. As Neel wrote in 1971, "All the insults and discrimination are just part of the terrible rat race to which the human race has been reduced"; see untitled statement, *Daily World*, April 17, 1971, p. 47. In a statement reproduced in Slatkin, "Alice Neel (1900–1984)," p. 263, Neel claimed, "I love to paint people torn by all the things that they are torn by today in the rat race in New York." Neel put the matter slightly differently in 1979: "I am like Chichikov in *Dead Souls*, a collector of souls. One of the primary motives of my work is to reveal the inequalities and pressures as shown in the psychology of the people I paint." Neel, quoted in Patti Goldstein, "Soul on Canvas," *New York* magazine (July 9–16, 1979), p. 76. And, finally, "I love people who are ruined by the city, psychologically and every other way. They're under this terrible strain that modern life imposes. I love to show the results of all that." Neel, quoted in Lynn F. Miller and Sally S. Swenson, *Lives and Works: Talks with Women Artists* (Metuchen, N.J., and London: Scarecrow Press, 1981), p. 124.

12. Alice Neel, "I Paint Tragedy and Joy," *New York Times*, October 31, 1976.

13. Hoban, *Alice Neel*, p. 24; Hills, *Alice Neel*, pp. 24–25.

14. Robert Henri, *The Art Spirit: Notes, Articles, Fragments of Letters and Talks to Students, Bearing on the Concept and Technique of Picture Making, the Study of Art Generally, and on Appreciation* (1923; repr. New York: Harper and Row, 1984), p. 111.

15. Hills, *Alice Neel*, p. 22. Neel regularly cited *Futility of Effort* as among her most important paintings.

16. See James K. Monte, *22 Realists*, exh. cat. (New York: Whitney Museum of American Art, 1970). This was one of many exhibitions at the Whitney and elsewhere in New York from which Neel's work was conspicuously absent, oversights that catalyzed feminists to lobby on her behalf in the 1970s.

17. Critic Hilton Kramer was especially skeptical of the artistic merits of Neel's technique. He offered one of his harshest assessments on the occasion of her 1974 retrospective at the Whitney Museum: "Beyond the subject's face . . . Mrs. Neel's attention diminishes and her ability to sustain a pictorial statement simply disappears. There are ineptitudes here—in the rendering of the figure, in the handling of design and in the over-all control of the motif—that are not a matter of style but of basic competence." Kramer, "Art: Alice Neel Retrospective," *New York Times*, February 9, 1974.

18. See Hoban, *Alice Neel*, pp. 241–42. Neel first compared herself to Balzac, according to Hoban, in her 1960 statement for *The Hasty Papers*, a Beat publication.

19. "Painting: Changing Scenes of Childhood," *Time*, January 3, 1969, p. 49.

20. These subjects were the topic of Hilton Als's revelatory 2017 exhibition, *Alice Neel, Uptown*. See Als, *Alice Neel, Uptown*, exh. cat. (New York: David Zwirner Books; London: Victoria Miro, 2017).

21. Gold, "Alice Neel Paints Scenes and Portraits from Life in Harlem," p. 11.

22. Ibid. This represents a misunderstanding of Abstract Expressionism on Neel's part. In truth, the artists of the New York School were committed to evoking the human condition albeit in abstract vocabularies.

23. Neel's FBI file chronicles the agency's surveillance of and suspicions about the artist between 1948 and 1959.

24. For more on the terms of this debate, see Francis Frascina, ed., *Pollock and After: The Critical Debate* (New York: Harper and Row, 1985); Serge Guilbaut, "Postwar Painting Games: The Rough and the Slick," pp. 30–79, and Benjamin H. D. Buchloh, "Cold War Constructivism," pp. 85–110, in *Reconstructing Modernism: Art in New York, Paris, and Montreal 1945–1964*, ed. Serge Guilbaut (Cambridge, Mass.: MIT Press, 1990); Matthew Cullerne Bown, *Art under Stalin* (Oxford: Phaidon Press, 1991); Okwui Enwezor, Katy Siegel, and Ulrich Wilmes, *Postwar: Art between the Pacific and the Atlantic, 1945–1965*, exh. cat. (Munich: Haus der Kunst; New York: Prestel, 2016); and John J. Curley, *Global Art and the Cold War* (London: Laurence King Publishing, 2018).

25. Neel more than once referred to this experience as the "awful dichotomy"; see Hills, *Alice Neel*, p. 29.

26. Neel's painting of James Hunter of 1965 was featured in the 2016 exhibition *Unfinished: Thoughts Left Visible*, at The Metropolitan Museum of Art. For more on "unfinishedness" as it applies to Neel and other artists, see Kelly Baum, Andrea Bayer, and Sheena Wagstaff, eds., *Unfinished: Thoughts Left Visible*, exh. cat. (New York: The Metropolitan Museum of Art, 2016).

27. "I draw and paint at the same time, which is essentially modern," Neel claimed. See Alexander Russo, "Alice Neel," in *Profiles on Women Artists* (Frederick, Md.: University Publications of America, 1985), p. 197.

28. Judith Higgins, "Alice Neel and the Human Comedy," *Art News* 83, no. 8 (October 1984), p. 77.

29. Stephen Porter Dunn, *Some Watercolors from Venice, and Other Poems* (Riverdale, N.Y.: Coalbin Press, 1994), pp. 61–62.

30. Helen Molesworth explores Neel's personal limits and contradictions in an episode of her Getty podcast. See Molesworth, with Simone Leigh and Moyra Davey, "Alice Neel: Viva la Mujer," November 12, 2019, in *Recording Artists*, podcast, 35:33, https://www.getty.edu/recordingartists/season-1/neel/.

## Political Creatures
### Kelly Baum

1. For more on Neel's position on the relationship between art and politics, see her comments in an interview with Judith Vivell, "Talking about Portraits," *Feminist Art Journal* 3, no. 2 (Summer 1974), p. 15. Later in life, Neel added, "I don't want to do political cartoons. But if I do–well, these poor that I did in Havana in 1926, that's a social commentary. But it's not completely obvious"; see Alexander Russo, "Alice Neel," in *Profiles on Women Artists* (Frederick, Md.: University Publications of America, 1985), p. 203. See also Wendy Slatkin, "Alice Neel (1900–1984)," in *The Voices of Women Artists* (Englewood Cliffs, N.J.: Prentice Hall, 1993), pp. 261–62.

2. For more information on these institutions, see the Greenwich Village Society for Historical Preservation's website: https://www.gvshp.org.

3. Neel's investment in racial justice was considerable. She recalled attending an event with Mamie Till-Bradley, the mother of Emmett Till, and later made a drawing of her; see Cindy Nemser, "Alice Neel," in *Art Talk: Conversations with 15 Women Artists* (New York: Icon Editions, 1995), p. 120. She also remembered donating money to the Black Panthers and attending a speech by Malcolm X; see Ted Castle, "Alice Neel," *Artforum* 22, no. 2 (October 1983), p. 39.

4. Patricia Hills, *Alice Neel* (New York: Harry N. Abrams, 1983), p. 53.

5. For more on the relationship between civil rights, Black liberation, and the CPUSA, see Gerald Horne, "The Red and the Black: The Communist Party and African-Americans in Historical Perspective," in *New Studies in the Politics and Culture of U.S. Communism*, ed. Michael E. Brown, Randy Martin, Frank Rosengarten, and George Snedeker (New York: Monthly Review Press, 1993), pp. 199–237; and Mary Helen Washington, *The Other Blacklist: The African American Literary and Cultural Left of the 1950s* (New York: Columbia University Press, 2014).

6. For more on Childress, see Washington, *The Other Blacklist*, pp. 123–64, esp. pp. 160–64. Neel's portrait was painted the same year Childress's acclaimed play *Florence* appeared in *Masses & Mainstream* 3, no. 10 (October 1950), pp. 34–47.

7. For more on Arroyo, see Denise Bauer, *Alice Neel's Feminist Portraits: Women Artists, Writers, Activists and Intellectuals*, exh. cat. (New Paltz: Samuel Dorsky Museum of Art, State University of New York at New Paltz, 2003), p. 14; and Mike Gold, "Alice Neel Paints Scenes and Portraits from Life in Harlem," *Daily Worker*, December 27, 1950, p. 11.

8. Along with others in the orbit of *Masses & Mainstream*, Neel attended monthly meetings of the Writers and Critics Group at the home of Annette T. Rubinstein; see Pamela Allara, *Pictures of People: Alice Neel's American Portrait Gallery* (Hanover, N.H.: University Press of New England [for] Brandeis University Press, 1998), p. 96; and Phoebe Hoban, *Alice Neel: The Art of Not Sitting Pretty* (New York: St. Martin's Press, 2010), p. 116.

9. Hoban, *Alice Neel*, p. 218. For more on Neel's attendance at the Jefferson School, see Hills, *Alice Neel*, p. 86; Hoban, *Alice Neel*, p. 116; and Andrew Hemingway, *Artists on the Left: American Artists and the Communist Movement, 1926–1956* (New Haven: Yale University Press, 2002), pp. 247–52. For Childress's relationship with the Jefferson School, see Washington, *The Other Blacklist*, p. 126. A 1956 class schedule for the school names Arroyo as the teacher of a course on "The Puerto Rican National Minority" (https://www.bibliomania.ws/details.php?record=46999).

10. Because only the second word in the periodical's title appears, it is also possible that Gold's hand rests near a copy of the journal's earlier manifestation, *The Masses*.

11. Neel's illustration for Bonosky's story "The Wishing Well" appeared in the May 1949 issue of *Masses & Mainstream*. Her courtroom sketch of the "Trial of the Twelve" was printed in the same journal in December (see Allara, *Pictures of People*, p. 99, for the circumstances surrounding these sketches). In the April 1950 issue, Neel published *Relief Cut*, and in January 1951 she created a drawing to accompany Bonosky's story "I Live on the Bowery." Neel contributed four drawings, including one of Georgie Arce, to the June 1958 issue of *Mainstream*. Also for *Mainstream*, Neel provided a portrait of W. E. B. Du Bois (February 1961) and lent her 1935 portrait of Kenneth Fearing to one of its covers (August 1961).

12. For Neel's comments on her portrait of Farmer, whose daughters she also painted, see Nemser, *Art Talk*, p. 120.

13. Hoban, *Alice Neel*, p. 136.

14. Hal Foster, "Towards a Grammar of Emergency," *New Left Review* 68 (March/April 2011), pp. 105–18.

15. See Michael (Mike) Gold, exhibition statement, in *Paintings by Alice Neel, April 23 to May 23*, exh. brochure (New York: New Playwrights Theatre, 1951).

16. In 1950 Neel spoke about the "extreme poverty" in Spanish Harlem, describing the neighborhood as a "battlefield of humanism" (Gold, "Alice Neel Paints Scenes and Portraits from Life in Harlem," p. 11). See also Neel's comment about the lack of bilingual education in Spanish Harlem in Barbaralee Diamonstein, *Inside New York's Art World* (New York: Rizzoli, 1979), p. 259. Finally, in an undated, handwritten statement, Neel praises the people of Spanish Harlem, "abandoned, despised, charged the most, given the worst," for their perseverance under conditions of extreme hardship (Folder Copies 1, Alice Neel Archive, Stowe, Vt.).

17. Neel is largely responsible for establishing the narrative of harmony between herself and her neighbors in Spanish Harlem. See, for example, Gold, "Alice Neel Paints Scenes and Portraits from Life in Harlem," p. 11; and Lynn F. Miller and Sally S. Swenson, *Lives and Works: Talks with Women Artists* (Metuchen, N.J.: Scarecrow Press, 1981), p. 125.

18. As Neel recalled to Nemser, Arce "had a rubber knife and used to pretend to cut my throat. This was just fun and games." She continues, though, by saying, "He once said to me, 'I don't like to play.' He was a desperate little character" (*Art Talk*, p. 111). For more on Neel's complicated encounters with her sitters, see Castle, "Alice Neel," p. 38.

19. Thomas Keenan, *Fables of Responsibility: Aberrations and Predicaments in Ethics and Politics* (Stanford: Stanford University Press, 1997), p. 2.

20. Judith Butler, *Giving an Account of Oneself* (New York: Fordham University Press, 2005), p. 136. See also Simon Critchley, *Infinitely Demanding: Ethics of Commitment, Politics of Resistance* (London and New York: Verso, 2007).

21. Neel also asserted her sexual agency in her writing. In the second stanza of an undated prose poem, for instance, she conflates desire and suffering, pleasure and guilt: "I have to tell myself that love is innocent–somehow I feel so hotflushy / guilty in a damp muddy place–a room of dark green bushes–earthy smell, / evening chill, delicate watery sounds plash plash paddling." It continues, "I am a pulse hot and pounding / A hot pulse on the cold black lake of evening / Oh I am melting but the earth repels me / I want a couch, a coverlet for my white false body / A hot room full of sensuous thots [*sic*]" (Folder Copies 3, Alice Neel Archive, Stowe, Vt.).

22. As Linda Nochlin argued, it was not until the 1970s that "the realm of erotic representation" was fully revolutionized, thanks to the growing political muscle of women; see "Eroticism and Female Imagery in Nineteenth-Century Art," in *Women, Art, and Power and Other Essays* (New York: Harper and Row, 1988), p. 143. By 1973, women were producing so much art with overt sexual content that Maryse Holder christened it a "movement"; see her "Another Cuntree," *Off Our Backs* 3, no. 10 (September 1973), pp. 11–17. If we understand the erotic in Audre Lorde's terms–as a power and a resource that patriarchy has long suppressed in women in order to enforce their secondary status–then Neel's determination to mobilize her sexual agency constitutes a political gesture; see Audre Lorde, "Uses of the Erotic: The Erotic as Power" (1978), in *Sister Outsider: Essays and Speeches* (Berkeley: Crossing Press, 1984), pp. 53–59.

**23.** According to Neel, she created *Joie de Vivre* while staying with John at a hotel on West 42nd Street (Hills, *Alice Neel*, p. 55). Bestiality also appears in an undated, untitled short story by Neel, in which a farmer engages in sexual acts with a black sow (Folder Copies 1, Alice Neel Archive, Stowe, Vt.).

**24.** According to Neel, she realized the true subject of *Alienation* in 1978, when she gave the watercolor its current title; see Hills, *Alice Neel*, p. 55.

**25.** See https://productioncode.dhwritings.com/multipleframes_productioncode.php.

**26.** Christine Stansell, *American Moderns: Bohemian New York and the Creation of a New Century*, 2nd ed. (Princeton: Princeton University Press, 2010), p. 227.

**27.** For more on this group of socialists and feminists, see June Sochen, *The New Woman in Greenwich Village, 1910–1920* (New York: Quadrangle Books, 1972); and Nancy F. Cott, *The Grounding of Modern Feminism* (New Haven: Yale University Press, 1987). The CPUSA was more conservative on issues of sexuality, marriage, and gender roles than socialism was. See Juliet Mitchell, "Women: The Longest Revolution," *New Left Review* 40, no. 1 (November/December 1966), pp. 22–23; and Robert Shaffer, "Women and the Communist Party USA, 1930–1940," *Socialist Review* 45 (May–June 1979), p. 105.

**28.** Even if Neel was unaware of the Greenwich Village feminists in the 1930s (which seems unlikely, given her friendship with Gold), she might have learned about them after the fact through Sochen's 1972 book (see n27).

**29.** Neel's 1978 exhibition at the Graham Gallery, *A Retrospective Exhibition of Watercolors and Drawings*, was the first time, according to my research, that *Joie de Vivre*, *Alienation*, and *José Asleep* were exhibited publicly, and the other works discussed in this section were not shown until much later. For more on the exhibition history of two of Neel's most provocative male nudes, *Joe Gould* and *John Perreault*, in the 1970s, see Randall Griffey's essay in this volume.

**30.** The phrase is borrowed from Elaine Showalter, *The Female Malady: Women, Madness, and English Culture, 1830–1980* (New York: Penguin Books, 1985).

**31.** Jacqueline Rose, *Women in Dark Times* (London: Bloomsbury, 2014), pp. ix, x.

**32.** "*Well Baby Clinic* makes my attitude toward childbirth very dubious," Neel once said (Hills, *Alice Neel*, p. 23).

**33.** Hoban was the first to connect this account to the "brutal imagery" that finds its way into *Well Baby Clinic*; see *Alice Neel*, p. 66.

**34.** Untitled statement by Neel, dated November 12, 1928, Folder Copies 10, Alice Neel Archive, Stowe, Vt.

**35.** As Neel told Nemser, "This painting was a combination of my own tragedy and that event" (Nemser, *Art Talk*, p. 100). See also Hills, *Alice Neel*, p. 22. As Neel said, "Into [*Futility of Effort*] went the amount of effort you put into having a child. Pregnancy. All the rest. Then the tragedy of losing it. Everything. Everything" (Eleanor Munro, *Originals: American Women Artists* [New York: Simon and Schuster, 1979], p. 125).

**36.** For Neel's own account of the events prior to her mental breakdown, see Munro, *Originals*, p. 125. On this period, see Hills, *Alice Neel*, pp. 32–40, as well as an undated text by Neel that begins "I want to paint," Folder Copies 8, Alice Neel Archive, Stowe, Vt.

**37.** "Frightful" is Neel's word; see Hills, *Alice Neel*, p. 33. Like her early erotica, Neel's particularly personal works of the 1930s seem to have first entered the public realm in the 1970s. *Suicidal Ward*, for instance, appeared in her 1978 retrospective at Graham Gallery, along with *The Intellectual*, *City Hospital*, and the watercolor *Kenneth Doolittle* (1931). See the review by Susan Grace Galassi, "Alice Neel," *Arts Magazine* 53, no. 6 (February 1979), pp. 20–21. Nemser reproduced *Futility of Effort* and *Well Baby Clinic* in "Alice Neel: Portraits of Four Decades," *Ms.* 2, no. 4 (October 1973), pp. 48 and 51, respectively.

**38.** From an undated note by Neel, written in 1931 or 1932, reproduced in Hills, *Alice Neel*, p. 40.

**39.** Hills, *Alice Neel*, p. 37. Although the title identifies the setting as Philadelphia General Hospital, at least one of the patients is from the Gladwyne Colony, the last hospital in which Neel was confined (ibid.).

**40.** Neel describes mental illness as a "cruel disease" in an undated note written in 1931 or 1932, reproduced in Hills, *Alice Neel*, p. 40.

**41.** Hills, *Alice Neel*, p. 38. Neel does not identify by name the psychiatrist she called an enemy, but it was a male doctor who worked in the suicide ward of Philadelphia General Hospital, so it was likely Breitenbach.

**42.** See Hills, *Alice Neel*, pp. 38–39. A female social worker eventually gave Neel access to pens and brushes. As Neel said of her recovery, "It was the drawing that helped me decide to get well" (Munro, *Originals*, p. 126).

**43.** See Allara, *Pictures of People*, p. 88; and Hoban, *Alice Neel*, p. 141.

**44.** For more on this exhibition as well as on *Childbirth*, which represents Neel's hospital roommate, Goldie Goldwasser, see Allara, *Pictures of People*, p. 91; and Nemser, *Art Talk*, p. 121. According to Robert Shaffer, the CPUSA press often addressed the dangers expectant women faced in capitalist countries ("Women and the Communist Party," pp. 93–94).

**45.** Neel routinely exhibited her work in mission-driven periodicals and exhibitions. In 1936 she exhibited *Nazis Murder Jews* in a juried exhibition sponsored by the American Artists' Congress at the ACA Galleries. In 1937 Neel's portrait of Pat Whalen appeared at the Waterfront Art Show, organized by the New School for Social Research and the Marine Workers Committee to coincide with a national strike of seamen and dockworkers; see Max Fraser, "Hands off the Machine: Workers' Hands and Revolutionary Symbolism in the Visual Culture of 1930s America," *American Art* 27, no. 2 (Summer 2013), p. 110.

**46.** This language is pulled from the same page in *Art Front* on which *Poverty* appears (p. 7).

**47.** Despite Allara's assertion in *Pictures of People*, p. 50, *Art Front* did not publish articles on child mortality, but the *Daily Worker* may have. Unfortunately, the outbreak of the COVID-19 pandemic restricted my research to issues available online, all from the 1920s. None of these included articles on child mortality, which is not surprising, given that the CPUSA did not start covering such topics regularly until the 1930s. See https://www.marxists.org/history/usa/pubs/dailyworker/index.htm.

**48.** "Money," undated, handwritten text by Neel, Folder Copies 1, Alice Neel Archive, Stowe, Vt.

**49.** Hills, *Alice Neel*, p. 22.

**50.** Nemser, *Art Talk*, p. 101.

**51.** Rose, *Women in Dark Times*, p. xi.

**52.** Neel's self-portraits are rare, but the few that do exist often represent her as either an expectant mother, as in *Flight into Egypt*, or as the mother of a young child, as in *The Family* (p. 141), *The Intellectual*, *Hartley on the Rocking Horse*, and *Alice and Richard* (1943). For more on Neel's pictures of and about mothers, see Denise Bauer, "Alice Neel's Female Nudes," *Woman's Art Journal* 15, no. 2 (Autumn 1994–Winter 1995), pp. 21–26; Denise Bauer, "Alice Neel's Portraits of Mother Work," *NWSA Journal* 14, no. 2 (Summer 2002), pp. 102–20; and Pamela Allara, "'Mater' of Fact: Alice Neel's Pregnant Nudes," *American Art* 8, no. 2 (Spring 1994), pp. 6–31.

**53.** As Neel wrote in an unpublished essay submitted to *Artforum* in April 1975 and quoted in Allara, "'Mater' of Fact," "The madonna has been replaced by abortion and the wife and helpmate has become woman the aggressor and so she should. Everything is questioned" (p. 7).

**54.** Hills, *Alice Neel*, p. 161. Although Neel's recollections to Hills about Carmen and Judy are characteristically candid and uncensored, she uses language that reads today as insensitive.

**55.** To my knowledge, Carmen and Judy are the only Black mother and child that Neel painted after leaving Spanish Harlem in 1962, and Judy is one of only two visibly disabled children she ever represented, the other being the boy Jonathan Perlis, who had cerebral palsy, shown with his father in *Don Perlis and Jonathan* (1982).

**56.** See Hilton Als, *Alice Neel, Uptown*, exh. cat. (New York: David Zwirner Books; London: Victoria Miro, 2017), p. 113. Overall, Als tends to romanticize the relationship between Carmen and Neel.

**57.** Very few artists before Neel represented pregnant women, even fewer pregnant nudes, and when they did, they often deemphasized the pregnancy out of a sense of discretion or cloaked it in symbolism. An incomplete list of precedents includes, in alphabetical order, Gustav Klimt's *Hope II*, 1907–8 (Museum of Modern Art, New York); Georges de La Tour's *Woman Catching Fleas*, 1630s (Musée Historique, Nancy); Paula Modersohn-Becker's *Self-Portrait on the Sixth Anniversary of Marriage*, 1906 (Paula Modersohn-Becker Museum, Bremen); Betye Saar's *Anticipation*, 1961 (Museum of Modern Art, New York); and Raphael Soyer's *Nude*, 1952 (Whitney Museum of American Art, New York).

58. Slatkin, "Alice Neel (1900–1984)," p. 263. For a masterful discussion of Neel's attention to the "plastic" qualities of the naked human form, see Mira Schor, "Some Notes on Women and Abstraction and a Curious Case History: Alice Neel as a Great Abstract Painter," *differences: A Journal of Feminist Cultural Studies* 17, no. 2 (2006), p. 149.

59. For Evans's recollection of her sitting, see Edith Newhall, "Neel Life Stories," *New York*, June 19, 2000, https://nymag.com/nymetro/arts/features/3409/.

60. Nochlin, "Some Women Realists," in *Women, Art, and Power*, p. 103.

61. Nemser, "Alice Neel: Portraits of Four Decades," p. 52.

62. Slatkin, "Alice Neel (1900–1984)," p. 263. When asked why she painted so many pregnant women, Neel replied, "Well, for one thing, I had children myself so I understand pregnancy. For another thing, I thought the whole picture of woman without including pregnancy was a very trivial picture. It's treating woman as a sex object. But you know sex results in something" (Diana Loercher, "Alice Neel: American Portraitist," *Christian Science Monitor*, March 4, 1974). According to Neel, moreover, a pregnant nude cuts against the grain of traditional nudes, insofar as a "pregnant woman has a claim staked out; she's not for sale" (Piri Halasz, "Alice Neel: 'I have this obsession with life,'" *Art News* 73, no. 1 [January 1974], p. 49). Later Neel claimed to have decided to paint pregnant nudes in order to "liberate" artists and society alike from their misplaced modesty about the pregnant body (Stephan Salisbury, "Oils and Vinegar: As a Painter and a Person, She Is an Original," *Philadelphia Inquirer*, March 4, 1984).

63. See Marjorie Kramer, "Some Thoughts on Feminist Art" (1971), in *Feminism–Art–Theory: An Anthology 1968–2014*, ed. Hilary Robinson, 2nd ed. (Chichester, West Sussex: Wiley Blackwell, 2015), p. 225. As Neel said of *Nancy and Olivia*, "You know why women's libbers always love that picture, because she looks so frightened" (Castle, "Alice Neel," p. 40). Additionally, *Pregnant Woman* was included in the 1973 exhibition *Women Choose Women* and then reproduced (with the caption "Breaking stereotypes") in a review of the show (Douglas Davis, "Women, Women, Women," *Newsweek*, January 29, 1973, p. 45). A roundup of exhibitions on Alice Neel mentions the same work (albeit with the incorrect date) in the same show, describing it as a "grisly prenatal odalisque," finding it clearly disconcerting, if not disgusting (Harry F. Gaugh, "Alice Neel," *Arts Magazine* 53, no. 7 [March 1979], p. 9). Nemser also reproduced it in her 1973 article "Alice Neel: Portraits of Four Decades," p. 48. Ann Sutherland Harris reproduced *Pregnant Maria* in "The Human Creature: The Portraits of Alice Neel," *Portfolio* (New York) 1, no. 6 (1980), p. 75. Of her pregnant nudes, Harris says that Neel shows "the way a woman's body is invaded" (ibid., p. 74). *Pregnant Julie and Algis* was included in Neel's 1968 exhibition at Graham Gallery (but not reproduced in its related pamphlet) and illustrated in Nemser's review, under the title *Reclining figures (Algis and Julie)* ("Alice Neel," *Arts Magazine* 42, no. 4 [February 1968], p. 60). *Margaret Evans Pregnant* appears in a photograph of Neel's studio in "The New York Artist in Residence," *Art News* 77, no. 9 (November 1978), p. 71.

64. Shulamith Firestone, *The Dialectic of Sex: The Case for Feminist Revolution* (New York: William Morrow, 1970), pp. 9, 81. See also Simone de Beauvoir, *The Second Sex*, trans. and ed. H. M. Parshley (New York: Vintage Books, 1989). Neel was vocal in her disagreements with de Beauvoir (see Castle, "Alice Neel," p. 37). As far as I have been able to ascertain, however, Neel never specifically mentioned de Beauvoir's position on motherhood.

65. Firestone, *The Dialectic of Sex*, pp. 219–31. Pregnancy, Firestone opined, is not only "barbaric" but also ugly (ibid., p. 226).

66. See, for instance, the contents of these anthologies: Deborah Babcox and Madeline Belkin, comps., *Liberation Now! Writings from the Women's Liberation Movement* (New York: Dell, 1971); Anne Koedit, Ellen Levine, and Anita Rapone, eds., *Radical Feminism* (New York: Quadrangle/The New York Times Book Co., 1973); and Redstockings of the Women's Liberation Movement, *Feminist Revolution: An Abridged Edition with Additional Writings*, 2nd ed. (New York: Random House, 1978). Only *Feminist Revolution* includes an essay that discusses motherhood as a lived, embodied experience in a way similar to Neel's pictures (R. L. Annchild, "Mother Love–Mother Work," pp. 115–17). Lucy Lippard speaks of the "curious" absence of pregnancy and childbirth in the work of feminist performance artists who otherwise use their bodies as tools to address personal experiences specific to women, although she provides no explanation for it; see Lippard, "The Pains and Pleasures of Rebirth: European and American Women's Body Art" (1976), in *The Pink Glass Swan: Selected Essays on Feminist Art* (New York: New Press, 1995), p. 112.

67. For more on feminist art and motherhood, see Andrea Liss, *Feminist Art and the Maternal* (Minneapolis: University of Minnesota Press, 2009); Cecilia Fajardo-Hill and Andrea Giunta, eds., *Radical Women: Latin American Art, 1960–1985*, exh. cat. (Los Angeles: Hammer Museum and DelMonico Books/Prestel, 2017); and Catherine Spencer, "Acts of Displacement: Lea Lublin's *Mon fils*, May '68, and Feminist Psychosocial Revolt," *Oxford Art Journal* 40, no. 1 (March 2017), pp. 65–83.

68. Adrienne Rich, *Of Woman Born: Motherhood as Experience and Institution* (1976; repr. New York: W. W. Norton, 1986), pp. xi, 13.

69. As Allara convincingly argues, "Neel's pregnant nudes thus address a double taboo–the subject's absence in the history of Western art and its conflicted status within feminist theory and practice" ("'Mater' of Fact," p. 10).

70. As Diane Cochrane recognized in 1973, Neel possessed a "rebellious unwillingness to conform to the going [feminist] philosophy," particularly when it came to granting visibility to mothers; see Cochrane, "Alice Neel: Collector of Souls," *American Artist* 37, no. 4 (September 1973), p. 63.

71. Neel's association with the Old Left continued apace even after the feminist movement was in full swing. The *Daily World* published two essays on Neel in the 1970s (Marla Hoffman, "Two Women Paint," *Daily World*, March 9, 1974, pp. 14–16, and Phillip Bonosky, "Alice Neel Exhibits Her Portraits of the Spirit," *Daily World*, October 4, 1973, p. 8). The June 7, 1979, issue of the *Daily World* identified Neel as "a workers' artist" and reproduced her portrait of David Gordon, the magazine's former cultural editor. In 1982 Neel donated a work to an auction that benefited the Reference Center for Marxist Studies (see brochure contained in the Alice Neel papers, 1933–1983, Archives of American Art, Smithsonian Institution).

72. Castle, "Alice Neel," p. 37. For Neel's self-proclaimed affiliation with feminism, see also Diamonstein, *Inside New York's Art World*, p. 261; Suzanne Muchnic, "Beneath the Skin with Alice Neel," *Los Angeles Times*, April 10, 1983; and Miller and Swenson, *Lives and Works*, pp. 123–24.

73. Miller and Swenson, *Lives and Works*, p. 129.

74. The portrait is based on a photograph of Millett, who refused to sit for Neel; see Nemser, *Art Talk*, p. 118. Millett's *Sexual Politics*, which decried sexism and patriarchy, served as a veritable manifesto for radical feminists, including some of those Neel painted.

75. For more on WAR and the founding of the Women's Interart Center, see Jacqueline Skiles and Janet McDevitt, eds., *A Documentary Herstory of Women Artists in Revolution* (Pittsburgh: Know, Inc., 1973).

76. "Hall of Fame" is one of the descriptive phrases used on the poster for the *Sister Chapel* (Alice Neel papers, 1933–1983, Archives of American Art, Smithsonian Institution). Apparently, Neel had originally planned to contribute a pregnant nude to the installation; see Andrew D. Hottle, *The Art of the Sister Chapel: Exemplary Women, Visionary Creators, and Feminist Collaboration* (Farnham, U.K.: Ashgate, 2014), p. 141.

77. For more on the exhibition in which Neel appeared, see Eunice Golden and Kay Kenny, "Sexuality in Art: Two Decades from a Feminist Perspective," *Women's Art Journal* 3, no. 1 (Spring–Summer 1982), pp. 14–15.

78. Neel's name appears on a list of advisory board members for the New York Feminist Art Institute in a brochure published in 1979, the same year the institute opened (Alice Neel papers, 1933–1983, Archives of American Art, Smithsonian Institution).

79. Mary Garrard, Ann Sutherland Harris, Kate Millett, Linda Nochlin, Adrienne Rich, and Faith Ringgold all belonged to the Women's Interart Center's board of advisers, and Irene Peslikis served on its board of directors.

80. For more on the generational differences between feminists, see Nancy J. Chodorow, "Seventies Questions for Thirties Women: Gender and Generation in a Study of Early Women Psychoanalysts," in *Feminism and Psychoanalytic Theory* (New Haven: Yale University Press, 1989), pp. 199–218.

81. Neel was also frustrated by the narrow definition of feminist art, especially its Eurocentric bias and its emphasis on white women. For more on Neel's complicated relationship to feminism, including

statements by the artist herself, see Allara, *Pictures of People*, pp. 191–216; Pamela Allara, "Alice Neel's Women from the 1970s: Backlash to Fast Forward," *Woman's Art Journal* 27, no. 2 (Fall–Winter 2006), pp. 8–11; Denise Bauer, "Alice Neel's Feminist and Leftist Portraits of Women," *Feminist Studies* 28, no. 2 (Summer 2002), pp. 374–95; Diamonstein, *Inside New York's Art World*, p. 258; Mary D. Garrard, "Alice Neel and Me," *Woman's Art Journal* 27, no. 2 (Fall–Winter 2006), pp. 3–7; Nemser, *Art Talk*, p. 118; and Russo, "Alice Neel," p. 206.

**82.** Alice Neel, "A Statement by Alice Neel," in *Alice Neel: The Woman and Her Work*, exh. cat. (Athens: Georgia Museum of Art, University of Georgia, 1975), unpaged.

**83.** Nemser, *Art Talk*, p. 105.

**84.** Alice Neel, handwritten statement, 1973, Alice Neel Archive, Stowe, Vt., included in the exhibition *Alice Neel: Freedom*, David Zwirner, New York, February 26–April 13, 2019.

**85.** Alice Neel, untitled statement, *Daily World*, April 17, 1971, p. 47.

**86.** Kate Weigand, *Red Feminism: American Communism and the Making of Women's Liberation* (Baltimore: Johns Hopkins University Press, 2001).

**87.** The relationship between feminism, women, and the CPUSA is extremely complicated. A male-dominated organization that embraced sexism and patriarchy within its ranks, the party tolerated feminism at best and disparaged it at worst. In its first decade and a half, it mostly sidelined issues specific to working-class women, but in the 1930s, in response to the Great Depression, it gradually began to consider the problems of the home alongside those of the factory, increasing its outreach to women and families. Some of Neel's ideological forerunners—the original red feminists, among them Ella Reeve "Mother" Bloor, Eleanor Flexner, Elizabeth Gurley Flynn, Josephine Herbst, Grace Hutchins, Mary Inman, Meridel Le Sueur, Betty Millard, and Tillie Olsen—were at the forefront of these and other important shifts. For more on the relationship between Communism and women's rights, see Rosalyn Baxandall, "The Question Seldom Asked: Women and the CPUSA," in *New Studies in the Politics and Culture of U.S. Communism*, ed. Brown, Martin, Rosengarten, and Snedeker, pp. 141–61; Barbara Foley, "Women and the Left in the 1930s," *American Literary History* 2, no. 1 (Spring 1990), pp. 150–69; Charlotte Nekola and Paula Rabinowitz, eds., *Writing Red: An Anthology of American Women Writers, 1930–1940* (New York: Feminist Press at the City University of New York, 1987); and Shaffer, "Women and the Communist Party," 73–119.

**88.** Weigand, *Red Feminism*, pp. 15–27.

**89.** In 1989 attorney Kimberlé Crenshaw introduced the term "intersectionality" to describe the interdependence of social status, race, gender, sexuality, nationality, and other categories of identity. As Crenshaw proposes, intersectional feminism considers sexism as part of a tightly woven pattern of inequality, in which one instance of identity-specific discrimination is compounded by another. See Sumi Cho, Kimberlé Williams Crenshaw, and Leslie McCall, "Toward a Field of Intersectionality Studies: Theory, Applications, and Praxis," *Signs* 38, no. 4 (Summer 2013), pp. 785–810.

**90.** These three texts are reproduced in *Public Women, Public Words: A Documentary History of American Feminism*, vol. 2, *1900 to 1960*, ed. Dawn Keetley and John Pettegrew (Lanham, Md.: Rowman & Littlefield, 2002).

**91.** Weigand, *Red Feminism*, pp. 90–91. See also Marvin E. Gettleman, "'No Varsity Teams': New York's Jefferson School of Social Science, 1943–1956," *Science and Society* 66, no. 3 (Fall 2002), pp. 339, 349.

**92.** Allara, *Pictures of People*, p. 66. Allara provides an incomplete list of the publisher's texts found in Neel's personal library (p. 278n14). Missing from this list (but not, perhaps, from the library) are the publisher's editions of books by Bloor and Childress. Unfortunately, because of the outbreak of COVID-19, I was unable to examine Neel's library, which remains more or less intact in her apartment at Broadway and 107th Street, before this catalogue went to press.

**93.** For more on the way Childress and Bloor triangulated gender, class, and, in Childress's case, race, see Washington, *The Other Blacklist*, pp. 123–64; and Kathleen L. Brown, "The 'Savagely Fathered and Un-Mothered World' of the Communist Party, U.S.A.: Feminism, Maternalism, and 'Mother Bloor'," *Feminist Studies* 25, no. 3 (Autumn 1999), pp. 537–70.

**94.** For more on New York Radical Women and the Redstockings, see Alice Echols, *Daring to Be Bad: Radical Feminism in America 1967–1975* (Minneapolis: University of Minnesota Press, 1989), pp. 72–101 and 139–58, respectively.

**95.** See ibid., pp. 4–5.

**96.** See https://www.redstockings.org/index.php/rs-manifesto.

**97.** Very few of Neel's clothed, adult female sitters pose with their legs apart. Some exceptions include *Wellesley Girls* of 1967 and *Ginny in a Striped Shirt* of 1969.

**98.** Neel was particularly supportive of antiwar and civil rights efforts in the 1960s and 1970s. Besides attending the protests mentioned in this essay, she contributed a small painting to the Artists' Tower of Protest in Los Angeles in 1966; participated in a January 1968 campaign at the Whitney decrying the absence of women and Black artists in the exhibition *The 1930's: Painting and Sculpture in America* (Ann Temkin, ed., *Alice Neel*, exh. cat. [Philadelphia: Philadelphia Museum of Art, 2000], p. 171); and exhibited her portrait *Stephen Shepherd* (1978), of a young Black man, at the exhibition *Voices Expressing What Is*, at Westbeth Gallery, sponsored by Action Against Racism in the Arts, an organization launched in 1979 after the opening of the show *The Nigger Drawings* at Artists Space. On the latter, see John Perreault, "Art Attacks," *Soho News*, February 18, 1981, p. 48. For Andrews's recollections of Neel, see Hoban, *Alice Neel*, p. 260; and Temkin, *Alice Neel*, pp. 72–73.

**99.** Alice Neel, untitled statement, in *June Blum, Audrey Flack, Alice Neel: Three Contemporary American Women Realists*, exh. brochure (Miami: Miami-Dade Community College, 1977), p. 11.

**100.** For a reading of the complicated power dynamic at play in *Isabetta*, see Meredith A. Brown's essay in this volume.

**101.** Alice Neel, undated and untitled statement, Folder Copies 3, Alice Neel Archive, Stowe, Vt.

## Siempre en la calle
### Susanna V. Temkin

**1.** Cindy Nemser, *Art Talk: Conversations with 15 Women Artists* (New York: Icon Editions, 1995), p. 100.

**2.** Used interchangeably in this text, East Harlem, Spanish Harlem, and El Barrio (translating to "the neighborhood") all refer to the Manhattan neighborhood bounded by 96th Street and 143rd Street, from Fifth Avenue to the East River.

**3.** See Jeremy Lewison and Barry Walker, *Alice Neel: Painted Truths*, exh. cat. (Houston: Museum of Fine Arts, Houston, 2010), esp. pp. 78, 179; and Gerald L. Belcher and Margaret L. Belcher, *Collecting Souls, Gathering Dust: The Struggles of Two American Artists, Alice Neel and Rhoda Medary* (New York: Paragon House, 1991), p. 177.

**4.** Examples of the increased attention paid to this period include the 1990s exhibitions *Alice Neel in Spanish Harlem*, presented at the Dia Center for the Arts in Bridgehampton, New York, in 1991, and accompanied by a catalogue with text by Henry Geldzahler; and *Alice Neel: The Years in Spanish Harlem,* held at the Robert Miller Gallery in New York in 1994. Hilton Als, *Alice Neel, Uptown*, exh. cat. (New York: David Zwirner Books; London: Victoria Miro, 2017).

**5.** These were *José* (1936), *T.B. Harlem* (1940), and *Black Spanish Family* (1950). See Lewison and Walker, *Alice Neel: Painted Truths*, pp. 112–13, 114–15, 220–21.

**6.** This popular metaphor draws from Puerto Rican poet and activist Lola Rodríguez de Tió's 1893 poem "A Cuba," which references the parallel history and culture of the two Caribbean islands.

**7.** For a more complete history on this period of Cuban art, see Juan A. Martínez, *Cuban Art and National Identity: The Vanguardia Painters, 1927–1950* (Gainesville: University Press of Florida, 1994). For more on Neel and Cuba, see Elvis Fuentes, "Havana–New York: A Missing Link in the History of Modern Cuban Art," in *Nexus New York: Latin/American Artists in the Modern Metropolis*, ed. Deborah Cullen, exh. cat. (New York: Museo del Barrio, 2009), pp. 70–71; and Pamela Allara, *Pictures of People: Alice Neel's American Portrait Gallery* (Hanover, N.H.: University Press of New England [for] Brandeis University Press, 1998), pp. 59–64.

**8.** Enríquez and Neel met in 1924 while attending a summer session at the Pennsylvania Academy of the Fine Arts at Chester Springs, where they had a whirlwind romance before Enríquez was expelled. The two married in 1925; Neel joined her husband in

Havana the following year. Later the winner of numerous national prizes in Cuba, Enríquez participated in the Museum of Modern Art's groundbreaking 1944 exhibition *Modern Cuban Painters*. For more on the artist, see Juan A. Martínez, *Carlos Enríquez: The Painter of Cuban Ballads* (Coral Gables, Fla.: Cernuda Arte, 2010).

**9.** Patricia Hills, *Alice Neel* (New York: Harry N. Abrams, 1983), p. 21.

**10.** Like Enríquez, Pogolotti studied in the United States, an experience that may have helped cement the trio's friendship. Dedicated to "revolutionary art," Pogolotti shared a deep sense of social commitment and politics with Neel. Although no letters between the two have been found, they reportedly maintained a lifelong correspondence, and in 1969 Neel visited Pogolotti, who at the time was living in Mexico.

**11.** Translated by the author from Martí Casanovas, "Almanaque: XII Salón de Bellas Artes," *Revista de Avance* 1, no. 3 (April 15, 1927), p. 67.

**12.** According to the catalogue, Neel exhibited *Sombrero negro* (*Black Hat*), *Naturaleza muerta* (*Still Life*), *Escena domestica* (*Domestic Scene*), *Paisaje* (*Landscape*), *Desnudo* (*Nude*), *Madre e hijo* (*Mother and Child*), *Calle* (*Street*), and *Contraluz* (*Chiaroscuro*). The works are not dated in the catalogue.

**13.** Neel was not the only non-Cuban participant: Russian-born Adja Yunkers took part in the exhibition as well. Also among Neel's often-overlooked contributions to Cuban art history is her role in a small scandal surrounding the *Exposición de Arte Nuevo*, when Enríquez's nude portraits of his wife were censored by the exhibition's host venue, the Asociación de Pintores y Escultores, over complaints of "exaggerated realism" and moved to an alternate exhibition space. The editors of the avant-garde magazine *Revista de Avance* (and the organizers of the exhibition) defended the inclusion of Enríquez's nudes; see "De un Realismo Exagerado," *Revista de Avance* 1, no. 5 (May 15, 1927).

**14.** Hills, *Alice Neel*, p. 21.

**15.** Significantly, when Neel presented this work in an Artists' Union exhibition, it was criticized in the press for the overt sign carried by one of the picketers. Other related protest paintings include *Uneeda Biscuit Strike* of 1936 and *Save Willie McGee* of about 1950. Emily Genauer, "New Fall Art Exhibits Feature by Tyros' Promising Efforts," *New York World Telegram*, September 12, 1936.

**16.** Susan Rosenberg, "People as Evidence," in *Alice Neel*, ed. Ann Temkin, exh. cat. (Philadelphia: Philadelphia Museum of Art, 2000), p. 43.

**17.** Nemser, *Art Talk*, p. 108.

**18.** This is a reference to the song "Que bonita bandera," a traditional Puerto Rican *plena* (a genre of folk music) that carries revolutionary undertones related to the colonial status of Puerto Rico. The song references the island's flag, which, along with other signs and symbols of patriotism, were banned under the notorious Law 53, passed by the Puerto Rican legislature in 1948 to suppress the independence movement.

**19.** Passage of the law, known as the Jones-Shafroth Act, coincided with the US entry into World War I and led to imposed mandatory conscription of Puerto Ricans into the armed forces. Although US citizens, Puerto Ricans do not have voting representation in the US Congress and cannot participate in federal elections, in keeping with other territories.

**20.** The history of the titles of Neel's canvases is complicated. According to the artist's daughter-in-law Virginia (Ginny) Neel, titles were given to her paintings when and if they were exhibited, usually long after they were first executed, and were often mainly descriptive. Although Neel may have helped assign titles, over the years, different and/or variant titles have sometimes been applied to the same work.

**21.** Carlos was not included in the composition because he was then recovering from surgery to treat his tuberculosis, a history Neel memorialized in *T.B. Harlem*. The title of this painting similarly omits the sitter's relationship to the artist. The high number of tuberculosis cases in East Harlem would later prompt revolutionary action by the Young Lords Party in the early 1970s; see note 42.

**22.** Allara, *Pictures of People*, p. 137.

**23.** Neel continued to correspond with Arce after he was imprisoned for murder in 1974.

**24.** This painting was at least the second image Neel painted of the fish market. According to Gerald and Margaret Belcher, Neel painted a similarly titled scene while employed by the WPA, but it was rejected by her supervisor, John Lonergan, because "[n]ot everyone likes blood as much as you do, Alice." Neel altered the image and resubmitted it for WPA acceptance, then later purchased the painting back and restored the blood. For more on the earlier work, see Belcher and Belcher, *Collecting Souls*, p. 173.

**25.** The Arthur Avenue Retail Market in the Bronx and the recently closed Essex Market on the Lower East Side were also part of this project.

**26.** Alex Mindlin, "Hope Amid the Plantains," *New York Times*, May 18, 2008.

**27.** Many of Neel's contemporaries, including John Storrs, Georgia O'Keeffe, Diego Rivera, and Margaret Bourke-White, created artworks inspired by these modern sites.

**28.** Allara, *Pictures of People*, pp. 149–60; Barry Walker, "Cityscapes," in Lewison and Walker, *Alice Neel: Painted Truths*, pp. 178–79; Rosenberg goes further by stating, "The implacable surfaces and obstructed views of Neel's paintings of building facades and alleys from this time . . . create a sensation close to that evoked by her portraits of her Spanish Harlem neighbors. In both, the impenetrability of the pictorial surface corresponds to the psychological impenetrability of the subjects and suggests the closetlike atmosphere of looking out from inside." See "People as Evidence," p. 47.

**29.** Michael (Mike) Gold, exhibition statement, in *Paintings by Alice Neel, April 23 to May 23*, exh. brochure (New York: New Playwrights Theatre, 1951).

**30.** Helen Molesworth, "Looking with and Looking at Alice Neel," in *Alice Neel: Freedom*, exh. cat. (New York: David Zwirner Books, 2019), see esp. p. 16.

**31.** Photography critic Max Kosloff has described this quality in Levitt's work as an ambivalence in the photographer's gaze; see the discussion in Vojislava Filipcevic, "In the Streets of Harlem: Race and Textures of Space in Helen Levitt's New York Photographs and the Levitt-Agee Documentary Films," *Columbia Journal of American Studies* 9 (Fall 2009), p. 116.

**32.** To hear Levitt speak about her technique, see Melissa Block, "Helen Levitt's Indelible Eye," *All Things Considered*, National Public Radio, January 17, 2002, https://www.npr.org/templates/story/story.php?storyId=1136521. Levitt briefly taught at a school in East Harlem, and her role as a teacher conveyed a level of authority and distance that contrasted with Neel's more intimate status as a neighbor. For more on Levitt's relationship to the neighborhood and its impact on her photographs, see Elizabeth Margaret Gand, "The Politics and Poetics of Children's Play: Helen Levitt's Early Work" (PhD diss., University of California, Berkeley, 2011), https://escholarship.org/content/qt2sf6765x/qt2sf6765x.pdf?t=mtfs2p.

**33.** A. D. Coleman, "Two Critics Look at Davidson's 'East 100th Street': What Does It Imply?," *New York Times*, October 11, 1970.

**34.** Philip (Felipe) Dante, "Two Critics Look at Davidson's 'East 100th Street': But Where Is Our Soul," *New York Times*, October 11, 1970.

**35.** Helen Levitt first exhibited her Spanish Harlem photographs at MoMA in 1943, in the show *Helen Levitt: Photographs of Children*.

**36.** Neel's work was not included in an exhibition at the Museum of Modern Art until the 1960s; the museum's only Spanish Harlem–era painting, *Georgie Arce* (1953), was acquired in 2017.

**37.** In the late 1960s and early 1970s, Neel took part in events organized by the Black Emergency Cultural Coalition to protest the absence of women and artists of color in exhibitions and public collections, including demonstrations in 1968 at the Whitney over *The 1930's: Painting and Sculpture in America*; in 1969 at The Met against *Harlem on My Mind: Cultural Capital of Black America, 1900–1968*; and in 1971 at the Whitney about *Contemporary Black Artists in America*.

**38.** Antwaun Sargent, "Why an Alice Neel Painting Is Stuck in This Artist's Psyche," *T: The New York Times Style Magazine*, May 28, 2019, https://www.nytimes.com/2019/05/28/t-magazine/jordan-casteel-alice-neel.html.

**39.** Als, *Alice Neel, Uptown*, p. 32.

**40.** Nemser, *Art Talk*, p. 112.

**41.** According to Madeleine Sims's study of the neighborhood, by 1967, nearly 171 acres of property had been razed. See Sims, "East Harlem: An Inquiry into Development" (undergraduate thesis, Fordham University, 2016), https://www.fordham.edu/download/downloads/id/5699/madeleine_sims_-_east_harlem.pdf.

**42.** The Young Lords of New York was established in 1969. A revolutionary group whose origins are linked with the Black Panther Party, the organization adopted radical gestures in an effort to secure health, education, food, and other public services in marginalized neighborhoods like East Harlem. For more on the Young Lords, see Darrel Enck-Wanzer, *The Young Lords: A Reader* (New York: New York University Press, 2010). It is tempting to imagine the portraits Neel might have created of the Young Lords' hip members. Instead, Maristany captured these images, as the unofficial photographer of the party and a member of its leadership.

## "I'll Show Everybody": An Artist-Mother at Home
### Meredith A. Brown

**1.** *Portrait of Alice Neel, 1976–1982*, directed by Michel Auder (1986; Collector's Edition 2000), VHS. Phoebe Hoban similarly begins her biography of the artist, *Alice Neel: The Art of Not Sitting Pretty* (New York: St. Martin's Press, 2010), p. 1, with a contemporary description of the apartment at 107th Street and Broadway, which the family maintains and which still contains many of the objects and furnishings from Neel's time there. Joan Kufrin also introduces the chapter on Neel in her book *Uncommon Women* (Piscataway, N.J.: New Century Publishers, 1981), pp. 133–34, by describing the apartment.

**2.** In the catalogue essay to their pioneering exhibition *Women Artists: 1550–1950*, Ann Sutherland Harris and Linda Nochlin note the various ways in which women throughout the history of Western art have been at a disadvantage. Nochlin, in her section of the essay, discusses women's lack of access to professional art training and studios and the societal assignation of women's "destiny as wife, mother, and guardian of the home." Linda Nochlin, "Women Artists After the French Revolution," in Ann Sutherland Harris and Linda Nochlin, *Women Artists: 1550–1950* (Los Angeles: Los Angeles County Museum of Art; New York: Alfred A. Knopf, 1976), p. 56.

**3.** Alice Neel in Auder, *Portrait of Alice Neel*, 24 minutes. Mead was, perhaps most famously, the subject of Warhol's 1964 film *Taylor Mead's Ass*. For more on Neel's relationship to Warhol and queer subjects, see Randall Griffey's essay in this volume.

**4.** Dorothy Thompson, "If I Had a Daughter," *Ladies' Home Journal* (September 1939), quoted in Stephanie Coontz, *A Strange Stirring: "The Feminine Mystique" and American Women at the Dawn of the 1960s* (New York: Basic Books, 2011), p. 46.

**5.** Alice Neel, interview with Cindy Nemser, 1971 or 1975, quoted in Helen Molesworth, with Simone Leigh and Moyra Davey, "Alice Neel: Viva la Mujer," November 12, 2019, in *Recording Artists*, podcast, 35:33, https://www.getty.edu/recordingartists/season-1/neel/.

**6.** Alice Neel in Patricia Hills, *Alice Neel* (New York: Harry N. Abrams, 1983), p. 19.

**7.** Ibid., 29. Louise Bourgeois gave an even more explicit description of her experience as an artist and a mother of young children in a 1995 interview. Discussing her 1943 drawing of a child in an adult's mouth, Bourgeois said, "I'm eating [the child], I'm stuffing my face with it, because I don't know what to do with it. . . . I want to abolish [children], because they are a fact, because they are such a huge burden. The only way of making them disappear is to eat them." Louise Bourgeois, "Interview with Marie-Laure Bernadac," in Louise Bourgeois, *Destruction of the Father/Reconstruction of the Father: Writings and Interviews 1923–1997*, ed. Marie-Laure Bernadac and Hans-Ulrich Obrist (Cambridge, Mass.: MIT Press; London: Violette Editions, 1998), pp. 295–96.

**8.** Susan Rubin Suleiman, "Writing and Motherhood" (1979), in *The (M)other Tongue: Essays in Feminist Psychoanalytic Interpretation*, ed. Shirley Nelson Garner, Claire Kahane, and Madelon Sprengnether (Ithaca, N.Y.: Cornell University Press, 1985), p. 363. Three years before Suleiman's essay–focusing on the particular difficulties of being a writer (or other type of creative professional) and a mother–the poet and essayist Adrienne Rich published one of the first feminist texts to tackle the issue of motherhood, examining it both as a personal experience and as "embedded in a political institution"; throughout, she analyzes maternal ambivalence, Neel's "awful dichotomy," as a product of patriarchal culture. Adrienne Rich, *Of Woman Born: Motherhood as Experience and Institution*, 10th anniversary ed. (New York: W. W. Norton, 1986), p. ix.

**9.** Suleiman, "Writing and Motherhood," pp. 363–64.

**10.** See, for example, Meredith A. Brown, Oriana Fox, and Frances Jacobus-Parker, "Making Art with Your Kids: Generation, Cooperation, and Desire in Parent-Child Artwork of the 1970s," in *Collaboration and Its (Dis)Contents: Art, Architecture, and Photography since 1950*, ed. Meredith A. Brown and Michelle Millar Fisher (London: Courtauld Books Online, 2017), pp. 134–57.

**11.** Neel said she gave herself "an extra arm because I was so busy with the little girl, and also an extra leg because I had to chase her." Neel in Hills, *Alice Neel*, p. 26. In a fitting twist of fate (and as a personal aside), one day while I sat at my computer writing this essay as I worked from home during the COVID-19 outbreak, my young daughter brought me a drawing she had made of me where I have four arms and a pronounced frown. "Because you're always so busy, Mama," she explained, "you need more arms."

**12.** Neel in Hills, *Alice Neel*, p. 50.

**13.** Bronze casts of this wax sculpture were made in 1922 following Degas's death in 1917. The Met acquired its bronze *The Little Fourteen-Year-Old Dancer* in 1929 as part of a bequest from Louisine and Henry O. Havemeyer. Neel may have seen the sculpture at The Met when it was featured in a 1930 exhibition celebrating the bequest.

**14.** Jeremy Lewison, "Showing the Barbarity of Life: Alice Neel's Grotesque," in Jeremy Lewison and Barry Walker, *Alice Neel: Painted Truths*, exh. cat. (Houston: Museum of Fine Arts, Houston, 2010), p. 41.

**15.** The uncomfortable dynamic of a mother depicting her own child nude has not lessened over time. For instance, from the mid-1980s into the early 1990s, photographer Sally Mann produced several prints of her prepubescent son and two daughters naked, which stirred controversy within and beyond the art world for their intimate, frank, and at times violent or sensual imagery. In 1992, critic Richard Woodward commented on the "worrying personal concerns" raised by Mann's art: "If it is [Mann's] solemn responsibility, as she says, 'to protect my children from all harm,' has she knowingly put them at risk by releasing these pictures into a world where pedophilia exists? Can young children freely give their consent for controversial portraits, even if–especially if–the artist is their parent?" Richard B. Woodward, "The Disturbing Photography of Sally Mann," *New York Times Magazine*, September 27, 1992, p. 30.

**16.** Neel biographer Phoebe Hoban and the artist's grandson, filmmaker Andrew Neel, have grappled with Neel and Isabetta's relationship. However, since both mother and daughter had died by the time of their research and few primary records exist, there is no way to gain further understanding of it. Hoban notes that it is not known how much correspondence there was between mother and daughter, or between Neel and Isabetta's aunts, who raised her. In addition to photographs taken during Isabetta's two childhood visits with Neel at the Jersey Shore, among Neel's papers in the Alice Neel Archive, Stowe, Vt., are a few letters from Isabetta written when she was a girl. For accounts of the relationship between mother and daughter, see Hoban, *Alice Neel*, pp. 72–73, 120–22, 145–46, 314–15, 352–62; and *Alice Neel* (SeeThink Films, 2007), a film by Andrew Neel that includes interviews with Isabetta's husband and children about her relationship with Neel.

**17.** Neel quoted in Jonathan Brand, "Fire and Alice," unpublished transcript of interview with the artist, ca. 1982–83, p. 13.

**18.** See Susanna V. Temkin's essay in this volume for more on Neel's move to Spanish Harlem and her relationship to Latino art and culture. This period of Neel's career was also the subject of the recent exhibition *Alice Neel, Uptown*. See Hilton Als, *Alice Neel, Uptown*, exh. cat. (New York: David Zwirner Books; London: Victoria Miro, 2017).

**19.** Neel in Hills, *Alice Neel*, p. 79.

**20.** Whitney Chadwick, *Women, Art, and Society*, 3rd ed. (London: Thames and Hudson, 2002), p. 324.

**21.** Alice Neel, "A Statement," in *The Hasty Papers: A One-Shot Review*, ed. Alfred Leslie (New York: Alfred Leslie, 1960; reprinted and expanded edition, Austin, Tex.: Host Publications, 2000), p. 91.

**22.** Chadwick, *Women, Art, and Society*, p. 324. See also Suleiman, "Writing and Motherhood," pp. 352–77; and Susan Rubin Suleiman, "On Maternal Spilling: A Propos of Mary Gordon's 'Men and Angels,'" *Signs* 14, no. 1 (Autumn 1988), pp. 25–41.

**23.** Mignon Nixon, *Fantastic Reality: Louise Bourgeois and a Story of Modern Art* (Cambridge, Mass.: MIT Press, 2005), p. 56.

**24.** Helene Deutsch, quoted in Suleiman, "Writing and Motherhood," p. 358.

**25.** Rich, *Of Woman Born*, p. 40.

**26.** In the 1970s, when Neel was a popular speaker at women's art events, colleges, and museums and the subject of many interviews, she strongly advised young women against the impulse to put their creative ambitions aside while their children were young. She told Cindy Nemser, "If you decide you are going to have children and give up painting during the time you have them, you give it up forever. Or if you don't, you just become a dilettante. . . . I don't think you can decide to stop for years and do a different thing. You get divorced from your art." Neel in Cindy Nemser, *Art Talk: Conversations with 15 Women Artists* (New York: Icon Editions, 1995), p. 109.

**27.** Hartley Neel, conversation with the author, September 30, 2019.

**28.** It is worth pointing out here that the issue of the artist working at home is as much a reflection of class as of gender. Neel was poor, and her Spanish Harlem apartment, while described as wider and lighter than most apartments in the neighborhood, was not especially spacious. And because it was a railroad flat, one had to walk through the boys' bedroom, then Neel's bedroom, to get to the living room, where she often painted and entertained. Women artists who were better off financially could establish their studios in separate rooms within their homes, if not in an outside building. Impoverished male artists often worked at home as well, although even then their female partners were expected to compromise their space. For example, when Jackson Pollock and Lee Krasner moved into their house in Springs, East Hampton, Pollock used the spare upstairs room as his studio while Krasner painted in the living room, her canvases and paints tucked away when she wasn't working so the room could be used for sitting and entertaining. Once Pollock took over the now-famous barn as his studio, Krasner was able to relocate to the upstairs room, painting in a space apart, dedicated solely as a studio, for the first time. After Pollock's death, Krasner moved her studio out of the house completely to the much larger space of the barn.

**29.** Michael (Mike) Gold, exhibition statement, in *Paintings by Alice Neel, April 23 to May 23*, exh. brochure (New York: New Playwrights Theatre, 1951); reprinted in Hills, *Alice Neel*, p. 89.

**30.** Not only the artist in the mirror but also the rocking horse had art historical precedents, although Neel was not aware of this when she painted her own domestic scene. Goya's portrait *José Costa y Bonells (died 1870), Called Pepito* (ca. 1810), which entered The Met's collection in 1961, shows a little boy dressed in military costume holding the reins of his toy horse. In an October 1975 interview Neel explained that seeing this painting by Goya with "a rocking horse in the background" at The Met gave her the courage to exhibit *Hartley on the Rocking Horse*. Alice Neel in "Art and Alice Neel," *Forum*, WGTV Atlanta, aired December 19, 1975, VHS, Archives of American Art, Smithsonian Institution.

**31.** In Neel's narrative of her own life, the mirror served as a locus of strength and mental transformation. Following her suicide attempts in the early 1930s, Neel spent several months at the Gladwyne Colony, a private sanitarium outside Philadelphia run by the experimental psychiatrist Seymour DeWitt Ludlum, who encouraged her to paint and draw as part of her recovery. "Dr. Ludlum was a wonderful person," Neel recalled in 1982. "He'd say: 'Why don't you look in the mirror and get well.'" And she did. The painted mirror, then, presents a portrait of the woman who marshaled the strength to "get well." Neel in Hills, *Alice Neel*, p. 39; and Kufrin, *Uncommon Women*, p. 145.

**32.** Neel was forced out of her apartment on East 108th Street when the owner decided to renovate the building and charge more money than Neel had been paying. The landlord showed Neel the Upper West Side apartment, which she did not hesitate to take because of its size and proximity to Columbia University, where both her sons were students at the time. Neel in Nemser, *Art Talk*, p. 112.

**33.** Neel rarely painted self-portraits before 1980, but when she did represent herself in her art—as in *The Family* (p. 140), *The Family* (p. 141), *Well Baby Clinic*, *The Intellectual*, or even *Hartley on the Rocking Horse*—she portrayed herself doing the physical work of mothering.

**34.** Suleiman, "Writing and Motherhood," p. 356.

**35.** Linda Nochlin, *Representing Women* (London: Thames and Hudson, 1999), p. 21.

**36.** Ibid., p. 17. See also Linda Nochlin, "Why Have There Been No Great Women Artists?," *ArtNews* 69, no. 9 (January 1971), pp. 22–39, 67–71.

**37.** For a discussion of Neel's relationship to feminism and to the women's art movement of the 1970s, see Kelly Baum's essay in this volume.

**38.** Ann Temkin, "Alice Neel: Self and Others," in *Alice Neel*, ed. Ann Temkin, p. 28.

**39.** Michel Auder, in "Undergoing Scrutiny: Sitting for Alice Neel," roundtable discussion moderated by Ann Temkin, Philadelphia Museum of Art, April 6, 1999, in *Alice Neel*, ed. Ann Temkin, p. 75.

**40.** Nochlin wondered in a 2004 lecture if Neel's rendering of the hands in this painting was not simply a record of how they were positioned but a "more general observation about the repressive relationship of mothers and children." Linda Nochlin, "Alice Neel: Lecture, Victoria Miro Gallery, London, May 2004," in *Women Artists: The Linda Nochlin Reader*, ed. Maura Reilly (London: Thames and Hudson, 2015), p. 286.

**41.** Ibid.

**42.** Tamar Garb, "'The human race torn to pieces': The Painted Portraits of Alice Neel," in Lewison and Walker, *Alice Neel: Painted Truths*, p. 30.

**43.** See, for example, E. F. Porter Jr., "Blithe Spirit, Collector of Souls," *St. Louis Post-Dispatch*, December 14, 1975; Paul Richard, "Alice Neel: Portraits and the Artist," *Washington Post*, October 8, 1976; and Patricia Burstein, "Painter Alice Neel Strips Her Subjects to the Bone—and Some Then Rage in Their Nakedness," *People*, March 19, 1979, pp. 63–64.

## Painting Fruit(s)
### Randall Griffey

**1.** Alice Neel, undated and untitled statement, Folder Copies 3, Alice Neel Archive, Stowe, Vt.

**2.** Johnny Misheff, "Visiting Artists: Geoffrey Hendricks," *New York Times Style Magazine*, May 15, 2012, https://tmagazine.blogs.nytimes.com/2012/05/15/visiting-artists-geoffrey-hendricks/. Hendricks revisited some of this information in a more detailed interview in 2016: Linda Yablonsky, oral history interview with Geoffrey Hendricks, August 17–18, 2016, Archives of American Art, Smithsonian Institution.

**3.** Hendricks recalled during his 2016 interview with Yablonsky that Buczak returned to Neel's apartment many times.

**4.** Buczak to Neel, undated letter (postmarked December 14, 1978), Alice Neel papers, 1933–1983, Archives of American Art, Smithsonian Institution.

**5.** Hilton Als speculates that *Stephen Shepherd* (1978) represents a gay sitter; see Als, *Alice Neel, Uptown*, exh. cat. (New York: David Zwirner Books; London: Victoria Miro, 2017), p. 129.

**6.** For Neel biographer Phoebe Hoban, Neel's late-career flourish was predicated in part on her portrayals of queer subjects: "During this decade [the 1970s], she produced some of her best pieces, including some gender-bending classics. She was particularly adept at navigating the subtle sexual nuances in the body language of transgender and gay couples." Hoban, *Alice Neel: The Art of Not Sitting Pretty* (New York: St. Martin's Press, 2010), p. 270. When it was sold at a Sotheby's auction in 2009, the painting *Jackie Curtis and Ritta Redd* set a then-record price for a work by the artist.

**7.** Neel quoted in Judith Vivell, "Talking about Portraits," *Feminist Art Journal* 3, no. 2 (Summer 1974), p. 15.

**8.** Neel's accommodation of gay and queer subjects has earned her a reputation as something of an ally, as suggested by Pamela Allara and Phoebe Hoban. "After 1969 [the year of the Stonewall Riots], . . . Neel, whose sympathies for gay men had been part of her sympathies for oppressed persons in general, explored the changing configurations of professional and sexual identity in her sitters." Allara, *Pictures of People: Alice Neel's American Portrait Gallery* (Hanover, N.H.: University Press of New England [for] Brandeis University Press, 1998), p. 164. "Neel's empathetic depiction of gay and transgender couples arguably stands alone in art history." Hoban, *Alice Neel*, p. 376.

**9.** As historian George Chauncey has written, "Attracted by the Village's bohemian reputation, gay men and lesbians . . . played a distinctive role in shaping the image and reality of the Village, for they became part of the spectacle that defined the neighborhood's colorful character, even as they used the cultural space made available by that character to turn it into a haven." Chauncey, *Gay New York: Gender, Urban Culture, and the Making of the Gay Male World, 1890–1940* (New York: Basic Books, 2008), p. 244.

10. "The place was so very popular," Cadmus later recalled, "it was full of beatniks, delinquents, minor gangsters of its day. . . . On Friday and Saturday men guarded the entrance to the toilets, allowing only one customer in at a time." Cadmus quoted in Lincoln Kirstein, *Paul Cadmus* (San Francisco: Pomegranate Artbooks, 1992), p. 26.

11. Neel quoted in Patricia Hills, *Alice Neel* (New York: Harry N. Abrams, 1983), p. 47. Hills's book is a compilation of transcribed interviews with the artist undertaken from 1979 to 1982.

12. On Jay/Latimer, particularly his relationship with Stevens, see, among other sources, George S. Lensing, *Wallace Stevens: A Poet's Growth* (Baton Rouge: Louisiana State University Press, 1986). Lensing's discussion of Jay/Latimer begins on p. 122.

13. Allara speculates that *Paul Kuyer* (1959) represents a gay subject, but, symptomatic of the time, evidence of Kuyer's sexuality is seemingly nonexistent; see Allara, *Pictures of People*, pp. 118–19. According to Virginia (Ginny) Neel, the artist's daughter-in-law, Neel maintained friendships with gay men throughout this period, including with Kuyer, who found her a supportive listener. Virginia Neel, correspondence with the author, September 15, 2020.

14. Cindy Nemser, interview with Alice Neel, May 14, 1975, audiotape, Box 27, R37a–b, Cindy Nemser papers, 2013.M.21, Getty Research Institute.

15. On the suppression and demonization of queer men especially during the Cold War, see John D'Emillo, *Sexual Politics, Sexual Communities: The Making of a Homosexual Minority in the United States, 1940–1970* (Chicago: University of Chicago Press, 1983), particularly Chapter 3, "The Bonds of Oppression: Gay Life in the 1950s," pp. 40–53.

16. Robert Shaffer, "Women and the Communist Party USA, 1930–1940," *Socialist Review* 45 (May–June 1979), p. 106.

17. Gold's most notorious homophobic critique appeared in "Wilder: Prophet of the Genteel Christ," *New Republic*, October 22, 1930, pp. 266–67.

18. Neel quoted in Hills, *Alice Neel*, p. 60.

19. On this critical environment, see Randall R. Griffey, "Marsden Hartley's Late Paintings: American Masculinity and National Identity in the 1930s and '40s" (PhD diss., University of Kansas, 1999).

20. Malcolm Cowley, *Exile's Return: A Literary Odyssey of the 1920s* (New York: Penguin Books, 1994), p. 190.

21. Neel made reference to Mayor Koch's pro-gay legislative activities in an interview with critic Barbaralee Diamonstein at the New School for Social Research in 1978; see https://www.youtube.com/watch?v=aLG2oNPQ5PA&t=362s. A transcript of most of this interview appears in Diamonstein, *Inside New York's Art World* (New York: Rizzoli, 1979), pp. 254–63.

22. Neel did not revere Warhol: "As an art-world personality, he represents a certain pollution of this era. I think he's the greatest advertiser living, not a great portrait painter." Neel quoted in Hills, *Alice Neel*, p. 138.

23. Brigid Berlin recorded the date of Warhol's sitting in her daybook; interview with the author, March 11, 2020. The author thanks Ms. Berlin for sharing her recollections of Warhol's initial sitting with Neel.

24. Breanne Fahs, *Valerie Solanas: The Defiant Life of the Woman Who Wrote SCUM (and Shot Andy Warhol)* (New York: Feminist Press at the City University of New York, 2014).

25. John Leonard, "The Return of Andy Warhol," *New York Times Magazine*, November 10, 1968, p. 144.

26. David Bourdon, *Warhol* (New York: Harry N. Abrams, 1989), p. 290.

27. Daniel Morris, *Remarkable Modernisms: Contemporary American Authors on Modern Art* (Amherst: University of Massachusetts Press, 2002), pp. 157–58.

28. Neel referred to Warhol as an androgyne on several occasions. See Alice Neel, interview with Werner and Yetta Groshans, March 20, 1979, Werner and Yetta Groshans papers, 1926–1997, Archives of American Art, Smithsonian Institution; and Hills, *Alice Neel*, p. 138.

29. Gerrit Henry, *Art International* 14, no. 10 (December 1970), p. 77.

30. Pat Hackett, ed., *Andy Warhol Diaries*, Sunday, March 29, 1982 (New York: Warner Books, 1989), p. 436. Even so, according to Hartley Neel, Warhol described the portrait in another context as "the greatest image anyone ever did of me." Hartley Neel, correspondence with the author, September 9, 2020.

31. Sandy Nelson, "Looking at Alice Looking at Us: Alice Neel in Los Angeles," *Images and Issues* 4, no. 1 (July–August 1983), p. 18.

32. Neel declared *Women in Revolt* a "masterpiece" during a 1983 visit to Los Angeles. Elaine Warren, "Her Work Bares the Souls of Her 'Victims,'" *Los Angeles Herald Examiner*, April 5, 1983.

33. Rosalyn Regelson, "Not a Boy, Not a Girl, Just Me," *New York Times*, November 2, 1968.

34. For Curtis's skepticism about the gay liberation movement, among other topics, see Vince Aletti, "Jackie," *New Times* 1, no. 1 (April 8, 1970).

35. The author thanks Penny Arcade for help in identifying Redd/Zollo in a conversation on January 22, 2020.

36. Ritta Redd, "Jackie Curtis: Andy Warhol's Bad Girl," publication unknown, ca. 1970, photocopy found in Andy Warhol's Time Capsule 7, Andy Warhol Museum Archives, Pittsburgh.

37. Neel's recollection of the circumstances surrounding this sitting corroborates Redd's secondary, almost incidental presence in the portrait. As Neel explained to journalist Sally Nelson, "Andy Warhol sent them up to pose for me. He really sent her [Curtis]; he didn't send the other one, but he was so attached to her, I thought I should paint him, too." Nelson, "Looking at Alice Looking at Us," p. 18.

38. The author thanks Penny Arcade for sharing her memories in a conversation on January 22, 2020.

39. Released in early 1971, the film made a splash at the Cannes Film Festival later that spring.

40. Craig B. Highberger, "Timeline of Jackie Curtis's Life," in *Superstar in a Housedress: The Life and Legend of Jackie Curtis* (New York: Open Road Integrated Media, 2015), p. 8.

41. This reading is consistent with Curtis's ongoing parody of marriage. Indeed, much of Curtis's life-as-performance-art project involved deconstructing bourgeois, heteronormative manifestations of romance, especially marriage, through camp appropriation. Between 1969 and 1984, Curtis staged at least eight weddings around the city, which were attended by many celebrants associated with Max's Kansas City, the popular hangout just north of Union Square. See Giulia Palladini, "Queer Kinship in the New York Underground: On the 'Life and Legend' of Jackie Curtis," *Contemporary Theatre Review* 21, no. 2 (2011), pp. 126–53.

42. Neel told this story in, among other contexts, Nelson, "Looking at Alice Looking at Us," p. 18.

43. Neel, interview with Patricia Hills, 1979–80, Patricia Hills papers, Box 9, Folder 1, Archives of American Art, Smithsonian Institution.

44. Given that Neel did not rely often on preliminary drawings, the sketch likely followed the painted portrait rather than preceded it. The author thanks Craig Highberger for sharing information about this sketch with him.

45. Hackett, ed., *Andy Warhol Diaries*, Tuesday, October 16, 1984, p. 608.

46. Bourdon, *Warhol*.

47. *Portrait of Alice Neel, 1976–1982*, directed by Michel Auder (1986; Collector's Edition 2000), VHS.

48. The author thanks Joseph Grigely for sharing his insights into Battcock's biography and personality.

49. While viewers of Neel's portrait of Bourdon and Battcock have often perceived it as showing a romantic couple, even "domestic partners," Battcock's voracious sexual appetite precluded that possibility. Sex was extraordinarily important to him, as suggested by his writing in *Gay*. "People keep trying to give me the impression that there's something sordid about traveling around and constantly picking up people. . . . Sexuality is an important area of communications media." Gregory Battcock, "The Last Estate," *Gay*, November 15, 1969, p. 22. Gregory Battcock papers, 1952–circa 1980, Archives of American Art, Smithsonian Institution. The feminist author Jill Johnston, a friend of Battcock's, recalled that he was "the only pure male homosexual chauvinist I know. He says he doesn't try to mess up his boyfriends' minds with love, security, false promises, fidelity, and the like." Jill Johnston, "The Making of a Lesbian Chauvinist," in *Admission Accomplished: The Lesbian Nation Years (1970–75)* (London: Serpent's Tail, 1998), p. 45.

50. For more on Battcock, see Joseph Grigely, ed., *Oceans of Love: The Uncontainable Gregory Battcock*, exh. cat. (London: Koenig Books, 2016).

51. "On the Cover," *Arts Magazine* 44, no. 6 (April 1970), p. 2.

52. David Joselit, "Transformer: Gregory Battcock," *Artforum* 51, no. 1 (September 2012), pp. 508, 510. The author thanks Meredith L. Lehman for sharing her discovery of the similarity between the Polaroid and Neel's portrait of Battcock.

53. Palladini, "Queer Kinship in the New York Underground," p. 134.

54. John Cheim, interview with the author, March 18, 2020. The author thanks Mr. Cheim for his insights.

55. John Perreault, "This Painting Is Not John Perreault," *NY Arts*, September 2000.

56. *John Perreault* evokes the words of pioneering art historian Linda Nochlin, who observed, "Nobody is ever quite relaxed in a Neel portrait, no matter how suggestive of relaxation the pose: some quivering or crisping of the fingers, some devouring patch of shadow under the eyes or insidious wrinkle beneath the chin, a linear quirk, a strategic if unexpected foreshortening dooms each sitter-victim to premonitory alertness as though in the face of impending menace." Nochlin, *Women, Art, and Power and Other Essays* (New York: Harper and Row, 1988), p. 102.

57. For a period account of women artists portraying the male nude, see Eunice Golden, "The Male Nude in Women's Art: Dialectics of a Feminist Iconography," *Heresies* 3, no. 4 (1981), pp. 40–42. Golden's analysis begins with a discussion of Neel's *Joe Gould*, an indication of the degree to which the artist's early male nude was seen as groundbreaking. Notably, Marion Pinto featured a number of male nudes in her exhibition *Man as a Sex Object* at the gay-centric Leslie Lohman Gallery in 1975.

58. Hoban discusses Sleigh's accusations of Neel's plagiarism in *Alice Neel*, p. 283.

59. See Chadwick Lee Roberts, "Consuming Liberation: Playgirl and the Strategic Rhetoric of Sex Magazines for Women 1972–1985" (PhD diss., Bowling Green State University, 2011).

60. Perreault, "This Painting Is Not John Perreault."

61. Carl Andre, Hans Haacke, John Perreault, and Cindy Nemser, "The Role of the Artist in Today's Society," *Art Journal* 34, no. 4 (Summer 1975), p. 331.

62. Pamela Allara likewise interpreted *John Perreault* as an emblem of gay liberation; see Allara, *Pictures of People*, p. 188.

63. Perreault, "This Painting Is Not John Perreault."

64. Jerry Tallmer, "Tornado with Paint to Burn," *New York Post*, November 4, 1978.

65. Neel's personal ambivalence about queer identity figures quite prominently in her 1978 interview with Diamonstein, where she admits her relief that her own sons are straight: "I just never wanted them . . . to belong to a little group in society," she explains, with parental concern, "because I think it's harder to live like that."

66. Helen Molesworth, with Simone Leigh and Moyra Davey, "Alice Neel: Viva la Mujer," November 12, 2019, in *Recording Artists*, podcast, https://www.getty.edu/recordingartists/season-1/neel/.

67. Neel quoted in Hills, *Alice Neel*, p. 41.

68. Neel, interview with Diamonstein.

69. Neel painted Millett (from photographic sources) for *Time* magazine, Rich for *Parnassus: Poetry in Review*, and Garrard as a commission from the sitter.

70. Neel quoted in Hoban, *Alice Neel*, p. 308. According to Virginia Neel, Neel was somewhat intimidated by the formidable Rich. Virginia Neel, correspondence with the author, September 15, 2020.

71. Mary D. Garrard, "Alice Neel and Me," *Women's Art Journal* 27, no. 2 (Fall–Winter 2006), p. 4.

72. Other authors have likewise detected Garrard's self-protective posture in Neel's portrait. See, as one example, Allara, *Pictures of People*, p. 140.

73. The author thanks Dr. Garrard for confirming that the drawing was derived from the same sitting as the painting, despite their distinct differences.

74. Garrard, "Alice Neel and Me," p. 4. Garrard points out that Norma Broude, another key feminist art historian, initially made this connection to Matisse.

## Alice Neel's "Good Abstract Qualities"

### Julia Bryan-Wilson

1. The literature on this subject is extensive; see the texts in Francis Frascina, ed., *Pollock and After: The Critical Debate* (New York: Harper and Row, 1985); Serge Guilbaut, ed., *Reconstructing Modernism: Art in New York, Paris, and Montreal, 1945–1964* (Cambridge, Mass.: MIT Press, 1990); and Okwui Enwezor, Katy Siegel, and Ulrich Wilmes, *Postwar: Art between the Pacific and the Atlantic, 1945–1965*, exh. cat. (Munich: Haus der Kunst; New York: Prestel, 2016).

2. Mira Schor, "Some Notes on Women and Abstraction and a Curious Case History: Alice Neel as a Great Abstract Painter," *differences: A Journal of Feminist Cultural Studies* 17, no. 2 (2006), pp. 132–60.

3. Ibid., p. 145.

4. Alice Neel, interview with Werner Groshans, 1979 and undated, Werner and Yetta Groshans papers, 1926–1997, Archives of American Art, Smithsonian Institution.

5. Mike Gold, "Alice Neel Paints Scenes and Portraits from Life in Harlem," *Daily Worker*, December 27, 1950, p. 11.

6. Neel, interview with Groshans.

7. Fred Moten, "The Case of Blackness," *Criticism* 50, no. 2 (Spring 2008), p. 200. Moten's essay delves into Mondrian's *Boogie Woogie* works and their complicated, generative relationship with Black culture.

8. For more on O'Keeffe's relationship to modernism and to gender, see Anne Middleton Wagner, "O'Keeffe's Femininity," in *Three Artists (Three Women): Modernism and the Art of Hesse, Krasner, and O'Keeffe* (Berkeley: University of California Press, 1996), pp. 29–103.

9. Typed undated notes, box 1, folder 21, Alice Neel papers, Archives of American Art, Smithsonian Institution.

10. Hilton Kramer, "Art: Alice Neel Retrospective," *New York Times*, February 9, 1974.

11. Neel, interview with Groshans.

12. See, for instance, discussions about Faith Ringgold and Harmony Hammond in Julia Bryan-Wilson, *Fray: Art and Textile Politics* (Chicago: University of Chicago Press, 2017).

13. For more on Thomas and other Black abstract painters in the 1960s and 1970s, including Howardena Pindell, whose abstract work directly references African textiles, see Kellie Jones, *Energy/Experimentation: Black Artists and Abstraction 1964–1980*, exh. cat. (New York: Studio Museum in Harlem, 2006).

14. Kobena Mercer, "Introduction," in *Discrepant Abstraction* (London: Institute of International Visual Arts; Cambridge, Mass.: MIT Press, 2006).

15. Af Klint's art was motored by her beliefs in spirituality, mysticism, and channeling; see Tracey Bashkoff, ed., *Hilma af Klint: Paintings for the Future*, exh. cat. (New York: Guggenheim Museum Publications, 2018).

16. Alice Neel, typed transcript of artist's talk at the Whitney Museum of American Art, December 2, 1982, Collection of the Whitney Museum of American Art Archives.

17. Clement Greenberg, "Towards a Newer Laocoon," *Partisan Review* 7, no. 4 (July–August 1940); reprinted in Frascina, ed., *Pollock and After*, p. 45.

18. Gold, "Alice Neel Paints Scenes and Portraits from Life in Harlem," p. 11.

19. Gerardo Mosquera, "Meyer Schapiro, Marxist Aesthetics, and Abstract Art," *Oxford Art Journal* 17, no. 1 (1994), pp. 76–80.

20. Eva Cockcroft, "Abstract Expressionism, Weapon of the Cold War," *Artforum* 12, no. 10 (Summer 1974), pp. 39–41. Many scholars have expanded on Cockcroft's basic premise and refined her claims; see, for instance, C. Oliver O'Donnell, "Meyer Schapiro, Abstract Expressionism, and the Paradox of Freedom in Art Historical Description," *Tate Papers* 26 (Autumn 2016), https://www.tate.org.uk/research/publications/tate-papers/26/meyer-schapiro-abstract-expressionism.

21. Neel, interview with Groshans.

22. Diego Rivera, "The Revolutionary Spirit in Modern Art," *Modern Quarterly* (Baltimore) 6, no. 3 (Fall 1932), p. 54.

23. Neel, artist's talk at the Whitney, 1982.

# WORKS IN PLATES

**All works are by Alice Neel (American, 1900–1984)**

**Harlem River at Sedgwick Avenue**, 1928
Oil on canvas
24 × 26 in. (61 × 66 cm)
Estate of Alice Neel
p. 117

**Men from Bleecker Street**, 1933
Graphite on paper
14 × 10 in. (35.6 × 25.4 cm)
Private collection
p. 118

**Investigation of Poverty at the Russell Sage Foundation**, 1933
Oil on canvas
24 1/8 × 30 1/8 in. (61.3 × 76.5 cm)
Pennsylvania Academy of the Fine Arts, Philadelphia, Art by Women Collection, Gift of Linda Lee Adler
p. 119

**Synthesis of New York – The Great Depression**, 1933
Oil on canvas
48 × 39 in. (121.9 × 99.1 cm)
Estate of Alice Neel
p. 120

**Ninth Avenue El**, 1935
Oil on canvas
24 × 30 in. (61 × 76.2 cm)
Cheim and Read, New York
p. 121

**Kenneth Fearing**, 1935
Oil on canvas
30 1/8 × 26 in. (76.5 × 66 cm)
The Museum of Modern Art, New York, Gift of Hartley S. Neel and Richard Neel, 1988
p. 122

**Dick Bagley**, 1946
Oil on canvas
30 × 25 in. (76.2 × 63.5 cm)
The Metropolitan Museum of Art, New York, Gift of Nina Baroness von Maltzahn, Betsy and Ed Cohen/Arete, A. Michael and Mercedes Hoffman, Michael and Beth Klein, Marjorie and Jeffrey A. Rosen, Familienstiftung Schultz-von Schacky (Berlin), Marlene and Dirk Ippen, Gahl Hodges Burt and Martin Indyk, Vedder family, Achim Moeller-Moeller Fine Art, 2014 (2014.456)
p. 123

**Pat Whalen**, 1935
Oil, ink, and newspaper on canvas
27 1/8 × 23 1/8 in. (68.9 × 58.7 cm)
Whitney Museum of American Art, New York, Gift of Dr. Hartley Neel
p. 124

**Longshoremen Returning from Work**, 1936
Oil on canvas
30 × 39 in. (76.2 × 99.1 cm)
Estate of Alice Neel
p. 125

**Nazis Murder Jews**, 1936
Oil on canvas
42 × 30 in. (106.7 × 76.2 cm)
Rennie Collection, Vancouver
p. 126

**Save Willie McGee**, ca. 1950
Oil on canvas
40 3/16 × 22 1/16 in. (102 × 56 cm)
Estate of Alice Neel
p. 127

**Fish Market**, 1947
Oil on canvas
40 1/8 × 27 1/8 in. (101.9 × 68.9 cm)
Estate of Alice Neel
p. 129

**Puerto Rican Girl on a Chair**, 1949
Oil on canvas
30 × 24 in. (76.2 × 61 cm)
The Brand Family Collection
p. 130

**Mercedes Arroyo**, 1952
Oil on canvas
25 × 24 1/8 in. (63.5 × 61.3 cm)
Collection of Daryl and Steven Roth
p. 131

**Dominican Boys on 108th Street**, 1955
Oil on canvas
41 7/8 × 48 1/16 in. (106.3 × 122 cm)
Tate: Presented by the American Fund for the Tate Gallery, courtesy of Hartley and Richard Neel, the artist's sons 2004
p. 132

**Georgie Arce No. 2**, 1955
Oil on canvas
30 × 22 in. (76.2 × 55.9 cm)
Collection of Lonti Ebers
p. 133

**Central Park**, 1959
Oil on canvas
44 × 34 in. (111.8 × 86.4 cm)
Estate of Alice Neel
p. 134

**Two Girls, Spanish Harlem**, 1959
Oil on canvas
30 × 25 in. (76.2 × 63.5 cm)
Museum of Fine Arts, Boston, Gift of Barbara Lee
p. 135

**The Black Boys**, 1967
Oil on canvas
46 1/4 × 40 in. (117.5 × 101.6 cm)
Tia Collection, Santa Fe, NM
p. 136

**Cityscape**, 1968
Oil on canvas
50 × 46 in. (127 × 116.8 cm)
Estate of Alice Neel
p. 137

**Fuller Brush Man**, 1965
Oil on canvas
40 × 27 in. (101.6 × 68.6 cm)
Collection of Diane and David Goldsmith
p. 138

**107th and Broadway**, 1976
Oil on canvas
59 3/4 × 34 in. (151.8 × 86.4 cm)
Private collection, Washington, D.C.
p. 139

**The Family**, 1927
Watercolor on paper
9 1/4 × 14 1/2 in. (23.5 × 36.8 cm)
Private collection
p. 140

**The Family**, 1927
Watercolor on paper
9 × 12 in. (22.9 × 30.5 cm)
Collection of Catherine Gund
p. 141

**Bathing in a Furnished Room**, 1927
Watercolor and pastel on paper
11 3/4 × 9 in. (29.8 × 22.9 cm)
Private collection
p. 142

**The Intellectual**, 1929
Watercolor on paper
10 7/8 × 15 in. (27.6 × 38.1 cm)
Collection of Marcia Rafelman
p. 143

**Alienation**, 1935
Watercolor on paper
10 1/2 × 9 in. (26.7 × 22.9 cm)
The Antonia Johnson Family Collection
p. 144

**Untitled (Alice Neel and John Rothschild in the Bathroom)**, 1935
Watercolor on paper
11 7/8 × 8 7/8 in. (30.2 × 22.5 cm)
Collection of Nancy Magoon
p. 145

**Spanish Harlem**, 1938
Oil on canvas
34 × 28 in. (86.4 × 71.1 cm)
Tufts University Permanent Collection, Medford, Mass., Gift of Richard Neel and Hartley S. Neel, M.D. M69
p. 147

**José**, 1936
Oil on canvas
23 × 18 in. (58.4 × 45.7 cm)
Estate of Alice Neel
p. 148

**Alice and José**, 1938
Watercolor and pastel on paper
11 3/4 × 9 in. (29.8 × 22.9 cm)
Estate of Alice Neel
p. 149

**Untitled (Alice and José)**, ca. 1935
Watercolor on paper
12 × 8 7/8 in. (30.5 × 22.5 cm)
Estate of Alice Neel
p. 150

**José Asleep**, 1938
Pastel on paper
12 × 9 in. (30.5 × 22.9 cm)
Private collection
p. 151

**Still Life with Fruit**, 1940
Oil on canvas
24 × 30 in. (61 × 76.2 cm)
Private collection, Los Angeles
p. 152

**Hartley on the Rocking Horse**, 1943
Oil on canvas
29 15/16 × 33 7/8 in. (76 × 86 cm)
Private collection
p. 153

**Cut Glass with Fruit**, 1952
Oil on canvas
21 × 31 in. (53.3 × 78.7 cm)
Estate of Alice Neel
p. 154

**A Spanish Boy**, 1955
Oil on canvas
20 1/2 × 27 in. (52.1 × 68.6 cm)
Museum of the City of New York, Gift of Thelma Hall and Lisa Dawn Simmons, 1980
p. 155

**Thanksgiving**, 1965
Oil on canvas
38 3/4 x 27 in. (98.4 x 68.6 cm)
The Brand Family Collection
p. 157

**Still Life, Rose of Sharon**, 1973
Oil on canvas
40 1/4 × 30 1/8 in. (102.2 × 76.5 cm)
Whitney Museum of American Art, New York, Arthur M. Bullowa Bequest
p. 158

**Black Bottles**, 1977
Oil on canvas
Framed: 40 × 30 × 1 1/2 in. (101.6 × 76.2 × 3.8 cm)
Collection of Equitable
p. 159

**Carlos Enríquez**, 1926
Oil on canvas
30 1/4 × 24 in. (76.8 × 61 cm)
Estate of Alice Neel
p. 160

**Elenka**, 1936
Oil on canvas
24 × 20 in. (61 × 50.8 cm)
The Metropolitan Museum of Art, New York, Gift of Richard Neel and Hartley S. Neel, 1987 (1987.376)
p. 161

**Christopher Lazare**, 1932
Watercolor and cut-and-pasted paper
12 1/2 × 9 1/4 in. (31.8 × 23.5 cm)
Estate of Alice Neel
p. 162

**Max White**, 1935
Oil on linen
36 × 26 in. (91.4 × 66 cm)
Smithsonian American Art Museum, Washington, D.C., Museum purchase
p. 163

**Phillip Bonosky**, 1948
Oil on canvas
30 × 25 1/4 in. (76.2 × 64.1 cm)
Louis-Dreyfus Family Collection
p. 164

**Alice Childress**, 1950
Oil on canvas
29 7/8 × 20 in. (75.9 × 50.8 cm)
Collection of Art Berliner
p. 165

**Mike Gold**, 1952
Oil on canvas
32 × 25 in. (81.3 × 63.5 cm)
Estate of Alice Neel
p. 166

**Sam**, 1958
Oil on canvas
32 × 22 1/8 in. (81.3 × 56.2 cm)
Estate of Alice Neel
p. 167

**Death of Mother Bloor**, 1951
Graphite on paper
9 3/4 × 13 3/8 in. (24.8 × 34 cm)
Estate of Alice Neel
p. 168

**Death of Mother Bloor**, 1951
Oil on canvas
26 × 35 in. (66 × 88.9 cm)
Defares Collection
p. 169

**Ay Ay Ay**, 1967
Ink and gouache on paper
22 × 30 1/2 in. (55.9 × 77.5 cm)
Private collection
p. 170

**Rita and Hubert**, 1954
Oil on canvas
34 × 40 in. (86.4 × 101.6 cm)
Defares Collection
p. 171

**James Farmer**, 1964
Oil on canvas
43 3/4 × 30 1/4 in. (111.1 × 76.8 cm)
National Portrait Gallery, Smithsonian Institution, Washington, D.C., Gift of Hartley S. Neel and Richard Neel
p. 172

**Henry Geldzahler**, 1967
Oil on canvas
50 × 33 7/8 in. (127 × 86 cm)
The Metropolitan Museum of Art, New York, Anonymous Gift, 1981 (1981.407)
p. 173

**Adrienne Rich**, 1973
Ink on paper
29 3/4 × 22 in. (75.6 × 55.9 cm)
Collection of Doug Woodham and Dalya Inhaber
p. 174 (left)

**Mary Garrard**, 1977
Graphite on paper
30 1/8 × 22 1/2 in. (76.5 × 57.2 cm)
Estate of Alice Neel
p. 174 (right)

**Marxist Girl (Irene Peslikis)**, 1972
Oil on canvas
59 3/4 × 42 in. (151.8 × 106.7 cm)
Collection of Daryl and Steven Roth
p. 175

**David Bourdon and Gregory Battcock**, 1970
Oil on canvas
59 3/4 × 56 in. (151.8 × 142.2 cm)
Blanton Museum of Art, The University of Texas at Austin, Archer M. Huntington Museum Fund
p. 176

**Geoffrey Hendricks and Brian**, 1978
Oil on canvas
46 3/4 × 36 3/4 in. (118.7 × 93.3 cm)
San Francisco Museum of Modern Art, Purchase, by exchange, through an anonymous gift
p. 177

**Jackie Curtis and Ritta Redd**, 1970
Oil on canvas
60 × 41 7/8 in. (152.4 × 106.4 cm)
The Cleveland Museum of Art, Leonard C. Hanna, Jr. Fund
p. 178

**Jackie Curtis as a Boy**, 1972
Oil on canvas
44 × 30 in. (111.8 × 76.2 cm)
Collection of John Cheim
p. 179

**Richard Gibbs**, 1968
Oil on canvas
64 × 50 in. (162.6 × 127 cm)
Private collection, Minneapolis
p. 180

**Robbie Tillotson**, 1973
Oil on canvas
58 × 38 1/8 in. (147.3 × 96.8 cm)
Museum of Contemporary Art, Los Angeles, Gift of Hartley and Richard Neel
p. 181

**Benny and Mary Ellen Andrews**, 1972
Oil on canvas
60 × 50 in. (152.4 × 127 cm)
The Museum of Modern Art, New York, Gift of Agnes Gund, Blanchette Hooker Rockefeller Fund, Arnold A. Saltzman Fund, and Larry Aldrich Foundation Fund (by exchange)
p. 181

**Well Baby Clinic**, 1928–29
Oil on canvas
39 1/4 × 28 3/4 in. (99.7 × 73 cm)
Minneapolis Institute of Art, The Christina N. and Swan J. Turnbald Memorial Fund, by exchange, and the Julia B. Bigelow Fund
p. 184

**Futility of Effort**, 1930
Oil on canvas
26 1/4 × 24 1/2 in. (66.7 × 62.2 cm)
Collection of Anne McNamara, Dallas
p. 185

**Suicidal Ward, Philadelphia General Hospital**, 1931
Graphite on paper
17 × 22 in. (43.2 × 55.9 cm)
Estate of Alice Neel
p. 186

**T.B. Harlem**, 1940
Oil on canvas
30 × 30 in. (76.2 × 76.2 cm)
National Museum of Women in the Arts, Washington, D.C., Gift of Wallace and Wilhelmina Holladay
p. 187

**Peggy**, 1949
Oil on canvas
18 × 36 in. (45.7 × 91.4 cm)
Collection of James Kenyon, Los Angeles
pp. 188–89

**Last Sickness**, 1953
Oil on canvas
30 × 22 in. (76.2 × 55.9 cm)
Philadelphia Museum of Art, 125th Anniversary Acquisition, Gift of Hartley S. Neel and Richard Neel, 2003
p. 190

**City Hospital**, 1954
Ink and gouache on paper
29 1/4 × 22 in. (74.3 × 55.9 cm)
Estate of Alice Neel
p. 191

**Randall in Extremis**, 1960
Oil on canvas
36 × 28 in. (91.4 × 71.1 cm)
Estate of Alice Neel
p. 192

**Robert Smithson**, 1962
Oil on canvas
42 × 24 in. (106.7 × 61 cm)
The Locks Foundation, Philadelphia
p. 193

**Andy Warhol**, 1970
Oil and acrylic on linen
60 × 40 in. (152.4 × 101.6 cm)
Whitney Museum of American Art, New York, Gift of Timothy Collins
p. 194

**Richard in the Era of the Corporation**, 1978–79
Oil on canvas
60 × 45 in. (152.4 × 114.3 cm)
Estate of Alice Neel
p. 195

**Kenneth Doolittle**, 1932
Graphite on paper
15 × 10 in. (38.1 × 25.4 cm)
Private collection
p. 196

**Joe Gould**, 1933
Oil on canvas
39 × 31 1/8 in. (99.1 × 79.1 cm)
Estate of Alice Neel
p. 197

**Ethel Ashton**, 1930
Oil on canvas
24 × 22 in. (61 × 55.9 cm)
Tate: Presented by the American Fund for the Tate Gallery, courtesy of Hartley and Richard Neel, the artist's sons 2012
p. 198

**Isabetta**, 1934–35
Oil on canvas
42 1/2 × 25 in. (108 × 63.5 cm)
The Brand Family Collection
p. 199

**Pregnant Woman**, 1971
Oil on canvas
40 × 60 in. (101.6 × 152.4 cm)
Private collection
p. 200

**Pregnant Maria**, 1964
Oil on canvas
32 × 47 in. (81.3 × 119.4 cm)
Private collection
p. 201

**John Perreault**, 1972
Oil on linen
38 × 63 7/8 in. (96.5 × 162.2 cm)
Whitney Museum of American Art, New York, Gift of anonymous donors
p. 202

**Cindy Nemser and Chuck**, 1975
Oil on canvas
41 1/2 × 59 3/4 in. (105.4 × 151.8 cm)
Collection of Lillian and Billy Mauer
p. 203

**Andrew**, 1978
Oil on canvas
30 × 24 1/4 in. (76.2 × 61.6 cm)
Estate of Alice Neel
p. 204

**Margaret Evans Pregnant**, 1978
Oil on canvas
57 3/4 × 38 1/2 in. (146.7 × 97.8 cm)
Institute of Contemporary Art, Boston, Gift of Barbara Lee, The Barbara Lee Collection of Art by Women
p. 205

**Self-Portrait**, 1980
Oil on canvas
53 1/4 × 39 3/4 in. (135.3 × 101 cm)
National Portrait Gallery, Smithsonian Institution, Washington, D.C.
p. 207

**Mother and Child, Havana**, 1926
Oil on canvas
26 × 18 in. (66 × 45.7 cm)
Estate of Alice Neel
p. 208

**Childbirth**, 1939
Oil on canvas
30 5/16 × 40 3/16 in. (77 × 102.1 cm)
Rennie Collection, Vancouver
p. 209

**The Spanish Family**, 1943
Oil on canvas
34 × 28 in. (86.4 × 71.1 cm)
Estate of Alice Neel
p. 210

**Mother and Child**, 1956
Ink on paper
14 × 11 in. (35.6 × 27.9 cm)
Collection of Francie Bishop Good and David Horvitz
p. 211

**Pregnant Julie and Algis**, 1967
Oil on canvas
42 × 64 in. (106.7 × 162.6 cm)
Estate of Alice Neel
pp. 212–13

**Mother and Child**, ca. 1962
Oil on canvas
40 1/8 × 27 1/4 in. (101.9 × 69.2 cm)
Private collection
p. 214

**Nancy and Olivia**, 1967
Oil on canvas
39 × 36 in. (99.1 × 91.4 cm)
Collection of Diane and David Goldsmith
p. 215

**Carmen and Judy**, 1972
Oil on canvas
40 × 29 7/8 in. (101.6 × 75.9 cm)
Oklahoma City Museum of Art, Westheimer Family Collection
p. 217

**Nancy and the Twins**, 1971
Oil on canvas
54 × 40 in. (137.2 × 101.6 cm)
Baltimore Museum of Art, Gift of the Childe Hassam Fund of The American Academy of Arts and Letters, New York
p. 218

**Linda Nochlin and Daisy**, 1973
Oil on canvas
55 7/8 × 44 in. (141.9 × 111.8 cm)
Museum of Fine Arts, Boston, Seth K. Sweetser Fund
p. 219

**French Girl**, 1920s
Oil on canvas
30 × 22 in. (76.2 × 55.9 cm)
Estate of Alice Neel
p. 221

**Addiction**, 1931
Watercolor on paper
12 × 8 1/2 in. (30.5 × 21.6 cm)
Estate of Alice Neel
p. 222

**Sunset in Spanish Harlem**, 1958
Oil on canvas
Framed: 39 × 22 × 1 1/2 in. (99.1 × 55.9 × 3.8 cm)
Collection of Equitable
p. 223

**Sunset, Riverside Drive**, 1957
Oil on canvas
50 1/8 × 25 3/4 in. (127.3 × 65.4 cm)
Estate of Alice Neel
p. 224

**Night**, 1959
Oil on canvas
32 1/8 × 18 1/4 in. (81.6 × 46.4 cm)
Estate of Alice Neel
p. 225

**Richard**, 1963
Oil on canvas
48 × 30 in. (121.9 × 76.2 cm)
Estate of Alice Neel
p. 226

**Black Draftee (James Hunter)**, 1965
Oil on canvas
60 × 40 in. (152.4 × 101.6 cm)
COMMA Foundation, Belgium
p. 227

**Hartley**, 1966
Oil on canvas
50 × 36 in. (127 × 91.4 cm)
National Gallery of Art, Washington, D.C., Gift of Arthur M. Bullowa, in Honor of the 50th Anniversary of the National Gallery of Art
p. 228

**View from the Artist's Window**, 1978
Oil on Masonite
29 × 19 in. (73.7 × 48.3 cm)
Private collection, Philadelphia
p. 229

**Blue House**, 1963
Oil on canvas
50 × 33 in. (127 × 83.8 cm)
The Brand Family Collection
p. 230

**Ginny in a Striped Shirt**, 1969
Oil on canvas
60 × 40 in. (152.4 × 101.6 cm)
Private collection
p. 231

**Ginny**, 1984
Oil on canvas
44 × 30 in. (111.8 × 76.2 cm)
Private collection
p. 232

**Elizabeth in a Red Hat**, 1984
Oil on canvas
48 × 36 in. (121.9 × 91.4 cm)
Estate of Alice Neel
p. 233

**Light**, 1980
Oil on canvas
50 × 36 in. (127 × 91.4 cm)
Collection of Barbara and Theodore Alfond
p. 235

# INDEX

Page numbers in *italics* refer to illustrations. All works are by Alice Neel unless otherwise indicated.

# PHOTOGRAPHY CREDITS

Archives of American Art, Smithsonian Institution: fig. 63; © 2020 Banco de México Diego Rivera Frida Kahlo Museums Trust, Mexico, D.F. / Artists Rights Society (ARS), New York. Bridgeman-Giraudon / Art Resource, New York: fig. 77; © 2020 Romare Bearden Foundation / Licensed by VAGA at Artists Rights Society (ARS), New York. Courtesy DC Moore Gallery, New York: fig. 78; © 2020 Estate of Paul Cadmus / Artists Rights Society (ARS), New York. Digital Image © The Museum of Modern Art / Licensed by SCALA / Art Resource, New York: fig. 56; ©1978 Barbara Carrasco: fig. 28; © Jordan Casteel, photo by Adam Reich: fig. 42; *Cosmopolitan*, Hearst Magazine Media, Inc., photo by Francesco Scavullo: fig. 65; © 2020 The Easton Foundation / Licensed by VAGA at Artists Rights Society (ARS), New York: fig. 51; © 2020 Helen Frankenthaler Foundation, Inc. / Artists Rights Society (ARS), New York. Courtesy Gagosian, photo by Robert McKeever: fig. 76; Getty Images, photo by Bettmann: fig. 36; © Emmet and Edith Gowin. Courtesy Pace Gallery. Princeton University Art Museum / Art Resource, New York: fig. 27; © 2020 Georgia O'Keeffe Museum / Artists Rights Society (ARS), New York. Photo by Minneapolis Institute of Art: fig. 72; © 2020 The Jacob and Gwendolyn Lawrence Foundation, Seattle / Artists Rights Society (ARS), New York. Image © The Metropolitan Museum of Art: fig. 10; © Helen Levitt Film Documents LLC. Courtesy Thomas Zander Gallery, Cologne: fig. 38; Courtesy Library of Congress: fig. 14; *Masses & Mainstream*, New York, 1949: fig. 3; © 1966 Hiram Maristany. Smithsonian American Art Museum, Washington, D.C. / Art Resource, New York: fig. 39; © 2020 Succession H. Matisse / Artists Rights Society (ARS), New York. Image © The Metropolitan Museum of Art: fig. 68; Courtesy Monique Meloche Gallery and David Antonio Cruz: fig. 43; Image © The Metropolitan Museum of Art: figs. 5, 6, 7, 23; Image © The Metropolitan Museum of Art, photo by Juan Trujillo: fig. 74; Digital Image © The Museum of Modern Art / Licensed by SCALA / Art Resource, New York: figs. 62, 71; Courtesy National Gallery of Art, Washington, D.C.: fig. 58; © The Estate of Alice Neel. Courtesy The Estate of Alice Neel and David Zwirner: figs. 1, 2, 4, 9, 12, 13, 15, 16, 18, 19, 20, 22, 24, 25, 26, 30, 32, 33, 34, 35, 37, 44, 45, 46, 47, 48, 52, 54, 55, 66, 69, 70, 72, pp. 2, 4, 6, 12, 118, 120, 123, 125, 130, 131, 132, 133, 134, 135, 136, 137, 138, 140, 141, 142, 148, 149, 150, 155, 159, 160, 164, 165, 166, 168, 169, 170, 172, 174, 175, 176, 177, 178, 181, 184, 185, 186, 187, 188, 189, 190, 191, 194, 198, 199, 200, 201, 202, 203, 214, 215, 217, 219, 223, 228, 231, 235; © The Estate of Alice Neel. Courtesy The Estate of Alice Neel and David Zwirner. *Art Front*, New York, 1936, p. 7: fig. 21; © The Estate of Alice Neel. Courtesy The Estate of Alice Neel and David Zwirner, photo by Sam Brody: figs. 49, 50; © The Estate of Alice Neel. Courtesy The Estate of Alice Neel and David Zwirner. Collection of John E. Cheim: p. 179; © The Estate of Alice Neel. Courtesy The Estate of Alice Neel and David Zwirner. Photo © Christie's Images / Bridgeman Images: pp. 151, 229; © The Estate of Alice Neel. Courtesy The Estate of Alice Neel and David Zwirner. Photo by Alfred Eisenstaedt / The *LIFE* Picture Collection via Getty Images: fig. 53; © The Estate of Alice Neel. Courtesy The Estate of Alice Neel and David Zwirner, photo by Mitro Hood: p. 218; © The Estate of Alice Neel. Courtesy The Estate of Alice Neel and Xavier Hufkens, Brussels, photo by HV-studio: fig. 57; © The Estate of Alice Neel. Courtesy The Estate of Alice Neel and David Zwirner. Courtesy Locks Foundation: p. 193; © The Estate of Alice Neel. Courtesy The Estate of Alice Neel and David Zwirner. *Masses & Mainstream*, New York, 1958, p. 48: fig. 17; © The Estate of Alice Neel. Courtesy The Estate of Alice Neel and David Zwirner, photo by Fred W. McDarrah / Getty Images: fig. 41; © The Estate of Alice Neel. Courtesy The Estate of Alice Neel and David Zwirner, photo by Kerry McFate: pp. 143, 144, 145, 196, 197, 204, 205, 209, 212, 213; © The Estate of Alice Neel. Courtesy The Estate of Alice Neel and David Zwirner. Image © The Metropolitan Museum of Art: pp. 161, 173, 227; © The Estate of Alice Neel. Courtesy The Estate of Alice Neel and Victoria Miro: pp. 192, 211; © The Estate of Alice Neel. Courtesy The Estate of Alice Neel, Victoria Miro, and Rennie Collection, Vancouver, photo by Stephen White, London: p. 126; © The Estate of Alice Neel. Courtesy The Estate of Alice Neel and David Zwirner. Digital Image © The Museum of Modern Art / Licensed by SCALA / Art Resource, New York: pp. 122, 183; © The Estate of Alice Neel. Courtesy The Estate of Alice Neel and David Zwirner, photo by Terje Östling: p. 207; © The Estate of Alice Neel. Courtesy The Estate of Alice Neel and David Zwirner. National Portrait Gallery, Smithsonian Institution: fig. 29; © The Estate of Alice Neel. Courtesy The Estate of Alice Neel and David Zwirner, photo by Ethan Palmer: pp. 117, 129, 154, 162, 195, 221, 222, 233; © The Estate of Alice Neel. Courtesy The Estate of Alice Neel and David Zwirner. Courtesy Pennsylvania Academy of the Fine Arts, Philadelphia: p. 119; © The Estate of Alice Neel. Courtesy The Estate of Alice Neel and David Zwirner, photo by Stephen Petegorsky: pp. 157, 230; © The Estate of Alice Neel. Courtesy The Estate of Alice Neel and David Zwirner, photo by Jan Van Ray: fig. 31; © The Estate of Alice Neel. Courtesy The Estate of Alice Neel and David Zwirner. Courtesy Aurel Scheibler Gallery: pp. 127, 224; © The Estate of Alice Neel. Courtesy The Estate of Alice Neel and David Zwirner. Smithsonian American Art Museum, Washington, D.C. / Art Resource, New York: p. 163; © The Estate of Alice Neel. Courtesy The Estate of Alice Neel and David Zwirner, photo by Greg Staley: fig. 67; © The Estate of Alice Neel. Courtesy The Estate of Alice Neel and David Zwirner. Courtesy Tufts University: p. 147; © The Estate of Alice Neel. Courtesy The Estate of Alice Neel and David Zwirner, photo by Malcolm Varon: pp. 121, 139, 153, 167, 171, 180, 208, 210, 225, 226, 232; © The Estate of Alice Neel. Courtesy The Estate of Alice Neel and David Zwirner. © 2020 The Andy Warhol Foundation for the Visual Arts, Inc. / Licensed by Artists Rights Society (ARS), New York: fig. 61; © The Estate of Alice Neel. Courtesy The Estate of Alice Neel and David Zwirner, photo by Bruce White: p. 174; © The Estate of Alice Neel. Courtesy The Estate of Alice Neel and David Zwirner, photo by Joshua White: p. 152; © The Estate of Alice Neel. Courtesy The Estate of Alice Neel and David Zwirner. Digital image © Whitney Museum of American Art / Licensed by Scala / Art Resource, New York: pp. 124, 158; © Philip Pearlstein. Courtesy Betty Cunningham Gallery, New York. Image © The Metropolitan Museum of Art: fig. 8; © 2020 The Pollock-Krasner Foundation / Artists Rights Society (ARS), New York. Image © The Metropolitan Museum of Art: fig. 11; © 1978 Sophie Rivera: fig. 40; © 2020 The Andy Warhol Foundation for the Visual Arts, Inc. / Licensed by Artists Rights Society (ARS), New York. *Arts Magazine*, New York, Art Digest Inc., 1970: fig. 64; © 2020 The Andy Warhol Foundation for the Visual Arts, Inc. / Licensed by Artists Rights Society (ARS), New York. © Vincent Fremont Enterprises, Inc. All Rights Reserved: fig. 59

This catalogue is published in conjunction with *Alice Neel: People Come First*, on view at The Metropolitan Museum of Art, New York, from March 15 through August 1, 2021, at the Guggenheim Museum Bilbao from September 17, 2021, through January 30, 2022, and at the de Young Museum, Fine Arts Museums of San Francisco, from March 12 through July 10, 2022.

The exhibition is made possible by the Barrie A. and Deedee Wigmore Foundation.

Major support is provided by the Adrienne Arsht Fund for Resilience through Art.

Additional funding is provided by Agnes Gund and the Jane and Robert Carroll Fund.

This publication is made possible by the Samuel I. Newhouse Foundation, Inc., Daryl and Steven Roth, Sueyun Locks, the Locks Foundation, and the Antoinette Kraushaar Fund.

**Published by**
**The Metropolitan Museum of Art, New York**
Mark Polizzotti, Publisher and Editor in Chief
Peter Antony, Chief Production Manager
Michael Sittenfeld, Senior Managing Editor

Edited by Anne Blood Mann
Designed by McCall Associates
Production by Lauren Knighton
Bibliographic editing by Kate Norment
Image acquisitions and permissions by
Josephine Rodriguez-Massop

Photographs of works in The Met collection are by the Imaging Department, The Metropolitan Museum of Art, unless otherwise noted.

Additional photography credits appear on page 255.

Typeset in Ambiguity Normate, Ambiguity Tradition, and District Pro
Printed on Arctic Volume White 150 gsm
Separations by Verona Libri, Italy
Printed and bound by Verona Libri, Italy

Jacket illustrations: front, *Elenka*, 1936; back, *Black Draftee (James Hunter)*, 1965
Page 2: *Jackie Curtis and Ritta Redd*, 1970; page 4: *Ethel Ashton*, 1930; page 6: *Mother and Child*, ca. 1962; pages 114–15: *The Black Boys*, 1967

The Metropolitan Museum of Art endeavors to respect copyright in a manner consistent with its nonprofit educational mission. If you believe any material has been included in this publication improperly, please contact the Publications and Editorial Department.

Copyright © 2021 by The Metropolitan Museum of Art, New York

First printing

All rights reserved. No part of this publication may be reproduced or transmitted in any form or by any means, electronic or mechanical, including photocopying, recording, or any information storage and retrieval system, without permission in writing from the publishers.

The Metropolitan Museum of Art
1000 Fifth Avenue
New York, New York 10028
metmuseum.org

Distributed by
Yale University Press, New Haven and London
yalebooks.com/art
yalebooks.co.uk

Cataloguing-in-Publication Data is available from the Library of Congress.
ISBN 978-1-58839-725-6